THE NEW NATURALIST

A SURVEY OF BRITISH NATURAL HISTORY

BRITISH MAMMALS

The aim of this series is to interest the general reader in the wild life of Britain by recapturing the inquiring spirit of the old naturalists. The Editors believe that the natural pride of the British public in the native fauna and flora, to which must be added concern for their conservation, is best fostered by maintaining a high standard of accuracy combined with clarity of exposition in presenting the results of modern scientific research. The plants and animals are described in relation to their homes and habitats and are portrayed in the full beauty of their natural colours, by the latest methods of colour photography and reproduction.

THE NEW NATURALIST

BRITISH MAMMALS

by

L. HARRISON MATTHEWS

WITH 16 COLOUR PLATES
48 BLACK AND WHITE PLATES
AND 92 FIGURES IN THE TEXT

COLLINS
ST JAMES'S PLACE LONDON

First impression 1952
Second impression 1960
Third impression 1963
Fourth impression 1968
Fifth impression 1972

ISBN 0 00 213021 1

Printed in Great Britain
Collins Clear-Type Press: London and Glasgow

CONTENTS

PLATES IN COLOUR

PLATES IN BLACK AND WHITE

It should be noted that throughout this book Plate numbers in arabic figures refer to Colour Plates, while roman numerals are used for Black-and-White Plates

EDITORS' PREFACE

As this book goes to press its author, Dr. L. Harrison Matthews, has left the University of Bristol where he has held a Research Fellowship to take up his appointment as the Scientific Director of the Zoological Society of London. It seems most appropriate that what is obviously a step in an interesting and distinguished career should coincide so closely with the publication of this book. For this book is itself an important step; indeed we can claim that it is the most important book on the British mammals that has ever been published, bringing together as it does an enormous number of facts into a new synthesis.

Scientific naturalists in Britain seldom agree among themselves about the correct bias of investigation, about the relative values of different advances in knowledge, about the relative merits of field-work or museum work, observational work or experimental work. Such disagreements are, of course, benign in that they simply stimulate the protagonists of the different points of view to greater effort! But on one important conclusion there has never been, during the present century, any disagreement among naturalists at all. It is the conclusion that the mammals have been badly served; and that the pursuit of knowledge about them has been, in many ways, a lost world of science, a lost art, perhaps even a lost enthusiasm. Now this remarkable book comes to put this right.

The neglect of the study of mammals for its own sake—of mammalogy—is really somewhat surprising and the reasons for it are not by any means easy to determine. Perhaps one of them is the fact that there is now no journal or magazine with a wide and regular circulation to which those interested in mammals can send minor notes on distribution and habits. The contrasting success of the study of birds must be at least partly due to the fact that there are several vehicles for the petty ornithological note: but petty mammal recording has

ix

suffered; indeed it has not taken place simply because there has been nowhere to record it.

It is clear, however, from Dr. Matthews' book, that while mammalogy may have been neglected the study of mammals has not. This is not a contradiction in terms, for much of our new knowledge of mammals has been conducted by ecologists and correctly described as ecology, or by physiologists as physiology or by anatomists as anatomy. This work has naturally been published in the journals appropriate for those sciences and not in a mammal journal—for there is no British mammal journal.

Dr. Matthews, then, has found himself in possession of a subject about which there is much knowledge, and on which there has been much recent research—but nevertheless a subject without a great following. We venture to think that this book will now create the following, and that mammalogy will come into its own again. Dr. Matthews has cast his net widely, for he is a very wide and general naturalist himself with interests in animals of all sorts in many parts of the world. He spent several years in antarctic and subantarctic waters with the Discovery expeditions and has written some of the official reports on animals resulting from those expeditions. He has been to South America, East Africa and Iceland. He has published papers on subjects as widely separated as the reproductive life of basking sharks and the habits of moles.

It is forty years since a complete text book on British mammals was published. This essay is not in the orthodox sense a text-book—no *New Naturalist* volume is intended to be. But it is a comprehensive synthesis of most of the important work that has been done on all the British mammals up to the present day. Readers in every walk of life, scientists, teachers, scholars, amateur naturalists and country-lovers generally will find that this book is something that a whole generation has been demanding and needing. Its publication will undoubtedly stimulate a renaissance of British mammalogy.

THE EDITORS

AUTHOR'S PREFACE

MANY books, some of them very good, have been written about the British mammals, and it is no aim of this one to repeat what has already been achieved. In the last twenty-five years a great quantity of research has been done upon mammals, British and others, in several directions of enquiry, and although results of the highest interest have been obtained, the accounts of them have for the most part remained inaccessible to the general reader in the scientific journals. This book attempts to present some of these results for the inspection of all, but the repetition of details such as minute accounts of the appearance, colour, and habits, that have been given so often and so well, is avoided as far as possible. Such well-known information has been included only where it is necessary for the sake of clarity and completeness. An exception has been made for the bats and for the whales and dolphins, orders of mammals that are little known to the general naturalist, where more detailed descriptions of the distinguishing characters of the species will, it is hoped, be interesting and useful.

It is obvious from a glance through the following pages that the information contained in them is drawn from many sources; the references to the bibliography show where these are to be found. The author believes that due acknowledgment has been made to all his authorities, and gratefully recognises his indebtedness to them. He would particularly like to thank his many zoologist friends for valuable criticism and other help; he is also grateful to the Editors of *Endeavour* and of *Zoo Life* for permitting the reproduction in chapters 4 and 11 of some matter which he has contributed to their journals. He is likewise very grateful to the editors for their helpful co-operation, and to Miss B. E. Wood who undertook all the hard work of compiling the index.

Throughout this book the term "British Isles" has been used solely in a geographical sense, and is to be understood as equivalent to

"Great Britain and Ireland"; similarly the term "British mammals" is intended to include the mammals of Ireland.

The drawings in the text figures, except Nos. 1, 2, 13, 14, 41 and 43, are original sketches from nature by the author.

L. HARRISON MATTHEWS

BRISTOL
February, 1951

CHAPTER I

MAMMAL NATURAL HISTORY
INTRODUCTION

"The investigation of our native animals must ever be a chief
source of sound zoological knowledge, for it is there only we can
watch, under favourable circumstances, for the observation of
their development, their habits, and their characters. The naturalist whose acquaintance is confined to preserved specimens
in a cabinet, can form but a vague idea of the glorious variety
of Nature... And unless we study the creatures living around
us, how can we gain that delightful knowledge?"

EDWARD FORBES. 1841

WILD MAMMALS, unlike birds, are not a characteristic feature of
the landscape almost everywhere in Britain; nevertheless
mammals, hidden from sight, are all around us, often within a few
feet, during our country walks. With the exception of a few kinds,
such as the rabbit, or seals or deer in suitable places, they are not
visible in the open, and are difficult to see at close quarters. Many of
them are nocturnal in their habits, and nearly all of them are expert
at concealing themselves.

Yet mammals abound in great numbers; the population of field-
mice alone probably exceeds in numbers that of man himself. But
though individuals are numerous, species are few, for we have only
about fifty species of land mammals in Britain; if the whales, and the
northern seals that rarely visit our shores, are added, the list extends
to about eighty at most. Some of our species have been isolated in our
islands from their neighbours on the continent long enough to have
become slightly different from them, and are recognisable as distinct
subspecies. So too have many of the populations of the smaller
mammals isolated on the islands off our coasts, and a considerable
number of subspecies has been described from them.

Mammals differ from other vertebrate animals in many ways, one of the most important being their comparatively high degree of intelligence, which is associated with the structure of their brains (see p. 28). To their intelligence they owe a great part of their evolutionary success; they are adaptable and, although they are to a large extent creatures of habit, they can alter their behaviour patterns to suit new circumstances.

Although we describe the biology of our species of mammals one at a time, the species are not isolated in nature, but all species, and all individuals, together make up the fauna, alteration to any one part of which affects all the others, though perhaps remotely and slightly. A crude example might be the destruction of small predatory mammals by man, leading to an increase in the numbers of small rodents, which in turn might destroy the grazing on which larger mammals subsist. Not only are the species making up the fauna interdependent, but the fauna as a whole is affected by changes in the environment, changes of climate, flora, and topography.

In undeveloped countries there is a constant see-saw in the state of the fauna with such periodical changes in the environment, but when human settlement comes profound and permanent alterations are quickly produced. Britain has been settled and cultivated for so long that most of the major changes due to human influences are already past—the large beasts of prey exterminated, and man's introduced species firmly established—and the whole character of the mammalian fauna is related to man and his works, and some sort of balance is struck.

From the earliest times many mammals have been of the greatest importance to man both as food and as the source of materials for his artifacts, at first as objects of the chase and later as domestic animals. His relations have been rather the reverse with the larger carnivores, which he generally regards as his enemies, though it may be doubted whether they have ever been a serious danger in thinly populated countries. Habitual man-eaters can exist only where men are numerous, and the suggestion that primitive man, in a country teeming with animals, was engaged in perpetual warfare against the large carnivores is probably exaggerated. In Africa today the pastoral nomadic Masai, who do not hunt the vast herds of game among which they live, kill such animals as lions, leopards, and hyaenas, only when their flocks and herds are harassed by them. But primitive man was a hunter, and his knowledge of the habits of his quarry must have been at the expense of Samuel Pepys, to whom the work is dedicated. What a treatise on mammals they might have left us had Willughby lived! Ray, however, left an important systematic treatise on mammals and snakes in his *Synopsis methodica Animalium Quadrupedum et Serpentini generis*, London, 1693, much of which was adopted by Linnaeus. But it was not until over seventy years later that another work treating solely of the British fauna was to appear, in the *British Zoology* of Thomas Pennant, of which five editions were published between 1766 and 1812. In the meantime Linnaeus had produced his *Systema Naturae*, in the tenth edition of which, published in 1758, he applied his binomial system to the whole of the animal kingdom; this edition consequently forms the foundation of all systematic zoology.

Until well on into the nineteenth century naturalists were mainly engaged in classifying and describing the outward appearance of the great numbers of new animals that were coming to their notice through the exploration of hitherto little known parts of the world. They produced such enormous works as the *Histoire naturelle* of Buffon which appeared in forty-four volumes between 1749 and 1804, and the twenty-eight volumes of *General Zoology, or Systematic natural history* of Shaw, 1800–26. At the same time the comparative anatomists were investigating the internal structure of all the new creatures that they could secure, the most celebrated British name of the eighteenth century being that of John Hunter, whose preparations were once the glory of the museum of the Royal College of Surgeons of England. On the continent Baron Cuvier, with his band of famous collaborators, investigated both systematic zoology and comparative anatomy, publishing the *Leçons d'anatomie comparée* and *Le règne animal*, the first of which went into several, the second into many editions.

During the first half of the nineteenth century the study of natural history became more and more separated into two channels, one the more anatomical and technical, in which the name of Owen is outstanding, leading to the modern science of zoology, the other more popular and more concerned with field study, giving rise, as far as mammals are concerned, to some excellent works as well as to many of a lower standard. Among the more popular publications William Bingley's *Memoirs of British Quadrupeds*, 1809 and John Fleming's *A History of British animals*, 1828, followed in the footsteps of Pennant, while the *General History of Quadrupeds* of Bewick, whose first edition was published in 1790, the eighth in 1824, is more famous for its unsurpassed wood-engravings than for its text (fig. 2). The numerous volumes on mammals in Jardine's *Naturalist's Library* were written by authors of repute and illustrated with charming hand-coloured engravings, that on the *British Quadrupeds* being the work of William MacGillivray who, however, was better known as an ornithologist. The best standard work of the century on British mammals

FIG. 2
Bewick's woodcut of the fallow deer

was undoubtedly Thomas Bell's *History of British Quadrupeds*, 1837, which was followed by a revised edition in 1874; and among the more technical treatises on mammals in general the relevant sections of Owen's *Comparative anatomy and physiology of vertebrates* 1866–68, and the *Introduction to the study of mammals living and extinct* of Flower and Lydekker, 1891, outshine all others. The last two were not written for popular reading but were addressed to the scientific worker, and in spite of their age, they are still constantly consulted by students of the subject.

About the middle of the nineteenth century there was a great increase of interest in natural history, and many popular writers produced books to encourage it, sound writers such as Gosse and Kingsley, and many others of less repute. Some of the popular books adopted the approach of the Bridgewater treatises which aimed at illustrating the *Power, Wisdom and Goodness of God as manifested in the Creation*, but others degenerated into anthropomorphism and sentimental anecdote. Among the popular writers who were not untouched by the latter blemishes was Frank Buckland, whose writings, however, showed an almost boyish enthusiasm, to say nothing of occasional naïvety, that gained them a wide circle of readers and did much to stimulate an intelligent interest in zoology among the non-scientific. Nevertheless they were not always esteemed in more technical circles, for the great Professor Newton[231] wrote of him after his death "... Buckland, for whom I personally had much regard. His great mistake was that he believed people when they told him he was a naturalist, while he was wanting in every essential of a naturalist, except zeal." Much of the anecdotal natural history of the time was produced by people whose first interest in animals was in killing them, and whose attitude of mind was that animals exist solely for the benefit and convenience of man, a point of view unsympathetic to objective observation.

The invention towards the end of the century of processes by which books could be illustrated with photographs gave a great impetus to the production of popular works on natural history. Some were published on the British mammals which, however, received much less attention than birds, and have never become involved in a cult comparable to "bird-watching." It is surprising that the authors of these books, with the new method and manifold opportunities for observation, achieved so little in the discovery of new knowledge. Of the more serious among the modern histories of British mammals by far the most sumptuous are the three thick folio volumes of Millais' *Mammals of Great Britain and Ireland*, 1904–06, which contain a great mass of information and many illustrations, some of them by Thornburn, who himself published some pleasing paintings in his *British Mammals*, 1920–21. But the most thorough, accurate, and scientific publication of the present century on the subject is the *History of British Mammals* by Barrett-Hamilton, publication of which in parts started in 1910 and continued to the 21st part in 1921. Thereafter it remained unfinished although the last six parts published were completed by Hinton after the death of the first author in 1914 while engaged on a zoological mission abroad. About half of this work remains unwritten, and if any zoologist ever completes it with the quality of that which has already appeared he will earn the gratitude of all interested in the British mammals. On the purely systematic side of the study of our mammals Miller's *Catalogue of the mammals of western Europe in the collection of the British Museum*, 1912, is the standard to which all serious students of the class must refer.

By the beginning of the twentieth century the scientific study of zoology had for the most part turned away from systematics and natural history to problems of genetics and cell-structure, stimulated thereto by the rediscovery of Mendel's experimental results, and to comparative physiology and experimental embryology. These were most profitable fields for research after the storm raised by Darwin's writings had subsided, leaving the idea of evolution to illuminate the biological sciences. But the knowledge gained in the laboratory is now being taken out into the field again, and applied to animals as they are in their natural environment, with the result that our understanding of the biology of the mammals has made great advances in recent years. Studies have been made in several directions, on the relation of the animal to its biological and physical environment, on behaviour and psychology, on population-numbers, and on the factors within and without the animal controlling the breeding cycle. And the knowledge of genetics won by experiment has led to the closer examination of the specific characters of our mammals, with the result that a large number of local races or subspecies has been recognised, careful study of which has thrown much light on the probable history of the British mammal fauna. The reports of these researches have appeared usually in the journals of learned societies, and the attempt is now made in the pages that follow to present them to the general reader in language burdened as little as possible with technicalities, and to correlate them with what was already known.

Systematic zoology, or taxonomy, deals with the classification of animals and provides the foundation of biology; for one cannot begin to talk of anything until it has a name that identifies it to the listener. After being despised as mere cataloguing for half a century this branch of science is at last beginning to take its proper place in the esteem of zoologists. Animals can obviously be sorted into groups containing different kinds of the same sort, such as the various kinds of deer or of mice; the work of the systematist aims at defining each different kind and giving it a name of its own, and in arranging the different kinds in order of affinity so that the system of classification resembles a family tree.

The unit of classification is the species or kind, a unit that is obvious enough when speaking of such distinct animals as the lion and

Plate 1 HEDGEHOG

the tiger, but which is not at all easy to define when considering, for instance, the different kinds of field-mice. So elusive is an exact definition of the concept of species that it has been facetiously said, "a species consists of those animals which a competent systematist considers to be one". The point cannot be more clearly expressed than it has been recently by one of our most distinguished systematic biologists[37] who says, "A species is an assemblage of animals which do not differ from one another more than the offspring of a single pair may do; which are not connected with the members of neighbouring assemblages by intermediate forms; which interbreed freely with one another but commonly do not (in the wild state) interbreed with other species, or, if they do, produce infertile hybrids; and which usually inhabit geographical areas distinct from those inhabited by the most nearly related species. It has to be admitted, however, that every term of this definition is subject to exceptions and qualifications."

The importance of the last of these criteria, that of geographical isolation, is stressed by Huxley, who defines a species as "a geographically definable group, whose members actually interbreed or are potentially capable of interbreeding in nature, which normally in nature does not interbreed freely or with full fertility with related groups, and is distinguished from them by constant morphological differences." But here again the definition is made with reservations, "with geographical speciation, one difficulty concerns the extent of morphological difference: there are bound to be borderline cases."

Species are assembled into genera, genera into families, and families into orders, a number of intermediate degrees being used, such as subfamily, tribe, and subtribe between family and genus, where large numbers of genera and species belong to a single order. Each species is designated by two names, that of its genus followed by the specific or trivial name, as *Homo sapiens* Linnaeus, the name or initial of the author who first named the species being appended; any descriptive implication in the trivial name need not necessarily be true in fact. Many species are divided into subspecies, which are usually geographically separated races. A subspecies from one extreme of the range of a species may differ markedly from that living at the opposite extreme, yet the two may be connected by a number of intermediate forms, so that the change from one to the other is gradual across the total range; such intergradations are known as 'clines' but a cline takes no place in the formal scheme of classification. The degree of difference accorded to subspecies, species, genera and so forth is influenced by the opinion of the systematist classifying any group; some systematists, the 'splitters', regard as species forms that others, the 'lumpers', consider to be at most no more than subspecies, and similarly with the higher categories. It must be borne in mind that species and subspecies are biological entities, but that all the higher categories are artificial groupings designed for convenience in classification, and to express the classifier's opinion on the degree of relation between species.

One of the main criteria of a species, as mentioned in the definition given above, is that it shall breed true, but in the course of evolution the species now living have descended from other different ancestral species; how can these two conflicting statements be reconciled? Every cell in the animal body contains a specialised part, the nucleus, which behaves in a peculiar way when the cell divides into two, the only method by which the number of cells can increase. At the time of cell-division the substance of the nucleus breaks up into a number of discrete bodies, the chromosomes, which, particularly because of their behaviour in the reproductive cells, are known to be connected with the transmission of characters from parents to their offspring. The chromosomes contain a number of units, termed 'genes', each of which exerts an effect upon one or more characters. As far as is known the external environment cannot normally exert any influence upon the genetic constitution of the chromosomes, and consequently there can be no inheritance of characters acquired by an individual in response to changes in its environment. Yet it is quite obvious that in many ways animals are adapted to their environment. It was Darwin who first pointed out how this apparent contradiction could be overcome, by his theory of natural selection.

No two animals are quite alike and consequently some individuals may have a slight advantage over their companions in the business of life, and their chances of survival and leaving offspring may be greater; they will be selected, because the others will be more easily eliminated, by the natural hazards of the environment. Should the characters which give these animals an advantage over the others be caused by a difference in the chromosomes, the characters could be transmitted to their offspring, and a strain more suited to the environment established. Changes in the chromosomes can be produced experimentally by very drastic methods, such as subjecting animals to the action of X-rays or radio-active materials, and such changes are inheritable, although most of them are of such a nature as to handicap the animals, and would quickly be eliminated by natural selection in a wild population. Changes of this kind in the chromosomes are known as mutations, and it is believed that small mutations which do not lead to harmful results sometimes occur in nature, providing new hereditable characters which can be acted upon by natural selection. It has therefore been proposed that the evolution of new species takes place by the action of natural selection on small random mutations, the accumulation of which in the course of time differentiates new species from their ancestors. Small inheritable changes thus produce a different survival rate, and a very slight differential may be sufficient to ensure the survival and production of offspring by its possessors.

The genes consist of deoxyribonucleic acid (DNA), a nucleoprotein with an enormous molecule arranged as a long chain of nucleotides to which bases are attached. DNA consists of two strands along which the bases are arranged in the same sequence, but the two strands are coiled spirally round each other head to tail so that the sequences are reversed. If suitable materials are to hand DNA is self-replicating; the strands separate and each makes an exact facsimile of its former partner so that the amount of DNA is doubled. There are only four different bases but they can be arranged in groups in an enormous number of alternative ways to produce a 'code' which controls the kind of protein or of enzyme that is made in the cell. This it does through the mediation of ribonucleic acid (RNA) which carries, by the arrangement of its bases, the coded message from the DNA to the place where protein is being made in the cell, thus determining what kind of protein is made.

The code-arrangement in the self-replicating DNA molecule is the basis of heredity, and is the means by which the characters of one generation reappear in the next. It is not the characters that are transmitted, but a message that tells the cells of the new organism what to do. In theory the message is copied exactly at every cell division, but in practice it is not very surprising that among so many million duplications a 'copyist's error' sometimes creeps in. If, during self-replication, a 'mistake' is made so that the sequence of bases is

altered, the coded message is changed and a mutation is produced.
It is possible to imagine conditions in which the probability of such a
mistake is enhanced by the nature and quantity of the bases that may
be available in the cell during self-replication. The nature and quantity
of the bases available could be determined by external conditions. If
such a theoretical situation is ever proved to occur in nature the whole
matter of the impossibility of inheriting acquired characters will need
radical re-examination.

Students of mammals are unfortunate in the name that has been
adopted for their branch of zoology. The term mammal, an animal
that suckles its young, is derived from *mamma*, a breast, hence the
word mammalogy can logically only mean the study of breasts, not
that of mammals. It has, however, been in use with the intention
of expressing the latter for so long that it is generally accepted for
this purpose, and the probability of the adoption of a sounder form
such as 'mammalology', or 'mastozoology' as proposed by Cabrera,[36]
is remote, not only from considerations of euphony. Even the
French, who have the excellent term "mammifère" descend to
"mammalogie". The uncouthness of the word is due to its hybrid
origin, for it is a mixture of Latin and Greek: Cabrera's proposal is at
least consistent with a pure Greek pedigree.

As a foundation before considering the details of the biology of our
different mammals, the next chapter deals with some of the salient
points in the structure of animals, and their functional meaning.

CHAPTER 2

MAMMAL STRUCTURE AND FUNCTION

"Before I take in pieces this Goodly Creature, it will not be amiss if I first give you an account of all these parts as they lie in order."

ANDREW SNAPE, *The anatomy of an Horse.* 1683

MAMMALS ARE generally considered to be the highest animals in the scale of evolution, perhaps partly because man is himself a mammal. Whether one agrees with this opinion or not it is certain that in their anatomy and physiology the mammals are among the most complex of animals, showing a degree of elaboration in these directions equalled only by those other warm-blooded animals, the birds. But they show a degree of evolutionary advance 'superior' to that of the birds in their development of intelligence, their method of reproduction, and the parental care in suckling their young. The mammals are one of the most diverse animal groups and include, in addition to a vast number of terrestrial animals, the bats and whales which are so different from the others that they are thought by simple folk to be birds and fishes.

Because of this diversity there are very few characters common to all the mammals by which the class may be defined. The old descriptive term 'quadrupeds' is not satisfactory, for it does not include the bats and whales, and furthermore it should strictly, include the many four-footed reptiles and amphibia; the name 'animals' will not do, for it has been extended zoologically to include all living organisms apart from plants and bacteria. There are in fact only about half-a-dozen diagnostic characters, most of them severely technical, any one of which definitely shows its possessor to be a mammal.

Within the great array or phylum of backboned animals, the vertebrates, the mammals are distinguished by the fact that the young are nourished for some time after birth on the milk secreted by the mammary glands of the mother, and from this feature the class takes its name. In no other class of vertebrates is the dependence of the offspring upon the parent so intimate, and in no other class does parental care develop, on the basis of the family, those complex social relations that reach their highest peaks, and lowest depths, in human civilisation.

The second diagnostic character of the mammals, after the possession of milk-secreting mammary glands, is the presence of a covering of hair on the surface of the body. Most mammals are nearly completely clothed with hair, and even the almost naked whales have, at least when young, a few hairs on the snout and chin forming a rudimentary moustache or beard. No other animals have hair of the same type; the hair-like structures found, for instance, among the plumage of birds are not true hairs but modified feathers.

The other characters diagnostic of the mammals are found in the details of their internal anatomy. In the skull of mammals the lower jaw consists of one bone only on each side; in other animals there are more. In the mammalian middle ear the small bones that transmit sound-waves from the outer to the inner ear are three in number; in other animals they are fewer. The joint between the head and the backbone in mammals is made by two rounded knobs at the back of the skull, the occipital condyles; in other animals, except some amphibia, there is only one. The body-cavity of mammals is divided into two parts by a sheet of muscle and tendon, the midriff or diaphragm, which separates the thorax containing the heart and lungs, from the abdomen containing the digestive and reproductive organs and the kidneys; a diaphragm is present in no other animal. In mammals the main artery leaving the heart curves round on the left side to form the aortic arch; in birds it curves to the right, and in other vertebrates one or more arches are present on both sides. Finally, the largest part of the brain in the mammals is more complex than in the other vertebrates, the part known as the fore-brain being comparatively greatly enlarged, and with this enlargement comes the development of intelligence. In the mammalian brain, too, there is an increased complexity in the cross-connections or commissures between the right and left halves, but the diagnostic feature is the presence in the mid-brain of a highly developed part, the corpora quadrigemina, connected with the functions of sight and hearing.

The class mammalia is divided into three subclasses, to a sub-division of one of which, the Eutheria, belongs the vast majority of living mammals. This subdivision contains sixteen orders of living mammals, and ten more of extinct ones; some of them, such as the Chiroptera (bats) or Rodentia, contain great numbers of species, others, as the Tubulidentata (aard-varks of Africa) or Sirenia (sea-cows),

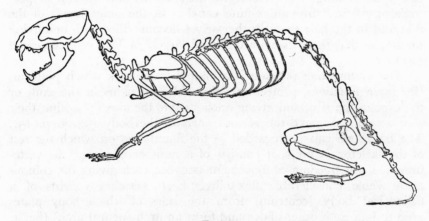

Fig. 3
Skeleton of a mammal (polecat).
The limbs and ribs of the near side only are shown

very few. The mammalian fauna of the British Isles is small, and contains members of only eight of the sixteen orders, none of them, apart from the whales, represented by more than about a dozen species. The eight orders are the Insectivora, Chiroptera, Carnivora, Lagomorpha, Rodentia, Ungulata, and Cetacea, to which might be added the Primates which are represented by man. Before considering the members of these orders in detail the remainder of this chapter presents a short sketch of the more important points in the anatomy and physiology of mammals in general, in order to avoid repeated explanations when matters concerning these subjects crop up later on.

The bodies of mammals, like those of all animals except the simplest, are built of an immense number of minute cells each a speck of living jelly, or protoplasm, contained inside a thin membrane. A smaller concentration of denser protoplasm, the nucleus, lies within each cell and contains the substances which control its growth and behaviour. There are many different kinds of cell, and usually those of each kind are massed together to form tissues such as muscle, brain, skin, or bone. The tissues contain non-living matter produced by the cells, and often deposited outside them, as in bone where the non-living part is a large proportion of the whole and the widely scattered cells lying among it are connected together by fine strands of protoplasm passing through minute canals. In the outer layers of the skin and in the hair the cells themselves become filled with non-living matter, so that these tissues are formed largely of dead cells cemented together.

The mammalian skeleton is a jointed framework which performs two main functions, protecting vulnerable organs as in the skull or the cage of the ribs, and giving anchorage to the muscles so that their contraction can move the various parts of the body (fig. 3, p. 15). The backbone can be regarded as the foundation on which the rest of the skeleton is built; it consists of a number of pieces, the vertebrae, a slight freedom of movement between each giving the column as a whole considerable flexibility. Each vertebra consists of a cylindrical body (centrum) from the sides of which bony plates arise to join each other above and form an arch (neural arch) (fig. 4, p. 17). From the summit of the arch a blade of bone, the neural spine, extends upwards giving attachment to muscles and ligaments, and from each side of the centrum a more or less horizontal blade (transverse process) extends outwards. When the vertebrae are in their natural position the joints are formed by the ends of the centra butting against each other, and are strengthened by the meeting of special parts (zygapophyses) of the neural arch. The successive neural arches form a tube, the neural canal, in which lies the spinal cord. The ribs, enclosing the chest, join the vertebral column with two attachments; the ends or heads join the centra, and roughened parts on the convex surfaces articulate with the transverse processes (fig. 5, p. 18).

The vertebral column is divided into regions; in the neck of most mammals there are seven (cervical) vertebrae with short centra, small spines, and very small ribs fused with the transverse processes. The first two differ greatly from the rest. The first (atlas) has no centrum, but very wide transverse processes and fused ribs; its front end bears two deeply concave surfaces for articulating

Plate 2 NOCTULE BAT   *Eric Hosking*

with the base of the skull. The second (axis) has a large neural spine overlapping that of the atlas, and the front end of its centrum projects forwards as the odontoid process. This is really the centrum of the atlas, detached from it and fused with that of the axis; it projects into the arch of the atlas and is held down by a strong ligament to form the floor of the neural canal. The thoracic or dorsal vertebrae follow the cervical series, and are the ones that carry the ribs; then follow the lumbar vertebrae, which have large transverse processes but no ribs. The number of ribs varies so that the number of thoracic vertebrae is not the same in all mammals, nor indeed, always the same in one species. But the the total of thoracic and lumbar vertebrae is constant not only in each species but in the larger divisions of mammals; the bats for example have seventeen, and the carnivores twenty or twenty-one. The ribs complete the cage of the thorax by joining the

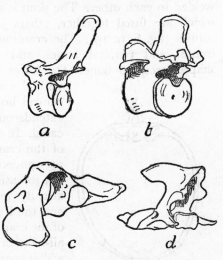

FIG. 4
Vertebrae.

a, from the chest, with facets for the ends of the ribs. *b*, from the loins. *c*, atlas. *d*, axis. (Bear)

breast-bone or sternum in front. The latter consisting of several more or less closely fused sections is fastened to the ends of the more forwardly placed ribs. The ribs farther back do not meet it, but each ends in a gristly rod that joins the end of the next rib ahead.

The sacral vertebrae follow the lumbar, and in most mammals are fused into a single mass to which the hip-bone is fixed. They vary in number between species from two to about a dozen, frequently being four or five; in many mammals as age increases one or more of the succeeding tail vertebrae become fused with them. The tail or caudal vertebrae decrease in size from before backwards, gradually losing their processes and neural arches so that the hinder ones are merely small rod-like centra. Their number varies according to the length of tail in each species, and even within species the number is not always constant.

At the fore end of the backbone lies the skull, consisting of the cranium, a box enclosing the brain, and the facial part, firmly welded to each other. The skull is made up of many bones, some of which are fused together, others joined by interlocking seams, the sutures (fig. 6, p. 19). The cranium is roofed by the large plate-like frontal and parietal bones, and completed behind by the ring-shaped occipital bone. The latter bears the condyles, for the joint with the atlas vertebra, on each side of the central hole through which the spinal cord extends out from the brain into the neural canal. In front of the occipital bone the floor of the cranium is formed by the basi- and pre-sphenoid bones, whose boundaries are not so easily made out as those of the bones already mentioned. Between these bones and the frontals and parietals the side walls of the cranium are built up of the squamosal, ali-, and orbito-sphenoid bones, and the front wall is completed by the ethmoid lying at the back of the nasal passage and invisible on the surface of the complete skull. Between the parietal, occipital, and squamosal bones lie the periotic and tympanic bones enclosing the inner and middle ear, the tympanic being expanded in many mammals over the middle ear to form a rounded box, the tympanic bulla.

FIG. 5

Vertebra and ribs, the latter joining the breast-bone in the middle line below

The largest bones forming the facial part of the skull are usually the paired maxillae, which carry the upper teeth, except the incisors. These bones join the frontals on each side, but are separated from each other on the upper surface of the skull by the paired nasal bones, which roof the nasal passage and meet the frontals between the maxillae. The latter extend to the undersurface of the skull and join each other in midline to form part of the roof of the mouth and floor of the nasal passage. The hinder part of the mouth-roof is formed by the paired palatine bones, and the foremost part by the premaxillae, which bear the upper incisor teeth and extend on to the front of the face, completing the nasal passage. A vertical plate,

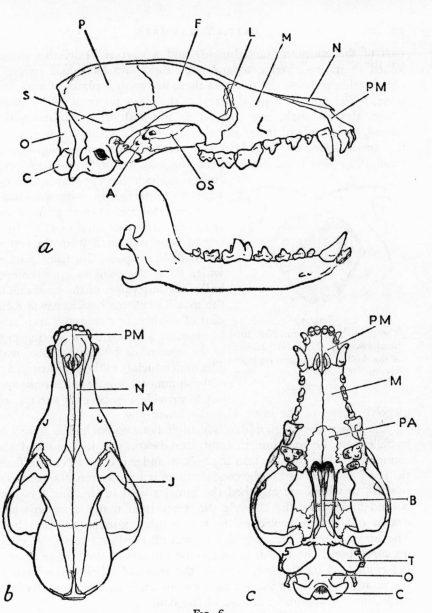

FIG. 6

Skull of dog, seen in side view, with lower jaw (*a*), from above (*b*), and from below (*c*). A, alisphenoid. B, basisphenoid. C, condyle. F, frontal. J, jugal. L, lachrymal. M, maxilla. N, nasal. O, occipital. OS, orbitosphenoid. P, parietal. PA, palatine. PM, premaxilla. S, squamosal. T, tympanic part of the ethmoid (mesethmoid) and a narrow bone, the vomer, joined to its lower edge separate the right and left nasal passages. On the side-walls of the passages there are several plates of very thin bone, rolled up into a scroll shape so that they fill most of the space. These, the turbinals, are covered in life with a membrane which warms, moistens and filters the air inspired, the scroll shape allowing the small space to hold a large area of membrane (fig. 7). A small lachrymal bone lies between the maxilla, orbito-sphenoid and frontal bones in the eye-socket, and extends on to the face in many mammals.

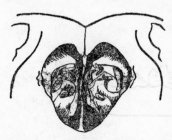

FIG. 7

The folded and scroll-like turbinal bones in the nasal passages of the skull of a lion, seen on looking into the nose opening from in front

The facial and cranial parts of the skull are further strutted together by a bar of bone separated from the rest of the skull by a space, the front part of which forms the orbit lodging the eyeball. The outer part of the hind end of the maxilla extends backwards to form part of the bar, or zygomatic arch, and is joined to a forwardly projecting part of the squamosal by the narrow jugal. The under-surface of the projecting part of the squamosal is more or less hollowed out to provide the bearing surface, or glenoid cavity, of the joint with the lower jaw.

The lower jaw or mandible is a single bone on each side, joined to its fellow in the mid line in front, and bearing at its hind end the rounded condyle that fits into the hollow under the squamosal to form the jaw joint. In front of the condyle there is a projection, the coronoid process, to which are attached the muscles used in shutting the jaw; behind and below the condyle the angle is in many mammals also drawn out into a projection to which other muscles are attached. The upper edge of the mandible carries all the lower teeth. A small unpaired bone, the hyoid, to which the muscles of the tongue attach, lies embedded in the flesh between the mandibles below the back of the mouth. A slender jointed rod of bone on each side connects it to projections on the under surface of the skull.

Although the teeth, set in sockets in the bones of the upper and lower jaws, are so closely associated with those bones, they are partly derived from the skin covering them. They are divisible into different kinds by their position, shape, and function (fig. 8). The incisors, lying at the front of the series, are usually small and often flattened; their function is seizing, biting, or gnawing the food. Next follow the larger eye-teeth or canines, one on each side above and below; they are particularly well developed in carnivorous mammals, but are absent from some orders, such as the rodents. Incisors and canines have single roots fitting the sockets in the jaw, but the cheek-teeth lying farther back have two or more. The latter teeth are of two

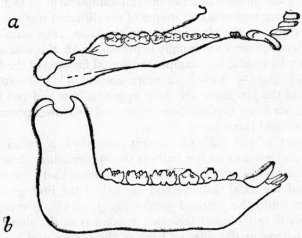

FIG. 8. The teeth in the lower jaw of a pig about 18 months old: *a*, from above, *b*, from the side. Three incisors lie at the front and are followed by a single canine, three premolars, and three molars. The fourth molar has not yet erupted. In the pig the first molar is not replaced

kinds, the premolars towards the front and the larger molars behind; the premolars of the adult dentition, unlike the molars, are usually preceded by milk teeth. The function of premolars and molars is to reduce the food to small particles suitable for swallowing; in some mammals their surfaces are flattened and ridged like miniature millstones for grinding hard vegetable substances, in others they are blade-like for cutting flesh or shearing bone. Although the molars are defined as having no milk-tooth predecessors, they usually form a single functional series with the premolars. In the upper jaw the incisors are carried by the premaxillae, the rest, beginning with the canines, by the maxillae; in the lower jaw the incisors oppose the upper incisors, and

and the canines bite in front of the upper canines when the jaw is shut.

Most mammals have two sets of teeth, the milk teeth of the young animal being lost after a longer or shorter period, and replaced by the more numerous permanent set. This arrangement allows the adult jaw to be filled by the teeth, for once teeth are formed they cannot increase in size and keep pace with the growth of the jaw as the young animal reaches its full stature. In some mammals, for example in the bats, the milk teeth are very different in shape from the permanent ones. Very few mammals have the full complement of teeth possible, and the relative numbers and shapes of the different teeth are valuable characters used in the classification of the class. The numbers of the different teeth present are usually expressed in an abbreviation known as the dental formula, for example the dental formula of the hedgehog: $i \frac{3-3}{2-2}$ $c \frac{1-1}{1-1}$ $pm \frac{3-3}{2-2}$ $m \frac{3-3}{3-3}$ or more simply, $\frac{3\ 1\ 3\ 3}{2\ 1\ 2\ 3}$ means that on each side of the jaw there are three upper incisors and two lower, one upper and one lower canine, three upper and two lower premolars, and three upper and three lower molars.

The part of the skeleton already described is called the axial skeleton; that supporting the limbs is the appendicular skeleton. Both fore and hind limbs are joined to a series of bones that form incomplete rings round the axial skeleton and are called the limb-girdles. That of the fore limb, the pectoral girdle (fig. 9, p. 23), is comparatively loosely joined to the axial skeleton; it consists of the shoulder-blades (scapulae) lying at the sides or back of the thorax and held in place only by muscles, and the collar-bones (clavicles) which join the lower ends of the scapulae to the fore end of the sternum. The clavicles are not present in all mammals; those mammals in which the fore limb has a wide range of movement have clavicles, but in those in which the limb moves mainly in the fore-and-aft direction they are reduced or absent. The clavicles serve to fix the shoulder-joint so that the limb can be moved freely on it in many directions; where they are absent muscular action pulls it forward and backwards, giving a long pace, but the other movements are restricted because there is no firm fulcrum for the limb. The lower end of the scapula carries a depression, the glenoid cavity (not to be confused with the glenoid cavity of the jaw joint) into which the upper end of the first bone of the limb fits to make the shoulder joint.

The pelvic girdle, supporting the hind limbs, which are generally the main propellors and supporters of the body, is very much more firmly fixed to the axial skeleton (fig. 10, p. 24). On each side it is formed of three bones, usually completely fused together. The largest is the hip-bone or ilium, which is attached very firmly to, and usually fused with, the transverse processes of the sacral vertebrae. Welded to it are the ischium, forming the hinder part, and the pubis, forming the front part of the girdle.

The pubic bones of each side usually, but not always, meet at the midline where they join together, and often fuse, at the pubic symphysis. At the point where the three bones meet there is a rounded cavity, called the acetabulum, which receives the head of the upper bone of the limb to make the hip joint.

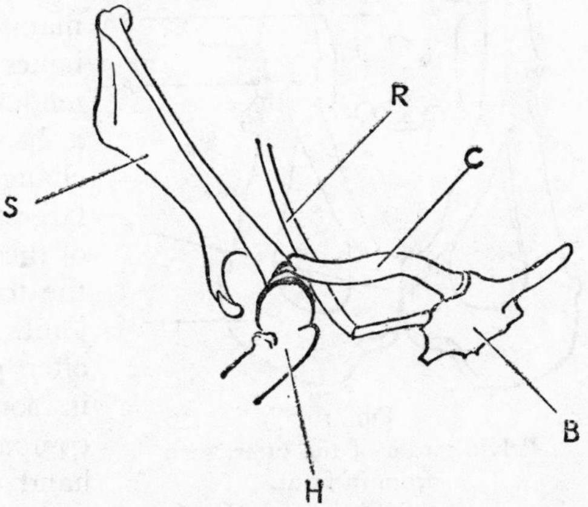

The fore and hind limbs have similar basic plans; in each the upper part contains one bone, the femur in the thigh, the humerus in the upper arm, forming

FIG. 9
The shoulder girdle of a shrew.
B, breast bone. C, collar-bone. H, upper end of the first bone of the arm. R, lower end of the first rib. S, shoulder blade (narrower in the shrew than in many mammals)

hip or shoulder joint above, knee or elbow below (fig. 11, p. 25). The lower parts each have two bones, the tibia and smaller fibula in the shin, the radius and smaller ulna in the forearm. In many mammals the lesser bone of either or both limbs is reduced to a small slip attached to the larger. At their lower ends these bones articulate with a number of smaller ones, tarsals to form the ankle, carpals to form the wrist. These small bones are bound together by ligaments, and vary greatly in shape and number between the different orders of mammals, but however much they may be modified in either direction their homologies can always be discerned. The tarsals and carpals are followed by a series of short straight bones, the metatarsals and metacarpals, one for each finger or toe, forming the main part of the foot and hand. Following these are the phalanges, short cylindrical bones, one for each joint of each digit. There is much diversity

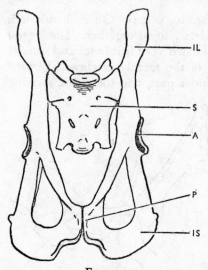

FIG. 10

Pelvic girdle of the otter, seen from in front.

A, socket for the hip joint. IL, ilium. IS, ischium. P, pubis, joining the corresponding bone of the opposite side in front. S, sacral vertebrae fused together and to the ilia

in the number of digits and in the form of the ankle and wrist bones, the digits numbering from five, as in man and many others, to a single functional one, as in the horse.

Bones occur elsewhere in the mammalian body; small (sesamoid) bones are often developed in the tendons of muscles, usually to give a bearing surface where tendons change their direction of pull. The largest and most constantly present of these is the patella (knee-cap) in the tendon passing over the knee-joint. Smaller sesamoid bones are often present in other tendons and in some mammals they reach a comparatively large size, as in the hand of the mole (see p. 54). In many mammals there is an os penis supporting the male organ, and in some of the larger ones there is an os cordis stiffening the partition dividing the heart.

The skeleton gives anchorage to the 'voluntary' muscles, the 'meat' of the butcher and the dining-table, each of which causes a specific movement by its contraction. Muscles consist of an immense number of elongated cells arranged parallel to each other and to the long axis of the muscle. They are in contact with nerve-endings, in response to stimulation from which a chemical change takes place, causing the cells to contract. At least one end of most voluntary muscles is attached to bone, and at its attachment the muscle-cells merge with those of the tough skin covering the bone; if the action of the muscle is transmitted to a distance, as from the forearm to the fingers, a tendon or sinew intervenes between the contractile part of the muscle and its insertion. The main groups of muscles correspond with the divisions of the skeleton; axial ones move the head and vertebral column, and move the ribs in respiration; appendicular ones move the limbs with respect to the trunk, and the parts of the limbs relatively to each other.

In addition to the skeletal voluntary muscles whose microscopic structure is characterised by numerous striations crossing each fibre, nearly every organ incorporates muscle fibres of another kind, without striations. These are the unstriped or involuntary muscles whose action is not consciously controlled, and cause contractions of the walls of the blood vessels, of the gut, of the reproductive tract, and many other parts.

The digestive system, alimentary canal, or gut of mammals fills most of the body-cavity (fig. 12, p. 26). Food is cut or ground up in the mouth, where it is mixed with saliva, which is delivered by special tubes or ducts, from several pairs of glands in the tissues near the mouth. Saliva has a slight digestive action on some foods, but its main function is to moisten and lubricate the food before it is swallowed. The food

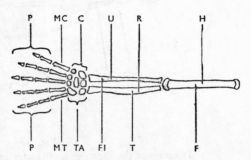

Fig. 11

Diagram of the bones of the limb of a mammal ; the upper letters refer to the fore limb, the lower ones to the hind. H, humerus. R, radius. U, ulna. C, carpal bones (wrist). MC, metacarpal bones (hand). P, fingers. F, femur. T, tibia. FI, fibula. TA, tarsal bones (ankle). MT, metatarsal bones (foot). P, toes

when swallowed passes along the gullet, through the chest, to the stomach lying in the abdomen close behind the diaphragm. The stomach can hold a mass of food, which may therefore be consumed in meals, and in it the process of digestion starts, numerous glands in the lining of the stomach secreting the gastric juice. The juice contains hydrochloric acid and the ferment rennin, which break down the complex food substances into ones chemically simpler, but no absorption of nourishment occurs in the stomach. In some mammals, as the ruminants and the whales, the stomach is not a simple bag but is divided into compartments; in the former the food goes to the first compartment and is later regurgitated, by way of the second, for chewing as the cud (see p. 281), after which it is re-swallowed and diverted to the third and fourth.

The end of the stomach is shut by a circular muscle (sphincter) that relaxes at intervals to allow small masses of food to pass into the

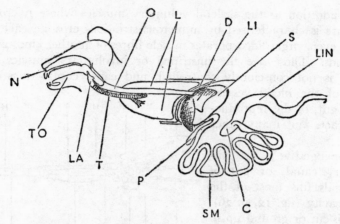

FIG. 12

Diagram of the digestive and respiratory organs of a mammal.
C, caecum. D, diaphragm, separating chest from abdomen. L, right lung
(the left is removed). LA, larynx. LI, liver. LIN, large intestine. N, nostril.
O, oesophagus. P, pancreas. S, stomach. SM, coils of small intestine.
T, windpipe, the branch to the left lung is shown as a cut stump. TO, tongue

first part of the small intestine, the duodenum. Here the food is acted
upon by the secretions from the liver and pancreas (sweetbread);
the liver lies close to the stomach and is pressed against the diaphragm,
the pancreas lies among the loops of the intestine. The liver-cells
make bile, which is delivered to the duodenum through the bile-duct;
in many animals there is also a gall-bladder for storing it. The bile
causes the fats of the food to break up into minute particles, and
increases the action of the intestinal juice. The pancreas makes a
secretion, delivered by the pancreatic duct, whose ferments act on the
partly digested food, breaking down the proteins, carbo-hydrates,
and fats. Digestion and assimilation are completed in the small
intestine, a long coiled tube that may reach a great length—about
five times the body-length in the dog, about 25 feet in man—whose
lining is covered with numerous small finger-like projections, the villi.
Between the villi many small glands secrete the intestinal juice, whose
ferments cause the final breakdown of the food to comparatively
simple chemical substances. These are absorbed by the cells covering
the villi, and passed to the circulation which distributes the nourishment round the body.

The small intestine opens into the much shorter large intestine; in most mammals by the time the food reaches the latter there is little remaining to be absorbed from it except water. At the junction of small and large intestines there is a blind side passage, the caecum, which is usually small, but is very large in herbivorous animals that do not chew the cud, such as rodents and horses. The digestive juices have no appreciable effect upon cellulose, but certain bacteria make ferments that break it down into simpler substances. Such bacteria live in enormous numbers in the caecum of those mammals that possess a large one, and, in digesting the cellulose of the food for their own use, break it down into substances and by-products that can be absorbed by the mammal. They are therefore termed 'symbiotic' bacteria, for though they depend upon the mammal for their food, the mammal equally cannot live unless they are present.

The contractions of the muscular wall of the whole of the digestive tube churn the food up so that it becomes well mixed with the digestive juices, and propel it slowly onwards. A thin semi-transparent skin lines the abdominal cavity, and a double layer of it forms a sheet wrapping round the gut and other organs and holding them in place.

The nourishment derived from the food finds its way into the blood, which is driven by the rhythmic contractions of the heart, situated in the chest. The heart of mammals contains four chambers, two auricles and two ventricles, which have muscular walls whose contraction pumps the blood onwards. Blood from the left ventricle enters the aorta, the main artery, which divides into smaller and smaller branches to supply blood to every part of the body. The ends of the arteries break up into a network of minute channels, the capillaries, whose walls are so thin that substances can be exchanged between the blood and the cells of the tissues. From the capillary network the blood passes to small veins, which join to form bigger and bigger channels, until the blood returns to the heart, entering the right auricle by the vena cava, the main vein into which the others drain. Thence it is passed to the right ventricle, and is pumped to the lungs. Here it passes through another network of capillaries, in which it is separated from the air by an extremely thin membrane. In these capillaries the blood gives out the carbon dioxide that it has collected from the tissues and takes up oxygen to be delivered to them. The blood returns from the lungs through a large vein to the left auricle, thence it goes to the left ventricle and enters the aorta on its journey round the body again.

The blood is a clear fluid in which float millions of cells, some of which are red and give it its colour. Much of the clear fluid oozes from the blood into the tissues through the thin walls of the capillaries. This fluid, the lymph, flows through great numbers of minute tubes that finally join to form a large duct, running along the back of the chest to the base of the neck, where it opens into one of the main veins and returns the lymph to the blood. The lymph is particularly concerned with the defence of the body against invasion by unwanted bacteria, and with carrying the products of digestion, especially the fats, away from the intestine.

The windpipe leads from the back of the mouth to the lungs; its entrance is guarded by a gristly flap, the epiglottis, which closes over it while anything is being swallowed. In the chest the windpipe branches to the right and left lungs, within which the branches divide many times forming smaller and smaller twigs, that finally end as minute blind pockets. Round each pocket is spread the capillary network through which the exchange of gases between the blood and the air occurs. The lungs contain immense numbers of minute end-pockets, and consequently their structure is compact and spongy; they are not mere hollow bags, and this arrangement gives an immensely increased surface area for the exchange of gases. Air is drawn into the lungs by an expanding movement of the chest-wall and a downward movement of the diaphragm.

In any activity of the body, the contraction of a muscle for example, the energy required is produced by oxidising the products of digestion; the energy is used up in doing work and producing heat, and by-products are formed that must be eliminated. One of these is carbon dioxide which passes out through the lungs, others, formed during the making-good of tissue wear and tear, and in the digestion of proteins, are complex ammoniacal substances. They are harmful to living cells, and are taken by a special blood vessel, the hepatic portal vein, direct from the gut to the liver, where they are converted into the comparatively harmless substance urea, which passes back into the blood and is carried to the kidneys. Here it is removed from the blood and, dissolved in considerable quantities of water, goes through a duct from each kidney to the bladder which is emptied periodically.

The brain and spinal cord constitute the central nervous system, which controls all the voluntary actions of the body and many others, such as breathing, that are automatic. They consist of immense numbers of nerve-cells, and are connected with all parts of the body by cells whose cell-bodies give off fibres of great length that form the ordinary nerves. Subsidiary chains of nerve-cells, the sympathetic and parasympathetic systems, are connected with the central nervous system and are particularly concerned with the activities of the viscera. Nerves are of two sorts, sensory and motor; sensory nerves run inwards from the eyes, ears, skin, and so on, bringing messages from the external surroundings and from the internal organs to the central nervous system; motor nerves convey impulses outwards to the muscles, so that action takes place in response to the stimuli received. In the simplest reactions the nervous path may be short, the inward impulse travelling only to the lower centres of the central nervous system, often no higher than the spinal cord, where it is handed on by other cells to the motor nerves which stimulate the muscles to action. Responses of this sort are known as reflex actions, and may take place even in an animal deprived of its brain. An example would be the quick withdrawal of the hand on running a splinter into it, very different from the complex actions involved in taking a pair of tweezers and pulling the splinter from the wound.

The interconnections of the nerves in the central nervous system, and especially in the brain, are of extreme complexity so that alternative responses can be elicited, thus providing the physical basis for the alternatives experienced as choice and free-will, allowing habits to be formed, and in the most elaborate type making language and thought possible. Even the simplest actions, such as standing up or walking, when analysed are found to be very complex. So too are many of the automatic ones, such as the contractions of the muscular wall of the intestine during digestion, which are quite beyond voluntary control and usually outside consciousness.

In addition to the nervous system, there is another method of controlling and co-ordinating the activities of the body, and this is by the action of the hormones, endocrines, or chemical messengers. These are substances produced in special 'endocrine' glands but not delivered to some external site of action by tubes, as for instance are the bile and the saliva; they go direct into the blood and produce their effects when it brings them to the organs capable of responding. The response to hormones is thus usually slower than that to nervous stimulation, but it generally persists longer. Hormones are made in many special parts of the body such as the pituitary gland at the base of the brain, the thyroid gland in the neck, the suprarenal bodies near the kidneys, the pancreas, the reproductive organs, and in many less specialised parts. The growth and proper functioning of all parts of the body depend upon the maintenance of a just balance in the proportions of the hormones present. The hormones play a very important part in the processes of growth and reproduction as well as in minute-by-minute regulation, and much has been learned about them in the last quarter-century.

The ultimate function of the life of any animal or plant is to reproduce its kind and leave a new generation of offspring to take its place. In some lower animals reproduction takes place by a complete new individual growing from the body of the old one, and becoming detached from it to live independently. The reproduction of higher animals differs from this asexual method in that the pieces detached from the old individuals to grow into new ones are single cells; these are the egg- and sperm-cells, produced by the females and males respectively, and the egg cannot develop into a new individual until it is fertilised by a sperm cell fusing with it, this method being sexual reproduction. In some animals, but not mammals, a state of parthenogenesis is reached in which the egg cell can develop without being fertilised.

During the course of maturation of reproductive cells the normal double set of chromosomes present in each cell of the body is sorted out into two single sets of various composition, so that there is only one set in each mature reproductive cell. Consequently fertilisation, or the fusion of egg and sperm, produces a cell with the full number of chromosomes ready to develop into a new animal. This sexual type of reproduction results in the recombination of the genetic material in the chromosomes, so that the units of the hereditary constitution are recombined in new ways; it is also this that is believed to allow the spread through a population of animals of new characters, or combinations of characters, on which natural selection may act with the ultimate formation of new species. The reproductive cells of both sexes are produced in the sexual organs or gonads; in all mammals the eggs are fertilised inside the body of the mother, and in all those higher than the egg-laying Duck-bill and Spiny Anteater of Australasia they develop there into the new individuals before they are expelled.

In the male the gonads are the testes, paired ovoid bodies that may lie inside the abdomen, as in elephants and whales, but are more usually accommodated in an external sac, the scrotum, as in man and many others. The testes contain a large number of closely packed tubules, the cells that line them being those that give rise to the motile male sex-cells, the sperms or spermatozoa. The spermatozoa pass from the testis through a much coiled tube, the epididymis, whose duct joins the passage leading from the bladder to the exterior, the ducts of each side opening into it close together. Glands of several sorts, such as the seminal vesicles and the prostate, provide by their secretions a fluid in which the spermatozoa swim, and in which they are transferred to the female during pairing.

In the female the gonads are the ovaries, solid masses of background-tissue in which are embedded numerous egg-cells or ova, each contained in a small envelope of cells, the ovarian follicle. When the eggs are ready for fertilisation the follicles contain a quantity of fluid that makes them bulge out on the surface of the ovary. At the appropriate moment the follicles burst, and the fluid gushes out carrying the egg-cells into the funnel-shaped opening of a tube that lies nearby. The tube is narrow and the eggs are wafted along it by the beating of hair-like projections, or cilia, of the cells lining it; it is while in this tube that the eggs are fertilised by the spermatozoa received from the male, and immediately start dividing to grow into the embryos and the membranes that surround them. At the end of their journey through the narrow tube they reach a very much larger one, the uterus, capable of great distension, where their development into young animals is to be completed. In most mammals the uterus-tube on each side of the body is separate from that of the opposite side, only the lower ends joining each other in the mid-line; in some species, including man, the two are partly or wholly fused into one. The lower end of the uterus, in all mammals higher than the pouched marsupials of Australasia and America, opens into an unpaired passage, the vagina, leading to the exterior, through which the young are born and the sperm received from the male. The urethra, the tube that drains the bladder, usually has a common opening to the exterior with the vagina, but in many of the smaller mammals the two openings are quite separate, the urethra opening at the end of a small structure resembling the organ of the male.

It is well known that most animals, including mammals, have seasonal breeding times, and do not breed all the year round. This time is marked in the female mammal by a willingness to mate, and

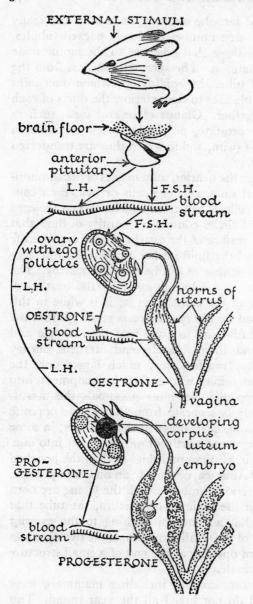

EXTERNAL STIMULI

brain floor →

anterior
pituitary

L.H.

F.S.H.
blood
stream

F.S.H.

ovary
with egg
follicles

L.H.

horns of
uterus

OESTRONE
blood
stream

L.H.

OESTRONE

vagina

developing
corpus
luteum

PRO-
GESTERONE

embryo

blood
stream

PROGESTERONE

Fig. 13
Diagram showing some of the
mechanism of the female breeding cycle

is known technically as oestrus or heat; at or shortly after oestrus, one or more eggs are released from the ovary, to be fertilised and to develop into young. Oestrus nearly always stops as soon as the eggs are fertilised and pregnancy starts; in many mammals it recurs soon after the birth of the young, but in others there is a long period of quiescence or anoestrus during and after suckling. Several litters may be produced in quick succession if oestrus is recurrent, but at the end of the breeding season anoestrus sets in until the beginning of the next, usually in the following year. This series of events, accompanied by great changes in the reproductive tract, is known as the oestrous cycle (fig. 15, p. 36); mammals having only one cycle in each breeding season are called monoestrous, those having a succession of cycles polyoestrous.

The course of the oestrous cycle is controlled directly by the state of the ovary. While the egg-cells are approaching maturity the follicles that contain them become distended with fluid secreted from the rapidly multiplying cells that line the follicles. The fluid contains a substance, oestradiol, the female sex-hormone, which passes into the blood and causes profound changes in the rest of the reproductive tract, and in the instincts and behaviour of the animal, stimulating the organs to functional activity and activating the nervous system to provide the psychological and behaviour changes character-istic of oestrus. The release of the egg-cells by the bursting of the follicles is spontaneous in some species when the egg-cells are ripe; in others it awaits upon the occurrence of mating, in the absence of which the follicles are retained and oestrus is prolonged.

The follicle collapses after bursting, and the lining cells increase greatly in size, though not in number, until the former follicle is transformed into a solid ball of cells, the corpus luteum. Its cells produce a hormone called progesterone, which, like other hormones, is released into the blood and carried round the body. Its primary action is, in conjunction with oestradiol, upon the lining of the uterus, stimulating it to a very active stage of growth preparatory to receiving and nourishing the newly fertilised eggs. This stage occurs while the eggs are being fertilised, and are travelling down the first narrow tube. The uterus is ready, soon after the arrival of the eggs, to take part in forming the special structure, the placenta, through which the growing embryo is nourished. This brings the circulation of the mother and offspring into very close proximity on a large scale, so that some

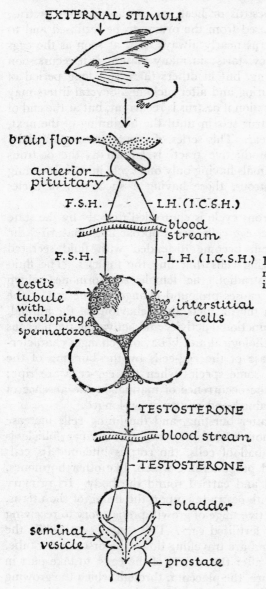

EXTERNAL STIMULI

brain floor→

anterior
pituitary

F.S.H. ——— L.H. (I.C.S.H.)

blood
stream

F.S.H. ——— L.H. (I.C.S.H.)

testis
tubule
with
developing
spermatozoa

interstitial
cells

TESTOSTERONE

blood stream

TESTOSTERONE

bladder

seminal
vesicle

prostate

FIG. 14
Diagram showing some of the
mechanism of the male breeding cycle. Drawing by Mrs. A.
J. Marshall.

substances can diffuse from one to the other, but the two circulations do not actually join and become mixed. The placenta remains attached to the lining of the uterus throughout pregnancy, and is connected to the embryo at the navel by a cord containing blood-vessels; at birth the cord is severed and the placenta is discharged shortly afterwards. In some mammals the corpora lutea produce hormone throughout pregnancy, but in others they stop functioning and disappear partly or wholly some time before the birth of the young. When their functional life is over they shrink in size and are gradually absorbed, so that eventually they can no longer be recognised.

In the males of many mammals there is a seasonal period of rut, when the sex apparatus and sex instincts are at their greatest activity, a period similar to the oestrus of the female, with the occurrence of which it must coincide to be biologically effective. In those species in which the male is potent at all times of the year, the limits of the breeding season are set entirely by the occurrence of oestrus in the female. The criterion of potency in the male is the production of spermatozoa in sufficient quantity by the testes, but the seasonal changes in the male are usually much more extensive than only this. In the testes the cells packed between the sperm-forming tubules, the interstitial cells, secrete the male sex-hormone, testosterone, into the blood. This hormone causes the development of the secondary sexual characters, such as the mane and antlers of the stag, and the thick neck of the bull and stallion, and induces the accompanying sexual behaviour. It also produces growth of the reproductive tract and its associated glands, and stimulates them to functional activity, especially in the smaller species whose males are seasonal breeders. In its absence, as in castrated animals, the secondary characters, such as the antlers of deer, are not produced.

One may well ask, what causes the seasonal activity of the gonads of both sexes so that they produce the hormones that have such profound effect? The answer to this question is not known completely, but much information about it has been discovered in recent years. The immediate cause of the activity is the presence in the blood of other substances, the gonadotropic hormones, which are secreted by the pituitary gland, lying at the base of the brain (figs. 13, 14, pp. 32, 34). The pituitary gland is a small gland of great functional complexity producing numerous hormones that affect the activity of many parts of the body. There are at least two gonadotropic hormones in the female, one stimulating the ovarian follicles to growth (follicle-stimulating hormone), and the other stimulating the formation of the corpora lutea after the follicles have burst (luteinising hormone); another hormone from the pituitary (lactogenic hormone) controls the production of milk when the young are born. Similar gonadotropic hormones act upon the gonads in the male, the equivalent of the follicle-stimulating hormone controlling the formation of spermatozoa by the tubules, and the interstitial-cell stimulating hormone, which may be the same as the luteinising hormone of the female, activating the interstitial tissue. The pituitary gland is divided into two parts, both of which make hormones, but it is the front or anterior part that produces the gonadotropic hormones.

But all this takes us only one step farther in the chain of causes, for we are still without an explanation of the seasonal activity of the pituitary. And here we come to a further complexity, for no one cause is known to produce this effect. In some mammals the amount of light falling upon the animals daily can be, in part at least, a cause of the seasonal activity. In the ferret, for example, the amount of light, and particularly the amount of ultra-violet light, that irradiates

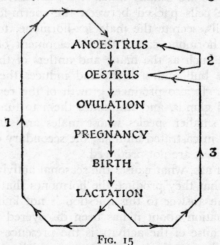

FIG. 15

Diagram showing the chain of events in the female oestrous cycle.
The cycle follows arrow 1 in monoestrous animals. In polyoestrous animals the cycle follows arrow 3 several times in succession and then switches to arrow 1. Arrow 2 shows the course of the cycle if mating is infertile or missed

the animal daily has a great influence on the activity of the pituitary gland. But this is in captive animals that can be given a measured amount of daily light; it is hard to see how the amount of light can have any effect upon wild animals that are nocturnal and spend the day in the dark recesses of their dens. And what of the animals whose pairing time is in late summer or autumn, such as the red deer? If the amount of daily irradiation has any effect upon them, it must be the decreasing daily quantity that produces the stimulation. Apart from direct physical agents, the activity of the pituitary gland is influenced by more subtle things, such as psychogenic stimuli that arise in the brain, or are built up there as a result of the reception of stimuli from the organs of special sense, those of sight, hearing, smell, and touch. The problem of pituitary activity is an extremely complex one which occupies the attention of many biologists; its intricacies are being gradually unravelled, and much has been discovered, but we still await a full explanation of seasonal activity and the causes that bring it about.

CHAPTER 3

MOLES, SHREWS, AND THEIR ALLIES
(INSECTIVORA)

"Other concerns there are of Molls . . . as the peculiar formation
of their feet, the slender Ossa Fugalia and Dogteeth, and how
hard it is to keep them alive out of the Earth. As also the ferity
and voracity of these animals; for though they be contented
with Roots and stringy parts of Plants or Wormes underground,
yet when they are above it will sometimes tear and eat on
another, and in a large glass wherein a Moll a Toad and a
viper were inclosed, we have known the Moll to dispatch them
and devour a good part of them both."

SIR THOMAS BROWNE, *Pseudodoxia Epidemica*

THE INSECTIVORES are regarded as the most primitive order of
mammals, many points in their anatomy showing their small
degree of divergence from the condition believed to have existed in
the original stock from which all the orders of placental mammals
are descended. These characters include the small size of the brain
and the comparatively large size of its lobes serving the sense of smell,
the plantigrade feet each usually with five toes, and many others.
On the other hand there are numerous specialised characters super-
imposed upon the more primitive ones, as for example, the peculiar
form and arrangement of the teeth in many species, or the extremely
specialised adaptations to digging and a fossorial existence seen in the
skeleton and muscles of the moles.

The insectivores are small mammals, the largest of them being no
bigger than a rabbit; most of them live on or in the ground, though a
few live in trees, and some are aquatic. The order is found throughout
most of the world, but in Britain its species are few, being the hedgehog, four species of shrews, and the mole; of these only the hedgehog
and one species of shrew are found all over the British Islands. The

insectivora are not confined exclusively to a diet of insects though the greater part of their food does consist of small invertebrates; most of them will attack any animal that they are large enough to overpower, and some also include food of vegetable origin in their diet though it usually forms no important part of it.

Both moles and shrews are very voracious, consuming more than their own weight of food every twenty-four hours; their whole life is an incessant hunt for food, only short intervals of repose punctuating their nearly continuous feverish activity. The necessity for almost continuous feeding is so great that if food is withheld the animals quickly die for want of it, usually within twelve hours. This high rate of food-intake is necessitated by their very high rate of metabolism when compared with other small mammals of similar size such as mice, but the causes of the high metabolic rate are not known. There may be some connection between the high rate of metabolism and the preponderance of protein over the comparatively small amounts of fat and carbohydrate in the diet, but no experimental investigation into the subject has been reported. Shrews and moles in captivity are better able to withstand a temporary shortage of food, as for instance overnight, if they are provided with plenty of warm bedding in which they can make a nest;[2] their early death from starvation is thus evidently connected with an inability to maintain their body-heat unless great quantities of food are continually available.

Shrews and moles are extremely quarrelsome and aggressive; a meeting between two individuals of the same species nearly always results in one attacking the other, except during the breeding season when the female is receptive to the male. This aggressive disposition appears to be correlated with the high metabolic rate that keeps the animals incessantly on the go. As a measure of the metabolic rate the consumption of oxygen during a given time may be taken; though no figures are available for our British insectivores some experimental results from the American shrew *Sorex cinereus* have appeared.[168] These show that the average consumption of oxygen per gram of body weight every hour is about five times as great as that of mice and small voles. This rate of oxygen-usage is believed to imply a correspondingly high production of heat, which is as rapidly lost, but, as already mentioned, the reasons for the high rate of heat-production and loss, and the means by which they are brought about, are not understood. The activity of the shrews and the mole contrasts strongly with that of the hedgehog, which is a very much more sluggish creature and is specialised in the opposite direction, being able to go without food for long periods during the winter when, unlike its relatives, it goes into hibernation.

Hibernation in the hedgehog is much less regular than in some other mammals such as the dormouse and many bats, for the animals often do not lie up for the winter until the end of the year, so that they may not be torpid for more than three months; but the time of starting hibernation and its duration vary between individuals and from season to season. Hibernating mammals are aroused by warmth, but none of them can withstand being frozen, hence the necessity for them to lie up in a protected nest where frost is excluded; the hedgehog usually hibernates underground in a hollow under old tree-roots or under accumulations of leaves and brush (Pl. II, p. 53). Hibernation in a warm-blooded animal such as the hedgehog is a very much more drastic process than in a cold-blooded one such as a snake or frog; the mammal has in effect to relinquish its temperature-regulation and become cold-blooded. Like all hibernating mammals, the hedgehog grows very fat before entering on the winter sleep, and the fat-deposits not only serve to keep the metabolism going at its reduced rate during the winter, but their presence in the autumn provides or helps to provide the stimulus that starts hibernation, though the means by which it does so are not known; in any case low temperatures and scarcity of food are not the primary causes. There is, in addition, a deposit of dark-coloured fat and lymph tissue round the blood-vessels in the chest, neck and elsewhere; it is large in autumn but decreases to very small proportions by the middle of summer. This has been termed the "hibernating gland", but its functions are obscure, for it decreases in size during hibernation more slowly than the general reserves of fat.

At the beginning of hibernation the general fat-deposits are very large not only under the skin, but also in the mesenteries, the thin sheets of tissue that anchor the viscera to their places inside the abdomen. It is these deposits that are used up first during hibernation, so that little fat is removed from the hibernating gland until the end of March.[40] In the hedgehog the part of the gland lying under the fore-arm is the largest; it is triangular and its apex extends forward, closely investing the external jugular vein. A smaller part extends up on to the back between the shoulder-blades and along the back of the neck

to the base of the skull, and another along the front of the neck close
to the thymus and thyroid glands.[38] In some other mammals large
parts of the gland accompany the aorta, the main artery from the
heart, through the chest into the abdomen, but such parts are small
or absent in the hedgehog. The gland is lobulated, and at the beginning of hibernation it is orange-brown in colour. Although portions
of the gland lie very close to the thymus gland and appear to be part
of it, a direct connection and structural similarity to it have been
denied; its structure is a mixture of lymphoid, glandular and fatty
tissues. But tissue similar to the hibernating gland is present in many
other mammals which do not hibernate ("brown fat tissue"), and it is
probable that all fat-tissue, during the course of embryonic development, goes through a stage in which it resembles the hibernating
gland; this fat-formation is very similar to the deposits of fat within
the lobes of the thymus.[144] Now the thymus gland is of great importance
during the growth-period of an animal, but becomes smaller and
apparently less active in the adult; it is therefore possible that in
hibernating mammals the hibernating gland does in fact have some
functions similar to that of the thymus. On the other hand recent
research has shown that the discharge of fatty material from the
aggregation of "brown fat" which lies between the shoulders of the
rat runs parallel to the discharge of similar material (adrenal cortical
lipids) from the outer layers of the adrenal bodies in the reaction to
alarm, and the conclusion has been drawn that the discharge is a
characteristic response during exposure to various kinds of mental or
physical stress.[187] But no reason has yet been discovered to explain
why these deposits of brown fat, which appear to be fat-storing glands
of internal secretion, are so large and conspicuous in rodents and
hibernating animals, nor why in some animals they should produce
large amounts of male sex-hormones. The precise function of the substances liberated from them in hibernating animals remains unknown.

The amount of water in the hibernating gland varies conversely
with the amount of fat, the fat being replaced by water as it is used
up although the animal does not drink throughout hibernation; this
water-logging of the tissues is similar to that seen in cases of starvation.[40]
The amount of water lost by the body during hibernation is reduced
by a slackening in the activity of the kidneys, in which a system of
short-circuits of the smaller blood-vessels comes into play. This
reduces the amount of blood flowing through the surface zone in which

most fluid leaves the blood in the formation of urine. Similar short-circuits appear to be present in the small blood-vessels of the kidneys in all mammals whether they hibernate or not, and they come into action in response to various stimuli of which a lack of oxygen is one. The reduced respiration in a hibernating mammal and the consequent oxygen-starvation of its tissues is probably the immediate cause of the short-circuiting of the blood in the kidney, and the diminution in the rate of urine-production.

In the hibernating hedgehog a great concentration of white blood-corpuscles has been found within the coats of the stomach; in some places near the larger blood-vessels they are so numerous and so closely packed as to form a gland-like mass. Carlier,[38] who investigated this matter says, "this great migration of white blood-corpuscles from the blood-vessels occurs at the very commencement of hibernation, just at the time when the temperature of the animal is beginning to decrease. That they come from the blood is borne out by the fact that up to this period there are from 18,000 to 20,000 white corpuscles per cubic millimetre of blood, which number falls suddenly at the very commencement of winter sleep to 1,000, 2,000 or 3,000 in the same volume; whereas the red corpuscles show if anything rather an increase in number." This author suggests that the great concentration is owing to the need of combating invasion by bacteria from the gut when the temperature is lowered at the beginning of hibernation, and adds that white corpuscles are present not only in the stomach but in vast hordes all along the alimentary canal, and in the tissue round the bile- and pancreatic-ducts.

Once the animal becomes cold-blooded and its temperature drops (see p. 43), the rate of respiration decreases and may become so slow that it is very difficult to detect any sign of breathing at all. At the same time the rate of the heart beat becomes very slow and the circulation of the blood round the body is greatly retarded. The blood itself is altered in composition, experiments on hedgehogs having shown that during hibernation the amount of sugar in the blood is less than half that present when the animal is active, and that the amount of magnesium is more than twice as great.[205] It has further been found that if active hedgehogs in summer are injected with insulin, which decreases the amount of blood-sugar and increases that of magnesium, and placed in a low temperature (but above freezing) an artificial hibernation is induced which may last for many days. When such animals are later removed to a warm temperature they awake in a normal manner and return to a warm-blooded state. Carlier,[39] who investigated the pancreas in the hibernating hedgehog, was surprised to find it in a more or less active state, and reported that the parts in which insulin is secreted (the islets of Langerhans) appeared to be fully functional, a finding which points to the probability that the maintenance of the secretion of insulin is one of the necessary conditions of hibernation in this animal. This observation has been confirmed recently, and in addition a decrease in the secretion of adrenalin during hibernation has been found,[16] the decrease probably helping to depress the general rate of metabolism.

There seems to be some doubt about the temperature of the body during hibernation, for most observers have recorded very low values by taking the rectal temperature; but if the temperature of the blood within the heart is measured, an operation which can be done with a fine thermocouple mounted within a small hypodermic needle, much higher values approaching the normal waking temperature, are found. There appears to be a temperature-gradient, the extremities being as cold as the surroundings but the centre remaining comparatively warm. Hibernation, however, is not entirely uninterrupted, for the hedgehog's sleep may last only a few days at a time, with intervals of activity, until the winter is well advanced.

None of the other British insectivores hibernates; they all pursue their ways with undiminished activity throughout the winter. Only one, the mole, lays up stores of food against times of scarcity, a procedure that is surprising in an animal of such voracity. For long the accounts of the storage of worms in larders near the mole's nest were regarded with scepticism, but the fact has now been established beyond doubt. Great numbers of worms have occasionally been found buried in the large heap of earth, sometimes called the mole's "fortress," in which its nest is placed. Stores of over a thousand worms have thus been found, not all in a single mass but scattered in bunches of up to about a dozen throughout the heap of earth. It was suggested that the worms had not been stored by the mole but had congregated in the loose earth of the heap during frosty weather when the surrounding ground was frozen. But careful examination of the worms showed that this could not be the correct explanation, for the front end of each worm had been injured so that, though not killed, it was unable to crawl away. L. E. Adams[2] appears to have been the first to clarify

the matter by experiments upon a captive mole. He fed the animal
with a great quantity of worms until it could eat no more, but instead
of then losing interest in food and ignoring the further worms that
were offered it pounced upon them, bit the front end and pushed
them beneath the surface of the earth, covering the place by scraping
earth over it with the paws. Adam's experiments have since been
repeated by other observers, especially on the continent, who have
confirmed his results. It is clear, then, that the mole does store worms in
the ground, first mutilating them by biting the front end so that they
cannot escape. The question remains, however, under what circumstances are so many worms available to the mole that it can eat to
satiation and yet leave an excess to be stored? The explanation seems to
be that a sudden frost restricts the movements of worms so that the
mole can capture large numbers of them in a short time and store those
that it continues catching after it can eat no more. This conclusion is
supported by the fact that stores of worms laid up by moles have most
frequently been reported during or after a spell of frosty weather. It
has been suggested, but there is no exact evidence, that at such times
worms leave their own burrows and enter those of the mole where they
are gathered by the inmate. This habit appears to be particularly
marked in the worm *Lumbricus terrestris*, for this species has been found
to form the chief content of the mole's larder although other species
have been more numerous in the surrounding earth.[69]

The differences already mentioned in habits, temperament, and
metabolism between the mole, the shrews and the hedgehog are
reflected in the anatomy of the animals, and in the classification
based upon it by systematists. The insectivores of the world, living
and extinct, are divided into eight superfamilies, only two of which
are represented in the British fauna; their grouping emphasises that
the moles and shrews are more closely related to each other than is
either group to the hedgehogs.

SUPERFAMILY ERINACOIDEA
    Family Erinacidae   Hedgehogs
SUPERFAMILY SORICOIDEA
    Family Soricidae   Shrews
    Family Talpidae   Moles (and Desmans, not
                           present in Britain)

FIG. 16
The Classification of the British Insectivora

The first and last of these families each contains a single British species, but of the Soricidae there are four species and one subspecies. The hedgehog, *Erinaceus europaeus* Linnaeus, is found over the whole of western Europe as far south as the Pyrenees and the Alps, the animals inhabiting Spain, Italy, and the Balkans being distinguished as several subspecies that differ from the typical race and each other in their depth of coloration and larger or smaller sizes. The mole, *Talpa europaea* Linnaeus (Pl. IVb, p. 69), is likewise distributed over Europe, but extends farther south to the shores of the Mediterranean; in the British Isles it is, however, absent from Ireland (see p. 377). Several other species of mole have been described from southern Europe, but it is questionable whether they differ sufficiently from *Talpa europaea* to be given full specific rank; it is more probable that they are no more than subspecies of the generally distributed species.

The four species of shrew found in Britain belong to three genera, *Sorex* (Red-toothed shrews), *Neomys* (Water-shrews), and *Crocidura* (White-toothed shrews). All the shrews are small mouse-like animals with long snouts, small eyes, and dense velvety fur; those of the first two genera can at once be distinguished from those of the last by the colour of the enamel on the crowns of the teeth, which is red or orange whereas in the latter it is white. There are two British species of *Sorex*, *S. araneus*, the common shrew, and *S. minutus*, the pygmy or lesser shrew, very similar to each other in general appearance but separable when adult by the smaller size of the latter (head-and-body length averages 56 to 64 mm., against 70 to 74 mm.), and the comparatively longer tail (0.7 of the length of head-and-body against 0.5). At all ages there is a difference in the teeth, the first three upper unicuspids (see p. 49) being approximately equal in size in *S. minutus*, but the third being smaller than the first two in *S. araneus* (fig. 17, p. 47). The common shrew of Britain (Pl. IIIa, p. 68), found over the mainland and on many of the nearer islands but not in the Outer Hebrides, Shetland, or Ireland, differs slightly in colour from that of the continent which is generally a trifle darker; the British race is therefore separated as the subspecies *S. araneus castaneus* Jenyns. On the continent several subspecies are recognised from different parts of Europe, including one peculiar to Jersey. In Islay there is a race that is larger than the mainland shrew of Scotland, which itself is slightly smaller than that of the south of England though otherwise indistinguishable. The Islay shrew differs in colour, the grey of the underside extending far up the sides and contrasting strongly with the dark upper surface, but the most striking character is the tendency for the second upper premolar tooth (the last or fifth upper unicuspid) to be absent on one or both sides of the jaw. This tooth is present on both sides in about 45 per cent, on one side in rather under 25 per cent, and absent on both sides in rather over 30 per cent of Islay shrews. When first discovered this shrew was named as a separate species, but it is undoubtedly to be regarded as a subspecies, *S. araneus granti*, Barret-Hamilton and Hinton. The shrews of Jura and Gigha are dark in colour and small in size, resembling *S. a. granti* in the former and *S. a. castaneus* in the latter characters; they are intermediate between the two forms, but are not sufficiently distinct to be recognised as definite subspecies. Because the forms from these two islands differ to some extent from the mainland one, at least one writer[153] has referred to them by the name of the typical subspecies of the Continent, *S. a. araneus*, a proceeding which is unnecessary and misleading, for it obscures the probable relationships between the races.

The pygmy shrew (Pl. IIIb, p. 68), *S. minutus*, the only member of the family found in Ireland, is distributed through Great Britain and most of the islands, including the Outer Hebrides, Orkney and Shetland. It is generally considered to be scarcer than the common shrew, or even rare, but it is found, usually in some numbers, wherever it is sought. The only figures[27] available show that among 1,218 shrews caught in North Wales and Kent 1,016 were *Sorex araneus* and 202 were *S. minutus*, the latter forming 16.6 per cent of the total. But in making this collection *S. minutus* was found to be much more common than *S. araneus* in some restricted localities. The species inhabits the whole of Europe and extends into Asia; throughout all this range only one subspecies has been recognised, in the south of Italy, the rest, including the British Islands, being inhabited by the typical race *S. m. minutus* Linnaeus.

The water-shrew (*Neomys fodiens*) (Pl. IVa, p. 69), larger than the common shrew, brownish or blackish grey above and whitish below, has a fringe of hairs round the edges of the feet and the toes, and another forming a keel along the under side of the tail. The fur of the ears, and a small spot above the eye, are sometimes white. The typical race, *N. f. fodiens* Schreber, inhabits the whole of continental Europe and extends into Asia, allied species distinguished by the absence of a keel of hairs under the tail being found in the south of Europe, where

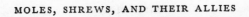

a

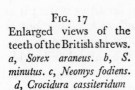

FIG. 17

Enlarged views of the teeth of the British shrews. a, *Sorex araneus*. b, *S. minutus*. c, *Neomys fodiens*. d, *Crocidura cassiteridum*

b

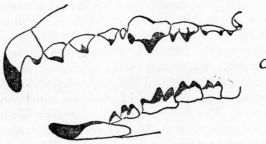

c

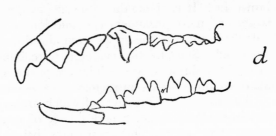

d

their ranges overlap. The British subspecies, which is found through-out Great Britain but is absent from most of the islands and Ireland, is distinguished by usually having the whitish underside suffused with brownish or buff, and is separated as *N. f. bicolor* Shaw. The water-shrew is subject to considerable individual variation in size, colour, and in the degree of development of the fringes on the feet and tail. Before this variability was recognised many different subspecies were named, some of them based upon characters which are merely seasonal differences; it was once believed that there was more than one species in Britain, a second named the "Oared Shrew" being described by the naturalists of the early nineteenth century,[19] who were misled by specimens with specially well-developed fringes. Though primarily an aquatic species the water-shrew is often found far from water; it is common in suitable habitats throughout England and Wales, but is said to be scarcer and more local in Scotland. Its food, like that of other shrews consists mostly of invertebrates, and the animal will tackle anything that it can overpower; vegetable matter is not usually eaten.

It is seldom that a zoologist has been able to announce the discovery of a mammal entirely new to the British fauna, one, too, belonging to a genus hitherto unrecorded. This unusual experience fell to Hinton[103] in 1924 when he determined certain shrews submitted to him from the Scilly Islands as a new species belonging to the genus *Crocidura*. There are many species of this genus, which is widely distributed throughout Europe, Africa and Asia, and includes *C. russula* Hermann, the common Musk-shrew of the continent and the Channel Islands. The new species, *C. cassiteridum* Hinton, differs slightly from that species, though they are very closely allied; the new one is almost certainly an offshoot from the old, and, indeed, might well be regarded as merely a subspecies of the latter. It can at once be distinguished from all other British shrews by its white teeth and greyish or silvery brown fur. It is about the same size as the common shrew, but has larger and more prominent ears and long scattered silky hairs on the tail; the number of the upper teeth also differs, there being only three unicuspids. Since the first examples were found it has been ascertained that all the shrews of the Scillies are of this species, and that none of the other three occurs on them.

The teeth, the characters of which are so useful in separating the species of shrews, show a high degree of specialisation in the insecti-vores, those of the shrews perhaps being most unlike the usual mammalian pattern (fig. 17, p. 47). In them the first incisor is a very large tooth that projects almost horizontally from the front of the jaw, that of the upper jaw being strongly hooked and bearing a second slightly smaller cusp behind the principal one. The first incisor of the lower jaw is long and blade-like, the cutting edge being raised into three distinct lobes. Behind the first incisor of both jaws follows a series of small teeth, each bearing a single cusp, and not differentiated functionally into incisors, canines and premolars. These teeth are often designated "unicuspids" because for long their homologies with the teeth of other mammals were considered to be uncertain. In the upper jaw the first two unicuspids are now generally regarded as incisors, the third as a canine, and the fourth and fifth, where they are present, as premolars; in the lower

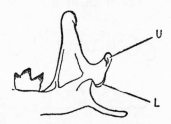

FIG. 18

Hind end of the lower jaw of a shrew showing the upper (U) and lower (L) joint surfaces

jaw the first is the canine and the second a premolar. The number of upper unicuspids present differs in the different genera; in *Sorex* there are five, in *Neomys* four, and in *Crocidura* three. In the lower jaw all three genera have only two unicuspids. Behind the unicuspids, in both jaws, come a number of molariform teeth; in the upper jaw the first of these is a premolar, the three behind it molars; in the lower jaw all three are molars. The dental formulae (see p. 22) of the genera are therefore *Sorex* $\frac{3.1.3.3.}{1.1.1.3.}$ (32), *Neomys* $\frac{3.1.2.3.}{1.1.1.3.}$ (30), and *Crocidura* $\frac{3.1.1.3.}{1.1.1.3.}$ (28), the progressive reduction being in the number of unicuspid premolars of which *Sorex* has two, *Neomys* one, and *Crocidura* none. The last genus is also distinguished by the absence of red-brown pigment from the enamel of the crowns of the teeth. The lower jaw of the shrews is further peculiar in having two separate bearing surfaces at the hinge where it forms a joint with the skull, but the mechanics of the functioning of this unusual arrangement do not appear to have been worked out (fig. 18).

In the hedgehog, too (fig. 19, p. 50), the first incisor in each jaw is a comparatively large tooth that projects forwards, though not placed so horizontally as in the shrews; there follow five unicuspids in the upper jaw, three in the lower. In the upper jaw the first two are incisors, the third the canine, the fourth and fifth premolars; in the lower jaw the first is an incisor, the second the canine and the third a premolar. In both jaws the unicuspids are succeeded by four molariform teeth of which the first is a premolar and the last three are molars: the dental formula is therefore $\frac{3.1.3.3.}{2.1.2.3.}$ (36).

The teeth of the mole approach the basic mammalian pattern more closely than those of the shrews and the hedgehog (fig. 20). In the upper jaw there are three small incisors, a large canine, three small unicuspid premolars followed by a larger one, and three molars. In the lower jaw there are three small incisors directed obliquely forwards, but the canine is very small and placed close to the incisors so that it appears to be one of them, the large caniniform tooth which follows them being an enlarged premolar. This tooth is followed by three normal premolars, and they again by three molars.

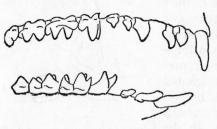

FIG. 19. Teeth of the hedgehog, showing the large front incisors and small canines. In this specimen the small second lower incisor has not yet been developed

An unusual feature of the dentition of the mole and hedgehog is that the upper canine, in the former always and in the latter sometimes, has two roots, for in most mammals this tooth has only a single root (fig. 21, p. 51). Further, in the hedgehog there is a tendency for the third upper incisor to be double-rooted, the root bearing a longitudinal groove as though it were in process of being split, just as does the canine in those individuals where it is not completely two-rooted. In the mole and hedgehog the zygomatic arch, the bar of bone connecting the back of the upper jaw to the rear part of the skull, is well developed as in most mammals, but in the shrews it is absent and represented only by a stump at the hind end of the upper jaw (fig. 22, p. 52). It is possible that this unusual feature is correlated in some way with the equally unusual feature of two bearing surfaces in the jaw joint.

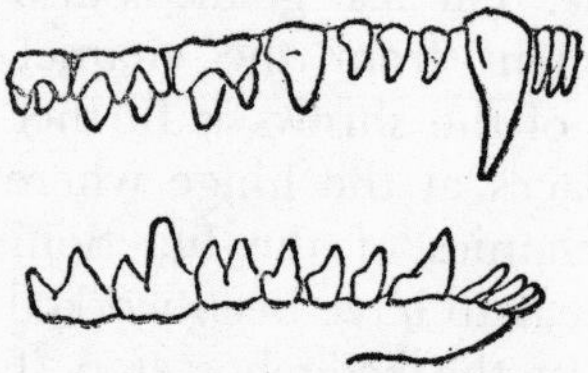

In the shrews and the hedgehog the

FIG. 20
Teeth of the mole, showing the small canine and enlarged first premolar in the lower jaw

skeleton is not greatly specialised in any one direction, but the same cannot be said of the mole in which the skeleton of the fore-limb is very highly modified. In this animal the foremost joint of the breast-bone is elongated so that the fore-limb is situated far to the front and the hand lies in front of the neck at the level of the back of the skull (fig. 23, p. 54). The under surface of this enlarged first breast-bone joint is produced into a keel which gives extended attachment to the muscles used in burrowing. The shoulder-blade is long, but very narrow, and the collar-bone is reduced to a small cubical mass which gives both strength and mobility to the limb. The bone of the upper arm, the humerus, is very short and wide so that it is quite unlike the corresponding bone in nearly all other mammals; its great lateral expansions give large areas of attachment for the muscles. The bones of the forearm, the radius and ulna,

FIG. 21

Front of the skull of a mole, the bone cut away to show the double root of the canine tooth

though short and stout are not so extremely modified from the more usual form. The hand is short, broad, and armed with stout claws; its breadth is increased by the presence of an extra bone in addition to the usual small bones of the wrist. This is a sickle-shaped bone on the inner side of the hand, giving increased breadth at the base of the thumb; it is not a true wrist-bone because it is developed in the tendon of a muscle, such bones being known as "sesamoid" bones. All these modifications are correlated with the burrowing habits of the mole, as is another skeletal character found in the skull: here the long snout of the animal is supported by a special bone developed from the plate of gristle which separates the two nostrils from each other.

The hands of the mole are often spoken of as "spade-like," but observation of a burrowing mole shows that they are not used as spades; their function is more nearly that of scrapers. When burrowing near the surface the mole pushed the earth upwards first with one hand then with the other, but when deeper in the ground it cannot do this. The hands are brought forward on each side of the snout alternately and the earth is scraped away and pushed back behind the body; the hind feet are used to help push the excavated earth backwards. When a plug of loosened earth has accumulated behind, the mole turns

round by turning a sort of somersault, a manœuvre that would seem
to be impossible but is quickly done although it must be a tight squeeze.
The animal then pushes the earth back to the nearest up-shaft by
holding one hand in front of itself and running on the other three legs,
every now and then changing hands. When it reaches the shaft it
pushes the earth up with one hand and then the other. The powerful

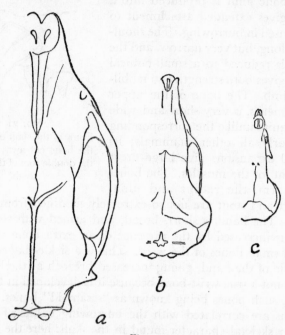

Fig. 22

Right half of skull of *a*, hedgehog, *b*, mole, *c*, shrew, seen from above.
The zygomatic arch is stout in the hedgehog, slender in the mole, and
absent in the shrew. All drawn to the same scale

muscles of the shoulders and forelimbs enable the mole to push up a
load of earth weighing much more than its own body. As a consequence of this method of turning out the earth the mole heap forms
like a volcano pouring out lava, the latest material coming up through
the centre and spilling down over the sides from the top. In shallow
runs where the ground is loose much of the earth is not thrown out

a. New-born hedgehogs with soft spines and unopened eyes

b. Mole-hills: heaps of excavated earth showing the course of the subterranean runs

Plate I

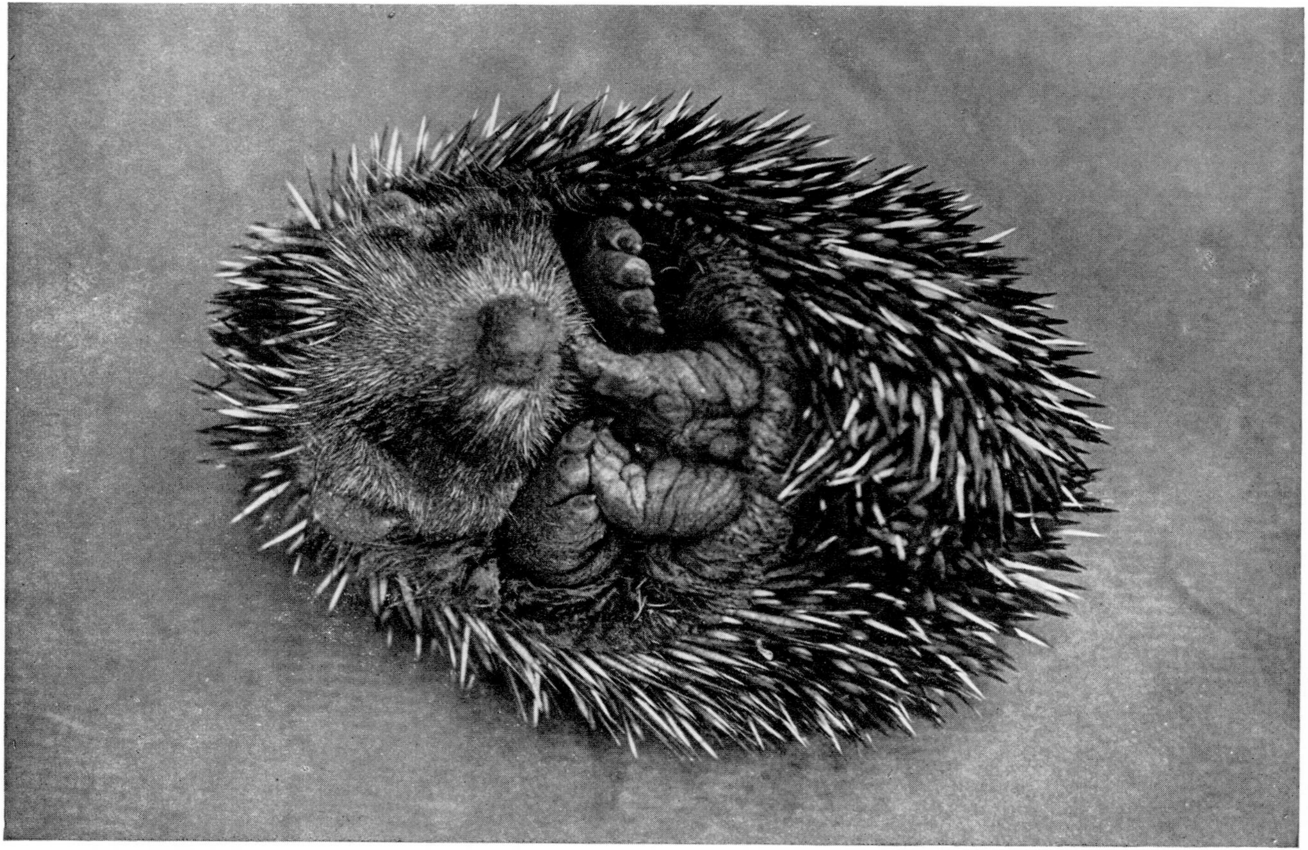

Plate II

A. R. Thompson

Hibernating hedgehog curled up asleep

is loose much of the earth is not thrown out at all, but is compressed on to the sides and roof, the latter being slightly raised so that a surface ridge marks out the course of the burrow. The speed with which a mole placed on a surface of turf can get beneath the ground is surprising, as also is the ferocious activity with which it appears to tackle the task. A rooting action of the head and snout and a few tearing strokes with the hands get the head and shoulders down, and with two or three strong heaves the rest of the body disappears after them. And once the shoulders are in, it is almost impossible to pull the mole out by the tail or hind part of the body without seriously injuring it.

Like most small mammals every mole has a territory to which its activities are, as a rule, confined; the mole's territory consists of a system of tunnels centred upon a nest placed beneath a mound of earth larger than the ordinary mole-heap of waste earth and often called the "fortress." The runs connected with the fortress of the female meander at random in all directions, but those of the male are arranged as side branches from a main "highway" that extends in a more or less straight line for some distance from the fortress, a difference that might be assumed to be no more than a popular fallacy were it not vouched for by Adams,[1] the naturalist who discovered most about the life of the mole (Pl. Ib, p. 52). But the territories of individual moles must obviously overlap very frequently, for it is well known that several moles may be caught in succession in a trap laid in one run. The nest chamber, just below ground level, is about six or seven inches in diameter and lies beneath the fortress mound which is about a foot high and three feet in diameter though sometimes much larger; a "bolt-hole" is often present, opening beneath the nest. The earth of the fortress is penetrated by a number of galleries, running in various directions, through which the loose earth is pushed out when excavating the nest-chamber and heaping up the fortress. These galleries are arranged in a completely haphazard manner, and not according to any fixed plan, as can be verified by anyone who carefully dissects a fortress. Nevertheless many of the older books show a diagram of the galleries in the fortress in which they are symmetrically arranged (as of course they may sometimes be), and either state or imply that all fortresses are similar, which is very far from the truth. This myth originated in the writings of de Vaux and Geoffrey St. Hilaire in the early years of the nineteenth century, and has been perpetuated by uncritical copying until the present day.

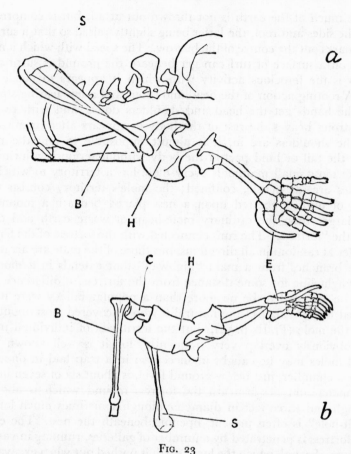

FIG. 23

Arm and shoulder girdle of the mole, *a*, from the side, *b*, from below.
B, foremost joint of the breast bone, keel-shaped for the attachment of
muscles. The lower ends of the first two ribs join its hind end. C, collar
bone. E, the extra (sesamoid) bone in the wrist that increases the width
of the palm. H, humerus. S, shoulder blade

The fortress appears to be regularly inhabited mainly during the
winter, and if the same one is used in successive seasons a new nest is
made inside it each year, the new one being placed on top of the old.
The nest completely fills the chamber and consists of a mass of dead
leaves and grass with no regular entrances. The leaves are collected

from the surface by the mole pushing its head out through the roof of shallow runs, seizing any within reach and dragging them down. The breeding nest of the female is placed in a fortress considerably smaller, and consequently containing fewer galleries, than that holding the winter nest. Mole's nests are always infested with fleas, one of the commonest mole-fleas, *Hystrichopsylla talpae*, being the largest and, as fleas go, one of the finest British species.

The mole, living underground and being an expert and rapid burrower, is well protected from potential enemies, though it is sometimes caught and eaten by carnivorous mammals or birds when working in shallow runs or when it emerges upon the surface, as it sometimes does. The shrews, on the other hand, have no effective defence against predators, and have to rely upon the cover of dense herbage for protection. It is true that they have a scent-gland beneath the skin of each flank that produces a secretion that is unpleasant to many animals, so that dogs and cats, for example, will seldom eat them, but that is little consolation to an animal once it has been killed. And the presence of the gland with its bad-smelling product does not prevent such predators from killing shrews even after repeated experiences of it. Nor does it protect shrews from carnivorous birds, for birds have little if any sense of smell, and shrews form a large part of the diet of owls.

The scent-gland consists of an area of skin that is thickened by the presence of a great number of large sebaceous and sweat-glands, the latter lying underneath the former and being the source of the scent.[62] There is no single duct, the secretion oozing out from the component glands onto the surface of the skin and matting the hair of the region together when it is abundant. Several explanations have been offered about the possible function of these glands; that of protection from predators, mentioned above, is inadequate because predators do not leave shrews unmolested. It has also been suggested that the scent serves to bring the animals together in the breeding season, and consequently that there may be some seasonal variation in the activity of the glands. This subject has not been fully investigated in the European shrews, but in the American *Blarina brevicauda* the glands have been found to be active in both sexes of all ages throughout the year.[167] The activity, as shown by the microscopical structure of the glands, is completely suspended in the female when she is in heat, pregnant, or lactating. It is therefore suggested that the secretion becomes rubbed off the fur of the shrews on to the walls of the tunnels inhabited by them and serves to mark out a territory and warn strangers that such scented burrows are tenanted. The absence of secretion from the female at the only times when she is receptive to the male would thus avoid warning off any wandering male that might enter her burrow. On this hypothesis the function of the scent is to keep these very quarrelsome and aggressive creatures apart from each other except when the female is in breeding condition.

Such information as is available about the glands in the European shrews, *Sorex araneus*, *S. minutus* and *Neomys fodiens*, indicates that the glands are most active in the breeding males, least in the pregnant and nursing females.[110] In the females, however, the glands are never so large as those in the males, nor are those of the immature animals. But though the amount of secretion produced by the males may be greatest in the breeding season it is not absent from those that are not breeding; the facts are thus not incompatible with the theory advanced to explain their function in *Blarina*. In *S. araneus* the glands of the male are conspicuous thickenings of the skin on the flanks, and reach from the fore to the hind limb; those of the female are more difficult to see but can be found in the dead animal by examining the inside of the skin, particularly if it is held against the light.

Shrews appear to have a slender hold upon life in spite of their high metabolic rate. The rapidity with which they die from starvation and cold has already been mentioned, and they seem also liable to die from fright; it is not uncommon to find a shrew that has sprung a nipper trap, but has not been caught in it, lying dead beside it with no visible sign of injury, the presumption being that the snap of the trap as it went off produced a sudden fright that was fatal.

Though shrews have little defence from possible enemies they are well provided with weapons of offence in their comparatively large and powerful teeth with which they can overcome any invertebrate that they are likely to meet, and even vertebrates as large as or larger than themselves. It is possible that they may have an additional weapon at their disposal. For long enough shrews have had a bad reputation in folk-lore in more than one respect; old Topsel says that the shrew "is a ravening beast, feigning itself gentle and tame, but, being touched, it biteth deep, and poisoneth deadly."[221] He devotes five folio pages to the subject of the poisonous bite of the shrew and the various alleged cures for it. Of course ancient tales of this sort are merely popular superstition, and are treated with the amused contempt that they deserve! But in 1889 C. J. Maynard[143] reported that when he was trying to catch one of the larger American shrews, *Blarina brevicauda*, the animal bit his hand. Although the skin was barely punctured a burning sensation was felt almost immediately, followed by shooting pains in the arm that decreased after an hour, though discomfort lasted more than a week. Nothing more was reported on this subject until 1942 when O. P. Pearson made some experiments to determine whether the saliva of this species has any poisonous properties.[165] Shrews were allowed to bite mice and voles, but not to injure them severely, the amount of the victim's tissues cut by the shrew's teeth being slight. "In a number of cases the mice were seriously affected and remained huddled in one corner of the cage in a depressed state for some time."

Pearson then made extracts from the salivary glands of the shrew and tested them for toxic effects. There are two main masses of salivary gland in the shrews, the parotid in the cheek and near the ear, and the submaxillary under the jaw and reaching down on to the neck and chest. The extract of the parotid gland was quite harmless when injected into the vein of a mouse, but that from the submaxillary gland was highly venomous. A dose containing the extract of only fifteen thousandths of a milligram of gland for every gram of the victim's weight was enough to kill seven out of nine mice in less than fifteen minutes; when the dose was raised to sixty-three thousandths of a milligram all the mice injected were dead within six minutes. Similarly a dose of extract from seven milligrams of gland for every kilogram of body-weight was lethal to a rabbit in less than five minutes. The poison appears to have properties similar to those of some snake venoms, its effect apart from the local reaction being to slow down the heart-rate, lower the blood-pressure and stop breathing. Pearson showed that the poison is not only present in the gland but is actually secreted in the saliva, and pointed out that it could be introduced into a wound along the groove between the two long lower incisor teeth, at the bases of which the ducts of the glands open. In the only species of the genus *Sorex* which he was able to test (*S. personatus*), he found that the extract of the submaxillary salivary gland was merely mildly toxic and not lethal to the mice on which he tried it.

The microscopic structure of the submaxillary salivary gland of *Blarina* is peculiar, containing a segment of coarsely granular cells in the secretory tubules of which it is presumed that the poison is produced. No similar segment of granular cells is known in any other mammal except the water-shrew, *Neomys fodiens*, of Europe. No experiments have been reported on the saliva or glands of this species, nor on those of any European species of *Sorex* or *Crocidura*, but the results obtained with the American shrew point to the high probability that something similar is present in some at least of these species, and that the ancient legends are not so far from the truth as has been supposed.

The poisonous shrew-saliva appears to resemble in its action the venom of the elapine snakes (the group including the cobra) which affects the nervous system, causing paralysis and respiratory failure.[121] On the other hand the painful local reaction resembles somewhat the effect of viperine venom, though the great swelling and haemorrhagic action characteristic of that venom were not produced. The poisonous action may be of use to the shrew in overcoming large prey such as mice, but it is more probably useful in minimising the struggles of large invertebrates. *Blarina* is known to store depots of food with such creatures as slugs and snails, and it is possible that these creatures are immobilised but not killed by the venomous bite. The British *Sorex* and *Neomys* are not known to make food stores, but what of the mole which certainly does store worms injured by a bite so that they cannot crawl away? This matter has not been investigated; all that can be said is that the mole possesses very large submaxillary salivary glands the nature of whose secretion is unknown: a study of the point might produce interesting results (fig. 24, p. 59). The only species of mole in which the saliva has been tested for toxic action is the American mole *Scalopus aquaticus*, and none was found; but that does not preclude the possibility that the salivary glands of the European *Talpa* may produce a venom. The venom of snakes contains, among other things, a highly active ferment that breaks down proteins, and it has been suggested that the saliva of shrews and other carnivorous insectivores may contain a similar substance, a suggestion that is plausible enough seeing that the diet of these animals consists almost entirely of proteins. The well known rapidity with which these animals decompose when dead might in part be owing to the action of such ferments on the tissues after death.

The protective coating of spines in the hedgehog is known to everyone, and forms its defence against predators (Pl. 1, p. 9). Although the hedgehog is well able to use its teeth against any attacker of its own size, it would be quite helpless against any of the larger carnivores. There are no stink glands to make it unpalatable, and the accounts of hedgehogs producing a formidable stench when put into water to make them uncurl appear to be due to the emptying of the intestine, possibly after the animal had been feeding upon carrion. The protection of the spines is highly necessary to the hedgehog which is

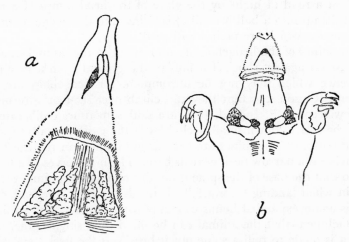

FIG. 24

The neck region of a shrew (*a*) and a mole (*b*) dissected to show the salivary glands. In the mole they are shaded, and in both animals the small oval bodies are lymph glands

a very acceptable meal to any flesh-eater, not excluding man himself, the opinion of one who has much culinary experience of the hedgehog being that it is "the best meat in England."* The spines are confined to the back of the animal, and when it rolls into a ball on being

---

* The classic way of cooking a hedgehog is to gut and stuff it with sage and onion, sew it up, and plaster it over with clay; then suspend it over the fire with a length of twisted worsted as a roasting jack, and when the clay cracks it is done. But this is not the best way because although the spines come away with the clay when it is broken open, the smaller hairs are not completely removed. It is better to singe the prickles and hairs off in the fire after gutting the animal, and then to scrape it with a very sharp knife before roasting it without clay. Another method is to gut and *skin* the animal, wash it well, and simmer it with seasoning in a little water for several hours; when cold the whole sets to a jelly, and the "pudding" can be cut into slices like pressed meat; this is very good.

alarmed the unprotected underparts are completely enclosed by the action of the skin muscle which runs from head to tail and draws the prickly skin close up to the edge of the way in (Pl. II, p. 53). Like many well protected animals, the hedgehog makes little effort to conceal itself, and will scuffle about among dead leaves or undergrowth making a noise that advertises its presence to all. But its confidence in its spines sometimes leads to its destruction, for if surprised on a road at night by the glare of the head lamps of a motor car it rolls up into a ball instead of running into the hedge, with fatal consequences which are plain to all road users.

The spines of the hedgehog are also useful to the animal in acting as a cushion against shock if it falls to the ground from a height, an occurrence which may not be uncommon, for hedgehogs are agile climbers; Ranson says that they can climb over six foot wire netting in a few seconds.[177] Indeed, they are said sometimes deliberately to throw themselves down small declivities as the easiest means of reaching the bottom. The spines are very firmly planted in the thick skin, and each has a narrow neck near its base. The neck serves as a flexible joint so that the base of the spine is not driven into the animal through the skin when landing from a fall. Beneath the neck, the base of the spine is again expanded hemispherically as an anchor, and so firm is the attachment that the animal can be lifted by a single spine. If an attempt is made to pull a spine out it breaks at the neck, leaving the root intact. Each spine is a highly modified hair and springs from a follicle in the skin containing at its base a papilla from which the spine is produced, just as is a hair in a hair follicle. The sharp end of the spine is solid and consists of the outer layer (cortex) only, but the body of the spine is hollow and consists of a thick medulla surrounded by a thin layer of cortex in which there are about two dozen longitudinal grooves (fig. 25, p. 61). The medulla contains a number of successive compartments filled with air and separated from each other by thin plates of material that serve as struts to keep the spine rigid. There are no sebaceous or sweat glands in the spiny skin, though they are plentiful in the skin of the hairy underside of the animal. There is one slight disadvantage in possessing a protective covering of spines, and that is, the animal is unable to groom the coat on its back; in consequence hedgehogs are always heavily infested with fleas and mites which disport unmolested among the prickles.

Most of the insectivores are rather noisy animals as far as their generally feeble voices allow them to be. Shrews squeak and chatter as they scurry about among thick herbage, but their notes are so high pitched as to be nearly inaudible to many people; because shrews are active by day as well as by night these hedgerow squeakings are familiar enough to country people. Less often heard is the very similar but more powerful squeak of the mole which, however, will squeak loudly if captured. The hedgehog when rooting about at dusk makes a lot of grunting and snuffling noises that are quite

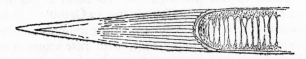

Fig. 25
The tip of the spine of a hedgehog greatly enlarged, the basal part cut in half lengthwise to show the internal structure. The point is solid, and the outside of the shaft is minutely grooved. The hollow of the inside is divided up by cross partitions

unmistakable; when it stands still it also makes a ticking or clicking sound that perhaps may be produced not with the voice but with the teeth. This sound is not heard when the animal is on the move and may merely be a sort of lip-licking finish to the devouring of some slug or insect. In addition the hedgehog sometimes makes a loud screaming cry that appears to be a sign of distress; it is said to make it when caught by the badger which sometimes pounces on a hedgehog before it has time to roll up completely. Country boys know how to make the hedgehog scream like this by sawing a stick backwards and forwards across the hamstrings just above the heel of the poor beast, the animal having first been made to uncurl by gently tickling or stroking the spines of the back by drawing the stick to and fro across them.

In the late summer and autumn shrews of all species are often found lying dead in the open; the bodies have so frequently attracted attention that it has been suggested that shrews are subject to some annual epidemic that destroys large numbers of them. The cause of this mortality has also been attributed to many other causes, from the action of predators, who find the carcass distasteful after killing the shrew, to "old age." An examination of large numbers of shrews caught in every month throughout the year throws some light on the question.[146] In *S. araneus* it is found that the percentage of adult animals in the catch falls rapidly in the autumn, and after November they occur only exceptionally. From December to April all the animals trapped are immature, and adults do not appear again until the following spring. The immature animals in autumn weigh from 7 to 9 grams, but during the winter they lose weight until they reach 5·5 to 7 grams, and it is not until spring that growth is resumed and completed to the adult weight of 10 to 13 grams. Similarly with *S. minutus*, where in one investigation[27] no adult males were found after August and only one adult female (on 12 October); from November to February there were only immature animals in the catches. It has therefore been concluded that, with rare exceptions, all the adults of both species die in the autumn, leaving only the immature animals to carry the race over the winter to the next breeding season. Individual shrews thus live about fourteen to sixteen months, barring accidents; survive only one winter, that following their birth; and experience only one breeding season, that of the year following their birth. There is less precise information about the water-shrew, but it, too, is believed to have a similar life history and longevity.

Against the suggestion that all the adult shrews die in the autumn the point has been brought that, in any species producing more than one litter of several young each season, the population will be greatly diluted by the young in the autumn, and the percentage of adults in it will thus necessarily be smaller.[166] This theory agrees with the facts in the population of *Sorex araneus* and *S. minutus* up to November, but its extension that claims there is no unusual mortality among the adults does not fit the facts for December to April when, with rare exceptions, there is a complete absence of adults. On the other hand no one has reported examining large numbers of the natural casualties to find out the exact cause of death and the approximate age of the animals. It is not to be expected that all the dead found in autumn are adults, for if there is a higher proportion of young than adults in the population, mortality is likely to fall more heavily upon the young simply because there are more of them. Further, young animals, owing to their inexperience and bodily immaturity, always have a high death rate, which decreases as they grow older. Thus even if all the adults do die, there is likely to be a large number of immature animals among those that die in the autumn. Indeed this is essential if the population is neither increasing nor decreasing, for although each female may give birth to numerous progeny during the summer, the total number of survivors after the winter must be equal to that of the last generation in the previous spring, if the population is to remain static.

When the short life span of the shrews was recognised, the fact that they are "annuals" was thought to be a very unusual phenomenon; but now that more is known of the biology of small mammals, and it has been shown that few of them ever survive more than one winter, the occurrences in the shrews seem less extraordinary. In many places there must be quite as many dead mice and voles as shrews to be disposed of, but their carcasses are very rarely seen, probably because they are quickly eaten up by the many animals that relish them; the shrews, which are much more unpalatable, are left and thus come to notice. In addition, it has been noted that captive shrews generally come into the open to die, unlike mice and voles which usually die in their nests or under litter. The life spans of mice and shrews are very similar, and the species differ only in the mortality of the adults in the latter being more complete in autumn, and in the resulting carcasses being less frequently eaten.

The diet of insectivores consists for the greater part of invertebrates, and consequently this group, unlike the destructive rodents, is wholly innocuous to man, and may be positively beneficial in reducing the numbers of harmful insects and their larvae. The hedgehog, which is more omnivorous than the shrews and mole, and includes some vegetable matter in its diet, is not recorded as seriously destructive to the crops of man. Even if the story of this animal carrying fallen apples away to its den impaled on the spines of its back were true it could not be held to show any hurt to man's interests. Hedgehogs do sometimes have leaves and vegetable fibres impaled on their spines, but it is almost certain that they have been accidently picked up, especially from the sleeping nest; when hibernating, hedgehogs are often thickly covered with the lining of the nest adhering to their prickles. The more or less omnivorous nature of the hedgehog's diet is reflected in the form of its molar teeth, where the cusps are much more rounded than those of the shearing molars seen in the shrews and mole. The only insectivore that can be claimed to be destructive to human affairs is the mole, though the damage it does is far outweighed by the benefits it confers. The mole, being exclusively carnivorous, does no direct damage to man's crops; any harm caused is indirect, and is the result of its burrowings in search of worms and insects. The result of its labours in a garden may be heartbreaking, but in the fields the mole is no more than an occasional nuisance; its mounds may at times hamper the mower, but in pastures they are positively beneficial if spread with the harrow. There really seems little reason beyond prejudice for the existence of the traditional trade of the mole-catcher, and the spectacle of one department of a ministry investigating means of poisoning and otherwise destroying moles, while others are seeking all ways of combatting insect pests, is fantastic.

Although the insectivores are in general harmless to human interests, the hedgehog may possibly be of some economic importance because, unfortunatly for itself, this species is susceptible to infection with the foot-and-mouth disease of cattle.[127] Diseased hedgehogs have been found during outbreaks of foot-and-mouth disease of farm stock, and it is believed that infected animals may sometimes spread the disease to cattle. The disease may be fatal to the hedgehog, but the animal is not thought to be of great importance in the spread of outbreaks because of the great ease with which the virus is carried accidentally by other animals, including man, which are not infected, or even by inanimate material. But because of its susceptibility the hedgehog is a very useful laboratory animal for use in research on the disease, and comparatively large numbers are now kept in captivity for the purpose. The other "crime" of which the hedgehog has been accused is that of sucking the milk from the teats of cows. Like many popular fallacies this story may have a background of truth in it; it is unlikely that a cow would tolerate the sharp teeth of the hedgehog, but there are some grounds for thinking that the hedgehog may occasionally lick up the milk oozing from the well-filled udder of a cow lying out in a summer pasture.[192]

The insectivores, like other mammals, are adapted for life in their particular habitats, but not all the characters which at first sight appear to be so are necessarily adaptive. The fur of the mole is velvety, the hair standing up at right angles to the skin and having no lay: this character is sometimes held to be an adaptation to living in a burrow, allowing the mole to move backwards as well as forwards in its tunnel without disarranging its coat. But the fur of the shrews is equally velvety, and these animals are not more nor less confined to burrows than our mice and voles whose coats are not velvety;

further, there is no evidence that the mole ever travels backwards in its burrow, though there is good reason for believing that it has more agility than it is usually credited with, and can turn round easily even in its smaller burrows if it wishes to retrace its steps. The minuteness of the eyes of the mole may be correlated with the under-ground habit; all moles have eyes, though in many individuals they are covered by the skin. The eyes of shrews too, are extremely small, and it is doubtful if they have the power of vision as we understand it; they may be able to distinguish bright light from darkness, but some experiments have made even that doubtful.[3] Vision is thus of little importance to moles and shrews, which rely upon their acute senses of smell and of hearing for information about their surroundings. Although the mole has no external ear-flaps its hearing is sensitive, and it is able to appreciate vibrations transmitted through the ground, perhaps by its sense of touch. In the shrews, ear-flaps are present though in many species they do not rise far, if at all, above the level of the fur. In the common and pygmy shrews the ear passages can be closed by a valve developed on the antitragus and working in conjunction with a fold on the inside of the ear-flap (fig. 26). In the water-shrew there are two valves, the second one being formed by an increase in the size of the fold. But this cannot be an adaptation to aquatic life, as might be thought, for the shrews of the genus *Crocidura*, which are terrestrial, have a similar arrangement. On the

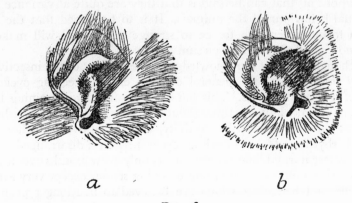

a   *b*

FIG. 26

Ears of the water shrew (*a*) and the pygmy shrew (*b*) showing the two valves guarding the ear hole within the main ear flap other hand, a special adaptation does appear to be present in the fringed feet and tail of the water-shrew.

Many of the insectivore characters, then, are not adaptive to special environments, but are such that they may be useful in several different habitats; the velvety fur, for instance, is equally suitable for life above or below ground, and also in the water. In the latter medium the fur of the water-shrew does not become wet, but traps innumerable bubbles of air that keep the water from the coat, so much so that when the animal is swimming below the surface it appears to be covered in a silvery layer of air. On emerging the coat is dry, though in the adverse conditions of captivity, when water-shrews are not always able to keep the fur well groomed, it may be wet and draggled after swimming.[113]

In spite of the well known savage disposition of shrews, more than one species has been reported to be gregarious on occasion. Barrett-Hamilton[14] mentions records of parties of the common shrew numbering from ten to over a hundred, and one consisting of nine or ten water-shrews. More recently an account has appeared of a "mass migration" of water-shrews in which some hundreds of the animals are said to have been seen swimming, packed close together, upstream in a narrow drain running through a pasture to join the river in Upper Teesdale. All too few details are recorded about these occurrences, and it is impossible to form any opinion about their cause or destination; all that can be said is that they are quite at variance with the usual behaviour of the animals. It is to be hoped that the next person fortunate enough to see so strange a spectacle will make an exact note of all the relevant circumstances.

Although much of our knowledge of the biology of the insectivores is very fragmentary, the general outlines of the breeding cycle are known in several species. This has been studied by examining large numbers of wild animals throughout the year, for moles and shrews are very difficult to keep in captivity, and in captive hedgehogs the normal rhythm of the breeding cycle becomes disarranged. The shrews whose normal life-span extends to only a few months over a year, can experience no more than one breeding season except very rarely; the mole and hedgehog which are believed to live longer probably go through more than one. In all these animals the breeding season is very sharply marked both physiologically and anatomically. Out of the breeding season the whole reproductive apparatus is very small, but at the onset of breeding it undergoes an enormous increase in size in both sexes, and afterwards decreases again at the end.

In the common shrew the breeding season, as shown by the occurrence of pregnant females, starts in May and lasts until September in the northern part of the country, and to the end of October in the southern counties.[25] As soon as the first litter is born the females become pregnant again so that a second litter is gestated while the first is being suckled. Thus there are at least two litters produced by each female, and probably more, though as the season advances females carrying a new litter while suckling the previous one become less common. The average size of the litter is just under $6\frac{1}{2}$ young, the number being less in the litters born after June than in those of the earlier part of the season. As in most mammals, there is some pre-natal mortality, the number of young born being smaller than the number of egg-cells released from the ovaries. The period of gestation is probably about eighteen days; it is certainly not less than thirteen nor more than nineteen days. The length of the period of lactation is the same, for after the birth of the first litter the two periods run simultaneously, and the young are therefore weaned at the age of about nineteen days. There is some indication that the period of gestation is slightly lengthened when it occurs while a previous litter is being suckled, through a delay in the development of the embryos after the egg-cells have been fertilised. In the shrew, contrary to what happens in many mammals, pairing practically always results in fertilisation and pregnancy; this is so constant an occurrence that it may indicate that the egg-cells are released only as a result of pairing, as they are in the rabbit and some others. An unusual phenomenon occurs about half way through the period of gestation, the passage in the female that leads from the uterus to the exterior becoming closed in its upper part by its walls growing together; it remains thus for some days until the passage is spontaneously opened again before the birth of the young.

Neither the males nor females breed in the season in which they are born, although in some of the females born early in the season there are signs of approaching sexual activity towards the autumn. But this precocious sexual development does not become functional and regresses again before the winter. From April to the beginning of November all the adult males are capable of breeding, but the females do not come into breeding condition until the end of April or the beginning of May. The onset of the breeding season is therefore determined by the condition of the females rather than of the males, as also probably is its end.

The reproductive tract is small in both sexes before breeding starts; with its onset there is a great increase in size of all the structures involved. In the female the passage leading from the outside opening to the uterus becomes elongated to such an extent that it is bent back upon itself in an S-shaped curve. In the male the growth of the parts is as great, the sex glands and the other glands accessory to the reproductive tract becoming relatively enormous, and the male organ itself being much elongated. The latter is not visible on the surface but is concealed beneath the skin and can be protruded through an opening much like that of the female, and, like it, opening into a common vestibule with the end of the intestinal canal. The protrusible part lying between the muscles of the body wall and the skin is so long that it is doubled up upon itself when stowed away. Pairing has never been observed in European shrews, but some particulars about it have been reported for the American shrew *Blarina*.[166] In this animal there is a similar arrangement of the anatomical structures and it results in the pair becoming locked together for about five minutes, the female towing the dismounted male tail-first behind her as she moves about. When released the male uses his mouth to return the long member to its sheath, and if he has been unsuccessful in mating he has to delay his pursuit of the female while he makes the readjustment with his mouth. Judging on purely anatomical grounds, it is probable that mating in the European shrews, and also in the mole, is similar.

The breeding cycle in the pygmy shrew is very similar in all particulars to that of the common shrew.[27] The season starts in mid-April, reaches a peak in June, and ends in October. The life span is as short as in the first species, and consequently individual animals experience one breeding season only. Each female produces two or more litters in the season; because it starts rather earlier than in the common shrew, and gestation is certainly not longer but probably shorter, it is likely that the females produce more litters than do those of that species. The litter size is slightly smaller, averaging just under six young for each female, and gestation of a new litter goes on simultaneously with the suckling of a previous one. As in the common shrew, the release of egg-cells from the ovaries may be dependent upon the occurrence of mating, for mated animals are invariably found to be

A. R. Thompson

a. Common shrew

Ray Palmer

b. Pygmy shrew

Plate III

Paul Popper Ltd.

a. Water-shrew

Eric Hosking

b. Mole

Plate IV

pregnant and no signs of infertile matings have been seen. The anatomy of the reproductive tract and the changes in size that it undergoes are similar in general to those in the common shrew, though in the male at least, the weight of the structures at the height of the breeding season is an even larger proportion of the total body weight than in that species.

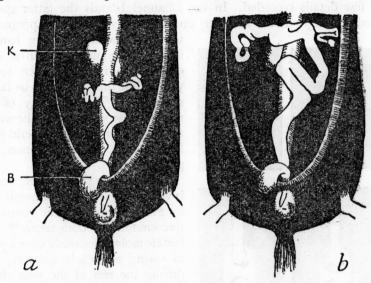

FIG. 27

The reproductive tract in the female mole (a) during anoestrus, and (b) at oestrus, showing the great increase in size during activity. B, bladder. K, kidney

Of the breeding cycle in the water-shrew there are few details recorded, but it is probably safe to assume that it is not greatly different from that in the species which have been carefully studied. The breeding nest appears to be more usually placed in a burrow, generally in the bank of a stream, whereas that of the other shrews is as often above ground, under the cover of thick matted vegetation, as below it in the shelter of a burrow. One peculiar point has been noted: after the egg-cells are released from the ovary and gestation has started, the ovary becomes entirely filled with a mass of luteal tissue, the glandular material that is produced in the follicles of the ovary

M.   F

from which the eggs are released, and in most mammals is confined to comparatively small localised aggregations. The cause and
effect of the extreme degree of development of luteal tissue in the
ovary of the pregnant female water-shrew are unknown. Nothing at
all is known of the breeding cycle of the Scilly shrew; it is probably
similar to that of its near relation the musk-shrew, of which again there
are few details recorded. In the Channel Islands the latter species
breeds throughout the summer, and all stages from early pregnancy

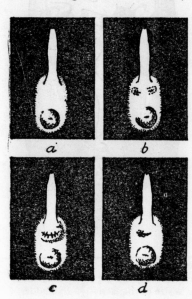

to newly weaned young can be
found in August. The litter sizes
observed were from three to six
young, but they may well be larger
sometimes. The anatomy of the
reproductive structures of the water-
and Scilly shrews is in general similar to that of the common and
pygmy shrews.

In the mole the breeding season
is very short and is accompanied by
by great changes in the reproductive anatomy of both sexes.[130] The
female mole breeds only once a year,
in spring and early summer, and
during the rest of the year she is
functionally asexual. The long
period of sexual quiescence is broken
by a brief, but very intense, sexual
season. This starts in mid-March
and lasts until the end of April when
most of the young have been born.
Pregnancy lasts about four weeks,
and suckling about three; the young
are weaned and the whole process
of reproduction is over by mid-
June. Very exceptionally litters
have been recorded in September,
but the details given have been very
scanty so that it is impossible to
judge whether such late litters

FIG. 28

Development of the reproductive
opening in the female mole.
a, non-breeding. *b*, at the approach
of the breeding season a small pit
appears at each side. *c*, the fully-
developed opening at oestrus.
d, the opening healing after the
birth of the young. The anal
papilla lies below, and the urinary
papilla above

represent second broods or precocious breeding by young of the year. The litter size averages three to four young, but occasionally reaches as many as seven. The young, which are naked at birth, grow rapidly and leave the nest by the time they are four weeks old, when the fur and the teeth are well grown. Unlike the shrews, which have three pairs of nipples on the abdomen but none on the chest, the mole has four pairs, two on the abdomen and two on the chest. They lie rather far out to the side, and the milk-glands which discharge through them spread from the front of the body on to the back behind the shoulder, and on each side of the hind leg to meet those of the opposite side above the tail.

The increase in the size of the genital tract at the breeding season is similar to that which occurs in the shrews, though rather greater in proportion (fig. 27, p. 69). In the female the sex passage is much elongated and folded upon itself, as is the intromittent member of the male; in the latter sex, also, the accessory glands and the testes are enormously enlarged. The passage of the female, which for most of the year measures about 20 per cent of the length of the body, elongates to no less than 70 per cent of the body length at the beginning of the breeding season when the female is receptive to the male; thereafter it decreases to about 30 per cent of the body length by the time the young are born, and then quickly regresses further to its normal size. Similarly in the male, all the structures rapidly grow to very large proportions and as quickly regress, becoming so small that the testes have been described as "atrophic" during the winter. In the female mole, as in many other mammals, especially some of the rodents, the sex passage has no opening to the outside in the immature animal, and the urine is discharged from the bladder through a member which looks much like that of the male, and lies just in front of the future opening; in this last respect the mole is unlike the shrews. As the breeding season approaches, the vagina, which ends blindly some distance from the surface, begins to extend and is joined by a depression that grows in from the outside, so that by the time the animal is ready for breeding the passage is fully established (fig. 28, p. 70). The first signs of the opening are two little pits that appear on each side of its future position; they gradually extend inwards and at the same time spread towards each other, and finally coalesce to form a transverse slit. Almost immediately after the birth of the young the opening closes again, the edges of the slit growing together, so that by the time

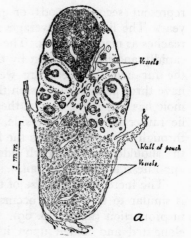

FIG 29

Slices across the ovary of the mole seen
under the microscope.

a, during the breeding season. The bodies
at the centres of the dark rings on each side
are egg-cells; the larger dark body above
is a corpus luteum; the lower lightly
shaded part is the mass of interstitial cells.
b, during anoestrus in the winter. The mass
of interstitial cells is greatly enlarged, and
the part containing egg-cells is the thin
layer on the upper edge

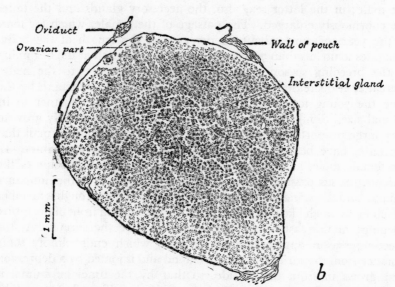

the young are weaned the site of the opening is represented only by a
transverse scar in which there are usually a number of small specks of
dark pigment. The old yarns which tell of the male mole savagely
pursuing the female and breaking open the passage by means of the
small bone present in the male organ are entirely imaginary; the

opening is formed quite spontaneously, and as spontaneously closed, while as for the bone, that is far from peculiar to the mole, a similar structure being present in the majority of mammals. The very complete closure of the passage in the female during at least nine months of the year has led to that other old country belief that "all moles are males until they are a year old, when they become separated into males and females," a belief which is of course quite erroneous.

The ovary of the female mole is very different from that of the other British insectivores, being divided into two parts, one producing egg-cells and the other containing a mass of glandular cells (interstitial cells). The part containing the egg-cells is small throughout most of the year, but increases considerably in size during the breeding season. In contrast the glandular part is very large, especially in the winter, but decreases in size when the other part enlarges (fig. 29, p. 72). In most mammals the glandular cells are comparatively few in number, and the function served by the large concentrated mass of them in the ovary of the mole is unknown. It has been suggested that the mass acts as a gland of internal secretion and produces hormones that may effect the seasonal changes in the external sex-organs, but there is no experimental evidence to support this theory, nor are those changes quite so unusual as was at one time thought, for similar though perhaps not quite such extreme processes are now known in other mammals.

In the hedgehog the peak of the breeding season occurs in May and June, and second litters of the season are born in July, August, and September.[53] The period of gestation lasts about a month, as does that of suckling, but a second litter is not started until the first is weaned.[99] There is thus little or no overlap of a new pregnancy with the previous lactation, and a new set of egg-cells is not released from the ovary until the end of suckling. The commonest litter size is five young, the number ranging from three to seven. The second litters are often born rather late in the season, for lactating hedgehogs are sometimes found in October. The release of the egg-cells from the ovary is spontaneous and does not depend upon the occurrence of mating; in the early part of the season as many as three to five sterile heat-cycles occur, in which mating is infertile and is not followed by pregnancy. It is unlikely that all female hedgehogs have two litters every year, and it is certain that the young do not reach maturity or breed in the season of their birth; those born late in the season do not

breed until late in the following one. There is complete sexual inactivity from October to April, and the ovary is very small during this
time, but it increases in size rapidly in the spring. The young are born
blind and have soft spines (Pl. Ia, p. 52) which do not harden until they
are about three weeks old, when they also assume the adult colour; they
are about three-quarters grown by the onset of hibernation. In the male
the seasonal increase in the size of the reproductive tract is very great,
particularly in the accessory glands; the complete tract reaches about
one-tenth of the total body-weight, a proportion greater than that
hitherto recorded in any other mammal.[4] The tissue of the testis is
active from April to August, after which regression is very rapid so
that complete quiescence is reached by the beginning of October.
From January to March there is renewed activity and full fertility is
reached by the beginning of the breeding season in April.

CHAPTER 4

BAT BIOLOGY
(CHIROPTERA)

"Come, now a roundel and a fairy song;
Then, for the third part of a minute, hence;
Some to kill cankers in the musk-rose buds,
Some war with rere-mice for their leathern wings,
To make my small elves coats."

A Midsummer Night's Dream

THE BATS form one of the largest orders of mammals, their vast number of species being exceeded only in one other order, by the multitudes of the rodents. Their headquarters are the tropics and subtropics, and though plentiful in temperate regions they do not extend into the colder parts of either hemisphere north or south of the limit of tree-growth. The British species belong to the insectivorous division of the order, the other division, which comprises the large fruit-eating bats or flying foxes, being confined to the tropics. Most, but not all, of the bats in the insectivorous division feed on insects; a few species have taken to other diets, the vampire of Central and South America feeds on the blood of other animals, another species feeds on fish which it snatches from the waves as it skims over the sea, and yet others are so-called 'cannibals', an unjust name, for though they feed on smaller species of bats, they do not attack their own kind. In the British Isles we have few species of bats compared with other countries, even nearby regions of the continent, there being but twelve species, of which only three are really widely distributed throughout the land. The rest are restricted to various parts of the country, most of them common within their own districts, but one or two universally rare.

Bats are the only mammals that have achieved true flight; some others can glide or parachute but are unable to propel themselves through the air as can the bats. The modifications that the body of the bat has undergone in correlation with this achievement are great. We know nothing of the evolutionary history of the bats; they are mostly small creatures whose fragile bones are not likely to be well preserved as fossils, and the few fragments that have been found show that even in Eocene times some fifty million years ago there were fully evolved bats little different from those of to-day. However, once the evolution had been accomplished and the air conquered, the bats made good use of the habitat that was now their monopoly among mammals, and branched off into a great number of different forms. Their general structure shows that the nearest relations of the bats are probably the insectivores.

The characteristic feature of the bats, the wing, consists of a double fold of skin stretched over the bones of the arm and hand (fig. 30, p. 77). The arm bones are elongated, especially in the forearm; here the radius is the main bone, the ulna being reduced to a rudimentary splint alongside the upper part of the radius, with which it is fused at the elbow-joint (fig. 31, p. 77). The wrist-bones are small and several of them are fused together (scaphoid, lunar and cuneiform); the bones of the hand and fingers except the first are slender and greatly elongated. The first finger (thumb) is short and provided with a strong claw; it is free and mobile, taking little part in the support of the wing-membrane, and serves for clinging to the surface when the bat alights. All the other fingers help to extend the wing like the ribs of an umbrella; none of them has a claw, and the bones of the second (index) finger, the outermost on the wing, are always reduced in number and sometimes completely absent, only the bone between wrist and finger (metacarpal) being present. The wing-membrane consists of two layers of skin back to back with no flesh between them, there being only a little connective tissue through which meander the blood vessels and nerves that supply it. The wing is thus merely an extension of the skin of the back and belly carried out from the side of the body. It starts in front of the shoulder so that a well developed ante-brachial membrane is formed between the upper arm and fore-arm, continues down the side of the body to the hip and extends down the leg to the ankle and thence to the end of the tail, at least in the British species, the interfemoral membrane lying between the legs and including the tail. In some foreign species the tail is only partly included in this membrane or is even quite free: in yet others there is

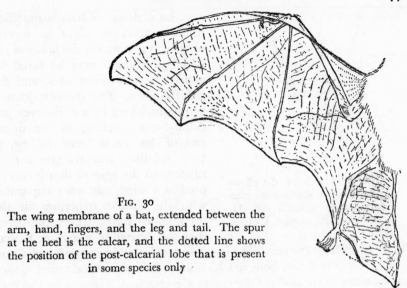

FIG. 30
The wing membrane of a bat, extended between the
arm, hand, fingers, and the leg and tail. The spur
at the heel is the calcar, and the dotted line shows
the position of the post-calcarial lobe that is present
in some species only

no tail at all. In order to spread the membrane fully the legs must
be widely opened, or rotated outwards, and in the course of evolution
the head of the femur has become so modified that the leg is in effect
twisted right round so that the foot faces backwards and the knee
bends in the direction opposite to that in most mammals. The knee
in a bat settled on a level surface thus bends upwards so that the leg
is held in a position like that of a grasshopper (fig. 32, p. 78). The
bones of the leg are slender but no so long as those of the arm; in the
lower leg the main bone is the tibia, the fibula being much reduced
and appearing only as a slender splint alongside the lower part of
the tibia near the ankle. The reduction of the fibula, like that of the
ulna, is correlated with the chief muscles of locomotion being those of
the chest and upper arm. The small ankle-bones are reduced in size
and number, and the foot consists of five small toes each of approximately equal length and each armed with a laterally compressed
claw. From the inner side of the ankle there springs a peculiar gristly
rod which helps to stiffen the free edge of the interfemoral membrane.
This is the calcar or spur, whose length and degree of straightness
or curvature varies from species to species. The tail in all British
species is well developed and in most of them it is comparatively long.

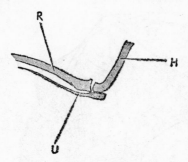

FIG. 31
The bones forming the elbow
joint of a bat, showing the ulna
reduced to a small slip. H,
humerus. R, radius. U, ulna

The skeleton of bats is modified
in adaptation to flight in several
other ways. Some of the joints of the
vertebral column may be fused together in fully adult bats, and the
ribs flattened. The shoulder-joint is
firmly anchored by a well-developed
collar-bone reaching to the upper
end of the breast bone (fig. 33, p.
79). All these features give a rigid
support to the arm so that it can be
used as a wing, and are comparable
with the similar structures in the
shoulder of birds, where, however,
they are carried to a greater perfec-
tion. Similar to the condition in birds, too, is the development of a central keel on the breast-bone to which the enlarged pectoral muscles, used
in the downward stroke of the wings, are attached. Here again the keel,
though similar, is proportionately very much smaller than in birds.
In the horseshoe-bats the strengthening of the fore-limb is carried
furthest. Here the last vertebra of the neck and the first of the back
are fused together to form a single bone, and this again is fused with
the first rib, the other end of which is fused with the tip of the breast-
bone. At its front end the second rib is fused to the first and may be
joined to it throughout most of its length. In these bats, then, the
forward end of the chest is enclosed in a solid ring of bone that
supports the wings and flight-muscles. And yet curiously enough the
horseshoe-bats are by no means the strongest fliers among bats,

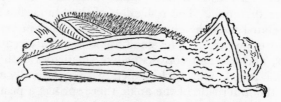

FIG. 32
A long-eared bat at rest showing the knee bent upwards and the foot
pointing backwards. The long ears are folded down under the wing,
and the tragus projects forwards

and compared with some of our other species, as for instance the noctule, they have a decidedly weak and fluttering flight. There is doubtless an explanation of this apparent anomaly, but no one has yet studied the flight of bats thoroughly enough to discover it.

In comparison with the high degree of elaboration of the fore-limb and its supporting structures, the hind limb and its girdle are feebly developed. The legs are used for supporting the animal when it is walking on all fours, and for suspending it when at rest, but though bats can scuttle about nimbly enough in their hiding places, the hind-limb never has the importance in loco-

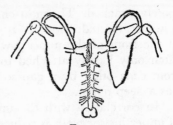

Fig. 33

The shoulder girdle of a bat, seen from in front.

The strong arched collar bones join the front end of the breast bone to the shoulder blades. The ribs are cut off close to their joints with the breast bone. The upper joint of the breast bone bears a keel for the attachment of flight muscles

motion that it has for other mammals or for most birds, the reason being that it has become involved in the flight-mechanism. The pelvis or hip-bone that anchors the hind-limbs to the backbone is therefore a comparatively weak structure. As in all mammals, it consists of three bones on each side fused together, the resulting single bone on each side usually being joined to several fused vertebrae (sacrum) at the back, and to its fellow at the front (fig. 34). But in the bats the joint between the two bones in front is generally incomplete; usually, and especially in the females, the two bones do not meet each other at all but are merely joined by some ligamentous tissue. This is in striking contrast to the conditions found in most other mammals where the joint in front is usually very firm to meet the need of a rigid support for the hind limbs during locomotion.

In the skull of bats the cheek-bone is a slender bar, and the ring of bone encircling the ear passage (tympanic) is not fused with the rest of the skull, but is comparatively

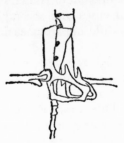

Fig. 34

The pelvic girdle of a bat, showing that though the two halves of the girdle meet in front they are not welded together loosely attached. The most characteristic feature of the skull of bats is, however, the reduction in size of the premaxillae, the two small bones at the front of the upper jaw that carry the incisor teeth. They are often only loosely attached to the rest of the skull and are separated from each other by a gap so that the front edge of the bony palate has a deep notch.

In correlation with the small size of the premaxillae the number of upper incisor teeth is reduced so that no bat has more than two on each side, the missing teeth being the first incisors, the innermost one on each side that belongs to the missing central part of the premaxillae (fig. 35, p. 81). In the horseshoe-bats the reduction in the number of upper incisors has gone further than in most bats, for the outer tooth (incisor 3) on each side also is absent, so that there is only a single incisor (incisor 2) present on each side. In these bats the pre-maxillae consist of tiny strips of bone loosely joined to the skull in the notch at the front of the palate. In the lower jaw the full number of three incisor teeth is present on each side in all the British bats except the horseshoes where the number is reduced to two on each side. All our bats have well-developed canine teeth, one on each side in each jaw, followed by a number of grinders that may be from four to six above and below on each side according to species, the number above and below not necessarily being the same. None of the bats has the full number of grinders characteristic of the higher mammals (4 pre-molars and 3 molars on each side), the first premolar above and below always being absent. The premolars, except the last upper one, which resembles the molars, are pointed like the canines but are much smaller. The molars bear three sharp-pointed main cusps and several minor ones, the molars of upper and lower jaws differing from each other in shape and details.

In action the jaws are worked with a slightly side-to-side move-ment, as well as up and down, so that the cusps of the upper and lower sets sweep past each other with a shearing action that cuts up the hard casings of the insects on which bats feed. This rotary action can be well seen in a tame captive bat rapidly crunching up mealworms or other insects, of which it will eat a surprising quantity at a sitting. The milk teeth of bats are quite unlike the permanent ones (fig. 36, p. 82). They are very small and all consist of slender pointed spicules that are usually shed early in life, in the horseshoe-bats generally before birth. It is thought that their only function is for holding tightly to the mother's fur as she flies; they certainly cannot be of any use in feeding. In the horseshoe-bats, where the new-born young have already lost the milk teeth, there is a different arrangement for clinging to the mother, described below, p. 98. When present, the milk teeth are generally recurved at the points, and occasionally some of them are not shed until the permanent teeth have cut through the gum, being so tiny that the latter can erupt alongside them without pushing them out (fig. 36, p. 82 & fig. 37, p. 83).

The fur of bats is characteristically long and silky with a denser underfur of fine down. The hairs stand out nearly straight from the

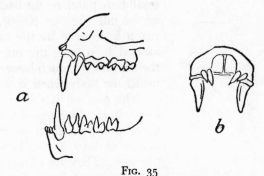

FIG. 35
The teeth of a bat (noctule).
a, from the side. *b*, the upper jaw from in front, showing the two incisors on each side of the gap left by the deficient premaxillae bones

surface of the body so that the fur has little direction or lay even on the face, except round the mouth and nose. The microscopic structure of the individual hairs is peculiar, the surface scales being arranged in a ring at regular intervals so that the hair has a saw-toothed edge and gives the appearance of a large number of cones with hollow bases fitted one inside another (fig. 38, p. 84). The pigment forms a continuous column within the hair-shaft. The colour of all the British bats is low in tone, as it is in bats generally, with the exception of one European and several tropical species that are marked with bright yellows and red-browns. There is frequently little countershading; that is to say, the under-surface is often not conspicuously lighter than the back, as it is in so many animals where the light underside neutralises the shadow of that region and helps to make the creature inconspicuous. But the lack of countershading is not universal in bats, and

among the British species those of the genus *Myotis* have characteristically light-coloured under-surfaces. The underfur is often different
in colour from the outer hairs and is usually darker and grayer. There
is little if any difference in pattern or coloration between the sexes
in any of the British species. The fur grows thickly all over the body
and extends on to the base of the wing-membrane and in some bats,
as the noctule, grows along the lower borders of the arm-bones on the
underside of the wing. In the horseshoe-bats, which carry their
characteristically short tails turned up
over the back when at rest there is a
small bare patch on the back at the base
of the tail (fig. 39, p. 86). This bare
patch is covered by the tail when the
animal is at rest; the other bats turn
their relatively much larger tails underneath the body when roosting.

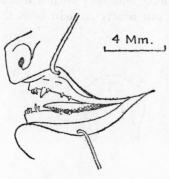

FIG. 36

The gums of a new-born bat
showing the milk teeth (magnified). The largest tooth is
the tip of the permanent canine
which is cutting the gum just
in front of the milk canine

The ears of bats are comparatively
large; in the long-eared bat they reach
their greatest development and are
nearly as long as the head and body
together. They are thin and membranous, not covered with fur, though they
bear small scattered hairs. Their internal gristly support is thickest on the
inner side and from this edge a number
of ridges and grooves extends towards
the outer margin, forming a pattern
which is characteristic of each species. In the Vespertilionid bats
(the family that contains most of the British species) a feature
of the ear distinguishes them from the Rhinolophid or horseshoe-
bats; this is the great size of the tragus, which is absent in the
latter. The tragus is the small lobe that lies at the front of the
ear-passage and, in man, partly covers it. In all the Vespertilionid
bats this is very large and stands up in front of the main ear-flap like
a small second ear (fig. 40, p. 86). It is generally, but not always,
narrow and pointed, and the details of its shape, like those of the
markings on the main ear-flap, are characteristic of each species. The
long-eared bat sleeps with its enormous ears folded back under the wings
but with the tragi remaining erect, looking like two little forwardly

directed spikes sticking out from the head (fig. 32, p. 78). The function of the large tragus in the Vespertilionid bats is not known but possibly has something to do with the reception of ultrasonic sound waves as described below (p. 104), perhaps acting as a diaphragm to increase the accurate perception of direction.

It is generally stated that the eyes of bats are small and that their sight is poor, a sweeping statement that is not wholly correct. It is true that in some bats the eyes are small, as in the horseshoe-bats,

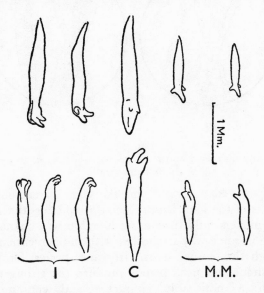

FIG. 37
The milk teeth of a bat (Leisler's) removed from the gums.
There are two upper incisors, but three lower. The line represents a
distance of 1 mm. I, incisors; C, canines; M.M., milk molars

but in many of the others they are not particularly tiny and there is no reason to suppose that they are not perfectly efficient. In the noctule for instance they are well developed and doubtless are used to good purpose, for this species flies at or before sunset while daylight is still quite bright. In the horseshoe-bats, on the other hand, where the eyes are comparatively small and the field of vision appears to be partly obstructed by the nose-leaf, sight is probably of much less importance to the animal.

Underneath the skin on the snout of bats, particularly in some of the Vespertilionids, there are large glands that form conspicuous folds round the lips and nose. These glandular masses are formed of great numbers of enlarged sebaceous glands, the skin-glands that are present in most mammals and produce a greasy secretion that

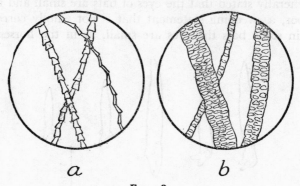

FIG. 38

Hairs, greatly magnified under the microscope, from *a*, greater horse-shoe bat, *b*, house mouse

serves to keep the skin supple and the coat waterproof. They lie round the roots of the long sensory hairs or whiskers that grow on the snout; until quite recently their exact function was unknown but was believed to be in some way connected with the perception of external stimuli through the sensory hairs. In some species, for instance the noctule, the snout and neck glands produce the strong rancid scent that is such a noticeable character and contaminates their sleeping places. It has lately been ascertained, however, that in addition to the skin-glands there are in the noctule large pads inside the mouth close to the angle of the lips.[94] The most characteristic feature of these buccal pads is the abundance of fatty substances contained within their cells. The function of the pads is unknown but they are believed in some way to be used in capturing or manipulating the prey; it has even been suggested that they may be sticky and, in effect, turn the mouth into a living fly-paper (fig. 41, p. 87). In many tropical species of bat the glandular pads of the snout are elaborated into fantastic shapes that give a most grotesque appearance to the face; in some, too, there are similar large skin-glands in a small pouch on the chest.

The horseshoe-bats are distinguished from the other British species

Plate V

Pipistrelle bat in flight, showing open mouth and partially closed tail-pouch

John Warham

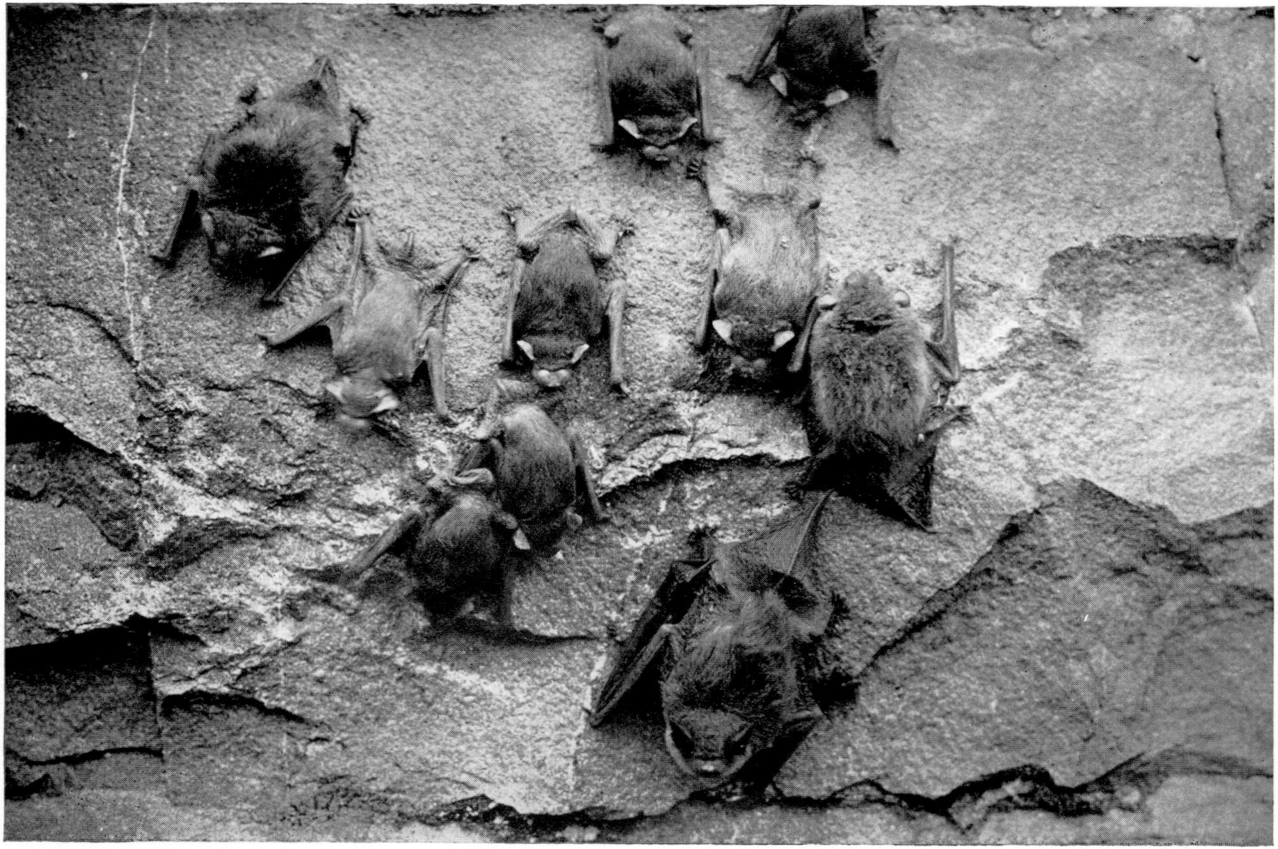

Plate VI *Eric Hosking*

A small colony of pipistrelle bats, with adults and young

not only by the absence of an ear tragus but also by the presence of the peculiar leaf-like appendage on the nose from which they take their name. This nose-leaf is an expansion of the skin surrounding the nostrils into a structure whose exposed area is greater than its area of attachment so that its free edges overlap the surrounding skin (fig. 42, p. 87). The lower part covering the upper lip and surrounding the nostrils is horseshoe-shaped and has a central notch in the lower edge. Above the nostrils it is produced into a pointed erect structure called the *lancet*, which is attached only by its base and so stands up free from the skin of the forehead. Both the horseshoe and the lancet are flattened from front to back, but between them, just above the nostrils in the centre line, there is another process, the *sella*, that is flattened from side to side and stands out in front of the rest of the nose-leaf. At the base of the sella a number of folds and ridges connect it with the lancet and horseshoe, their shape and arrangement differing in each species. Round the lip, just beyond the free edge of the horseshoe, is a row of small pimple-shaped papillae, and several more are present round the base of the sella, from which a number of long tactile hairs grow. Under the skin between the upper edge of the horseshoe and the eye there is a gland which produces a dark oily secretion that sometimes oozes out in such quantity as to mat the hair together on the cheek below the eye.

The function of the nose-leaf and these associated structures is unknown. It has been suggested that they enable the bat to exercise a kind of touch-sense at a distance so that it can feel nearby objects without touching them. This is however pure speculation; all that can be said with certainty is that they obviously serve some sensory function in some way, the details of which are not understood. The size of the nerves connected to the nose-leaf shows that it is an important organ of sensation; the branches of the fifth cranial nerve supply it; they are large and on reaching it break up into a vast number of fine ramifications. The great numbers of sweat and oil glands present are thought to maintain the surface of the nose-leaf in a highly sensitive condition. It is possible that the tactile hairs and glandular pads on the snouts of Vespertilionid bats serve some similar function, though they are much less specialised.

The character of the flight varies widely between different species of bats. At the one extreme the noctule has a vigorous and powerful flight, wheeling rapidly through the air at a considerable height with

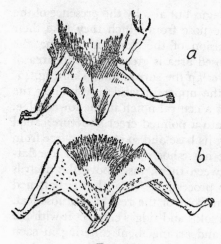

FIG. 39
The short tail of a horseshoe bat.
a, seen from above. *b*, seen from behind,
and showing the bare patch that is
normally covered by the tail being
turned back over it

sudden swerves and dives, in some ways reminiscent of the powerful flight of swifts. At the other extreme is the fluttering flight of the horseshoe-bats which do not ascend to great heights but sail butterfly-like near the ground. Correlated with these different manners of flight is the shape of the wing, narrow and pointed in the noctule, broad and with rounded end in the horse-shoe-bats. Intermediate in style between these two extremes is the flight of the smaller Vespertili-onid bats most of which do not rise to great heights, though there are exceptions, such as the sero-tine. A constant feature of the flight of many of the smaller bats is the habit of following a regular beat, hawking up and down between fixed turning points. Such a beat may be alongside the edge of a wood, up and down a section of country lane, or among buildings. One can take advantage of this habit if one wishes to obtain a specimen; it is very difficult, and almost impossible except by a fluke, to shoot a bat during its irregular flight, but if the shooter lies in wait at the end of the beat it is not so difficult to kill the the animal as it turns; the difficulty is then to find the corpse, which is very tiny when the wings are not extended and is easily lost among quite sparse herbage. Dust-shot from a .22 rifle is the best ammunition for securing a speci-men without knocking it to pieces. In spite of the extraordinary ability possess-ed by bats of avoiding obstacles in the dark it is not difficult to knock down a hawking bat with a stick. If a very long

FIG. 40
Head of Natterer's bat show-ing the ears each with a long narrow tragus, and the glandular pads near the nostrils on the snout

flexible rod such as a bamboo is rapidly waved too and fro in its path it often happens that a bat will come to grief by flying into it.

The type of flight of the different bat species depends largely upon the habits of the particular insects on which they feed; Daubenton's bat for instance concentrates so much upon insects with aquatic young stages that it is sometimes called the water-bat from its constant habit of skimming low over pools and rivers as it hunts. Its near relative Natterer's bat is also frequently seen hunting low over the surface of water. This species is, however, not so exclusively a hawker over water and

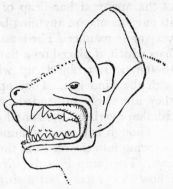

FIG. 41
Mouth of the noctule bat showing the glandular pad inside the lip below the eye and ear. (Adapted from Harrison & Davis 94)

often hunts amongst trees, where it not only takes flying insects but pauses hovering to pick them off the leaves. This hovering habit is particularly pronounced in the long-eared bat which characteristically glides round the foliage pausing every now and then to snap up an insect at rest.

Graceful as is a bat in flight, its movements are not so elegant when it alights. When it moves on a flat surface, horizontal or vertical, it folds its wings, and supports itself on the hind feet and wrist, using the claws of the toes and of the short thumbs for gripping. In spite

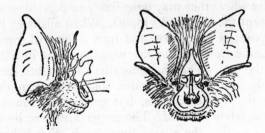

FIG. 42
Side and front views of the head of a horseshoe bat to show the nose-leaf. The ear has no tragus, the lobe sticking up at the base of the ear is the anti-tragus

of the apparent handicap of the wings and inter-femoral membrane its movements are anything but clumsy, and it can scramble about in a very agile manner. The least accomplished walkers are the horseshoe-bats which, if placed on a flat surface, at once shuffle along backwards to the nearest object, up which they climb by feeling for toe-grips with the hind feet. They appear to be acutely uncomfortable until they are safely suspended from a vertical surface or hanging freely from an overhead horizontal one.

Though bats usually launch into flight from a height they are able to spring into the air from the ground, even the less nimble horseshoe-bats. The jump into the air is so quickly done that it is difficult to follow the process, but a single spring with the arms and legs simul-taneously appears to give them sufficient ground clearance for an unobstructed first stroke of the wings. When alighting at the entrance to their homes, usually a hollow in a tree or crannies in rocks or a building, and it is necessary to alight on a more or less vertical surface, the Vespertilionid bats nearly always pitch head upwards, clinging on with thumbs and toes. Then they immediately shuffle round until they are head downwards and sleep hanging from their toes with the wings folded alongside the body. As a rule, however, they do not hang freely suspended, but prefer to hang on a vertical surface, facing towards it, often clinging to it with the thumbs as an additional security. This is when they are sleeping in a rather exposed position and not, as often, wedged tightly into some crevice (Pl. Xb, p. 105).

Quite different is the habit of the horseshoe-bats when alighting. They make their homes in caves or the roofs or cellars of buildings and do not creep into crannies like the Vespertilionid bats, but always choose a place where they may hang freely suspended without touching anything except the overhead support. When alighting they approach the chosen point of suspension and turn a forward somersault in the air, at the same time closing the wings, so that in a flash they are hanging by the toes. When hanging they do not shut the wings along-side the body with the membranes folded between the supporting bones as do the Vespertilionids, but wrap them round the body so that it is completely covered. The upper arms are brought together over the back so that the elbows touch each other behind the root of the tail, and the forearms lie side by side over the mid line of the back. This brings the wrists over the top of the head, while the fingers, slightly diverging from each other, are pressed against the front and

sides of the body so that the membranes completely enclose it, one
wing slightly overlapping the other in front. The tail, turned up
over the back, meets the elbows and completes the covering behind
by bringing the interfemoral membrane into contact with the edges
of the folded wings. A sleeping horseshoe-bat is thus completely enclosed in the flight membranes, and when suspended from an object
above looks like the pod of some strange fruit or the cocoon of an

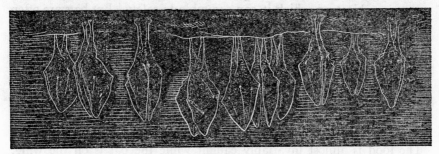

FIG. 43
Hibernating horseshoe bats

enormous insect (fig. 43). In contrast to the Vespertilionid bats,
which flatten themselves as much as possible against the surface to
which they cling, a sleeping horseshoe-bat has a plump rounded
appearance.

The position of the head also is characteristic of the horseshoe-bats
when at rest. When they are active the head is carried, as it is in the
other bats, stretched out with its basal axis more or less in a straight
line with the spinal column. But when the bat hangs up asleep this
axis makes a right angle with the vertebral column so that the animal
looks to the front instead of ahead, and the tips of the ears are about
level with the wrists. This attitude of the head is not adopted by the
other bats when at rest. The horseshoe-bats show an amazing agility
when alighting upside down, and are able to cling to the smallest
inequalities or roughnesses of the surface of wood or stone, being aided
in this by the very sharp claws on their toes. Not only can they
seize on such inconspicuous toe-holds but they can manoeuvre in very
restricted spaces so that they can hang up underneath a boulder or
other object where the ground-clearance is only a matter of inches
and certainly less than a foot.

It has been recorded that some species of bats can swim, a statement that perhaps implies rather more than the facts warrant. No species of bat willingly takes to the water, to which medium it is as ill adapted as it is well adapted to the air. But if by accident a bat falls on to a water-surface it floats with partly extended wings; and in its struggles it makes the only movements that it can, chiefly a beating of the wings, which drive it along so that if fortunate it reaches the bank or some object up which it can scramble to safety. But bats are often found drowned in water-butts in which they have probably come to grief while catching mosquitoes and other insects hovering over the surface, so that they are by no means always able to extricate themselves from the accident of being caught in the unfamiliar medium. It is, however, interesting to notice that the two American fish-eating bats can, if knocked into the water, not only swim but take off from the surface.

The British species of bats feed exclusively on insects, of which the total bat population must consume an immense weight annually. The food is almost invariably caught while the bat is on the wing, and is usually eaten there, no doubt a simple enough action if the insect is small. But when a large insect is taken that needs more manipulation before it can be eaten a difficulty arises because the bat has no hands available for this purpose. When this happens the tail is curved forward underneath the body so that the interfemoral membrane forms a pouch into which the insect is pressed and rapidly manipulated with the mouth so that the juicy body of the insect is eaten, and the dry wings bitten off to float to the ground (Pl. V, p. 84). All this is done with great rapidity and without interrupting the flight. But this action is not possible to the horseshoe-bats which have comparatively short tails and small interfemoral membranes. When a bat of this kind catches a large insect it tucks it into the wing-membrane under the arm, pressing it against the wing while it manipulates it with the mouth. In addition, the horseshoe-bats often alight holding large prey in the mouth in order to deal with it more easily, and sometimes they bring it into their daytime sleeping places to eat it.

But horseshoe-bats are not the only ones that alight to deal with large insects. Both the pipistrelle, long-eared, and the whiskered bats, and probably some other species, retire to some favourite perch on such occasions, and large quantities of insect remains may accumulate on the ground beneath these places—which are not necessarily the day-time roosts.[176] The parts dropped are the wings of moths and the wings and wing-cases of beetles together with the harder parts such as heads, large legs and so on. The evidence of these remains shows that moths form a very large part of the diet of several species,[158] no less than seventy-two species of moth having been identified from a single bat-roost,[107] forty-five of these being noctuids. The preference of bats for moths is also shown by their competition with entomologists round the baits, natural or artificial, that attract moths at night. Several species of bat have been identified hawking over sallow blossom, particularly the pipistrelle and whiskered bats, catching the moths visiting the catkins. They have also been recorded as shaking the upper twigs by fluttering among them as they took the moths, but it is probable that this was merely accidental and not purposely done to put up the insects.[106] Bats also steal the moths attracted to entomologist's sugar-patches; most of the species capture the moths as they approach the bait, but the long-eared bat takes those which have actually settled upon sugared trees. This is in accordance with the well-known habit of this bat of catching moths and other insects at rest on foliage and elsewhere. Bechstein's bat has also been recorded as taking insects at rest, but the hovering habit is said to be less pronounced in this species. Entomologists' light-traps for moths are also visited by bats which take the moths as they approach them;[8] Daubenton's bat is recorded as being particularly attracted in this way. The species that have been found visiting sugar and light include the pipistrelle, the whiskered, barbastelle, long-eared, Natterer's, Daubenton's, Bechstein's and the lesser horseshoe-bats. The horseshoe-bats, too, sometimes take prey that is not flying, for the remains of the cave-spider *Meta menardi* have been found in their droppings. It is not known whether the spiders are taken while the bat is at rest, or whether they are picked off the sides of the caves while the bat is hovering, but the latter is the more probable. These bats are also known to eat the moths that hibernate in caves, particularly the herald-moth *Scolipteryx libatrix*.[46, 47] The fluttering flight of horseshoe-bats as they reconnoitre the crevices of a cave before settling would suggest that they probably take these insects from the cave sides while they are hovering.

In spite of popular belief to the contrary bats are cleanly animals and thoroughly dress their fur and wing-membranes. The toilet is performed when the animal is at rest hanging upside-down, and the bat goes through surprising contortions to reach the various parts of the body. In the horseshoe-bats the process is usually carried out while hanging by one foot only, the other being used as a comb. The wings and interfemoral membrane are thoroughly washed by being licked all over on both sides with the tongue, and the fur is combed by scratching with the toes. And a very good comb the toes make, for they are all of approximately equal length and the sideways-flattened claws lie close together. The whiskers are combed by the claws after they have been licked with the tongue, but the rest of the fur is merely combed without being licked. At frequent intervals during the grooming the toe-combs are cleaned with the lower incisor teeth. All the movements during the toilet are very rapid and carried out with restless energy. The mobility of the hind-limb is well seen during this process, for while hanging from one foot the other can be brought up over the back behind the wings to scratch the back of the head, or under the wings on the front of the body to scratch the face. When the toilet is complete a grip with both feet is resumed, the wings are shaken and then carefully folded, and the bat relapses into sleep.

In spite of the careful and thorough toilet, bats are commonly infested with parasites in their fur. On the wings or ears, a few small mites are often to be found, and among the fur live species of fleas peculiar to bats. But the strangest bat parasite is a highly modified species of fly of the family *Nycteribiidae*. This fly has no wings, a rather small body, and long legs armed with hooked claws; it feeds by sucking the blood of its host (fig. 44, p. 93). Flies of this sort are very quick runners and very nimble at avoiding capture; it is very peculiar to see one disturbed by the bat combing its fur appear on the surface, run a few steps and then dive down among the hair again. The bat appears to be unaware of the presence of the Nycteribiids and makes no effort to comb them out, carrying on with its grooming as though they were not there. Most bats carry one or two of these flies, sometimes more, and it is remarkable that they tolerate the presence of such comparatively huge insects; it is as if we would put up with several large shore-crabs lurking among our clothing.

Most bats are gregarious, living crowded together in colonies that may total several hundred individuals. The gregarious habit is particularly well-developed in the pipistrelle, noctule and horseshoe-bats, in which the composition and location of the summer and winter colonies may differ widely. Pipistrelles often inhabit the same homes throughout the year, and not only inhabit caves and house roofs but creep into the crevices in cliffs, behind thick ivy, and similar places (Pl. VI, p. 85). Numbers have been found between a signboard and the wall to which it was attached, and behind loose rough-cast on the outside wall of a cathedral. Such places are typical of those inhabited by the pipistrelle, which shows a decided preference for

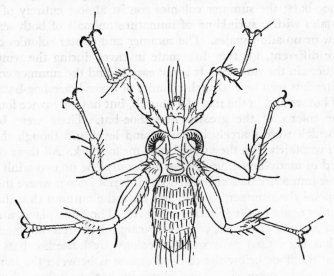

FIG. 44

A wingless nycteribiid fly parasitic on bats, magnified.
It is about three-sixteenths of an inch long

crowding into small crannies. In early summer such colonies usually consist almost entirely of adult females and it is not known where the adult males go at that time: perhaps they are not then gregarious and are scattered widely in small numbers. Immature bats of both sexes occur in small numbers with the adult females, but it is not until after the females have given birth to their young in July that the adult males again join the colonies. The bats in a large colony wake up about an hour before sunset and there is a good deal of activity before they start emerging for the evening flight.[227] This starts at sunset at the height of summer, but is rather later at the beginning and end of the season. Dull weather delays the time of emergence, and low temperature or gusty winds discourage it so that only small numbers emerge and some of the colony does not fly at all; if the temperature falls below 40° F there is usually no emergence.[223]

There is a similar segregation of the sexes in the colonies of several other species. In the noctule, for example, whose colonies are very often in hollow trees, the summer roosts are usually crowded with pregnant females without any adult males among them. So also with the horseshoe-bats; the summer colonies consist almost entirely of breeding females with a sprinkling of immature animals of both sexes but very few or no adult males. The summer and winter colonies of these bats are different, for they hibernate in caves during the winter but desert them in the summer. It is not easy to find the summer colonies; the writer has seen several such colonies of lesser horseshoe-bats in the roofs of houses and in the roof of a church, but has only twice found the summer colony of the greater horseshoe-bat. These were both in crypts which were scarcely below ground level and though the light in them was fairly dim they were by no means dark. All these colonies consisted of many breeding females with only one or two adult males, and some immature bats of both sexes. It is not known where the adult males spend the summer, for it is not until the autumn that they join the females again in the hibernating caves. The same places are used, either in summer or winter, year after year; the church roof mentioned above has been used as a summer colony by horseshoe-bats for so long that the floor below the roof—the roost is between the inner and outer roofs—is some six inches deep in bat droppings that have disintegrated into a dry dust composed entirely of the undigested fragments of insect exoskeletons and the wing scales of moths. Bat guano forming deep deposits in caves is mined for agricultural use in several parts of the tropics.

Horseshoe-bats are notoriously difficult to keep in captivity; even when they have been induced to feed and seem to be doing well they inexplicably die without warning. It has been suggested that the humidity of the air is of great importance to their health, and this certainly seems probable in view of the saturated atmosphere of the caves in which they hibernate, so damp that the tips of the hairs are often beaded with moisture (cf. Pl. Xa, p. 105). Such an atmosphere is certainly not always necessary for them in the summer colonies, for on a hot summer's day the temperature, in the dry and dusty church-roof for example, becomes sweltering, certainly well over 100°F, and yet the bats, both lesser horseshoe and pipistrelle, flourish and are very active in it. Several other species of bat are, unlike the horseshoe-bats, quite easy to keep in captivity, soon becoming tame and making most interesting pets. The long-eared bat is one of these, and may be fed on plenty of mealworms or other insects, for bats have voracious appetites; and there must always be clean water available for drinking. Noctules too are tolerant of captivity and if well fed sometimes become so fat and lazy that it is difficult to get them to fly.

Though there is a limited local migration from summer to winter quarters and back, none of the British bats are known to undertake migrations comparable with those of birds, nor are any known regularly to leave this country or to visit it from abroad. On the continent some of the species that are also found in this country have been known to wander great distances, up to several hundred miles, but it has not been shown that these journeys are proper migrations and not haphazard wanderings. There is a continental species, not found in Britain, that migrates regularly between Scandinavia and south Germany, and several species in America regularly migrate over long distances in spring and autumn. The assumption that no migration between Britain and the continent takes place has led to an attempt to distinguish two subspecific races of bats peculiar to Britain. These are the horseshoe-bats, which have had the subspecific names *Rhinolophus ferrum-equinum insulanus* and *Rhinolophus hippodideros minutus* bestowed upon them. But the subspecific distinctness of the British horseshoe-bats is at least doubtful, the alleged differences from the continental specimens lying in the measurements of the body, which are said to be slightly smaller. But the range of individual variation in both races overlaps that of the other so far that it would be impossible to assign unlabelled specimens to their appropriate subspecies. That being the case, to call them distinct subspecies is quite wrong and useless. No one has had the temerity to describe any of the other British species as distinct from the corresponding species of the continent. As might be expected in such highly mobile animals the distribution of each of our species is very wide outside the British Isles. Most of them are found all over Europe at least as far north as the Baltic, and the majority extend into both Africa and Asia, some reaching as far as China and Japan.

The hibernation of bats is a well-known phenomenon, and in the absence of migration to a warmer climate, is a necessity to animals that feed on flying insects and inhabit the temperate zones. During the summer bats feed enormously so that by the end of autumn they are greatly loaded with fat that forms a thick layer almost completely covering their bodies underneath the skin. This deposit of fat has to provide the energy needed for their reduced metabolism during the period when they are inactive. There is in addition a deposit of dark-coloured fat and lymphatic tissue round the blood vessels in the chest, neck and elsewhere. This has been termed the "hibernating gland," but its functions are obscure and it decreases in size more slowly during hibernation than do the general reserves of fat. In hibernation the animal becomes torpid, the heart-beat and rate of breathing are greatly reduced as are all the metabolic processes. The temperature of the body, at least of the extremities and the outer surface, drops almost to that of the surrounding air, but the temperature in the heart is not likely to reach so low a level, though no exact observations have been made on this point in bats. So great is the reduction in metabolism during hibernation that the oxygen consumption is then only about one-hundredth of that of the same bat when awake and active.[168] It takes from thirty to sixty minutes to wake up a torpid hibernating bat so that it becomes sufficiently active to fly. During that time the temperature rises from about 47° or 48°F to the normal of just over 98°F. While torpid the bat breathes at the rate of about 25 to 30 breaths a minute for some three minutes and then pauses for three to eight minutes without breathing; when it becomes active the rate goes up to about 200 a minute without any pauses. One of the most peculiar facts is that during torpidity the spleen swells up to as much as seven times its normal volume, being distended with blood and acting as a reservoir to store it while it is not being vigorously pumped round the body by the heart.[70]

Even during the summer a bat when asleep often becomes torpid and passes part of the way into the hibernating state. Not every bat asleep during the day in a summer colony does this, but generally several will be found that are unable to wake up quickly and escape if they are disturbed, whereas the rest are at once active. When they thus become semi-torpid, though not hibernating, the temperature and metabolic rate drop far below the values for normal activity, and the oxygen-consumption may be only a tenth of what it is when the bat is active. So great is the difference between the active and resting metabolism that one hour of activity would use up as much food or fat stores as over twelve hours at the torpid rate. When bats are active their appetites appear to be as voracious as those of shrews, and.

were they active all the time, they would, like shrews, need to eat their own weight of food daily. But the periods of deep sleep and torpidity during which the metabolism is greatly reduced spare them this necessity and allow for the expenditure of the energy required during flight.

Contrary to what might be expected, the stimulus leading to hibernation is probably not the autumn drop in temperature nor the seasonal decrease in food supply. It is more likely to be an internal stimulus correlated in some way with the amount of fat laid up as stores under the skin and elsewhere. Temperature may perhaps play a part in starting the onset of the state by reducing activity at the usual feeding-time, for as noted above (p. 93) there is a definite threshold temperature below which bats do not generally emerge from their roosts. But the most important factor is certainly within the animal and not external. Although a hibernating bat is so deeply torpid that it has nearly ceased living, the state is not uninterrupted during the winter. At irregular intervals life returns and the bat wakes up and moves about in its winter den, sometimes actually emerging and flying about on mild days. The pipistrelle and whiskered bats frequently do this even in the middle of winter. Among the horseshoe-bats, too, winter activity is common, for though a visit to a hibernating cave generally shows all the inhabitants hanging up cold and stiff, another visit a week later will often reveal that many of them have altered their positions and are hanging in different places. They must therefore wake and fly about at least within their caves even if they do not emerge into the open. It is during these intervals of winter activity that horseshoe-bats may feed occasionally on the spiders and hibernating moths that share the caves. It is certain that food-remains are to be found in their intestines during the winter, and it is unlikely that these are the remnants of food taken before hibernation.[159]

Young bats are born in the summer from late May to early July according to species. They are naked and uncoloured at first (fig. 45, p. 98) and are carried about by the mother, clinging to her fur, for two or three weeks until their own fur has grown and their permanent teeth have erupted. When too large to be carried about, just before weaning, they are left in the roost by the mothers while foraging. Young bats in their first coat are generally greyer and lighter in colour than the adults, though they are darker in some species, and the ears and wing membranes are not so darkly coloured; indeed at weaning the bases of the ears may still be pinkish-white where the pigment has not yet been laid down. At parturition the young is delivered into the pouch formed by the interfemoral membrane, at least in the Vespertilionid bats. As soon as it is born it is licked all over by the mother who eats the placenta when that follows. The young clings to the fur of the mother's under surface and is suckled at the nipples which are placed on the chest.

FIG. 45
A new born Leisler's bat. The body is naked and un-coloured, but the face, ears and wings are darkly pigmented. Total length 4.5 cm.

The mammary glands, one on each side, extend under the skin round the side of the body right up on to the back. In the horseshoe-bats in addition to the pair of chest nipples connected with the mammary glands there is another pair in the groin, one on each side of the sex opening (fig. 46, p. 99). These anchoring nipples or false teats are not connected with a mammary gland, but they evidently belong to the original milk line which has here become suppressed, for, at least in some species, they contain ducts exactly like the milk-ducts of the true nipples although there is no milk to flow through them. These anchoring nipples appear to be grasped in the mouth of the young to obtain a firm hold on the mother, and there is presumably a correlation between their presence and the early loss of the milk teeth before birth in the horseshoe-bats. The young may grasp the false teat thus during flight, but when suspended in their roosts the writer has always found that the young of the lesser horseshoe-bat are not anchored to the false teats, but are clinging to the mother in the suckling position with the head pointing in the same direction as hers.

The gestation period of bats is about six weeks,[58] the young being born in early summer, and yet pairing occurs in the autumn before hibernation, seven or eight months previously. The sperm received from the male is thus stored in the uterus of the female during hibernation, the uterus of a hibernating female bat being not only filled but actually distended with living sperm. This is a most unusual happening among mammals, for the life of the sperm within the female is generally strictly limited. But this is not the strangest part of the

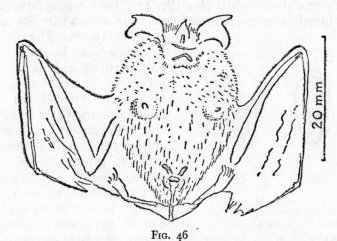

FIG. 46

A lactating horseshoe bat showing the mammary glands on the chest, and the false teats towards the tail. The infant bat anchors itself by grasping the false teats in its mouth

process, for when the bat finishes hibernation in the spring the stored sperm do not always, in many species of Vespertilionids, fertilise the egg that is to become the offspring of the coming summer. The stored sperm is lost, presumably expelled, and another season of pairing takes place in the spring; and it is the sperm of the spring pairing that fertilises the egg.[90] But the sperm received during the spring has also been stored—in the male; for the testis of the male produces sperm actively during the autumn but not during hibernation or spring. After the autumn activity of the testis its long coiled duct, the epididymis, a tube of small calibre but great length closely coiled up to form a compact body, is distended with sperm and acts as a reservoir which is drawn upon in the spring pairing.

In the horseshoe-bats the process is different. There is an autumn pairing and sperm passes into the uterus, but in lesser quantity, so that the latter is not so greatly distended. In these bats the vagina, the passage leading to the uterus, is comparatively very large and wide.

perhaps partly in correlation with the large size of the terminal part of the male organ, which in the Vespertilionid bats is minute.[132] Be that as it may, the upper end of the vagina of the female forms a pouch in front of the uterus, and in this during the winter there is a relatively enormous vaginal plug (fig. 47). Such a plug is formed in many animals after pairing and consists of a firm jelly-like mass of

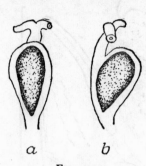

a   *b*

FIG. 47

Part of the reproductive tract of a horseshoe bat made semi-transparent by soaking it in oil, to show the vaginal plug. *a*, from in front. *b*, from the side. The two limbs of the uterus are cut off short, and the plug is the body with a dark border in the enlarged vaginal pouch

coagulated mucus. The plug in the horseshoe-bats, however, is not only relatively large in size but is very hard in consistency, resembling gristle. It is semi-transparent, its outer layers consisting of hardened cells from the female passage, and its inner mass of clear hard jelly. It appears to be derived mainly from the very large glands on the urethra of the male, which are not present in Vespertilionid bats; at the centre of the plug is an opaque mass of sperm. It is not certain whether there is a spring pairing in the horseshoe-bats, but there is some evidence that sometimes there may be. But female horseshoe-bats have been found in which fertilisation had already occurred while the vaginal plug of winter was still in place, so it is apparent that, in these bats at least, fertilisation can be brought about by the sperm stored during the winter. After hibernation the plug is expelled, and sometimes if a horseshoe-bat is disturbed during hibernation the plug is discharged as a small body of crystalline appearance about the size and shape of an orange pip.[133]

All our species of bat give birth, as a rule, to only a single young one each year in the British Isles, but the same species are known to produce a small percentage of twins on the continent. This is known, perhaps, because they have been much more closely studied by competent zoologists there than in Britain, where the careful work of many amateur naturalists has been little supported by professional zoologists. If it is indeed a fact that twins are very rarely, or never, produced in

Plate VII

Long-eared bat

Eric Hosking

a. Daubenton's bat   *Eric Hosking*

b. Serotine bat at rest   *Eric Hosking*

Plate VIII

the British Isles there is here a real difference from the continental races more definite and significant than the alleged difference in size on which subspecific names have been based. A point that would be interesting if settled is whether the twins produced on the continent are identical (uniovular) twins derived from a single egg, or whether ovulation is sometimes multiple so that the twins are derived from separate eggs. If the latter alternative were established it would indicate a tendency towards a return to more primitive conditions, for the evolution of bats has undoubtedly tended towards a reduction in the number of young produced at a birth. So much so that in the horseshoe-bats, which occasionally have twins on the continent, the reproductive tract has become asymmetrical and is partly degenerate on one side of the body. For in these bats the pregnancy always takes place in the right side of the divided uterus, the left side being smaller than the right even in the immature bat, and the left ovary appears never to be functional, all the eggs shed coming from the right one.

The low reproductive rate of not more than one offspring a year has a bearing upon the age attained by bats. If the numbers of a species are not to decline each female must leave at least one surviving daughter. If the ratio of sexes born is roughly equal this means that each female must leave at least two surviving offspring and, to allow for the accidents inevitable to any animal, more than that number must be produced. At a bare minimum, then, each female must give birth to at least three offspring in her lifetime. A female bat born during the summer does not normally breed in the following autumn or spring so she must be at least two years old at the time when she gives birth to her first young. She must live then to the age of at least four-and-a-half years in order to rear three offspring; and this being the least possible average span, many individuals must live much longer. This conclusion is upheld by observations made on marked bats on the continent. In a Vespertilionid bat of a species not found in Britain 7 per cent of the animals marked as adults of unknown age were alive and in good health five-and-a-half to six-and-three-quarter years afterwards; and a lesser horseshoe-bat was similarly recorded over seven years after being marked.[24] These ages are in very striking contrast to the short life-spans of most small mammals, many of which are little more than annuals or at most biennials. On the other hand when it is remembered that some species of bat spend

M.   H up to nine-tenths of their life in summer asleep, and all of it during the winter in hibernation, it can readily be appreciated that the animal machine will not wear out so quickly as in mammals that are active for a higher proportion of the twenty four hours daily.

Until it was overshadowed by the announcement of the harnessing of atomic energy, the subject of radar appeared as one of the outstanding scientific inventions of the war of 1939–45. But the principles underlying radar are not new, and they have been put to practical use for the last fifty million years. For it is by using these principles that bats are able to find their way about when flying in the dark, and fully evolved bats are known as fossils from the Eocene rocks. There is, moreover, no reason to think that these remote ancestors differed in their habits and structure from their descendants of the present day. Radar, and echo-sounding as used by ships for finding the depth of the sea, are both founded on the same fact—that if a short burst of energy is sent out by an observer and the time taken for an echo to come back from an object is noted, then, if the speed at which the energy travels is known, the distance of the object can be calculated. Furthermore, by pointing the energy sent out down a narrow beam in different directions the bearing of the object from the observer can be found. In radar the energy used is in the form of electromagnetic waves— the same waves that are used in short-wave wireless broadcasting—and in echo-sounding ordinary sound waves can be used. Bats also use sound waves in their echo-location; not ordinary ones, but ultrasonic waves, that is vibrations of such high pitch, or frequency, that they are inaudible to human ears.

The range of frequencies that the normal human being can hear as sounds is from about 16 vibrations a second to 30 or 40,000—middle C being 256 vibrations a second, and the highest note of the orchestra, the top D of the piccolo 4,752 a second. The frequency of the ultrasonic waves used by bats ranges from about 30,000 to 70,000 a second, and thus lies above the human upper limit in the sound spectrum. But bats are not the only animals that can hear ultrasonic vibrations, for it has long been known that dogs, at least, can hear these inaudible sounds. Some people train their dogs to come on the blowing of a Galton whistle, named after its inventor, and sometimes known as a "silent whistle" that gives forth ultrasonic sounds of so high a pitch that they are audible to a dog but not to its master.

One of the most interesting problems that have so long been a puzzle is the way that bats can fly at night, and catch the insects upon which most of them feed, without colliding with the objects they encounter. It seemed unlikely that animals with eyes so small that they are proverbially called blind, could make any use of the sense of sight while executing aerobatics among trees or around buildings, in the gloom of a dark night. Late in the eighteenth century an Italian naturalist, the Abbé Spallanzani, made the experiment which proved that bats do not find their way about by sight. He released blinded bats in a room in which various obstacles had been placed to obstruct the way, and found that they flew about as easily, and avoided collisions as well, as if they had been uninjured, but he was able only to guess at the means by which they were able to do so. Here things rested for a century and a half; many were the speculations, but nothing definite was found out. It was suggested, and regarded as probable by many naturalists, that the wing-membranes, the large ears, and the structures known as "nose-leaves" on the snout of many bats were very sensitive to changes in atmospheric pressure, so that bats would be able to feel objects near to them without actually touching them. Some people even went so far as to suggest that bats possessed an unknown sixth sense of location, though they were unable to suggest in what sense-organ this faculty might lie.

In the summer of 1920 Professor Hartridge was burning the midnight oil in his rooms at King's College, Cambridge, and was visited by numbers of bats that flew in through the open and uncurtained window, probably in pursuit of moths and other insects attracted to his light. He, being a biologist, was fascinated by the beauty of their flight, and was interested to find that they continued flying from one room to another even when the lights were switched off and the door was partly closed. But he found that if he nearly shut the door, so that only a very narrow gap was left, the bats flew up to the crack but never attempted to pass through if it was too narrow for them; and they were obviously able to recognise, without seeing or touching, whether the space was large enough for them to pass through or not. Professor Hartridge was then working on problems of vision and his laboratory contained a light-proof room in which he was conducting his experiments, so he was able easily to investigate further the problem of the bats' flight in the dark. He satisfied himself that vision had no part in helping bats to avoid obstacles, and by a process of elimination he was able to suggest that bats, when flying in the dark, were probably made aware of the position of surrounding objects by means of reflected ultrasonic sounds emitted by the animals and reflected to their ears. He put this forward as the probable explanation of the phenomenon, but being busy with other matters, he did not go on to prove it; this was rather a pity, because in due course his suggestion was found to be right. Professor Hartridge published his conclusions in a short scientific paper in 1920,[97] but another twenty years were to elapse before the subject was carried farther.

It was not until after the outbreak of the late war and the development of radar to an operational system that Griffin and Galambos[88] in America were able to solve the riddle of the bats' flight; and it seems likely that their attention must have been attracted to the problem by their knowledge of the principles of radar. Their first experiments were simple: they confirmed that blindfolded bats are not handicapped in flight; and then found that if the bats' ears are covered they are not able to avoid collisions when flying, and are in fact very reluctant to take to the wing at all. If one ear only is covered the bat can fly with moderate success but makes some collisions, showing that its efficiency in locating its surroundings is impaired. These experiments proved that bats are made aware of neighbouring objects that they cannot see by means of sound waves reflected from them. The experimenters then covered the nose and mouth of the bats, but left the ears uncovered, and found that again the animals were unable to fly without collisions, thus proving that the sound-waves reflected from objects are produced by the vocal apparatus of the bats themselves.

Griffin and Galambos[81] then went on to investigate this interesting discovery in more detail. They made use of an apparatus known as an ultrasonic* analyser, which consists of a microphone sensitive to ultrasonic vibrations, an amplifier to magnify them and to convert them to vibrations of a lower frequency, and either a telephone to give an audible sound, or a recorder to trace a graph on paper when ultrasonic sounds impinge on the microphone. The apparatus was also able to measure the frequency of any ultrasonic vibrations that it

* The confusion arising from the indiscriminate use of the terms 'supersonic' and 'ultrasonic' has recently led physicists to agree that supersonic shall mean speeds greater than that of sound and ultrasonic, vibrations of a frequency above the audible limit.

Plate IX

Bechstein's bat

Mondiale

a. Three Daubenton's bats sleeping in a cave. their fur covered with drops of moisture

b. Natterer's bat

Eric Hosking

Plate X

might pick up. By using this machine the investigators found that bats make ultrasonic squeaks at frequent intervals nearly all the time. The frequency of the vibrations given forth varies, but is most commonly about 50,000 a second; at this pitch each squeak lasts for about two-hundredths of a second or less. When bats are at rest they make ultrasonic squeaks about ten times a second, but as soon as they start flying the squeak-rate goes up to about thirty a second; obviously the faster the squeak-rate the more information about the position of surrounding objects will be obtained in a given time—and a bat in flight needs the information much more urgently than one at rest. Then a most interesting fact came to light: Griffin and Galambos arranged one of their experiments so that there was a narrow aperture for the bats to fly through, and found that as the bats approached the hole the squeak-rate became faster and faster, and then returned to normal when the bat was safely through. Now, we have already pointed out that the higher the squeak-rate the more the information, but there is a limitation; and that depends on the distance of the bat from the object it is sounding. The time between squeaks must be long enough for the echo of one squeak to come back before the next squeak is sent out, otherwise echoes and squeaks would become hopelessly confused: in fact, the squeaks must be so spaced that the sequence is Squeak 1, Echo 1, Squeak 2, Echo 2, and so on, and not Squeak 1, Squeak 2, Echo 1, Squeak 3, Echo 2, or even worse. So the closer a bat gets to a gap it wants to pass through, or any object it intends to approach closely, the quicker can be the squeak-rate since the echo-time is shorter.

In a radar set, which consists of a transmitter and a receiver, corresponding to a bat's vocal organs and ears, it is found necessary to prevent the signal sent by the transmitter from getting into the receiver direct: it must only come in as an echo from a distant object. The receiver is suppressed while the transmitter sends because, if it were not, the direct signal would momentarily paralyse it, and spoil the reception of the echo, just as a very loud sound temporarily deafens the ear. And something exactly comparable to this happens in the bat. Griffin and Galambos found that the contraction of a minute muscle in the bat's ear puts it out of action for a moment while the squeak is being made, so that the bat's hearing is not temporarily paralysed by the loudness of its own squeak, but is eagerly awaiting the reflected echo.

Imagine a room, or a dark cave, with a number of bats flying about in it: as they will all be giving out ultrasonic sounds, will that not lead to complete confusion, like a room full of schoolboys all shouting at once? Two things prevent such a state of chaos from occurring. First, the attenuation of ultrasonic waves in air is great; that is to say they do not travel far, but quickly die away, just as an ordinary sound gets fainter and finally fades out as distance increases. The distance from which the ultrasonic squeaks of bats are able to return a useful echo is only about five yards, so that unless the bats are close together they do not interfere with each other's echo-location. This probably explains also the amazingly quick swerves and aerobatics that bats indulge in, for they have to be very quick to turn when flying at full speed if they get warning of an impending collision when they are only five yards or less away from an object. The second thing that prevents confusion is that the frequency of the vibrations made by any two bats is not necessarily the same. In fact it is extremely unlikely that they will be of exactly the same pitch. A difference of quite a few vibrations a second is probably enough to distinguish them, so that if many bats are flying together there is no danger of confusion because each will recognise its own voice.

Anyone who has ever tried playing the instrument known as the "tin whistle" will remember that you blow quite gently to get the lower notes and harder to get the higher ones, and that in going up the scale when all the notes have been played you can go an octave farther by blowing harder still. That is to say, the higher the note and the greater the frequency, the more energy there is in the vibrations. There must, therefore, be much more energy in the ultrasonic cries of bats than in the lower notes of ordinary animal noises. And if we examine the vocal organs of bats we find that they are very different from those of other animals. The larynx—the Adam's apple—in most animals is made up of gristly cartilage, but in bats it is a very stout structure in comparison with the size of the animal and is made of bone. In addition, the muscles that operate its different parts are, comparatively, very large and strong. The exact method by which the ultrasonic vibrations are produced is not yet known, but the very strong build of the bat's larynx together with its small size—the smaller the organ-pipe, the higher the note—are obviously special adaptations to this end. Another interesting point found by the American investigators was that bats give out audible sounds as well as ultrasonic ones. The bat's ordinary voice, apart from its echo-location noises, is well known as a very high-pitched squeak, so high that it is not audible to all people: this may be called the conversational tone. But they found that in addition to this sometimes a buzzing noise was produced, and this turned out to be a side effect of the echo-location. The ultrasonic sounds are given out in short bursts and the sequence of these bursts itself produces a note,

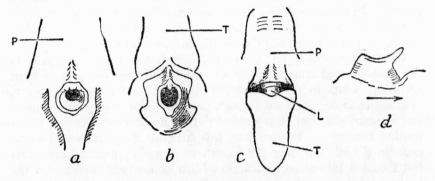

FIG. 48

The larynx of the horseshoe bat. *a*, the internal opening of the nasal passages at the hind end of the palate, P, surrounded by a ring which grasps the tip of the larynx. *b*, looking down on to the larynx which lies behind the tongue, T. *c*, looking into the open mouth at the back of the throat. The ring of the palate, P, grasps the tip of the larynx, L, behind the tongue, T. *d*, side view of the larynx; the epiglottis projects towards the base of the tongue on the right

whose pitch is determined by the repetition rate of the echo-location bursts, the repetition rate being low enough to produce an audible sound. If a horseshoe-bat is watched while it is hanging up after it wakes before taking to the wing this effect can be observed. When awake and alert the wings are half opened and the bat rapidly twists about, apparently looking in all directions, sometimes swinging round so far that the legs are crossed. All the time an intermittent vibration of the ears and nose-leaf is kept up, and it is probable that this vibration, which accompanies the audible low buzz, is produced by the rapid succession of ultrasonic pulses.

So far we have been dealing mainly with facts: now we come to speculation, for there are many points about the behaviour of bats that are still obscure. For one thing, do bats emit their ultrasonic sounds through the mouth or the nose, or both? Bats catch their insect food while in flight: the insects are usually flying too, but at least one species, the long-eared bat, is also in the habit of picking insects off the foliage of trees and bushes while hovering. When a bat shuts its mouth whilst catching an insect, does it stop echo-location and fly blind or does the echo-location go on through the nose? The matter is unsettled, but there is one piece of evidence that is a pointer. In the horseshoe-bats the larynx—the tip of the voice-box—does not open into the back of the mouth as in most animals, but projects up into the roof of the mouth and fits into the hinder opening of the nasal passages (fig. 48, p. 107). It is not immovably fixed in this position and can probably be withdrawn, but the arrangement certainly points to the probability that the supersonic sounds are, or at least can be, given out through the nose. The function of the nose-leaf is unknown, but it is suggested that if the echo-location trans-mission takes place by the nose, this structure may in some way be concerned with directing the sounds so that they are not broadcast but focussed into narrow beams, with a consequent increase in the bat's appreciation of the direction of objects.

It has been suggested that the tragus, present in Vespertilionid but absent in the horseshoe-bats, is in some way connected with the facility for direction-finding, and this of course may be so. But it is not likely that it is concerned with focusing the received ultrasonic vibrations into the ear, because it is too small in physical dimensions when compared with the wave-lengths concerned. Nevertheless one cannot help suspecting that the tragus and the nose-leaf, which are not usually found together in the same species of bat, must in some way serve similar functions. In the bats without nose-leaves, too, there occurs a great development of glandular and fatty pads, well covered with whiskers, on parts of the face. It has been suggested that they are cushions to protect the bat when it collides with objects in the dark, but that theory is made extremely unlikely by the discovery of the bat's ability for echo-location.

In spite of echo-location there may still be something in the old theory that bats have some sort of tactile sense acting at a distance, for if any object is brought near to a sleeping horseshoe-bat it reacts by bending the knees so that it is drawn up towards the object from which it hangs. This happens while the bat is still so torpid that if disturbed it is unable to fly; and it happens in response to the approach of any object, not only for instance the hand of an observer, the heat from which might be the cause of the reaction. It does seem probable that the wing-membranes that wrap the body while the bat is asleep are sensitive to a nearby object which is not touching them, for while the bat is torpid there is no question of its using its echo-location.

CHAPTER 5

BRITISH BATS

" The Reremouse or Bat, alone of all creatures that flie, bringeth
forth young alive: and none but she of that kind hath wings
made of pannicles or thin skins. She is the onely bird that
suckleth her little ones with her paps, and giveth them milke;
and those she will carrie about her two at once, embracing them
as she flieth .... No flying foule hath teeth, save only the bat
or winged mouse."

PLINIUS SECUNDUS, *Historiae Naturalis* Libri XXXVII
Trans. Philemon Holland. 1601

BATS are not easily identified by the non-expert who has not collec-
tions of specimens at hand for comparison. The key for the
identification of the British species that follows has been devised
by Mr. T. C. S. Morrison-Scott of the British Museum (Natural
History), by whose kind permission it is inserted. It should enable
anyone to make a correct identification of any specimens he may
encounter.

KEY TO THE BRITISH BATS (MORRISON-SCOTT)[155]

Barrett-Hamilton gives a key to the external characters and to the
skulls, but he arranges his key as a 'natural key,' keeping the members
of each genus together; this system creates extra difficulties, with the
result that the key based on external characters is of little use, even
to the expert. As for the key based on skull characters, this is not at
all easy to use for those unacquainted with the teeth of mammals.
The following key has been designed for use by one who has never
previously handled a bat; there is no need to examine the teeth.

1. Nose bears 'nose-leaf'; tragus absent (the tragus is a separate earlet within the ear and should not be confused with the antitragus which is an extension of the lower border of the ear and well developed in the horseshoe-bats) 11

   Ordinary nose; tragus present 2

2. Tragus broadest at end 3

   Tragus elongated and broadest at middle or base 4

3. Wing-span (from tip to tip of outstretched wings) 353–387 mm. (13.9–15.2 in.); forearm 49–54 mm. (1.93–2.12 in.) . . . *noctule*

   Wing-span 289–318 mm. (11.4–12.5 in.); forearm 38.5–44.5 mm. (1.52–1.75 in.) . . . . *Leisler's*

4. Bases of ears joined together on top of head; nostrils opening upwards 5

   Ears not joined together; nostrils opening forwards 6

5. Huge ears, 34–38 mm. (1.34–1.50 in.) long; fur on back grey-brown . . . *long-eared*

   Ears moderate, 13–16 mm. (0.51–0.63 in.) long; fur on back almost black, but with slight yellowish tinge . . . . *barbastelle*

6. Wing-span 348–381 mm. (13.7–15.0 in.); forearm 49–54 mm. (1.93–2.12 in.). Tail projects about ¼ in. beyond the tail membrane. . . . *serotine*

   Wing-span less than 320 mm. (12½ in.); forearm 45 mm. (1¾ in.) or under 7

7. Post-calcarial lobe (see fig. 30) present; wing-span 203–232 mm. (8.0–9.1 in.); forearm 27.5–32.2 mm. (1.08–1.23 in.) . *pipistrelle*

   No post-calcarial lobe 8

8. Inter-femoral membrane fringed with short hairs . . *Natterer's*

   Inter-femoral membrane not fringed 9

9. Ears long, when laid forward extend about 13 mm. (½ in.) beyond tip of the nose . . . . *Bechstein's*

   Ears moderate, when laid forward extend about 3 mm. (⅛ in.) beyond tip of the nose 10

10. Middle finger with second and third joints equal to each other in length; calcar extending half-way from the heel to the tail; foot half as long as the shin-bone . . . . . . *whiskered*

    Middle finger with second joint longer than the third; calcar extending two-thirds of the way from the heel to the tail; foot more than half as long as the shin-bone . . . . . . *Daubenton's*

11. Wing-span 330–355 mm. (13.0–14.0 in.); forearm 51 mm. (2.0 in.) or over . . . . *greater horseshoe*

    Wing-span 254 mm. (10.0 in.) or under; forearm 39 mm. (1.54 in.) or under . . . . *lesser horseshoe*

In using this key it should be noted that the wing-span measurements should be taken as a rough guide only; different observers' results are apt to vary, and moreover many of these measurements have been taken from specimens in alcohol, which are often too stiff to be fully expanded. The length of the forearm is a much more reliable guide. It should also be noted that females are nearly always slightly larger than males. Juvenile specimens may be recognised by the fact that the finger-joints appear to be complex instead of just a simple joint as in the adults.

The systematic and biological notes that are given in the next section set out the chief points in the natural history of each species and will, it is hoped, enable an enquirer to check an identification made with the aid of the Morrison-Scott key. This useful key applies to bats in the hand; a key to field identification of flying bats is extremely hard to devise.

It is generally very difficult to identify with any certainty bats when they are upon the wing, except for one or two species whose flight has well marked characteristics. The habit and flight-character of many species are so varied, and those of different species so similar, that identification in the field is often unreliable. The following key has been devised as a help towards identification, but it can be no more than a guide, and any results produced by its use should be accepted with the greatest caution.

Flight sustained, or even powerful. Wings not markedly rounded.
    Flight in general high.
        Rapid; twists and turns between straights; starts well before dark: large bat . . . . *noctule*
        Similar; but smaller bat: flight often a series of gradual rises with sudden drop back to original level . . . . . *Leisler's*
        Rather fluttering, with sudden dives to low levels . . . *serotine*

    Flight in general low.
        Habitually over water.
            Skimming low, often touching the surface . . *Daubenton's*
            Slow, without sudden twists . . . . *Natterer's*
        Not habitually over water.
            Hovering among foliage and trees.
                Gliding, and hovering to pick off insects . . . . *long-eared*
                Slow and steady; pick off insects . . . . . *Natterer's*

John Markham

Barbastelle bat, showing the ears meeting over the forehead

Greater horse-shoe bat

Not hovering among foliage.
    Rapid; much twisting and turning . . . . . *pipistrelle*
    Slow and steady . . . . *whiskered*
Flight fluttering. Wings markedly rounded.
    Large bat . . . . *greater horseshoe*
    Small bat . . . . *lesser horseshoe*

It will be noted that one species, Natterer's bat, comes into this key twice, for it is as likely to be seen flying over water as among trees. On the other hand the key does not include either Bechstein's bat or the barbastelle, the flight of both species being low and without salient characters suitable for inclusion in a key.

FAMILY VESPERTILIONIDAE

Bats with an ear tragus and without a nose-leaf. The tail is comparatively long so that the interfemoral membrane can be used as a pouch. Ten species of the family are British.

NOCTULE (*Nyctalus noctula*), Pl. 2, p. 16

This is the largest of the British bats, having a wing span of 13 to 15 inches. The ear is rounded, nearly as broad as long, the outer edge having a notch below the tragus and ending just behind the angle of the mouth. The tragus is short and broad, the terminal lobe wider than the basal stalk. The ears are spaced widely apart. Teeth $\frac{2123}{3123}$; the lower incisors are crowded and overlap each other, and the first premolar is minute. The colour of the velvety fur is yellowish- or golden-brown above and below, the hair extending some way out from the body on both surfaces of the wing and interfemoral membrane; a band of hair is usually present along the hind edge of the wing bones on the inner side as far as the wrist. The noctule inhabits all temperate Europe and Asia, and in Britain it is common as far north as Yorkshire and north Wales, but north of that it rapidly becomes scarcer and has rarely been found in Scotland. It has not been recorded from the Isle of Man or Ireland. Its colonies are usually in holes in trees or buildings, hollow trees being specially favoured during summer; it has rarely been found in caves and then only singly. It is very gregarious, the colonies often containing many individuals, even up to one or two hundred. In summer the females form separate colonies when bearing and rearing their young. Noctules feed upon any insects that they can catch but appear to prey specially on the larger sorts of beetles. The young are born about the end of June after seven weeks' gestation; there is no good record of more than one young at a birth in Britain. They are blind and naked when born but grow rapidly and are independent of their mothers in little more than a month. After the first week the mothers usually leave them parked in the dens when they come out to feed. The evening flight starts a little before sunset and lasts only about an hour, seldom as much as two hours, the colony emerging from the den in small parties at short intervals. There is sometimes a second flight of about an hour's duration by some individuals of the colony from one to two hours before sunrise. Hibernation generally lasts from October to the middle or end of March, but individuals may be active both later and earlier in the year.

LEISLER'S BAT (*Nyctalus leisleri*)

This bat closely resembles the noctule in general appearance but is much smaller, the wing span being from 10 to 12 inches. The shape and proportions of the ear are similar to those of the noctule as is the dental formula, $\frac{2 1 2 3}{3 1 2 3}$, the first premolar also being minute. The lower incisors are less crowded than those of the first species and overlap each other very little if at all. The colour is a darker and not such a golden brown, the outer ends of the hairs fading to a rusty brown in spring and early summer, especially in the males. The fur of the under surface is a lighter shade of the same colour. The range of Leisler's bat extends right through Europe and temperate Asia from Ireland to China. In the British Isles its range is imperfectly known, probably because it has often been confounded with the noctule. In England it has been found in some numbers in Yorkshire, Cheshire, and along the valley of the Warwickshire Avon; it has also been recorded from Hampshire, Cambridgeshire, Gloucestershire and Somerset.[141] It probably occurs elsewhere and may be commoner than is usually thought. In Ireland it is locally abundant in the eastern half of the country; absence of records from the west does not mean that it may not be found there. Leisler's bat is often gregarious, living in holes in trees, and roofs or holes in buildings; the colonies may number up to a hundred, but the bats are sometimes solitary, especially when hibernating. The rancid smell so strong in the noctule is much less noticeable in this species, though it is sufficient to taint the dens. The evening flight starts just after sunset and lasts about an hour, during which time the bat feeds on moths, flies and other insects so rapidly that the stomach is crammed with food when the animal returns to the roost. A second flight of about an hour's duration ends about half-an-hour before sunrise. The flight of this bat is strong, but not at such a great height as that of the noctule. The young are born in June and are not known to exceed one to each mother here, though two is said to be the usual number in Germany. Hibernation lasts from the end of September to about the last week in April.

PIPISTRELLE (*Pipistrellus pipistrellus*), Pl. V, p. 84; Pl. VI, p. 85

This is the smallest British bat, the span being only 8 to 8½ inches. The ears are widely separated, longer than broad, and the external edge is definitely, though not deeply, notched and ends just behind the angle of the mouth. The tragus is bluntly pointed and its hind edge is rounded. Teeth, $\frac{2123}{3123}$; the inner upper incisor is bifid, and the first upper premolar though smaller than the other teeth, is not so extremely minute in comparison with them as in the genus *Nyctalus*. The fur is long and extends on to both sides of the wing and on to the back of the interfemoral membrane; on the underside of the latter it is usually restricted to the neighbourhood of the tail and thighs. The colour of the fur varies from dark to light, almost reddish, brown; and the under side is slightly lighter. The colour is, however, subject to much individual variation.

The pipistrelle occurs all over temperate Europe and extends far into Asia, probably to China; a closely allied subspecies inhabits eastern North America. In the British Isles it is the commonest bat everywhere both in country and town, and extends from the south of England to the north of Scotland, the Orkneys and Shetlands, and from the West of Ireland to East Anglia. Pipistrelles live in large or small colonies, or sometimes singly, hiding by day in cracks and crevices in buildings, cliffs and trees, behind loose bark and under ivy stems, but rarely in caves. Where the accommodation is big enough the colonies are often of large size and may contain several hundred bats, especially in summer. The bats emerge about dusk, coming out from crowded roosts in small parties which break up on taking to the wing, and the flight usually lasts all night, the return home being about an hour or less before sunrise. The flight is not very high, the bats usually fluttering up and down a regular beat round buildings, along a lane or among trees. Bats are sometimes seen flying during daylight and it is generally stated, mostly by guesswork, that this is the species concerned. The food consists chiefly of the smaller kinds of insects, and particularly of gnats, but larger insects are also taken and held in the tail pouch while being eaten. One young is born each year, usually in July, sometimes a little earlier or later. In the northern parts of the country hibernation lasts from before the end of October to nearly the end of March, but in the south hibernation is much less complete and individual pipistrelles may fly on any mild night throughout the winter.

SEROTINE (*Eptesicus serotinus*), Pl. VIIIb, p. 101

This large bat, about the size of the noctule, has a very limited distribution in Britain. The wing-span is 14 to 15 inches, and the wings are considerably broader than are those of the noctule. The oval ears are longer than broad, spaced far apart, and the unnotched but sinuous hind margin ends between the base of the tragus and the angle of the mouth. The tragus is fairly long, bluntly rounded at its tip, and has a curved hind edge. Teeth, $\frac{2\ 1\ 1\ 3}{3\ 1\ 2\ 3}$, the anterior premolar being absent from the upper jaw and small in the lower one. The fur is longer and less velvety than in the noctule; it does not extend far on to the upper surface of the wing nor on to the under surface of the inter-femoral membrane both of which are, however, sparsely sprinkled with very fine hairs. A band of hair extends along the under side of the arm bone towards the wrist. The colour is dark brown above and a lighter shade of brown beneath. Bats of this or closely allied species have a very wide distribution throughout temperate Europe and Asia, but the British Isles are on the extreme limit of the range. The species is locally abundant in Kent, Surrey, Sussex, Hampshire including the Isle of Wight, and parts of Devon. Elsewhere it is either unknown or very rare, but it has been recorded from Cambridgeshire, Cornwall, Essex and Suffolk. The serotine lives in small colonies of up to twenty individuals, frequently in the roofs of houses. It emerges quite early, as soon as the sun has set; the flight lasts little more than an hour and

Plate 3 NATTERER'S BATS
John Markham

there appears to be no second flight before sunrise. The flight is at no great elevation and is rather heavy and fluttering. The food consists of beetles, especially cockchafers, and moths, and doubtless other insects are also taken. On the continent the single young is said to be born at the end of May; nothing is known about its breeding in this country. Hibernation lasts from the end of October to early April. The natural history of the serotine in Britain is very imperfectly known.

GENUS MYOTIS

DAUBENTON'S BAT (*M. daubentoni*), Pl. VIIIa, p. 101; Pl. Xa, p. 105

Wing-span 10 to 10½ inches, the wings comparatively rather short and broad. The ears are well spaced, rather long and pointed, the hind edge very slightly notched and ending just in front of the base of the tragus. The tragus is narrow and half as long as the ear, widest at its middle, straight, and bluntly pointed at the tip. The teeth are $\frac{2\ 1\ 3\ 3}{3\ 1\ 3\ 3}$, the first two premolars in upper and lower jaws being smaller than the rest of the teeth, and the lower incisors broad and flattened. The fur is short and extends a short distance on to both surfaces of the wing. The colour is a grizzled warm brown on the upper surface, lighter brown below, where the hairs are tipped with yellowish white, giving the under surface a distinctly lighter colour. The range of Daubenton's bat extends throughout Europe from southern Scandinavia southwards, and eastwards half-way across Asia. In Great Britain it is generally common wherever there are woods near stretches of water, its restriction to the neighbourhood of water having gained it the name of 'water-bat.' It extends from southern England to Scotland as far as the Great Glen, but it appears to be scarce or unknown in the counties bordering the mouth of the Severn. It is probably widely distributed in Ireland though records are few. This species is very gregarious, the daytime dens in caves, trees or buildings near water often containing large numbers of bats—a hundred or more; they generally creep into small crannies but are sometimes found hanging in large clusters. The food consists chiefly of ephemerid or caddis-flies of small size caught as the bat flies close over the surface of water. The quivering slow flight as the bat skims very close to the water is characteristic. The bats start foraging over the water about an hour after sunset and the flight lasts all night, until rather less than an hour before sunrise. The single young is born in the second half of June. Hibernation lasts from the end of September to the middle of April, and takes place usually in caves or buildings, the summer roosts being then deserted. Bats of this species are usually solitary while hibernating.

WHISKERED BAT (*M. mystacinus*)

This is a small species, little exceeding the pipistrelle in size, the wing-span being about 8½ inches. The ear is comparatively long and narrow, the notched outer edge ending below the tragus. The tragus is slightly over half as long as the ear, straight, widest a little above its base, and pointed. Teeth, $\frac{2}{3}\frac{1}{1}\frac{3}{3}\frac{3}{3}$, the first two premolars in each jaw small; the first two lower incisors broad, but the third narrower. The fur is long and thick; it extends a short way on to both surfaces of the wings and the upper surface of the interfemoral membrane. The lips are fringed with long hairs, but not more so than are those of Daubenton's bat. The upper surface is dark or smoky brown, sometimes nearly black; the under surface lighter, the dark hairs there being tipped with whitish. The distribution of the whiskered bat covers all Europe and Asia from about 60° to 65° north latitude southwards. In Great Britain it is common from the south coast north to Scotland, but it is very rare in East Anglia, and has not often been recorded from South Wales. It is practically absent from Scotland, widely spread and probably plentiful throughout Ireland. This species is usually solitary, but colonies of up to a hundred or more have occasionally been found. In summer it usually makes its den in holes in buildings and the roofs of houses, but in winter it is commonly found hibernating in caves, which it deserts in summer. The food consists of flies, moths and small beetles. The flight superficially resembles that of the pipistrelle but is slower and steadier and often confined to a narrower beat. This species emerges rather early in the evening, often before sunset, and probably remains on the wing most of the night. The young are born in June or early July, but detailed information is lacking. Hibernation lasts from November to March and, at least in the south, is often interrupted in mild winter weather by a flight in full daylight. Flying by daylight is not confined to the winter, day-flying being probably as common in this species as in the pipistrelle.

NATTERER'S BAT (*Myotis nattereri*), Pl. 3, p. 117; Pl. Xb, p. 105

This is a medium-sized bat, the wing-span being about 11 inches. The ear is long and narrow, the outer edge notched about one third of the distance from the tip, and ending below the tragus. The tragus is long and narrow, about two thirds of the length of the ear, widest at its base, and pointed; there is a deep notch at the base of its hind edge. The ears are widely spaced. Teeth $\frac{2}{3}\frac{1}{1}\frac{3}{3}\frac{3}{3}$; the upper pre-molars are very small, the lower incisors wide and overlapping. The thick fur is rather long and in colour is greyish brown above and whitish below, the line of separation being distinct and running from the mouth to the fore edge of the wing. Distinctive are the rows of short stiff hairs on the edge of the interfemoral membrane between the end of the calcar and the tail (fig. 49). Natterer's bat occurs all over temperate Europe and Asia from Ireland to Japan. In England and Wales it has been found in practically every county, plentifully in many of them, but it has only

FIG. 49
Tip of the tail of Natterer's bat showing the fringe of hairs on the edge of the web near it

once or twice been reported from Scotland; it is widely distributed over Ireland. It is a gregarious species living in holes in buildings and trees, and in caves, particularly using the latter for hibernation. Natterer's bat emerges early in the evening, often before sunset, but the duration of its flight is not known. The flight is slow and steady, usually round trees, and carried out at a moderate height. The tail is carried extended behind the body during flight and not bent downwards as in the other Vespertilionid bats. The food consists of flies, small moths, and beetles, the bats often picking insects off foliage as well as catching them flying. The single young is born towards the end of June. Hiber-nation finishes about the end of March, but the approximate date on which it starts in autumn is not recorded.

BECHSTEIN'S BAT (*M. bechsteini*), Pl. IX, p. 104

This, the rarest British bat, is the largest of its genus. The span is about eleven inches, the wings rather narrow and pointed towards the tips. The ear is very long, with a rounded end, and the tragus is long, narrow and curved outwards. Teeth, $\frac{2133}{3133}$; the first upper premolar larger than the second, and neither extremely minute. The fur is long and woolly, and extends only a short way on to the wing and interfemoral membranes. The colour is dusky brown above, whitish beneath. Bechstein's bat occurs over the greater part of Europe south from Scandinavia but has very rarely been found in Great Britain, and then always in the southern counties, mainly Sussex and Hampshire including the Isle of Wight. It is gregarious, living in small colonies of up to about twenty in holes in trees. The flight is slow and near the ground, the bats emerging rather late in the evening. The young are said to be born about the middle of June in Germany. Very little is known of the natural history of this bat on the continent, and practically nothing of it in this country.

For (*Myotis myotis*) see footnote*

LONG-EARED BAT (*Plecotus auritus*), Pl. VII, p. 100

A medium-sized bat with a wing-span of about ten inches. The ears are enormously long; their inner edges meet each other on the top of the head, and their outer edges end just behind the angle of the mouth. The tragus is long, narrow and pointed. The ear is folded back under the arm when the bat is asleep, leaving the long tragus standing up alone. During flight the ears are carried pointing forwards. The teeth are $\frac{2123}{3134}$, the first upper premolar being very small. The fur is long and silky, extending a short way on to the surfaces of the wings. The colour is dusky brown above, shading into light brown or dirty white below. The distribution of the long-eared bat includes all temperate Europe and Asia to Japan and extends into Egypt, Palestine and northern India. In Great Britain it is one of the commonest and most widely distributed bats, being scarce only in the highlands of Scotland. It is gregarious and often found in large colonies of fifty to a hundred or more in the spaces under house and church roofs, both in summer and winter. It also hibernates in caves in which it is more solitary in habit, single individuals creeping alone into crevices. During the summer large companies of breeding females, sometimes a hundred or more, often take up temporary quarters in some building while they are nursing. The food consists of flies, moths and beetles, which are generally picked off the foliage of trees and not caught on the wing. The flight among foliage is a gliding one, with

*Michael Blackmore has recently (1957) discovered a colony of the Mouse-eared bat (*Myotis myotis*) established in Dorset.

another tree the flight is swift, strong, and close to the ground. The flight starts about half-an-hour after sunset and lasts until about an hour before sunrise. The single young is born in June or July. Hibernation lasts from the middle of October to early April, but it is not so complete as in some other species, for long-eared bats often emerge in winter when the weather is mild, or shift their quarters within the hibernation cave without coming out into the open.

BARBASTELLE (*Barbastella barbastellus*), Pl. XI, p. 112

Medium in size, the wing-span about ten inches. The ear is about as broad as long with a conspicuous notch on the outer edge. The inner edges of the two ears join each other above the eyes and the outer edges end between the eye and the mouth so that, in effect, the eye lies within the ear. The tragus is half the length of the ear, wide at its base, narrow and pointed at the tip, with two notches towards the base of the hind edge. The teeth are $\frac{2123}{3123}$, the first upper premolar is minute, and the first lower premolar is only half as big as the second. The fur is long and extends well on to both surfaces of the wing and interfemoral membrane. The colour is very dark, almost black, with a grizzled effect caused by the light tips of the hairs; the colour of the under surface is slightly lighter. The distribution of this species includes all Europe from southern Scandinavia, and a large part of temperate Asia. In Britain it is widely distributed in small numbers south of the Wash. North of that it is infrequent and it is unknown in Scotland and Ireland. Although this species is often found solitary it is sometimes gregarious to the extent of forming small colonies of half-a-dozen or so. In summer it creeps into crevices in buildings or trees but it appears to hibernate only in caves. The flight is slow and flapping, usually not far from the ground, and starts early in the evening, not later than sunset. The duration of the flight is unknown, as are the breeding habits. Hibernation lasts from the end of September to early April.

FAMILY RHINOLOPHIDAE (*Leaf-nosed bats*)

Characterised by the presence of a nose-leaf and the absence of a tragus. The two British species have been named as subspecies, the alleged difference being the smaller size as compared with continental specimens. The differences are so slight that the subspecific distinctions are not adopted here.

GREATER HORSESHOE-BAT (*Rhinolophus ferrum-equinum*), Pl. XII, p. 113

This is one of our larger bats, the wing-span being 13 to 14 inches and the wings broad with rounded ends. The ear is large, broad at the base, and tapers to a sharp point, the front edge being curved so that the point is directed backwards. The hind edge has a well-developed lobe, the antitragus, at its base; there is no tragus. The teeth are $\frac{1123}{2133}$, the upper incisor, and the first upper, and second lower premolars being minute. The fur is thick and woolly and extends a short distance on to both surfaces of the wing membrane. The colour is medium brown above, rather lighter below, often with a yellowish or pinkish cast. The range of the species extends from south England through central Europe and Asia to Japan. In Britain it is confined to the south of England and it is not known in Scotland or Ireland. It is most plentiful in the south-west and south Wales where it is a constant inhabitant of the limestone caves. Summer colonies sometimes occur in house roofs, cellars and perhaps hollow trees, the caves in which hibernation takes place being deserted at that season. The species is gregarious and there is a segregation of the sexes in the colonies at least during the summer. The food consists of the larger as well as smaller insects, and especially beetles. Large prey is pouched against the wing-membrane during manipulation since there is no tail-pouch; and it is often taken to the roost to be eaten. Wingless and other insects are often picked up off the ground, the flight frequently being only a few inches above it. The single young is born in late June or July and probably does not breed until it is three years old. Hibernation lasts from October to the end of March, but within the hibernating caves the bats often shift their quarters at intervals during the winter, when it is possible that they feed upon insects hibernating in the caves.

LESSER HORSESHOE-BAT (*Rhinolophus hipposideros*)

This species resembles the last very closely in all but size. It is one of our smaller bats, the wing-span being about 8½ inches. The ears are pointed and have a well-developed antitragus very similar to that of the greater horseshoe-bat on a smaller scale, but there are small differences from that species in the details of the form of the nose-leaf. The colour is a rather greyer brown without the yellowish or pinkish shade, and the fur is proportionately longer, silkier and less velvety. The underside tends to be lighter in colour and the fur extends on to the base of the wing membranes. As in the larger species there is a bare patch at the base of the tail on the upper surface. The teeth are $\frac{1\,1\,2\,3}{2\,1\,3\,3}$, the upper incisors, and the first upper, and the first two lower premolars being very minute. The range extends from Ireland to the Himalayas and north Africa and includes all Europe south of the Baltic. In the British Isles it is common in the south and west from Kent to Cornwall, though scarcer in Sussex and Hampshire. It is found throughout Wales and the border counties but not in east Anglia or north of Yorkshire. In Ireland it is confined to the west. The lesser horseshoe-bat is gregarious, the summer colonies occurring in house and church roofs and perhaps in hollow trees. The winter colonies are nearly always in caves, but the species is not then closely gregarious, individuals usually hanging up at some distance from their neighbours. They do not always hang in the roof of the cave and often choose the undersides of projecting points or boulders where they are only a few inches from the ground. The summer colonies show a segregation of the sexes and usually consist mainly of adult females, some immature bats of both sexes, and a few adult males. The flight is rather fluttering with frequent glides, and usually fairly near to the ground. The food consists of the smaller insects; moths appear to form a large part of the diet judging by the vast mass of lepidopterous scales in the guano deposits in the dens. The single young is born in June or July, the breeding season being rather protracted. Hibernation lasts from early October to the beginning of April, but it is frequently interrupted, the bats shifting their quarters within the hibernating cave and perhaps feeding upon the gnats which are usually found in them; but they are not known to come out into the open in the winter. Wherever caves are used by the greater horseshoe-bat for hibernation this species is found too; but because its range in Britain is much wider, it is also found in many caves outside the range of that species.

CHAPTER 6

RABBITS, HARES, AND RODENTS
(LAGOMORPHA AND RODENTIA)

"It was soon known among the neighbours that I was pleased with the present, and the consequence was, that in a short time I had as many leverets offered as would have stocked a paddock ... Puss grew presently familiar, would leap into my lap, raise himself upon his hinder feet, and bite the hair from my temples ... Finding him extremely tractable, I made it my custom to carry him always after breakfast to the garden, where he hid himself generally under the leaves of a cucumber-vine, sleeping or chewing the cud till evening ... Puss was tamed by gentle usage; Tiney was not to be tamed at all; and Bess had a courage and confidence that made him tame from the beginning ... I should not do complete justice to my subject, did I not add, that they have no ill scent belonging to them; that they are indefatigably nice in keeping themselves clean, for which purpose nature has furnished them with a brush under each foot; and that they are never infested by any vermin."

WILLIAM COWPER. 1731–1800. *Letters*

THE TWO orders Lagomorpha and Rodentia were formerly classified as one, the Lagomorpha forming merely a subdivision of the Rodentia. Modern research, however, has shown that they should be separated, for fossil forms of both orders are now known from as far back as the Paleocene, and even then they were quite distinct. They probably evolved independently of each other, and are not closely related, although superficially they show many points of resemblance that are due to convergence. The affinities of neither of these orders with other orders of mammals are known.

There are numerous species of these orders in the British Isles (fig. 50, p. 125). Of the Lagomorpha there are the rabbit and three species of hares, two of the latter being closely related and little more

Order LAGOMORPHA   Rabbits and hares
          Family *Leporidae*   Rabbit, Hare

Order RODENTIA
          Suborder *MYOMORPHA*   Mouse-like rodents
                    Family *Cricetidae*   Voles
                    Family *Muridae*   Mice and rats
                    Family *Gliridae*   Dormice
          Suborder *SCUIROMORPHA*   Squirrel-like rodents
                    Family *Sciuridae*   Squirrels
          Suborder *HYSTIRCOMORPHA*   Porcupine-like rodents
                    Family *Capromyidae*   Coypu

FIG. 50

The orders, suborders and families of the British Lagomorpha and Rodentia

than subspecies of the same basic stock. The Rodentia proper are divided into three suborders, the Myomorpha including the mice and rats, the Sciuromorpha, or squirrels and the Hystricomorpha, the porcupines and their relatives. All of our native rodents except the squirrels, belong to the first of these suborders; two species of squirrel, one native and the other introduced, represent the second; and the third, though without any native members, makes a slender contribution to the British fauna through the presence in some places of the coypu, an introduction from South America that has escaped from captivity, though it has become fully naturalised only in a restricted area. Of the Myomorpha we have thirteen species, two species of dormouse, one native, the other introduced; one species (four subspecies) of bank-vole (*Clethrionomys*); one species (two subspecies) of water-vole (*Arvicola*), and two species of field-vole (*Microtus*) each divided into five subspecies. Of field-mice (*Apodemus*) there are two species, one of which should probably be divided into not more than four subspecies; of the house-mouse one species; and of the harvest-mouse one species. Lastly, there are the two species of rat, neither aboriginal natives; and a recently introduced vole, the musk-rat, which it is to be hoped, has now been successfully exterminated.

The rodents are the largest order of mammals; there are more species of them than of all the other mammals put together, and the world population of rodents likewise probably exceeds that of all other individual mammals collectively. With few exceptions they are small or at most medium-sized animals, and they have been adapted to all possible environments except the sea. Although they are essentially feeders upon vegetable matter, they are not at all particular in their diet, and many of them are quite omnivorous. Most of them are rapid breeders, and this together with their adaptability, has led to their radiation into a vast number of species throughout the world.

Both Lagomorpha and Rodentia are gnawing mammals and are characterised by the nature of the teeth, especially the incisors. These teeth are chisel-shaped in both orders; in the Rodentia they are coated with enamel, which is often yellow or orange in colour, on the outer surfaces only; in the Lagomorpha the enamel, though thickest on the front surface, extends round the sides to the back of the teeth. The dentine, which forms the bulk of the tooth, is softer than the enamel, and wears away more quickly, leaving the enamel projecting to form a sharp cutting edge. The incisors are long and set in very deep sockets from which they are continually growing, just like human finger nails, to compensate for the constant wearing-away of the free end with use. Not only the sharpness of the edge, but the length and shape of the tooth are determined by the amount of wear it receives; if one tooth is accidentally broken the opposing one is not worn away, and grows to such a length and shape that the animal may be gagged and die of starvation (fig. 51, p. 127).

In the Rodentia there is a single pair of incisor teeth in both upper and lower jaws, but in the Lagomorpha there is in the upper jaw a second pair, very much smaller than the first, set immediately behind, and not beside, the first ones. This character at once separates animals belonging to the Lagomorpha from those included in the Rodentia. In the Rodentia the sharp and constantly growing incisor teeth are not merely part of the eating apparatus, but are efficient tools ready to hand for many purposes, a good example being seen in the beaver, which uses its incisors for carrying out large scale engineering works. This order probably owes a great part of its evolutionary success to the possession of these characteristic incisor teeth.

No less characteristic than the incisors is the arrangement of the other teeth in the jaws. There are no canines, and there is always a wide gap, or diastema, between the incisors and the cheek teeth. This gap is of special importance when the incisors are being used as tools to gnaw something that is not edible, for instance in opening the shell of a nut to get at the kernel. The hind part of the lips at the angle of the mouth is then pinched in on both sides so that the opposite halves meet in the centre line of the mouth. The inedible chips shaved off by the incisors are thus prevented from entering the mouth and fall away on each side; a rat gnawing a hole through a wainscot does not have to spit out the chips produced by its work (fig. 52, p. 128). In some foreign rodents this mechanism is so highly developed that

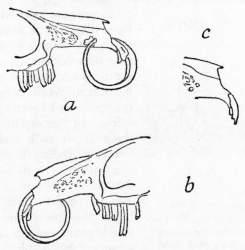

FIG. 51

The upper teeth of a rabbit whose left lower incisor had been broken off. *a*, from the right. *b*, from the left. The left upper incisor, having nothing to wear against, has grown in a circle and entered the bone of the right side of the jaw. The right upper incisor, being compressed by the overgrown tooth, has stopped growing. The molar teeth have grown to an abnormal length to meet the lower molars, because the overgrown incisor prevented the mouth being properly shut. *c*, side view of normal upper incisors, showing the small second incisors behind the front pair.

the lips on each side are fused with each other behind the incisors, the diastema being thus lined with fur and the functional opening of the mouth lying behind it. In correlation with this arrangement the hinge of the jaw joint is rather flattened so that a wide range of movement is possible. The lower jaw can thus be pushed forward to bring the incisors into action for gnawing, or it can be drawn back to bring the molars into opposition for chewing.

Similar as are the incisor teeth throughout the two orders, the cheek teeth differ widely and show many different forms. In many species, though rather large in size, they are greatly reduced in number; in some they have open roots and continue to grow throughout life, but in others they are less specialised. In the Lagomorpha the cheek teeth are short but wide, and have a pattern of transverse ridges. They are comparatively large in number, being six in the upper, and five in the lower jaw on each side (fig. 53, p. 129). The upper

a   b

FIG. 52

The mouth of a rodent (Guinea pig) showing the cheeks pinched in on each side behind the incisor teeth, separating front and hind mouth cavities. a, the jaws closed b, the jaws half open

tooth rows are more widely separated than those of the lower jaw, so that when the mouth is shut the lower rows lie inside the upper, and the jaw is moved with a crossways or rotatory movement when chewing to bring the upper and lower rows into opposition. In this order, too, there are three upper milk molars, and two lower, preceding the corresponding front teeth of each row, which are therefore premolars. The incisors are also preceded by milk teeth; the first upper and lower ones by rudiments which never cut the gum, and are absorbed before birth. The second upper milk incisors, however, are functional, and are lost about three weeks after birth, at the same time as the milk molars. It is commonly stated that in none of the Rodentia are any of the incisors preceded by milk teeth, but this is not quite correct, for in some species minute rudiments, which are absorbed before birth, are present.

In the Rodents can be traced a series showing the progressive specialisation and reduction in number of the cheek teeth. In the squirrels there are two upper premolars and one lower, all preceded by milk teeth, and three molars in each jaw. All these teeth have permanent roots, and their crowns are flattish, with low cusps at their edges, connected to each other by low transverse ridges. In the dormouse there is only one premolar, preceded by a milk tooth, in each upper and lower series, followed by three molars. All these have permanent roots, and have a very peculiar crown-pattern consisting of a number of close transverse ridges, from two to seven according to the tooth, quite unlike that found in any other of our rodents.

In the mice and rats (*Mus, Epimys, Micromys, Apodemus*) there are only three molars on each side in each jaw and no premolars at all; in consequence there are no milk teeth, all these animals having only one set during their lifetime, a condition described as monophyodont. In these genera the crowns of the molar teeth are low, and have a basic pattern of nine cusps, arranged in three rows of three along each tooth. Not all the teeth show the full nine, for in the smaller of the teeth some of the cusps fail to be developed. All the molars of these animals have permanent roots (fig. 54, p. 130).

In the voles, whose diet is much less omnivorous than that of the other rodents, consisting almost exclusively of the comparatively hard stems and leaves of grasses, the teeth are very different. As in the others, there are no milk teeth nor premolars, and there are only three molars in each row. Each molar consists of several small columns

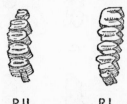

R U   R L

FIG. 53
Crowns of the molar teeth of the right side in the rabbit. RU, upper jaw. RL, lower jaw

of dentine set one behind another and joined together by narrow connecting pieces, the whole enclosed in a layer of enamel. The tops of the columns are worn down to form a flat surface, so that a top view of the tooth shows the ends of the columns joined to each other by narrow waists. The three teeth are placed close to each other without spaces between them, so that they appear to form an unbroken row of column-tops, the absence of connecting waists between the individual teeth being very inconspicuous. The shape of the pattern formed by the tops of the columns and waists is used as a character in classifying the different species of voles. In the bank-vole (*Clethrionomys*) the molars have two well-developed roots in the adult, so that in later life growth stops and the crowns of the teeth become worn down. In the field- and water-voles (*Microtus* and *Arvicola*) the molar teeth are permanently rootless, and consequently growth never stops and, since growth replaces the loss due to wear, the crowns do not become worn down even in old age (fig. 55, p. 131).

The Lagomorpha and the Rodentia are rather defenceless animals, and are preyed upon everywhere by carnivorous mammals and birds, of whose diet they often form an important part. They owe their ubiquitous abundance in the face of this drain upon their numbers to a combination of several factors. Their senses, especially of hearing and scent are acute, giving good warning of the approach of danger

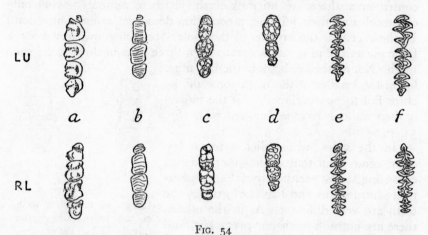

FIG. 54
Crowns of the cheek teeth in rodents. Left upper jaw above, right lower
jaw below.

a, squirrel; two premolars in upper, one in lower jaw; three molars.
b, dormouse; one premolar in upper jaw, one in lower; three
molars with transverse ridges in each jaw. *c*, brown rat. *d*, long-tailed
field mouse. In *c* and *d* three molars only in each jaw; basic pattern of
the cusps, three rows of three. *e*, bank vole. *f*, water vole. In *e* and *f*
three molars only in each jaw

and allowing safety to be found in flight; many species are nocturnal, and many live in burrows where they are comparatively safe from attack. The burrowing habit leads to a concentration of numbers of animals in places where the substrate is suitable for excavation, and this in turn leads to the development of some form of community and of social structure in the colony. Although co-operation between individuals may not reach a high level, increased safety is brought about by the transmission of danger-warnings. This may occur merely by one frightened animal being noticed by the others who also dash for safety, the warning being passed on quite without intention. On the other hand there may be deliberate danger signals, as in the rabbit and hare among the Lagomorpha, where an animal suspicious of danger thumps on the ground with the hind feet, giving a signal that brings all the others within hearing distance on to the alert.

Numbers are also maintained by the high rate of breeding; since the animals are omnivorous or herbivorous there is, until numbers become very great indeed, almost no limit to the amount of food available, and the food supply thus provides little check on the size of the population. Nearly all species produce large litters of young that make rapid growth, and are soon able to fend for themselves. As soon as they are weaned the young can find their own food, and do not need to have it caught and brought to them during their adolescence as do the young of, for example, the carnivores. The family is thus soon off the mother's hands, so that she is able to rear several broods in quick succession. In many species the female comes into oestrus shortly after the birth of the young, in some mice within an hour or two, so that she is pregnant and gestating a second litter while she is suckling the first. The suckling period is compara-

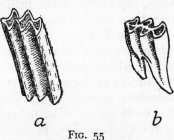

FIG. 55

First upper molar of *a*, water vole, *b*, bank vole, showing the columnar structure. In the water vole the tooth has no roots and is open at the bottom; in the bank vole the tooth has two roots which are closed

tively short and, as mentioned above, many species have no milk dentition so that the young animal is fully equipped for adult life at an early age. Further, the young reach sexual maturity very early in life, and frequently breed long before they have attained to their full physical growth. The rapid production of a succession of litters is correlated with the habit of burrowing, and as a rule it is only in animals that have solved their housing problem in this or some similar way, and are able to shelter their young from the elements and predators, that large litters are found.

Apart from the animals killed by predators, and those lost by the various accidents of wild life, there would appear to be no limit to the numbers reached by a population until they overtake the available food supply. And in nature something of this sort actually occurs; the numbers tend to increase for some time until a phase of great abundance is reached, and then a crash intervenes, there is very great mortality, and the population is reduced to a minute fraction of its former abundance. The crash is not, however, always or even generally caused by a lack of food, nor by the increase of predators which accompanies the attainment of high numbers; it may sometimes be caused by an epidemic of some kind, but in general the factors responsible for it appear to be complex and not easily ascertained. Cycles of abundance and scarcity following each other at regular intervals are known in many species; they are very conspicuous in some of the voles, especially in the field-vole (*Microtus*) where, as shown below, they have been extensively studied.

In the Lagomorpha, local cycles of increase followed by a crash sometimes occur in the rabbit, but they do not recur with any regularity. Although in many places there appears to be nothing, beyond the human rabbit trapper, to prevent the numbers of this species from becoming overwhelming, the population carries within itself what at first sight appear to be the seeds, if not of its own destruction, at least of its own limitation. For our knowledge of this, and other phenomena concerning the breeding of the wild rabbit, we are indebted to the long series of researches of Professor Rogers Brambell and his colleagues.[26, 29, 30] Their results refer particularly to the rabbits of north Wales, but have been confirmed by examination of rabbits in East Anglia, Scotland, and elsewhere, and thus there is every reason for believing that they apply equally everywhere.

In the rabbit there is a small amount of sporadic breeding in all months throughout the year but the vast majority of the animals conform to the limits of a very well defined breeding season. This extends from January to June inclusive, starting gradually in the first month or month and a half, reaching its height during March and April, and declining in the second half of May and in June. These dates are those of the starting of pregnancy, and not merely those of mating, which extends over a much longer period. During the quarter of the year preceding the breeding season, in November, December and the beginning of January, mating occurs frequently, although the does are not in heat, but pregnancy does not follow as a rule. The bucks also mate with females in all stages of their pregnancy, and especially in the earliest part. The female rabbit is thus an exception to the general rule that female mammals are not receptive to the male unless they are in oestrus. This great sexual activity of the males is not continuous throughout the year, for in this sex, too, there is a periodic breeding maximum, which is shown by the variation in the weight of the testes. In adult rabbits the testes reach their maximum weight in April, and then rapidly decrease in size until they reach a

Plate 4 YOUNG WILD RABBIT

minimum in July, after which they slowly increase again. The decline in April starts at the height of the breeding season, a month before the decline in the pregnancy rate of the does. The onset of the breeding season is thus determined by the physiology of the female, for although mating takes place frequently for several months before it starts, pregnancy does not occur; and the end of the breeding season is determined by the physiology of the male whose potency declines while the females are still in full breeding condition.

Litters succeed each other with great rapidity, for the female mates again about twelve hours after the birth of her young, and as gestation last 28 to 30 days, a new litter will be produced roughly every month. In the rabbit the eggs are not released from the ovary spontaneously at oestrus, and are shed only in response to the act of mating, usually about twelve hours after it occurs. Consequently it is almost unknown for the eggs to miss being fertilised, and a high breeding efficiency is assured. Thus from about the middle of March to the middle of May more than 90 per cent of the female wild rabbits in north Wales were found to be pregnant, and for the greater part of this period nearly all of them had already been pregnant at least once before in the same season. The reproductive rate is further increased by the occurrence of breeding in young rabbits during their first year. Those that are born early in the year are capable of breeding before they have reached their full adult size, at a body weight (cleaned) of 800 gm. (1 lb. 10 oz.) (Pl. 4, p. 132), the average body weight (cleaned) of adults being 1,150 to 1,200 gm. (2 lb. 5 oz. to 2 lb. 7 oz.); the average weight of the young at birth is 40 to 45 gm. (1¼ to 1½ oz.).

This very high potential rate of increase is reduced in a most remarkable manner by an event that is quite unknown as a regular feature in the biology of any other mammal except the hare, though it does happen sometimes in individual cases. At least 60 per cent of all the litters conceived are never born, the developing embryos dying before they reach full growth. They are not expelled as abortions, but broken down within the uterus of the mother and absorbed, the material forming them being taken back into the body of the mother. Most of the litters that are lost in this way die at a fairly early age, the majority at about the twelfth day of development; but between 1 and 3½ per cent of litters are lost entirely at the very earliest stage, before the embryos have become attached inside the uterus of the mother.

M.   K

Not every litter is necessarily lost entirely, for some of the embryos may survive to birth when the others are lost and reabsorbed; the average loss in litters that live to be born is between 9 and 10 per cent. The probability of any litter suffering total or partial loss does not depend upon the size of the mother, whether she is suckling or not, or whether the litter is the first of the season or not; nor is a mother that has already lost a litter more prone to lose another. The likelihood of loss is, however, related to the initial number in the litter, unusually high or low numbers being the most probable sufferers. The average number of eggs released from the ovary at each oestrus period is a little over five, and the initial litter size most productive of embryos likely to survive to birth is five or six. In spite of this enormous mortality before the birth of the young, it is estimated that the average number of young produced by any adult female rabbit during each year is between 10 and $11\frac{1}{2}$.

When a litter is lost by the death of the embryos the process of reabsorption is extremely rapid, so rapid that the remains are completely removed in about two days. When this has taken place the female is ready to start another pregnancy, and in fact does so, but this does not occur merely by the onset of another oestrus period. As the reabsorption is completed the animal's physiology behaves as though a successful pregnancy had just ended, entering for a short interval into a state of false-pregnancy, so that milk is produced in the mammary glands; and then oestrus occurs, just as it does in a female that has given birth to a living litter and is starting to suckle it.

The cause of this peculiar pre-natal mortality remains obscure; it is certainly not any form of infection or disease, and it does not appear to be any deficiency of nutrition or of the glands producing hormones. In some animals there are recessive genetic factors that, when inherited in certain ways, cause the death of the offspring: these are known as "lethal genes." It is possible that something of the sort is concerned here, but it would need breeding experiments on a large scale, which have not been attempted, to resolve the matter. At first sight it seems surprising that natural selection in the course of time has not eliminated this character, apparently so unfavourable to the continuance of the species. But further consideration leads to the conclusion that it is possibly not unfavourable; a smaller number of young produced may have a better chance of surviving to reach breeding age, and the pre-natal mortality factor may thus actually be perpetuated by natural selection.

Although the basic cause of the phenomenon is unknown, something has been discovered about the circumstances in which the death of the embryos takes place.[30] At a very early stage of development the yolk-sac, a small membranous bag lying outside the embryo but connected by a tube with the future gut of the animal, becomes filled, and even distended, with fluid. Normally this fluid is quite clear, but in the embryos that will die at about the twelfth day, the fluid becomes gelatinous and cloudy at the eighth or ninth day. The cloudiness is due to a sort of precipitate, which consists of fibrin, the solid substance produced in blood when it clots. It is practically certain that the liquid precursor of the fibrin passes into the yolk-sac from the blood of the mother, and is then solidified to form the clot.[29] The way in which this is fatal to the embryo is not known; and

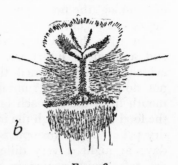

Fig. 56

The nostrils and mouth of a rabbit.

a, at rest. *b*, the centre flap between the nostrils raised to show the sensory pad at the entrance of each nostril

there, until further research has been carried out, the story ends.

It might well be thought that in an animal so common, so familiar, and so long domesticated as the rabbit, there would be few new facts to be discovered. Yet within the last ten years two important points, one anatomical, the other physiological, and hitherto unknown, have been revealed.

The nostrils of the rabbit are elongated and narrow, and set lengthways on the snout. Normally they are concealed by hairy folds of skin that overlap them; if these folds are held apart the nostrils are seen lying in a groove that is hairless, or practically so. Just in front of the nostril the hairless skin is raised into a characteristic pattern on a small oval pad.[101] The front part of the pad is covered with minute pimples set in longitudinal rows, but the hinder third bears five or six ridges running from before backwards, and fading away at the edge of the nostril (fig. 56, p. 135). Similar, but not quite identical, structures occur in the nostrils of hares; and in the rodents the corresponding pads are often developed to a comparatively large size, and sometimes bear complex patterns of ridges or pimples, comparable with the human finger-print. The function of these structures is quite unknown; their discoverer[102] has called them 'tactile organs', and well they may be, but it is also possible that they are 'distant-receptors' of some sort, for the well-known habit in rabbits and rodents of 'winking' the nose appears to be an alternate exposing and covering of this organ, as though testing the air.

In 1939 the habit of 'refection' was rediscovered in the rabbit, and announced under the headline, "Do rabbits chew the cud?", evidence being provided that, in effect, they do so.[128, 208] This is not done, as in the ruminant mammals, by returning food to the mouth from the stomach for chewing, but by passing practically all the food twice through the intestine instead of only once. The familiar dry pellet-shaped droppings of rabbits are produced only during the day; at night a very different form occurs. The night droppings are soft, moist, coated in mucus, more or less spherical, and generally small though varying from 1/12 to nearly ½ an inch in diameter. But they are not dropped; the rabbit takes them direct from the vent and swallows them without chewing, and in the morning they may form as much as half the total contents of the stomach. It has been found experimentally that over 80 per cent of the food may thus be refected. If a rabbit is provided with a large thin wooden collar so that it cannot reach its vent the night droppings are not eaten, and may be found in the morning on the floor of the hutch if it is provided with a grating. The production of the two kinds of droppings is due to an intestinal rhythm; and refection is a perfectly normal part of the rabbit's behaviour, being in no way a pathological or depraved habit. It is believed that B-vitamins are formed by bacteria in the food within the large intestine of the rabbit, and that refection allows them to be absorbed in large quantities in the upper intestine when the food is passing through for the second time.[117]

This information has been obtained by observation on domestic rabbits, in which the natural rhythm of activity has been changed; they have no enemies to fear, and food is offered to them by day, so that they are practically diurnal animals. But in the wild rabbit, which is crepuscular, if not wholly nocturnal, the production of night

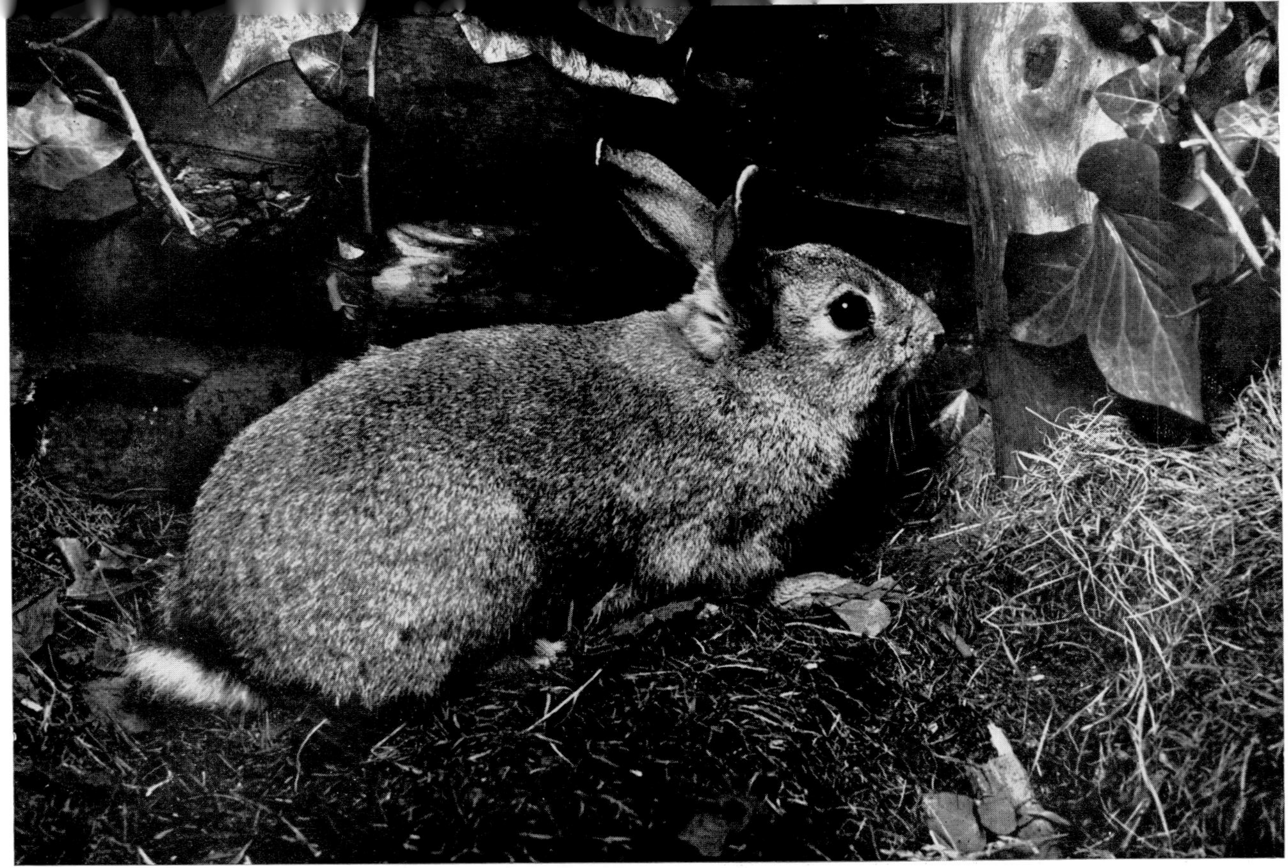

Plate XIII *John Markham*

Adult wild rabbit

Oliver Pike

Plate XIV

Mondiale

Hares

and day-droppings is reversed, and refection occurs during the day when the animals are in their burrows.[194] During the middle hours of the night also, when there is little activity, there is a further period of refection. Refection thus takes place twice in the twenty-four hours, the periods being separated by the morning and evening grazing times. It is peculiar that the phenomenon of refection has been overlooked for so long, especially since an account of it was published so far back as 1882,[154] in a paper which, though published in a veterinary journal, seems to have been completely forgotten until the rediscovery of the habit in 1939.* Refection also occurs in the hare, a fact that was published in 1895,[61] and likewise appears to have been unknown to most students of mammals. But it is possible that this habit has been known for very much longer; the hare is forbidden as food to the Hebrews, in *Leviticus* xi, 6, "because he cheweth the cud but divideth not the hoof," a statement which might be taken as referring to refection.

A close study by H. N. Southern[193] of the wild rabbit (Pl. XIII, p. 136) in an undisturbed warren has provided some interesting results. A proportion of the rabbits was trapped (harmlessly), marked with conspicuous identity discs fastened to the ear so that each animal could be individually recognised, and released. The life in the warren was then watched through a telescope from a hide, without upsetting its normal activities. The warren, containing about 150 rabbits, was in the middle of a field and covered about half-an-acre; the feeding grounds occupied the surrounding two acres, of which the inner acre was intensively grazed. Grass was the main food, but during frost, and when snow lay, trees and saplings in a nearby hedge were severely damaged by having the bark nibbled off. In normal feeding, the grass is cropped by the rabbit grazing the semicircle in front that it can reach by turning the head, then a step forward is taken and another semicircle grazed. Cropping is frequently interrupted while the rabbit, chewing vigorously, raises the head to look round for danger. Rabbits seem to react to changes in barometric pressure, for they feed voraciously and without interruptions before thunderstorms or heavy rain. Feeding activity is little affected by rain unless it is heavy, or by low temperatures, but a high wind causes a marked decrease. Sunshine has no effect on feeding, but rabbits like to lie outside the burrow in the early morning, washing themselves and basking in the

* But Gesner in 1602 wrote, "Cuniculus aliquando vorat urinum et stercus suum."

sun. Like some other animals, rabbits deposit their droppings in definite latrines, at a short distance from the burrow, in a patch of grass that becomes discoloured, or on an old mole-hill.

There were thirty-six does in the warren, and about 280 young lived long enough to be weaned and to come out and feed; this gives a production of nearly eight young for each doe during the season. They comprised at least two litters, the second being the larger and containing about five as against the first one's three. The breeding season in this warren lasted from February to June. Of the 280 young no less than 252 disappeared during the season, many of them probably being killed during their first week above ground at the age of three to four weeks, though a number were believed to have wandered away to other warrens, from which they were expected to return later. Further, of the seventy adults, fifty-nine disappeared, most of them believed killed. In spite of the large number of young brought above ground the total population of the warren never rose above 162. There is thus a great annual loss of breeding stock that has to be made good from the yearlings, and it is probable that most wild rabbits do not live much longer than one year.

Adult rabbits are very sedentary, and do not go far from their own warren; a small number of young move into adjacent warrens, but even they do not travel far. If an adult goes to a strange warren it is given a hostile reception, but the young ones seem to be more readily accepted. Warrens are enlarged by the does making their breeding stops on the outskirts; for the young are not born in the warren, but in special burrows whose mouth the doe stops-up when she is not at home suckling her litter. After the young have left the stop, it is enlarged and incorporated in the rest of the warren. If the stop is some distance from the warren it may thus become the centre of a new, subsidiary one, and small isolated warrens started in this way may become confluent by growth to form a single large one. Cover, either of trees or tall weeds, appears to be an attraction in starting a warren, and open warrens are often developed as over-flows from warrens in hedge banks.

Rabbits, as is well known, are in many places a serious pest to agriculture and forestry; there are few places where they are not plentiful, and the amount of damage that they do is enormous. The damage is not confined to planted crops, for rabbits are equally destructive to pasture and hill grazings; by their burrowing, too, they destroy hedgerows and field boundaries, and their warrens encourage the growth of weeds such as nettles and ragwort. Rabbits are, in effect, large-scale landscape gardeners.

Rabbits damage pasture not merely by grazing off the herbage that should be eaten by stock, but by the change in the character of the vegetation that is brought about by their activities. They graze very close so that the herbage is reduced to less than an inch in height, and, where they are numerous, the lateral buds of the plants are destroyed, and so little is left that normal regeneration cannot occur.[207] The valuable pasture grasses and clovers are thus progressively extirpated, and are replaced by species that are useless to the farmer. The final stage in the process of deterioration is reached, where the land is not too dry, when a continuous carpet of luxuriant mosses, which are not eaten even by rabbits, is established. Similarly on mountains rabbit pressure destroys the heather and whortleberry, that are replaced by low plants useless for sheep-grazing, and these in turn are followed by mosses, and finally lichens.[73] The enormous influence exerted by rabbit-grazing on the character of downland turf is strikingly shown if a small area is fenced off so that rabbits are denied access to it. Equally serious is the damage to young trees, which are killed or deformed by having the bark and the buds of the leaders nibbled off. It is for this reason generally impossible to restock woodlands with natural seedlings, and plantations of young trees must be enclosed within rabbit proof fences until they have grown beyond their vulnerable stages.

The rabbit population of the country must obviously be very large, but no attempt at an accurate estimate can be made. Nevertheless the figures showing the weight of rabbits consigned from railway stations in only three counties of west Wales in 1948 are illuminating.[60] The weight totalled no less than 3,320 tons, which represents about $4\frac{1}{2}$ million rabbits; figures for the whole country are not available but in the same year over 800 tons of rabbits were shipped from both Devon and Cornwall, and amounts between 200 and 799 tons from five other counties. It is believed that rather fewer native wild rabbits are sold than imported ones. Of the latter the imports in 1948 were over 32,000 tons valued at over 2 million pounds, and representing neary 36 million animals; if the number of natives approaches this figure the rabbit population of the country must equal or exceed the human one in size.*

*Before the arrival of myxomatosis.

Rabbit control is a complex matter that has received much attention of late years from the Ministry of Agriculture and Fisheries and the Agricultural Executive Committees. The complete extermination of rabbits cannot be expected, for many reasons, not the least of which is the market value of the animals. It is difficult to convince people that the damage done by rabbits greatly outweighs their commercial value, when the cheque received from the trappers goes far to paying the rent of many a holding. However, the Minister of Agriculture now has power, delegated to county agricultural committees, to require an occupier of land to take such steps as may be necessary for the destruction of rabbits, if it appears expedient to do so for preventing damage to crops, pasture, foodstuffs, hedges or practically anything else.

Trapping, though the traditional method, is not an effective way of clearing the land of rabbits, for trappers stop operating as soon as the numbers caught fall below what pays them, and it has been found that this level may be reached when no more than about a third of the population has been caught. Trapping may actually encourage the survival of a rabbit population, for a reduction of numbers in the autumn may allow a larger population than would otherwise do so to survive the winter, and thus be ready to start breeding at the beginning of the new year. At best trapping can only be considered a temporary check on rabbit populations, and not a method of eradication; it is less effective since the Agriculture Act 1947 makes it illegal to set traps in the open, and permits their use only in the mouths of burrows, because setting traps in the runs allowed of a much greater number being put down in a given area. Snaring, netting, ferreting and shooting can only be considered as ways of catching rabbits, not of exterminating them, for though great numbers may be taken by these means, there are always some left to breed and replenish the stocks.

Great hopes of effective control of rabbit numbers were raised when it was found possible to inoculate the animals with a fatal disease.[124] This is caused by a virus, *Myxomatosis cuniculi*, which after an incubation of some days, causes a feverish condition, with inflammation of the nose and eyes from which exudes a discharge that transmits the disease to other rabbits by contact. It is usually fatal, but any rabbits that may recover are practically immune to further infection. As far as is known it is specific to rabbits and cannot infect any other animals. Although this disease has been found to give complete extermination in experimental warrens, it has been a failure when used at large, for sick animals in the contagious state tend to wander away from the warren, and lie out in the open where they are picked up by predators, so that the disease dies out instead of spreading.

Myxomatosis is not endemic to Britain, but another contagious disease affecting rabbits and hares occurs naturally. This is rabbit syphilis, caused by the spirochaete *Treponema cuniculi*, indistinguishable in appearance from *T. pallidum* which is pathogenic to man. The disease causes hard raised scabs on the skin of affected animals, but whether it is fatal or whether the victims can recover is not known. Outbreaks of the disease are often very local, being confined to animals of one warren or hedgerow, but the distribution of it throughout the country in general is wide. Although the disease is said to be innocuous to man, there are reports that trappers have developed sore hands and arms after handling affected rabbits.[147]

The most successful modern method of control is by gassing;[195] into the burrow is introduced a powder that releases hydrocyanic gas when it comes into contact with the damp air inside. The powder is either pumped in, or a spoonful is placed inside the mouth of the burrow, and all the holes are stopped. The gas is very fatal, but even so some rabbits in a warren are likely to survive in pockets of clean air in recesses of the tunnels. Rabbits can be completely exterminated only by carrying on a campaign over a wide area from which most of them are first removed by trapping, ferreting, snaring and netting, and then finishing off the residue by gassing; thereafter constant vigilance is needed to prevent re-infestation.

The genus *Oryctolagus* contains only one species, *O. cuniculus* L., the rabbit, but the other European lagomorph genus *Lepus*, contains many species and subspecies of hares, three of which are found in the British Isles. Apart from the larger size and black ear-tips in the hares, the external differences between the hares and the rabbit are indefinite; the exact criteria are found in the skull. In *Lepus* the palate is short, its length being less than the width of the posterior nares, the postorbital process is broad and triangular, and the sutures of the interparietal bone are fused in the adult; all these characters are the reverse of the corresponding ones in *Oryctolagus* (fig. 57, p. 142). Biologically the two genera differ in that the young of the rabbit are

blind and helpless at birth, whereas those of hares are active, fully
furred, and have the eyes open.

The brown hare of Britain, *Lepus europaeus occidentalis* (Pl. XIVa, b,
p. 137), is a race peculiar to this country, distinguished from the
typical continental race by its darker and browner colour. It is larger

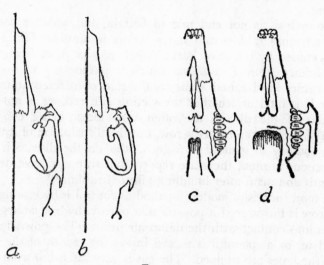

FIG 57.
Skull of rabbit *a, c*, compared with that of hare *b, d. a, b.* from above to
show the narrow post-orbital process in the rabbit, the more triangular
one in the hare. *c, d*, from below to show the narrow hind opening of the
nasal passage in the rabbit, the wide one in the hare

than the other hares of the British Isles and can at once be distinguished from them by the colour of the tail, which is black on the upper
surface; in the others it never is. The upper parts are a mixture of
brown and grey, the sides and legs more buffish, and the underside
white; the tips of the ears are black. There appear to be two moults
a year, in spring and autumn, the latter being the more clear cut, the
former protracted and gradual. The colour of the winter coat sometimes differs considerably from the summer one, the buffish colours of
summer being replaced by a light grey, but usually the difference is
less marked. The assumption of the grey winter coloration appears
to be uncommon, but there is no precise information available about
its frequency or geographical distribution.

The brown hare is found all over Great Britain, except in the more mountainous parts of Wales and Scotland; it has been introduced by man into Orkney, Shetland, the inner and outer Hebrides, the Isle of Man, and several parts of Ireland. It is a common animal wherever there is cultivation, and is destructive to crops both of field and garden, but, since it does not swarm everywhere in excessive numbers, it is not such a serious pest to agriculture as the rabbit, and presents no similar problem of control. Unlike the rabbit, the hare is native to the country.

The blue hare is confined to the mountains of Scotland, where it is plentiful above the level of cultivation; it is also found in most of the larger of the Hebrides, where it has been introduced, but not in Orkney or Shetland. It has been introduced in parts of the north of England and of Ireland, and in north Wales. It is distinguished from the brown hare by the shorter ear and tail, the latter never being black on the upper surface. The Scottish race *Lepus timidus scoticus* Hilzheimer (Pl. XVI, p. 145), is smaller than the others found in various parts of Europe. The winter coat of this species is typically white, except the palms and soles which are brown, and the tips of the ears which are black. In the Scottish subspecies the coat is never wholly white, an area of grey of larger or smaller size extending over the back, and the outer half of the ear below the black tip remaining brown (Pl. XVII, p. 148). The summer coat is rather greyer than that of the brown hare, but otherwise very similar.

The Irish hare is another subspecies, *L. timidus hibernicus* Bell, distinguished by its rather larger size, and much redder brown colour, and by rarely turning white in winter. It is confined to Ireland, where it is common in the mountainous parts, and is sometimes found also on lower ground; it has been introduced into north Wales and into Mull. The winter coat usually differs little from the summer one, but is often conspicuously greyer on the rump.

A characteristic feature of *Lepus timidus*, of which both the blue and Irish hares are subspecies, is the change to winter whiteness in most of the races. In those of the Alps and northern Scandinavia the change is most complete; in Southern Scandinavia some change to white, others to greyish; in Scotland some grey is always present on the back in the white winter coat, and often the change is very incomplete; in Ireland the complete change is uncommon. Little exact observation on these changes has been recorded, though much guesswork has been indulged in, but in an allied American species, *Lepus americanus* Erxleben, some very instructive experiments have been done on the subspecies *L. a. struthopus*.[125] The experiments show that the change is brought about by moulting, and not, as has often been claimed, by a loss of pigment in the coloured hairs by a fancied process of phagocytosis.

In the American species the hair follicles begin to contain a pigment-producing ferment at least two months before the spring moult, so that the new coat is coloured as soon as it starts to grow. The animals are thus physiologically brown for some time before they cease to be externally white. In the autumn there are two moults, a preliminary one that produces a coloured coat, and a final one that gives the white coat. After the preliminary autumn moult the hair follicles contain no pigment-producing ferment, and consequently the winter coat is white. In the experiment it was proved that the amount of light received by the animals determined the colour change, rather than the temperatures to which they were subjected. The most important points established were that reduction in the amount of light stimulated the preliminary autumn moult, but that the final autumn moult to white can be arrested by increasing the daily illumination. If similar effects are produced in the closely related European *Lepus timidus*, here is a complete explanation of the different degrees of assumption of a white winter coat in the various subspecies. It appears very probable that the spring and preliminary autumn moults always occur in this species, but that the final autumn moult to white is suppressed, partly or even wholly, in some of the geographical races; or else the amount of illumination received is so great that the winter coat, partly or wholly, is pigmented. Further, the varying stages of completeness of change between the individuals within each subspecies would be due to the individual responses to varying amounts of illumination. The white hairs of the winter coat are almost completely grown before the autumn coat is shed; when shedding starts it is rapidly completed, so that the animal appears to change with startling speed. The spring change appears to be much slower because the shedding of white hair starts before the coloured ones have grown out, and there is thus no sudden transformation. The change from the white coat to the coloured one in spring is bound up with the resumption of breeding activity. It was found that if hares in the white coat were injected with extracts of pituitary gland, containing the hormones that stimulate the sex glands to activity, there was a copious

Plate XV

Leverets

Plate XVI

Blue hare in summer coat

shedding of the winter coat and a development of dark colour. The chain of events thus appears to be that the amount of light falling upon the eye affects the activity of the pituitary gland which is the place of origin of the hormones. Investigation along similar lines of the coat-changes in the European species still awaits the attention of zoologists.

The details of the breeding processes in the hares are not known with anything like the completeness that they are in the rabbit. In the brown hare, breeding appears to take place at any time of year, the litter being divided and cared for in several forms, visited by the female for suckling (Pl. XV, p. 144). In the blue hare the litter is similarly divided, but the season is more restricted and young are not as a rule born in winter. It is peculiar that, although breeding is thus not confined to a restricted season, there is a great increase in the sexual activity of the males of both species in the spring. At this time the males lose much of their caution, and career about the countryside in broad daylight chasing and fighting with each other, and pursuing the females (Pl. XIVa, p. 137). Perhaps, as in the rabbit, there is sporadic breeding throughout the year, and a season of intense breeding activity in the spring.

As in the rabbit, too, the phenomenon of reabsorption of the developing embryos occurs, at least in the subspecies of the brown hare inhabiting the Caucasus, and the Moscow region of Russia.[116] In the Caucasus, breeding occurs all through the year, but most intensively in the spring and early summer; in the late summer and autumn it is reduced because of drought. The average number of embryos in each female ranges from 3.7 in summer to 1.7 in winter, but the number of living young is very much less because of the death and reabsorption of the early embryos. The loss ranges from 7 per cent in spring to 25 per cent in autumn, leaving an average of only about 2½ young for each litter, and a total of nine or ten young yearly produced by each female in four litters. In the Moscow area, only two litters are produced yearly, with an average of three embryos in the spring and five in the winter. But here the amount of reabsorption is less, so that about seven living young are born by each female every year. The pre-natal mortality rate in the hare is thus considerably lower than in the rabbit, being only about one quarter of the rate in that species. Nothing is known of these matters in the brown and blue hares of the British Isles, and they, too await investigation by zoologists.

Little, likewise, is known of the phenomenon of refection in the hares, beyond the fact that it does occur as a regular habit in the brown hare, and that the droppings refected are different from the ones discarded, resembling those eaten by the rabbit. Refection takes place mainly during the day, when hares lie up in their forms; most of the feeding occurs during the night between 7 p.m. and 7 a.m., especially between 9 p.m. and midnight. It is peculiar that the rediscovery of the habit came as such a surprise to zoologists in 1939, seeing that not only had a paper on the subject in the rabbit been published in 1882,[155] but that it was described for the hare in 1895 by Drane,[61] whose observations were quoted in full by Millais in his great work published in 1904.

The present geographical distribution of the blue, Irish, and brown hares is explained by a consideration of the pleistocene fossil remains of hares that occur in England. The animal found in the fossil state belonged to a subspecies, now extinct, closely related to the blue and Irish hare, and named *L. timidus anglicus* by Hinton. This form appears to have been widely distributed throughout the land, and to have been the ancestor from which the two living subspecies are descended. Both of these have diverged from the original stock, and the two populations, isolated in Scotland and Ireland respectively, are now clear-cut subspecies. The brown hare, on the other hand, is a comparatively late post-pleistocene arrival that was not present in Britain until long after Ireland and the islands were cut off, so that it was absent from them until introduced by man. Where the brown and blue hares compete for a living the former ousts the latter, not by any deliberate hostility, but by crowding it out in some way not understood; and this is what has happened in Britain, the blue hare being banished to the high ground of Scotland, where the brown hare apparently finds it is not able to compete successfully.

*   *   *   *   *   *   *

Of the rodent suborder Myomorpha there are in the British Isles numerous species and subspecies belonging to three families. These are the Cricetidae containing the voles, the Muridae containing the rats and mice, and the Gliridae containing the dormice. The division of these animals into subspecies is inclined to be puzzling to the field naturalist, and in the account that follows an attempt is made to show the reasons for these subdivisions and the relations of the subspecies to each other.

The British Cricetidae consist, in addition to the introduced muskrat, of the bank-vole, the short-tailed vole, the Orkney vole and the water-vole, all of which are represented by more than one sub-species, and all of which fall into the subfamily Microtinae. The word 'vole' is of northern origin and means a field; it is properly used as in the name 'vole-mouse', but such an expression as 'field-vole' is etymo-logically ridiculous. 'Vole' as applied to an animal is in origin entirely a book-name, but it has now become so generally accepted in this sense, and, let it be admitted, is so useful, that it is perhaps rather pedantic to insist, as did Barrett-Hamilton, on discarding it in favour of such names as 'grass-mouse', 'bank-mouse' and so on.

The Microtinae are burrowing rodents, usually of small size, with small eyes and ears and comparatively short tails. The profile of the head is rounded, so that the snout appears blunt, and not pointed, in side view. The crowns of the cheek-teeth, which are built of suc-cessive columns of dentine surrounded by an envelope of enamel, form characteristic patterns. In the genus *Clethrionomys*, containing the bank-voles, the outer angles of the columns tend to be obtuse or rounded, a feature that distinguishes it from the other genera, as

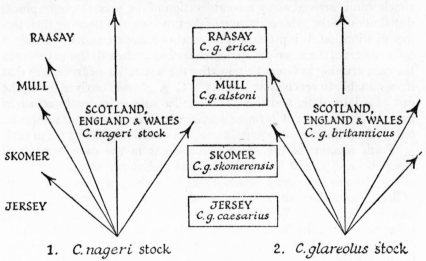

1. *C. nageri* stock   2. *C. glareolus* stock

Fig. 58
Diagram to show the origins of the population of the Bank vole.
1. Original invasion of the British Isles, by *C. nageri* stock. 2. *C. glareolus* stock replaces *C. nageri*, remnants of which are cut off in islands and become separate subspecies.

does the fact that in the fully grown adult these teeth are rooted so that growth is not continuous throughout life. The general coloration of the upper surface of the bank-voles is reddish brown, the underside buffy or greyish white. They are vegetable-feeders, but are not so restricted to a diet of grass as are some of the other genera, nor are they so strictly terrestrial, being good climbers and often seeking their food in low shrubs and hedgerows. The different subspecies are separated on the characters of the teeth, coat-colour, and body size, but individual specimens of a subspecies often show characters of an intermediate nature, so that a study of the various geographical races is possible only with long series of animals, from which the average characters can be determined.

The bank-vole, *Clethrionomys glareolus* Schreber, is divided into a number of subspecies inhabiting Europe, some of which are found in Great Britain; these subspecies fall into two groups, one centring round the sub-species *C. g. glareolus* Schreber, the other round *C. g. nageri* Schinz. Of these the *nageri* group appears to be the older, and to be less vigorous than the *glareolus* group, for wherever a subspecies of the *glareolus* group invades a territory occupied by one of the *nageri* group it replaces it. This conclusion is arrived at by a consideration of the present geographical distribution of the subspecies, and of the fossil remains showing their former distribution. It is probable that most of Europe was once inhabited by members of the *nageri* group, which spread westwards from a centre in the east, arriving in Great Britain after the separation of Ireland so that it was unable to reach that country*. *C. g. glareolus* arrived from the east at a later date, and though a smaller subspecies, replaced *nageri* over the greater part of its range, leaving the remnants of that subspecies only in Scandinavia, on mountain tops, or isolated islands (fig. 58, p. 147).

Fossil remains of the *nageri* group occur in the cave deposits of Great Britain, and it is only in the late pleistocene that the remains of the *glareolus* subspecies occur. Since its arrival, and the cutting-off of Britain from the continent, the *glareolus* form has become differentiated from its continental allies and is distinguished as *C. g. britannicus* (Miller), being rather smaller in size and duller in colour than the typical race (Pl. 5, p. 153). It is distributed all over England and Wales and the low-lands of Scotland, but is not found on the higher mountains; in the Scottish highlands it is confined to the valleys. It is not found in Ireland, or any of the islands except Wight, Anglesea and Bute; it is common

*The Bank-vole has now been found in Ireland—probably artificially introduced.

Plate XVII

G. B. Kearey

Blue hare

S. Crook

S. Crook

a. Opened nest revealing young

b. Female removing her babies to
safety from a disturbed nest

c. Short-tailed vole

John Markham

Plate XVIII

in most places, so that it is surprising that it was not recognised as a member of the British fauna until a little over a century ago.

So completely did *C. g. britannicus* replace the *nageri* group in Britain that the representatives of the latter are now found only on a few islands that were cut off from the mainland before the arrival of the former. They too, in the course of time have differentiated into distinct subspecies, and being small populations living in isolation, they have become more different from their parent stock, and from each other, than *C. g. britannicus* has from *C. g. glareolus*. On the continent *C. g. nageri* and its allied subspecies are found on mountains, having, presumably, been replaced in the plains; but no comparable mountain subspecies are known in Great Britain. Three subspecies of this group are British, *C. g. alstoni*, *C. g. erica*, and *C. g. skomerensis*, all inhabiting small islands. They are all larger in size than *C. g. britan-nicus*, and differ between themselves in colour, skull and tooth characters. *C. g. alstoni* (Barrett-Hamilton & Hinton) is confined to the island of Mull; it is a rather darkly coloured subspecies, the underside being strongly tinted with buffish. *C. g. erica* (Barrett-Hamilton & Hinton), found only on Raasay off Skye, differs from *C. g. alstoni* in its larger size and more robust build, and its much darker underside. Both are closely similar to the subspecies of the *nageri* group in Norway.

Dr. D. Steven[202] and his colleagues have recently made some interesting studies on the Raasay bank-vole, and kindly allow some of the unpublished results of their work to be presented here. A comparison was made between a series of Raasay voles and a series of bank-voles from Reigate, Surrey. The lengths of head-and-body of these animals were as follows:

Raasay, 24 mature males. Head-and-body length, 108.1 ± 1.59 mm.
  „ 9 „ females. „ „ 115.9 ± 1.18 „
Reigate, 20 „ males. „ „ 91.0 ± 0.88 „
  „ 20 „ females. „ „ 92.6 ± 1.45 „

Significance tests, by Fisher's "*t* distribution" method, show that a difference of this magnitude would occur by chance in fewer than 1 in 10^4 similar series. In the accompanying diagram (fig. 61, p. 154) of the size distribution of the Raasay and Reigate series, the lengths of the males and females of both have been combined, although mature females are a little larger than the males in both series. The diagram shows that the *largest* Reigate voles do not attain the *average* length of the Raasay ones, and there is in fact very little overlap of the two distributions.

M.   L

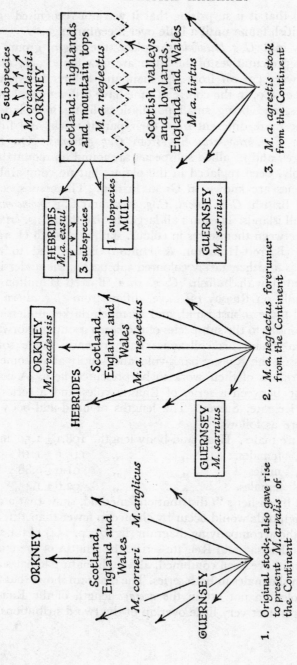

FIG. 59

Diagram to show the origin of the population of the Short-tailed vole.

1. Original invasion by stock which gave rise to the extinct *M. corneri*, and *M. anglicus*, to present *M. arvalis* of the continent, and to *M. sarnius* and *M. orcadensis*. 2. *M.a. neglectus* replaces original stock, remnants of which are cut off in Orkney and Guernsey. 3. *M.a. hirtus* replaces *M.a. neglectus* in southern part of country. *M.a. neglectus* gives rise to Hebridean subspecies; *M. orcadensis* gives rise to 5 subspecies in different islands

Similarly it was found that the mature Raasay voles are about twice the weight of the mainland ones, the figures being as follows:

Raasay, 24 mature males. Average weight 33.4 g.
       ,,   9 ,, females.   ,,   ,,   43.3 g.
Reigate, 20 ,, males.   ,,   ,,   18.6 g.
      ,,   20 ,, females.   ,,   ,,   19.8 g.

The original describers of the Raasay vole made much of the differences in skull proportions in their Hebridean voles. The chief points of distinction are in the heavier jaw apparatus—heavy jugals, broad zygomatic arches and larger cheek-teeth. They thought this to be an adaptation for eating coarser herbage, but it seems likely to prove an effect of allometric growth, automatically associated with the larger skull-size. Complete series are not yet prepared, but the skull of an adult bank-vole from the Edinburgh district seems quite indistinguishable from that of an immature Raasay vole of approximately the same size. Both Mull and Raasay voles are darker above than mainland bank-voles from round Edinburgh. Whereas the latter are a decidedly bright chestnut red along the back, the island forms are a rather dull russet. Tufts of hair under the microscope show no obvious differences in the pigment distribution in individual hairs, but there is a much greater proportion of long black hairs on the island specimens.

Dr. Steven summarises the matter as follows: "The size difference between the Raasay and mainland bank-voles amounts to between 15 and 20 per cent in length and about 100 per cent in weight (just about the same as between the largest and smallest races of man). The other differences, with the possible exception of the coat-colour, are probably allometric effects directly related to the size-difference. I think that the question whether they should continue to be regarded as separate species should depend upon an analysis of the results of several generations of crosses, if we manage to make them. Personally the more I see of these island voles, especially when put beside the ones we have taken round Edinburgh, the more I incline to the theory that they are remnants of an old stock, now represented by the Alpine and Norwegian races of *C. g. nageri*. The Raasay and Mull voles are so much alike, and so strikingly different from the mainland ones that I find it difficult to swallow the alternative that they have evolved along exactly parallel lines from a typical mainland form in the past few thousand years. However I do not wish to prejudge the question; that is what we are setting out to test by cross-breeding."

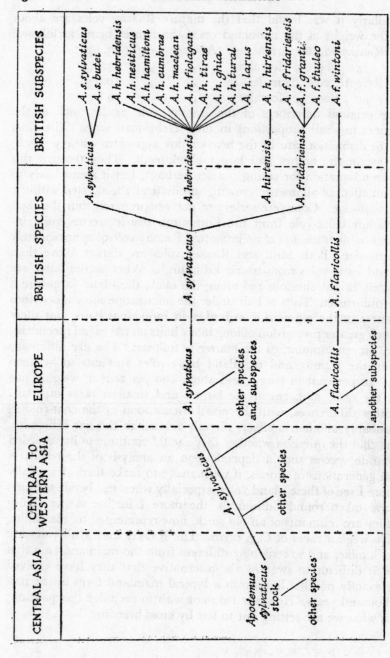

FIG. 60

Diagram to show the geographical relations of the species and subspecies of the *Apodemus sylvaticus* group

Black-and-white photography by John Markham, coloured

Plate 5 BANK-VOLE

Dr. Steven adds, " 'erica' is something of a misnomer for the Raasay vole. The original five specimens from which the species was described were trapped in deep heather, but most of our specimens of the last two years have been taken in the sort of places in which one would expect to find them anywhere. Our Raasay voles in captivity, however, do show some differences in behaviour and temperament from our local Edinburgh ones."

Clethrionomys glareolus skomerensis is a very distinct subspecies of large size, with very light, bright-coloured upper side (Pl. XIXa, p. 164); it is found only on Skomer off the coast of Pembrokeshire. In addition to its physical characters, the Skomer vole differs genetically from its relatives in its confiding and inoffensive disposition. As soon as voles of this subspecies are taken from a (box) trap they will sit quietly in the hand and eat a proffered crumb and then sit up and wash their faces, behaviour very different from that of the other subspecies, which bite, jump to the ground and run like stags if released, although they soon become tame after a short time in captivity. On Ramsey, an island only a few miles along the coast from Skomer, but much closer to the mainland and therefore more recently cut off, the bank-voles appear to be inseparable from *C. g. britannicus*, although there is some indication that they are smaller, and duller in colour. On Skomer's neighbour island of Skokholm there are no voles, nor are there any on Grassholm which lies a few miles farther out to sea. These islands may have been cut off before the voles arrived—or voles may have died out on them: it is impossible to be definite. In the Channel Islands there is another representative of the *nageri* group, the large and dark *C. g. caesarius* Miller, confined to Jersey.

The British forms of the short-tailed vole, or short-tailed field-mouse (genus *Microtus*) are much more numerous than those of the bank-vole. Each of the more closely related groups of subspecies is a subdivision of one of two separate species. As in the bank-vole, we find that invaders have driven out the pre-existing species, whose descendants have become differentiated into recognisable geographical races on isolated islands; but in this genus there have been at least two separate invasions at different times. The subspecies are classified as divisions of the species *Microtus orcadensis* and *M. agrestis* (fig. 59, p. 150).

The short-tailed vole is generally browner and greyer than the bank-vole; the tail is shorter, and the ears are hidden in the fur which is proportionately longer. The crowns of the cheek-teeth tend to have sharply defined acute angles on the sides of the columns; these teeth are without roots and continue growing throughout life. The food of the animals in this genus is much more strictly confined to the hard stems and leaves of grasses, and the permanently growing cheek-teeth are correlated with this diet which wears their grinding surfaces away rapidly. The animals (Pl. XVIIIc, p. 149) inhabit shallow burrows beneath the surface of the ground, or surface runs below a thick mat of grass-stems.

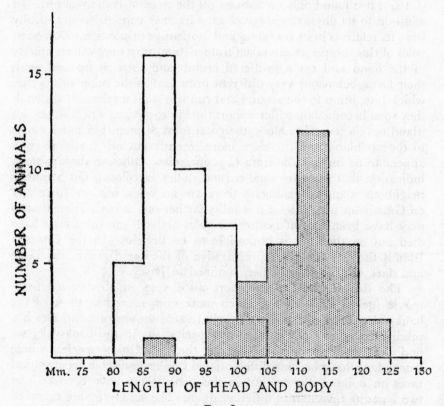

FIG. 61

Distribution of head-and-body lengths of 33 Raasay voles (shaded) compared with that of 40 bank voles from southern England (unshaded). All animals mature. The difference in size between the two subspecies is evident. (Figures by courtesy of Dr. D. Steven)

M. orcadensis (Pl. 6, p. 160) is a large, rather dark species that is confined to Orkney, and whose nearest relative is the species *M. sarnius* peculiar to Guernsey. Though widely separated from each other these two species are connected by an intermediate (or possibly ancestral) form, *M. corneri*, extinct since the pleistocene, whose fossil remains have been found in England. All these forms, together with another extinct species, *M. anglicus*, are believed to be offshoots of the group typified by *M. arvalis*, the numerous subspecies of which are found throughout continental Europe, though none of them occurs in the British Isles. It is therefore suggested that the ancestral form came into Britain from the south-east and penetrated to all parts of the country, but was later driven out by the arrival of another species. It was only in those islands that became separated from the mainland after the ancestor had colonised them, but were cut off before the arrival of the competing species, that its descendants have survived; and there they have become differentiated into distinct species and subspecies.

There are five subspecies of *M. orcadensis*, distinguished from each other by small differences in the details of the skull and teeth; and two are separable from the others by the coat-colour. *M. o. orcadensis* Millais, which inhabits Orkney Mainland, is dark in colour, as are the subspecies living on South Ronaldshay and Rousay (*M. o. ronaldshaiensis* Hinton and *M. o. rousaiensis* Hinton), whereas those from Westray and Sanday (*M. o. westrae* Miller and *M. o. sandayensis* Millais) are distinctly lighter, and are believed to have been cut off from the rest of the stock at an earlier period than the others, the sea depths between these islands and the mainland being greater than those separating the others. In captivity the Orkney vole is noticeable for its pugnacious disposition and its readiness to bite; why then should it have been replaced by a smaller and apparently less aggressive species? Barrett-Hamilton gives it as his opinion that the extermination was at least in part caused by the "attacks of carnivora, from which large and palatable mice inhabiting shallow burrows can only escape in the presence of moderately deep snow," attacks which, presumably, the replacing species was more adept at avoiding.

If this suggestion about the way in which the Orkney vole became confined to its present habitat is correct, and the evidence provided by the distribution of allied forms and by the fossil record supports it, the species responsible for banishing it to the north is the Scottish short-tailed vole, *M. agrestis neglectus* (Thompson). This subspecies of *M. agrestis* or its forerunner arrived in Britain in late pleistocene times, as is shown by the fossils from cave deposits, and presumably it spread northwards driving the *M. orcadensis* group before it. In the invading species, too, isolated populations became cut off in the Hebrides, where they have become differentiated into a number of subspecies, but on the mainland yet another invader has restricted its distribution, though it has not exterminated it.

M. a. neglectus is a smaller and more brightly coloured species than the Orkney vole, and is distinguished by the character of the second upper molar, which has a small extra column at its hinder end. The subspecies is restricted to Scotland, where it is found in the highlands and on the hilltops of the lowlands, and in nearly all the Hebrides. The subspecies of the Hebrides are regarded as more primitive than that of the mainland; because in them there is no reduction in the complexity of the first molar; they therefore appear to be more in the nature of relicts of the original stock rather than new lines of development, though at least one worker (Montagu)[153] on the group has denied the systematic value of the tooth-character. The Hebridean vole, *M. a. exsul* Miller, is found in most of the Hebrides except Lewis, but the animals of Islay, Eigg and Gigha are sufficiently different to be separated as *M. a. macgillivraii* Barrett-Hamilton & Hinton, *M. a. mial* Barrett-Hamilton & Hinton and *M. a. fiona* Montagu respectively. Apart from the detailed skull and tooth characters which distinguish these subspecies, the coat of the Islay vole is shorter and darker, those of the Eigg and Gigha voles longer and shaggier, than that of the Hebridean vole, itself a rather full-furred subspecies. All the Scottish subspecies of short-tailed voles are closely related to the Scandinavian subspecies *M. a. agrestis*, and of them all the Islay vole, being the most primitive, is probably nearest to the original stock, and the mainland form *M. a. neglectus*, the farthest removed. The Hebridean vole is intermediate between these extremes; so too is the Scandinavian form, but this does not necessarily imply a Scottish origin for the Scandinavian subspecies, which may well have followed a parallel evolutionary path that has not led it so far from its origin as has that of *M. a. neglectus*. The island of Muck contains voles, but very few specimens have been examined. The Muck vole has been named *M. a. luch* Barrett-Hamilton & Hinton, and is believed to be derived directly, as a dwarf form, from *M. a. neglectus*, and not from the *M. a. macgillivraii, mial, exsul* group. Similarly the vole of Bute, which has not been given a separate name, is barely distinguishable from *M. a. neglectus*.

Just as the Scottish subspecies of short-tailed voles expelled the Orkney voles, so have they themselves been pushed away to the north by a more recent arrival which did not appear in Britain until post-pleistocene times. This is the common short-tailed vole of England, *M. a. hirtus* (Bellamy), which, although classified as a subspecies of *M. agrestis* parallel with the Scottish subspecies, is probably much more distantly related to them than they are to one another. In order to emphasise this point Barrett-Hamilton raised this form to a full species, *Microtus hirtus*, an action quite unjustified biologically, in which he has not been followed in the latest works of systematists. It is much smaller than any of the other subspecies of *Microtus* found in Britain, and its coat-colour is much redder in tint, sometimes even approaching near to the colour of the bank-vole; a very closely allied subspecies inhabits the greater part of western and central Europe. *M. a. hirtus* has invaded the whole of England and Wales, the Isle of Wight and Anglesey, and the lowlands of Scotland, but does not extend into the highlands. The line of separation between the ranges of *M. a. hirtus* and *M. a. neglectus* is not exactly known, but where their territories meet the populations appear to remain separate, for *hirtus* occupies the valleys and *neglectus* the hilltops. It is notable that each of the larger species and subspecies has been driven out by successively smaller forms. Although fossils of voles occur in British deposits as early as the late pliocene, none of the present species is very closely related to them; all the living forms are comparative newcomers which colonised the country after the separation of Ireland, for none of them is found in that country.

This interpretation of the interrelations of the subspecies of the bank, Orkney, and short-tailed voles, and the outline of their probable history, is based entirely upon the study of the fossils, and of the characters and geographical distribution of the living subspecies, both British and continental. The bewildering variety of fossils has been reduced to order in the classic researches of Hinton,[104] and the living animals have been closely studied by that author, Barrett-Hamilton,[14] Miller,[151] and others. But it is important to remember that it is an interpretation of the available evidence; that it may be the whole story, but on the other hand it may have to be modified in the future when more detailed research has been done on the genetics of voles.

This is particularly emphasised by the conditions found in another species of vole in this country, the water-vole.

The water-vole, or water-rat, is a large vole of rather dark colour both above and below, the tail a little longer than half the length of head and body (Pl. XIX, p. 164). It lives all over Europe, and is divided into several species and subspecies, not all of them aquatic in their habits. The species found in Great Britain, *Arvicola amphibius*, is peculiar to that country, and occurs as two subspecies *A. a. amphibius* (Linnaeus) and *A. a. reta* Miller, which between them cover the whole of England, Wales, Scotland, the Isle of Wight and Anglesey, but are absent from Ireland. *A. a. reta* is the subspecies found in Scotland north of the Clyde and Tay, *A. a. amphibius* everywhere else. The former is distinguished by its slightly smaller size and its considerably darker colour; completely black (melanic) examples are quite common in this subspecies. Black examples are rare in the southern subspecies (*A. a. amphibius*), except in parts of East Anglia, where colonies of black water-voles are known to occur both in Norfolk and Cambridgeshire. The exact status of these black populations of the fens has not been determined by systematists. Thus in the water-vole, as in the short-tailed vole, the race inhabiting northern Scotland differs from the southern one; but in this species there is no suggestion that a smaller, darker race once existed all over the country, and that it was driven out of the southern part of its range by the advent of the larger, lighter form. Nor is it probable that the black water-vole of the eastern counties is an isolated surviving population of *A. a. reta*, which for some reason has been able to resist replacement by the other subspecies; it appears to be merely a black form of *A. a. amphibius*. *A. a. reta* is believed to have become differentiated in the northern part of Scotland from *A. a. amphibius*, its particular characters probably being linked with a better ability to cope with its own environment and having been segregated by natural selection, but the cause of the isolation of the northern animals, that must have occurred for the subspecies to be evolved, is not known. As far as is known, the black water-voles of the fens are no better fitted for their environment than their normal-coloured relations; it thus appears possible that a local dominant mutation for blackness has occurred in their genetic constitution. If the black coloration is of no disadvantage to the animals, or if it is merely linked to some other character, which need not necessarily be anatomically obvious but may give a physiological advantage, it will tend to spread through the population from its centres of origin. On the other hand if the advantage occurs only in relation to some purely local environmental conditions, it would be expected to spread until the area subject to those conditions was covered, and not to spread beyond its limits. This last alternative may apply to the fen water-voles, where the black population, which has long been known, appears to be stationary in its distribution. The phenomena in the water-vole underline once again the desirability of extensive breeding experiments by geneticists, so that the genetic constitution of all the subspecies of our small mammals may be determined, and the obscurities of their interrelations illuminated.

Rodents of the family Muridae, the mice and rats, are much less specialised than those considered above, especially in the character of their cheek-teeth which have permanent roots and bear cusps arranged in a basic pattern of three longitudinal rows of three. Although the dentition is less specialised there is only one set of teeth, the milk teeth being entirely suppressed or represented only by some minute rudiments that disappear before birth. In correlation with the less specialised character of the teeth we find that the mice and rats are very much more omnivorous in their diet, and more versatile in their habits, than the voles. They are in consequence, for the most part, a very successful group, and their numbers in Britain probably exceed those of all the other mammals, including man, put together. This abundance, owing to their adaptability, in the field- and house-mice and in the rats, contrasts with the dwindling numbers and restricted distribution of the harvest-mouse, which is much more specialised in its way of life and is, apparently, unable to adapt itself to the changed methods of modern agriculture. It is in animals that owe their success to adaptability that plasticity of structure, as well as of behaviour, is to be expected, and this is strongly shown by our native species of field-mouse (genus *Apodemus*) (Pl. XXI, p. 180).

Up to the present, seventeen subspecies of field-mouse have been named from different parts of the British Isles; they are all closely related to each other, and are difficult to distinguish even to the expert systematist. Indeed, Hinton[14] says that the identification of the subspecies is a matter of much difficulty, "calling for great patience, skill, and an accuracy of skull measurement and calculation, which in most cases will probably be beyond the powers of an ordinary field naturalist." On the mainland of Great Britain and Ireland, and on the larger islands, there is one widely distributed and very common species; in parts of England there is a second, less common, species of more restricted distribution. But on the Scottish islands the first of these has given rise to a great number of subspecies or incipient subspecies, the mice from nearly every island being recognisable as a distinct geographical race, if enough skill, care and patience is devoted to their examination.

Allied but separate species can be defined as 'sympatric' if they remain distinct although their geographical ranges overlap or coincide; or 'allopatric' if they exclude each other geographically. Unfortunately many of the island races of the field-mouse were named early in this century before these differences were appreciated; and it is now very doubtful whether some of these refer to true biological entities. The mice inhabiting any island are not sympatric with those of other islands or the mainland, but on the other hand, neither are they allopatric. Each does not exclude the others from its own island, the sea-barrier does that; it is almost certain that they would not remain separated did that barrier not exist. The correct way of classifying the island races is, then, to regard them all as subspecies of a single widely spread species (see p. 152).

But so many names have been bestowed, many of them without justification, that in order to arrange them methodically some systematists have raised certain groups of names to the status of species, the subspecies belonging to each radiating from it. These 'species' are not nearly so different from each other as are, for example, the species of voles in the genus *Microtus* and, were the insular forms not distinguished, these species would certainly be classified as subspecies of the widely distributed field-mouse, *Apodemus sylvaticus*. But it would be much too unwieldy a classification to have sub-subspecies with four latin names (although that is what the insular forms really are), and the alternative has been to promote the next higher rank from subspecies to species. This is quite unwarranted on any biological grounds, and is an entirely artificial arrangement; until we have very much more information on the interrelations of these alleged forms it would be better to discontinue using many of the names. However, because these names are to be found in the literature dealing with British mammals, where they cause much confusion to some naturalists, in

Plate 6 ORKNEY VOLE

John Markham

the following pages the artificial classification of these named forms
is set out to show their theoretical arrangements; but the reader
must remember that the so-called species have not been proved to be
more than artefacts of the systematist, and that they are not real
biological entities. The arrangement which is justified by the facts
as far as they are known is discussed below (see p. 163). A
defence of the splitting of the field-mice into species and numerous
subspecies might run:—

"Field-mice of the genus *Apodemus* are common all over temperate
Europe and Asia, and those of our familiar species, *A. sylvaticus* and
its close relations, forming the "*sylvaticus* group," extend far to the east.
The distribution of a less close relation, the yellow-necked mouse,
A. flavicollis, which is our second, less common English species,
overlaps that of *A. sylvaticus* all across Europe into Asia; but the
farther east in Asia that these species are traced the less distinct they
become, until east of northern India only a single form can be recognised. This relationship is shown in fig. 60, p. 152, which is a diagram
showing the geographical (not the chronological) relationships of the
British species and subspecies, and of their allies, from the Scottish
islands across the Eurasiatic continent to their eastern limit. All the
subspecies shown are peculiar to various parts of the British Isles,
except *A. sylvaticus sylvaticus* which is the typical subspecies and whose
range extends eastward across Europe into Asia.
"*A. s. sylvaticus* (Linnaeus), the long-tailed field-mouse, is common
practically everywhere throughout England and Scotland, and is
widespread in Ireland; it occurs in nearly all the larger islands off the
coasts of these countries. The brown coloration of the upper parts
is brightened by the admixture of much yellowish or reddish which
becomes more distinct on the flanks where it forms a line separating
the coloration of the upper and under sides. The underside is silvery
white, sometimes suffused with greyish, and a patch of reddish-
yellow is often present on the chest between the arms; this patch may
extend as a streak along the centre line of the belly, or may form a
collar by uniting with the coloration of the sides of the neck. The
tail is about as long as the head and body, the hind foot is rather slender,
and the ears comparatively large; the eye is large and prominent.
Although only one subspecies has been named, Hinton has found
"slight but quite tangible" differences in the shape and proportions

of the skull in field-mice from different parts of England, Wales, Scotland, and some of the islands; differences which suggest that local populations are differentiated to some extent, possibly as a result of selection by local ecological peculiarities. A very close and exhaustive study of a great number of carefully collected specimens would be needed before any opinion could be formed on the desirability of regarding any of these forms as subspecies meriting separate names. Only on the island of Bute has *A. s. sylvaticus* become sufficiently modified to be recognised as subspecifically separate; *A. s. butei* Barrett-Hamilton & Hinton, has the tail and ears shorter than in the typical subspecies, and the general coloration is darker. Hinton, however, finds that the *A. s. sylvaticus* from Skye and the Highlands appear to be intermediate in character between *A. s. butei* and *A. s. sylvaticus* from England.

"The Hebridean field-mouse, *A. hebridensis*, is found in all the larger Hebridean islands except Skye, the latter being inhabited by a form of *A. s. sylvaticus*. The Hebridean species differs from *A. sylvaticus* in its larger size and heavier build; the feet are comparatively longer, the tail and ear shorter. The colour is variable, being darker in some races, more rufous in others; the underside, too, varies from clear silver to a considerable suffusion with yellow, and the chest spot may be prominent or absent. The proportions and characters of the skull also serve to distinguish the various races. There are ten named subspecies of *A. hebridensis*, detailed descriptions of which can be found in the writings of the systematists who originally separated them; no purpose would be served in repeating the catalogue of their minute differences here, but a list of the subspecies and their localities follows. To the average field naturalist the island from which any example comes will be the most useful datum in identifying any subspecies. The named forms are: *A. h. hebridensis* de Winton, Lewis; *A. h. nesiticus* Warwick, Mingulay and Berneray; *A. h. hamiltoni* Hinton, Rum; *A. h. cumbrae* Hinton, Great Cumbrae; *A. h. maclean* Hinton, Mull; *A. h. fiolagan* Hinton, Arran; *A. h. tirae* Montagu, Tiree; *A. h. ghia* Montagu, Gigha; *A. h. tural* Montagu, Islay; *A. h. larus* Montagu, Jura.

"The St. Kilda field-mouse, *A. hirtensis* Barrett-Hamilton, is another large species closely related to *A. hebridensis*, from which it is distinguished by its comparatively large feet and ears, larger size, and larger skull. The coloration is variable and may resemble that of

A. sylvaticus fairly closely or, in a minority of examples, be considerably yellower on the under surface. The species is found on the islands of Hirta, Soay, and Dun of the St. Kilda group, and has not differentiated into subspecies. Its ancestors were probably accidentally introduced by man soon after the islands were first inhabited.

"The field-mouse of Shetland is represented by three subspecies, the first of which to be recognised was that of Fair Isle; the name of this island was bestowed upon it, and consequently the field-mice of Shetland are classified as subspecies of the Fair Isle field-mouse, *A. fridariensis* (Kinnear). Like the Hebridean and St. Kilda field-mice this species is larger than *A. s. sylvaticus*, and has shorter ears; the skull characters are distinctive, and the colour is darker. Of the three subspecies *A. f. fridariensis* and *A. f. granti* agree in having the hind foot comparatively smaller and more slender than that of *A. s. sylvaticus*, a condition exactly opposite to that in *A. hebridensis*. But in the third subspecies, *A. f. thuleo*, the hind foot is larger than in any other British form; nevertheless the sole-pads and the coloration are as in *A. f. fridariensis*, and consequently Hinton considers that it is best treated as a subspecies of *fridariensis*. The subspecies are thus: *A. f. fridariensis* (Kinnear), Fair Isle: *A. f. granti* Hinton, Yell, (and probably Mainland, Shetland, from which the field-mice which are known to exist have not been critically examined); *A. f. thuleo* Hinton, Foula."

If we are to be scientifically honest, however, we must admit that the evidence upon which all this is raised is not good enough. The diagnoses of many of the island forms have been drawn up after the examination of much too few specimens, so that we do not know the range of individual variation that may occur in them. Even the limits of variation in the mainland form are not defined with accuracy, nor have the skull characters, which are much used in diagnosis, been studied in the light of the allometric growth principle. Allowing that some of the island forms can be distinguished, though only with difficulty and by experts, in the absence of information about their provenance, it appears that there are at most four reasonably distinct subspecies. They are:—

1. *A. s. sylvaticus.*   All the mainland of England, Scotland and Ireland, and the larger islands, but not those of Scotland except the isles of Skye and Bute. The

forms from the latter two may differ slightly, but not enough to merit parallel subspecific rank.

2. *A. s. hebridensis.*   The Hebrides. Some of the nine other named island forms may differ enough to be worth parallel subspecific rank, but more information about them is required. Any that turn out to be distinct would be parallel subspecies of *A. sylvaticus*, e.g. *A. s. hamiltoni, A. s. ghia*, etc.

3. *A. s. hirtensis.*   St. Kilda. Possibly not more entitled to subspecific rank than some of the nine island forms of *A. s. hebridensis*, but given the benefit of the doubt because of its (possibly) longer isolation, and rather more distinct characters.

4. *A. s. fridariensis.*   Shetland. Should either of the two other named forms from Shetland be finally recognised as good subspecies they would rank as subspecies of *A. sylvaticus*, e.g. *A. s. thuleo*, etc.

The yellow-necked field-mouse, *A. flavicollis*, is larger than *A. s. sylvaticus*, and more brightly coloured; the upper parts are redder and the underparts whiter, usually with a large chest-spot, and the greater development of the temporal ridges on the skull, in which also there are differences of proportion, makes the cranium more angular. These differences in the skull may be caused by an allometric growth gradient, and be no more than correlations with large size of body. The subspecies found in Britain, *A. f. wintoni* (Barrett-Hamilton) (Pl. XXII, p. 181) differs from the continental *A. f. flavicollis* Melchior, in having the chest-spot well-defined and nearly always expanded to form a collar uniting the upper coloration of the two sides, and in the underside being a more slaty and less pure white. *A. f. wintoni* is widely distributed throughout the southern and midland counties of England, but has not been found farther north than Northumberland. It occurs in the same places, both regions and habitats, as *A. s. sylvaticus*, but is restricted to local centres of population which, apparently, are not in continuity with each other. It is said to interbreed with *A. s. sylvaticus* and thus to produce all stages of intermediate forms; the two species also are alleged to be found in the same colonies.[109] On parts of the continent, however, the two species are said to be

John Markham

a. Skomer vole

A. R. Thompson

b. Water-vole

Plate XIX

a. Musk-rat

Plate XX

b. Coypu

segregated, *A. sylvaticus* living in the plains, *A. flavicollis* on the mountains, and intermediate forms in the region between. In Russia[206] a difference in the habits of the two species has been recorded, *A. flavicollis* being more vegetarian and less omnivorous than *A. sylvaticus*. If these differences of food and habitat are really constant, they lend much support to the view that the two forms are valid species. On the other hand the mixture of *A. s. sylvaticus* in the sporadic populations of *A. f. wintoni*, and the absence in England, as far as is known, of any difference in habits, lend support to those (and high authorities are among them) who consider that there is no specific difference between the two. Much experimental work is needed to determine the normal limits of variation and the genetic constitution of both forms, and of their subspecies.

Some interesting information on the question of local races has recently been produced. A study of mouse populations in restricted localities has shown that the differences in size from year to year and from place to place, the growth and survival rates, and the distances of individual travel, all suggest that there are no closely inbreeding local communities within a main region.[91] On the other hand, there appear to be constant differences in size between mice from different parts of the country; but the survival-rates are different in summer and winter, few mice surviving from one winter to the next, and the limit of growth, differing from place to place, is reached by young of the early part of the breeding season in summer, and by young of the later part in autumn. The differences in size may thus be correlated merely with differences in age. Here again it would be desirable to know how much of the differences is determined genetically, and how much by the influence of the environment on the individual during its growth.

The interrelations of the British forms of *Apodemus* can be regarded in two quite different ways, as pointed out by Hinton. Fossil forms believed to be closely allied to *A. flavicollis* because of their large size are known from British deposits, but they do not occur until the late Pleistocene, and consequently this species may be regarded as a comparatively late invader of the territory of *A. sylvaticus*. On the other hand, although fossil forms resembling *A. sylvaticus* are known from as far back as the late Pliocene, none are known from deposits between the early and late Pleistocene; consequently the earlier forms may have died out and been replaced much later by new immigrants

M. M

entering at the same period as did *A. flavicollis*. The older and original *sylvaticus*-like stock may therefore have given rise to the large insular 'species' and subspecies of the north, and then either have died out before, or have been driven out after, the arrival of the new stock in the late or post-pleistocene, thus forming a parallel with the replacement of large species by smaller invaders from the south, in voles of the genera *Clethrionomys* and *Microtus*.

The subdivisions of our only other truly native species of murine, the harvest-mouse (*Micromys minutus*) (Pl. XXIII, p. 184), are less complex. One species only is known throughout its entire range from Great Britain to eastern Asia; the animals inhabiting western Europe are included in the subspecies *M. m. soricinus* Hermann to separate them from the typical subspecies which is found in Russia, and from another race inhabiting Hungary and Rumania. The species appears to be eastern in origin, and to be a comparative newcomer to Britain and Europe generally.

On the other hand our introduced murines, the house-mouse and the black rat, both form extremely complex mazes of subspecies, the complexity increased by the crossing of races made possible by the inadvertent transport given to the animals by man. An interesting attempt to sort out the endless forms of the house-mouse (*Mus musculus*) throughout the world has recently been made by Schwarz and Schwarz.[186] These authors find that there were originally four wild subspecies of this mouse, some of which have branched out into the great number of subspecies commensal with man, often but less appropriately called parasitic on him. Three of these wild subspecies have given rise to commensal forms that are more or less dependent upon man's houses and cultivation, some being indoor and some being outdoor commensals; in some places members of commensal subspecies return to the wild and become feral.

All the truly wild forms have the tail short, its length being less than that of the head and body, the back brownish buff, and the underside white. They inhabit dry steppes or even desert areas, and are essentially feeders on seeds and grass. When the wild forms become commensal with man they tend to adopt omnivorous habits, and develop into new forms in which the tail is longer than the head and body, the underside is grey, and the upper side is dark. The coat-colour of the most completely commensal forms is the darkest, and the genetic factors responsible for it are the most recessive; there is however another type of darkening that occurs in both wild and commensal forms, this being a dominant mutation. In the commensal races, too, there is a shortening of the facial region of the skull, and a reduction in the size of the molar teeth.

The diagram in fig. 62, p. 168 is constructed from the Schwarzs' data, and shows the relations that are believed to exist between the commensal subspecies derived from two of the wild subspecies. A third wild subspecies that is confined to Japan has given rise to one main commensal subspecies, with a number of minor geographical forms, in those islands. The fourth wild subspecies *M. m. spretus* found in Spain and north-west Africa has produced no commensal forms, and the suggestion is made that it was unable to do so because when man came to those regions he brought already existing commensal forms with him so that the commensal habitat was preoccupied. Leaving aside Japan, which has its own wild and commensal forms, the diagram shows that apart from eastern Europe, the Caucasus and Siberia, all the *musculus*-mice of the world are derived from *M. m. wagneri*, the wild subspecies of Russian Turkestan, which has developed commensal forms in two main trunks, one eastern, the other western. In south Russia and Hungary a second wild subspecies, *M. m. specilegus*, has produced the commensal form that inhabits Scandinavia, eastern Europe and Russia, and overlaps the range of the western house-mouse in central Germany, where the two races interbreed. It will be seen from fig. 62, p. 168 that the house-mouse of the British Isles is *Mus musculus domesticus* Rutty (Pl. 7, p. 166), which, though properly an indoor race, is often found outside. It should be noted that the forms shown in fig. 62 are only the main and more distinct ones, and that a number, larger than that shown, of additional forms characterised by minor differences has been named, a fact that is not surprising in a species that is so universally distributed and so plastic.

These races of minor importance are in the nature of sub-subspecies, or should even rank lower in the scale than that. When, therefore, one considers the species *Mus musculus* as a whole, and its distribution throughout the world, it is obvious that it is not logical to raise to the status of a full species the house-mice formerly living on St. Kilda, but now extinct since the island was abandoned by its human in-habitants in 1930.[74a, 95] This small population of *M. m. domesticus* was distinguished from the animals of the mainland under the name

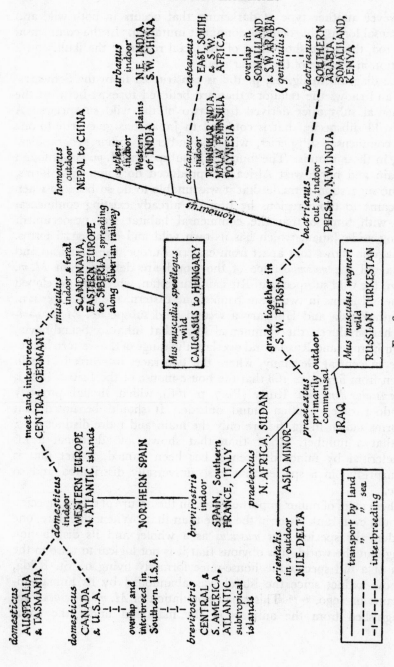

FIG. 62

Diagram to show the geographical relations and distribution of two subspecies of *Mus musculus*

domesticus
AUSTRALIA
& TASMANIA

domesticus
indoor
WESTERN EUROPE
N. ATLANTIC islands

meet and interbreed
CENTRAL GERMANY

musculus
indoor & feral
SCANDINAVIA,
EASTERN EUROPE
to SIBERIA, spreading
along Siberian railway

homourus
outdoor
NEPAL to CHINA

tytleri
indoor
Western plains
of INDIA

homourus

castaneus
indoor
PENINSULAR INDIA,
MALAY PENINSULA
POLYNESIA

castaneus
EAST, SOUTH,
& S.W.
AFRICA

urbanus
indoor
N.E. INDIA,
S.W. CHINA

overlap in
SOMALILAND
& S.W. ARABIA
(*gentilulus*)

bactrianus
out & indoor
PERSIA, N.W. INDIA

bactrianus
SOUTHERN
ARABIA,
SOMALILAND,
KENYA

Mus musculus spcilegus
wild
CAUCASUS to HUNGARY

grade together in
S. W. PERSIA

Mus musculus wagneri
wild
RUSSIAN TURKESTAN

praetextus
primarily outdoor
commensal

IRAQ

domesticus
CANADA
& U.S.A.

overlap and
interbreed in
Southern U.S.A.

brevirostris
indoor
SPAIN, Southern
FRANCE, ITALY

NORTHERN SPAIN

praetextus
N. AFRICA, SUDAN

ASIA MINOR

brevirostris
CENTRAL &
S. AMERICA,
ATLANTIC
subtropical
islands

orientalis
in & outdoor
NILE DELTA

transport by land
" " sea
interbreeding

Plate 7 HOUSE-MOUSE   *John Markham*

Mus muralis, by its slightly lighter belly, and slightly more robust feet and tail; it should, however, be regarded as a subspecies, *M. m. muralis*. The St. Kilda house-mouse lived in the grain stores—the 'cletts'—as well as dwelling-houses, but there is no evidence that it was tending to become feral, a state that has been reached by some of the subspecies in the Faeroes, which have diverged from *M. m. domesticus* both in coloration and increased size. These island races of mouse are particularly interesting in showing the rate at which isolated wild populations can develop new genetic characters, for it is definitely known that their forerunners could not have been introduced into the Faeroes less than two hundred and fifty or more than about a thousand years ago.[59, 72]

The black rat also is found throughout the world as a number of subspecies, some wild and some commensal, that have been very puzzling to systematists. The original home of the wild species appears to have been India, where it became commensal with man and produced several subspecies. Some of these were unwittingly carried to other parts of the world where they, too, have given rise to further subspecies of various degrees of commensalism. Crossing between the different subspecies has led to such diversity of appearance that in many places, especially in the larger eastern cities, it is a hopeless task to attempt the assignation of specimens to any subspecies. The genetic situation, in fact, is closely similar to that in various human populations.

The wild subspecies are brown above, white below; the less commensal races are brown, with dusky bellies; and the completely commensal ones are black above, with dusky bellies. Forms resembling the subspecies of all three kinds are found in Britain, always commensal, and all confined to ports or their neighbourhood. Their restriction to ports seems to show that they are unable to maintain their position without frequent recruitment of the population from abroad. The species is not indigenous, but was accidentally introduced during the middle ages. It quickly became established and flourished for several centuries until the introduction of the brown rat early in the eighteenth century. In most places the new arrival soon replaced the old black rat, which disappeared everywhere except at the ports.

The black rat was imported to Britain from Asia Minor whence commensal or partly commensal subspecies, different from those of

India, penetrated through north Africa and south Europe. These races are *Rattus rattus frugivorus* Rafinesque, the tree-rat, which has the wild coloration, white-bellied brown (Pl. 86, p. 176); and *R. r. alexandrinus* Geoffroy, the Alexandrine rat, which is brown with the belly dusky. These races on reaching temperate and northern Europe are believed to have given rise to the black rat, *R. r. rattus* Linnaeus (Pl. 8a, p. 176). This race appears to be better adapted to commensal life in the cooler parts of Europe, and Hinton suggests that it may have arisen from the other subspecies "perhaps on many distinct occasions." *R. r. rattus* should thus be our characteristic subspecies, and the fact that we also have the other two subspecies points to the probability of repeated new importations. Breeding experiments have shown that the colour of *R. r. frugivorus* is a simple mendelian dominant to that of *R. r. alexandrinus*, and that *R. r. rattus* is dominant to both; the breeding experiments also produced some new colour patterns, unknown in nature, which are probably less viable and therefore eliminated by natural selection when they occur outside captivity.

It is only biologically realistic to regard the species in London and certain other ports in Britain as being polymorphic with three main colour types that resemble quite closely the three main world sub-species, but have an almost infinite range of intergradation between them. Of course *Rattus rattus* can support itself in London away from the port area: it has established itself in some of the best known clubs of London, and is the commonest rat in the Oxford street area where it is found in every office block, there being practically no *R. norvegicus*. It is also common in modern blocks of centrally heated flats, and in theatres and cinemas.

Just as there are brown forms of the black rat, there are black ones of the brown rat (*Rattus norvegicus* Berkenhout) (Pl. XXVIa, p. 193), that came from central Asia, north of the Himalayas, by way of Russia, whence it was probably introduced direct into Britain by shipping. But the black examples of the brown rat (Pl. XXVIb, p. 193) are not like the different forms of *R. rattus*, for they occur sporadically in all range, and are probably produced by recessive factors which become segregated in locally inbred populations. These black examples are dark grey above and dusky beneath, in contrast to the brown upper side and white belly of the normal ones; they evidently have no advantage over the others, either from their coloration or from any linked physiological characters, for if they had, natural selection would be expected to have produced one of three alternatives from them. If they had a general advantage they would have replaced the normal type everywhere; or if a regional advantage, they would have produced a cline; or finally if only a local advantage and some of them were geographically isolated, they would have produced a subspecies. These animals were formerly regarded as at least a separate subspecies and later given a specific name (*hibernicus*) which however is unjustified.

CHAPTER 7

MORE ABOUT RODENTS

" Wee, sleekit, cow'rin', tim'rous beastie,
O, what a panic's in thy breastie!
Thou need na start awa' sae hasty,
 Wi' bickering brattle!
I wad be laith to rin an' chase thee
 Wi' murd'ring pattle!

" Thou saw the fields laid bare and waste,
An', weary winter comin' fast,
An', cozie here, beneath the blast,
 Thou thought to dwell,
Till crash! the cruel coulter past
 Out-thro' thy cell."

BURNS *To a Mouse*

PLAGUES of mice, in which countless thousands of the animals swarm over the countryside destroying the crops and vegetation, have long been known, and accounts of them are to be found throughout recorded history, from the writings of Aristotle and Herodotus onwards. In northern Europe these plagues are usually caused by *Microtus arvalis*, and in Britain, where they occur less frequently, by *M. agrestis*. There is an account in the *Brut y Tywysogion* telling that in the summer of A.D. 893 "vermin of a strange species were seen in Ireland, similar to moles, with two long teeth each; and they ate all the corn, all the pasture, and the roots of grasses, and the hay ground, causing a famine in the country, and it is supposed the Pagans [Danes] took them there, and wished likewise to introduce them into the isle of Britain; but by prayer to God, alms to the poor, and righteous life, God sent a sharp frost during the summer weather, which destroyed those insects." On the face of it this story describes the outbreak of a vole plague, but the vermin must have been something other than voles, for there are none in Ireland.

A vole plague is characterised by a gradual increase in the numbers of the animals over several successive years, until finally they reach a peak so that the voles overrun an area of greater or less extent, doing great damage; and then suddenly, when farmers are facing ruin and everyone is at their wit's end to know how to cope with it, a crash comes and the voles vanish, leaving only a few survivors from which in time the numbers can again build up. The build-up in numbers occurs through an increase in the local breeding—or in the survival-rate or both and not through immigration from elsewhere; similarly the crash occurs through the death of the voles on the ground, and not through emigration. The biological problems involved in this cycle of events are so interesting, and from an epidemiological and economic point of view so important, that much time and work have been devoted during the last twenty years to their elucidation, chiefly by the team of researchers at the Bureau of Animal Population in Oxford, whose director, Charles Elton, has fully recounted the results of the work in a fascinating book,[65] on which the following paragraphs about vole-plagues are, for the greater part, based.

On the continent plagues of *M. arvalis* are frequent, and much work and large sums of money have been expended in combatting them with, however, only limited success. Direct killing of the animals, and even ploughing up the ground, have no appreciable effect in diminishing the numbers; dogs and cats become so surfeited that they lose interest in catching them. About fifty years ago a French biologist isolated an infectious bacterium that was causing a fatal disease in wild voles; he was able to cultivate this in the laboratory and to use it for killing the animals during an outbreak, by infecting them with it from baits soaked in the culture. The use of this organism was at first believed to be the perfect method of control, because it was thought to be harmless to man and domestic animals, and to be specific to rodents, and because it was hoped that the disease would spread throughout the population from the animals infected by taking the prepared baits. This bacterium is a strain of *Salmonella enteritidis*, causing mouse typhoid, and a similar disease is produced by an allied organism *Salmonella typhimurium* (*aertrycke*) that has been cultured for the same purpose; these bacteria are the infective agents in the miscalled 'viruses' used for destroying rodents. Much has been discovered about these bacteria since their first isolation, and they are not now regarded as so innocuous to man and domestic animals as was at first claimed; in fact their use is not approved in many countries and is actually forbidden in some. Their effectiveness, too, is doubtful; if the original claim had been fulfilled vole plagues should now be unknown, but they are as frequent as ever. It is probable that there is little spread of the disease from one animal to another, and that the good results obtained in some outbreaks of voles were due to the great quantities of infected bait laid, so that a very high proportion of the animals died from the primary infection obtained by eating the bait.

Plagues of voles on a large scale are uncommon in Great Britain; the two most recent of which there are fairly full records were in 1875-6 and 1891-2, and both occurred on the sheep-walks of the southern uplands of Scotland. In these, great damage was done to the sheep grazings, the grasses being destroyed and the ground riddled with burrows, so that had not the sheep been fed with imported fodder large numbers would have died. As it was, the mortality among ewes was above the normal, and the crop of lambs was smaller than usual, on the worst affected farms; nevertheless the drop in the total sheep population of the district was not great, though the financial losses in preserving it were serious. These outbreaks caused a great local outcry, and in 1892 led to the appointment of a Government Commission of Investigation which recorded evidence and issued a report. But no effective control measures were undertaken to deal with either of these vole-plagues, and before action could be decided upon and taken, the crash came, the voles disappeared, and the matter was forgotten.

Little is known of the ultimate cause of vole-plagues, nor of the crash which brings them to an end. It was alleged that the decrease in the numbers of predatory birds and mammals brought about by intensive game-preserving was, at least in part, responsible for the spectacular plagues just mentioned; and it is certain that there was a great influx of predators, especially birds, to the affected areas at the height of the outbreaks. But the absence of predators is as unlikely to have been the cause of the plagues as their presence the cause of the ends. It has been pointed out that both these plagues occurred in an area of high rainfall, but seeing that plagues occur on the continent in areas of many different types of local climate it is improbable that the correlation is significant. Although devastating plagues on a large scale are uncommon in this country, local cycles of abundance and scarcity are continuously running their courses, and these have been, and are, the subject of intensive research by the Oxford Bureau.

Microtus agrestis prefers grass country; and an area where the preferred grassy and rushy conditions are not periodically disturbed by agricultural operations, or by grazing, has to be found if extended research lasting over a number of years is to be undertaken. Such areas are provided in the lands planted by the Forestry Commission, where the required conditions last for about fifteen years before the density of cover kills the undergrowth. In these places, where grass-burning is not practised, and which are fenced off from grazing and the trampling of sheep, so that there is no competition for food or disturbance of the ground, the voles find an ideal habitat; and there the vole population undergoes a cyclic increase and decrease in numbers, the peaks of abundance occurring every four or, less commonly, every three years. The planting of forest areas during the last twenty years has increased the vole population of the country by hundreds of thousands and probably by millions, and in the young forests the voles, not content with the grass and other herbage, have become serious pests, for they damage the young trees by nibbling off the bark thus either killing or deforming the trees. The damage done in some years runs into hundreds of thousands of pounds.

In studying a vole population it is necessary to have some idea of the numbers of the animals on the ground; a census can be taken by trapping selected areas, a laborious process that takes up much time, although it may give reasonably accurate results. Population-densities have in this way been shown to vary from less than fifty voles per acre, before an increase in numbers, to five hundred per acre at the peak of a cycle; a number that is, however, trifling when compared with that found during a true plague. A quicker way to estimate the density of the population, although it does not give the absolute numbers, is to take a trace-census. This is based on the fact that voles generally leave their droppings on the surface of the ground and not in their burrows when there is a dense grass cover, that fresh droppings are easily recognised, and consequently, if a number of two-yard circles selected at random throughout an affected area are examined, the number of circles containing fresh droppings gives an indication of the number of voles present. This method of making a census is possible because of the high rate at which food passes through the body of voles; a female weighing 27 grams was found to pass 1,057 pellets in one day, and it is calculated that voles eat their own weight of dry food in about ten days. The occupation-index produced by the trace survey may be anything from o to 100 per cent, depending upon the stage in the cycle of numbers reached by the population. That the density of the population revealed by this method is a true one, and is not obscured by voles wandering about the territory, is attested by the sedentary habits of *Microtus agrestis*, for the animals nearly always stay near home, and marked examples are commonly retrapped within a few yards of the original spot of capture after a lapse of many months. In one area, during a peak, the occupation-index for February and March was over 90 per cent, and after the crash came in May the figures for June were under 10 per cent.

The breeding season lasts from February or March to September or (exceptionally) to October, the start of the season being determined by the physiological state of the females, for the males are capable of breeding fully a month earlier.[28] Light rather than temperature determines the limits of the breeding season, which occurs during the months that can expect to have a total of 100 hours' sunshine, but not in those with less. If the amount of light is sufficient, low temperatures do not stop breeding, nor does the absence of green summer food; in fact voles kept at winter temperature and on winter diet (dry grasses and seeds) but given adequate illumination, bred more successfully in the laboratory than those given summer conditions.[10, 11] It was also found experimentally that voles feed on and off throughout the whole twenty-four hours; periods of two to three hours' activity and feeding alternate with periods of rest and sleep about ten times during the day and night, each of the night periods of activity being rather longer than the day ones. The normal span of life in nature is short, and averages less than one year. The animals born early in the season breed later on in the same year, overwinter, and breed again the next spring, but are all dead before the end of the summer. Animals born later in the season do not breed in the year of their birth, and so experience only one breeding season, that in the following spring and summer, after which they die. Only exceptionally does a vole, usually a female, reach the age of two years.

Just as the cause of the build-up in numbers to a peak is not yet understood, so the cataclysmic crash after the peak remains a mystery. Several reasons have been suggested, but none of them have turned out to be the right explanation. Mouse typhoid, from which the

a. BLACK RAT, *Rattus rattus* (*rattus* form)   *John Markham*

b. BLACK RAT, *R. rattus* (*frugivorus* form)   *John Markham*

Plate 8

original 'viruses' used in the hope of controlling outbreaks were isolated, has not been found as an epidemic since it was first noticed. In at least two minor outbreaks in this country the voles were found to be dying from an affection causing convulsions and paralysis of the hind limbs. This was traced to an obscure organism named *Toxoplasma*,[74] which is perhaps a protozoan, found in the brain, where it formed small cysts. Although the natural method of infection is unknown, a preparation from the brain of affected voles could be transmitted to others, in which the same symptoms were later developed; but toxoplasma is believed not to be the cause of the crash, for it has not been possible to find any trace of its presence in other outbreaks. Recently a form of tuberculosis has been found infecting field-voles, bank-voles, field-mice and common shrews; it is the first naturally occurring tuberculous disease of wild mammals to have been discovered.[229] The infection can be carried from one animal to another in food or water contaminated by an infected one, but the most probable method of transmission in the wild is through cannibalism; voles are very quarrelsome amongst themselves and intolerant of strangers; they will attack, kill and eat a trespasser into the community, a procedure that has been shown experimentally to be a sure way of spreading the disease if the victim should be infected. Though voles dying with the disease may be grossly infected, it does not follow that it is of any importance in reducing numbers, for it is very chronic, and voles riddled with the infection may be active and appear quite normal to within a few hours of death; infection does not appear to lessen a vole's expectation of life.

Voles can be the hosts of one or more of a long list of parasites, both external and internal, but the presence of parasites does not appear to bear any relation to the cycle of numbers.[67] So far from causing the mortality of a crash by their presence in high numbers, parasites are actually fewer in a dense population of wild voles. This is because parasites reach their highest numbers in the older voles, and when the population approaches its peak it necessarily contains a larger and larger proportion of young voles that have not had time to develop heavy infections.

Wherever a population of voles is building up towards peak numbers there is an increase of predators, especially of predatory birds, among which the most characteristic is the short-eared owl. There is an influx of these birds into the affected district, and they may stay to breed for a couple of years, disappearing when the crash comes. This species of owl is so closely connected with *Microtus* that it has even been suggested that without an adequate supply of voles as food it is unable to nest successfully, or at least to rear the usual number of young, perhaps because it obtains some accessory food-factor, essential for its breeding, from the voles. But although a short-eared owl may eat about 2000 voles in a year, the effect of owl pre-dation on a population of voles must be negligible. In an area that carried a population nearing its peak, calculation showed that the increased number of short-eared owls that had assembled on the ground was not likely to kill more than from two to five hundredths of one per cent of the voles daily.

Thus it has not been possible to show that the crash in numbers of voles is due to disease, to parasites, or to the attacks of predators. It is not due to all the food being eaten up, for although great damage is done and the vegetation bears a blasted and moth-eaten appearance, there is still plenty of food, though some essential factor necessary in minute amounts may be missing.[66] On the other hand overcrowding may foul the ground, so that the chemical nature of the vegetation is altered and toxic substances are produced in it; the land may be 'vole-sick' just as pastures are said to be 'sheep-sick' when, usually through overgrazing, some change that is not understood occurs and sheep no longer thrive on them. This suggestion is supported by the fact that many voles captured at the time of a crash are found to be less viable than normal; nothing can be found wrong with them; but they die soon after being caught and will not flourish in captivity as well as voles do usually. Overcrowding may have other effects; it may in some way upset the reproductive rate, or prevent the successful rearing of litters by harassing the nursing mothers. In this connection some figures on the reproductive rate and life-span, worked out by Leslie and Ranson,[123] are of interest.

These authors showed that in the laboratory the females can start breeding at the age of three weeks, the males at six weeks; but breeding does not necessarily start at so early an age in the wild, indeed there is definite evidence that frequently it does not. Gestation lasts three weeks, and the females become pregnant again either immediately after the birth of the litter, or about nine days later; the average number of young in the litter is five (Pl. XVIIIa, b, p. 149). The rate of increase is thus 87.7 per thousand per week, which is equivalent to

multiplying the population ten times in six months. The expectation
of life at birth is about thirty weeks, though individuals may live much
longer, and 94 per cent of the population is less than twenty-four weeks
old. Because of the short life-span the rate of increase during the
summer breeding season must be very high in order to produce quite
a small addition to the total numbers; if the season lasts fifteen weeks
and the population is unchanged in size at the end of a year, the
original population must have increased between three and four times,
and most of it must have died. Leslie and Ranson conclude that a
population subject to a life-table of this sort must necessarily be very
sensitive to any changes in the environment that might affect the
length or intensity of the breeding season. Anything tending to increase them would lead to peak numbers and a plague, and, once
numbers were high anything to the contrary would lead to a crash.
There is a critical period in the spring when the population consists
of middle-aged animals, all of which have a low expectation of life,
and it is thus quite possible that when the crash occurs it is brought
about by a slight decrease in fertility. The animals that die, and are
not replaced by new crops of young, would therefore not be the
victims of any epidemic, but would have merely reached the end of
their natural span.

Biologists are now (1950) tending to adopt the opinion that the
crash at the end of a cycle of abundance is due to the exhaustion of
the adreno-pituitary system of the animals throughout the affected
population. In a rapidly expanding population the increasing pressure
on food supplies, cover, and individual territories, and the consequent
disturbance and competition between individuals for these necessities
leads to a condition of stress throughout the population. As a reaction
to stress the adrenal glands of each animal are thrown into a condition
of over-activity that, if prolonged, leads to great disturbances of
metabolism, especially to an abnormally low level of sugar in the blood
and liver. Such a condition, with other attendant symptoms, is known
as 'shock-disease,' and has been found in the snowshoe-hares of America
when a population crash occurs. The reaction of the adrenals is
stimulated by the adrenocorticotropic ('ACTH') hormone secreted
from the anterior pituitary gland, which in turn becomes overworked.
With the approach of the next breeding season a great strain is thrown
on the anterior pituitary gland because it has then to produce the
gonadotropic hormones that stimulate the sex glands. "Hence at a

time when stresses are maximal, we suddenly have an increased pituitary load, and the animals begin to succumb with symptoms of exhaustion of the adreno-pituitary mechanism, and the periodic decimation is in full swing."[42a] The reproduction rate of the species determines the length of the population cycle, animals that breed rapidly building up to peak proportions more quickly than the slower breeders.

Cycles of abundance alternating with scarcity are known to occur in most of our species of small rodents, but much less is recorded about them than about those in *Microtus*. This is because the latter animal is particularly suitable for the study of cycles in those habitats mentioned above, where it occurs as the dominant animal in almost pure culture, with very little admixture of other species. *Microtus* is, of course, common in most other places as well, but the problem is much more complex in a varied environment where there is possibly competition from other species, such as the bank-vole and the field-mouse. Little is recorded of the population dynamics in the bank-vole (*Clethrionomys glareolus britannicus*), but some interesting studies have been made upon its breeding and life-history.[31, 181] The breeding season starts quite suddenly in the middle of April, rises to a peak in June, and then subsides gradually to its end late in October. In some winters a limited amount of breeding takes place in all the months from November to March, but there is great variation in the amount of winter breeding from year to year, and it appears to be more usual for breeding to stop completely from November onwards. Females born early in the season become mature and breed in the same year. These survive the winter and breed again in the following season, but the females born late in the season do not breed until after wintering. It is very improbable that any of either group survive a second winter or breed for a third time.

Although two breeding seasons is the maximum that any female can experience, the reproductive rate is nevertheless high, for each can produce four or even five litters in a season, each litter averaging four young. This is possible because, as in so many rodents, the female can mate again immediately after the birth of the young, so that nursing females are often at the same time pregnant with the next litter. In June and July over 90 per cent of the females are pregnant, and in these months the litters are largest, averaging nearly $4\frac{1}{2}$ young each; before June the average is not quite four, and after July it falls

Plate XXI

Young long-tailed field-mouse

John Markham

Plate XXII   *John Markham*

Yellow-necked mouse

to less than three. The onset of the breeding season is determined by the physiological state of the females, for at its beginning they may come into oestrus three times or more without mating, although the males are perfectly fertile at that period. The reason for this is not understood, nor is it known why the males should be ready for breeding more than a month before the females. In the winter months the males are usually completely infertile, and it is not until the beginning of March that sexual activity starts and the weight of the testes begins to increase; the growth of these organs is so rapid and so great that their average weight in June is more than seventeen times that of their average winter weight.

Towards the end of the breeding season the reproductive rate is reduced, not only by the smaller average size of the litters, but also by an increase in the length of gestation. In the late breeders it has been found that there is some delay in the implantation and early development of the embryos in the uterus, if the mother is nursing a previous litter. Another point of interest is that, although the average litter-size at the height of the breeding season is rather over four, litters larger than this are common. In these larger litters there is a higher incidence of death among the young before birth than in the smaller ones; the incidence being much higher when six or more eggs are released from the ovaries, than when the number is five or less. This mortality during gestation appears to be due to the inability of the mother to provide sufficient nourishment for all the embryos to complete their development, rather than to mechanical overcrowding within the uterus. It appears to be possible that some such mechanism as this may be one of the causes of the crash when a vole population is at its peak. The reproductive rate may tend to increase to such an extent that an excessive number of egg-cells are released from the ovaries, and the consequent pre-natal mortality may reduce the number of live births to a level at which the numbers of the population are not maintained.

The breeding season of the water-vole (*Arvicola amphibius*) starts at the end of March and lasts until the second half of September.[172] As in the bank-vole, the start of the season is determined by the female, for the males are fertile as early as February; and as in that species, the females often experience oestrus, sometimes several times, at the beginning of the breeding season, without pregnancy following. The number of litters produced by the female in a single season is not known, but it is certainly more than one, for after the birth of a litter the females are often found to be pregnant with another while they are still nursing the former. The average number of young in a litter is just under six, the average in the earlier litters, up to the end of June, being slightly over six, that for the later ones being less than five. The young of the first litters of the season begin to be out and about during May. The breeding season of the males begins to decline in August, and by the end of October nearly all males are infertile.

Although the water-vole is a considerably larger animal than the short-tailed or bank-voles, its expectation of life appears to be no longer than in those species, and few, if any, survive a second winter. Animals born early in one season may breed later in the same year, but those born late, do not breed until the spring of the year following. In this country the water-vole has never been known to increase in numbers sufficiently to become a plague, indeed it appears to be a remarkably inoffensive animal of little direct economic importance to man. Its food consists largely of reeds and other water-plants; its grazing on the grassy banks of rivers does not extend far from the water, though it may keep the margin close clipped for a foot or two from the edge.[52] About the worst that can be said of it is that its burrows give harbourage to the brown rat, though that species would be quite capable of making its own were none provided. Its burrowings in the banks are not sufficiently extensive to cause any serious damage in this country, but on the continent the numbers sometimes build up to plague proportions. It is trapped for its fur in Russia, and in that country it has been found to carry the virus of the dangerous disease tularaemia, which has been caught by many of the trappers and others who handle the animals.

In very different relationship to man and his works stands, or in this country stood, another species of water-vole, the alien musk-rat, a native of north America that became naturalised in Britain in the late nineteen-twenties.[6] The musk-rat (*Ondatra zibethica*) is a large vole, its head and body, without the tail, over a foot long, dark reddish-brown in colour above and lighter beneath. The tail is peculiarly flattened from side to side, its upper and lower keels carrying a fringe of dense stiff hairs (Pl. XXa, p. 165). Similar fringes on each side of the large hind feet and toes serve to increase the surfaces opposed to the water in swimming. The animal takes its name from the musky scent of the secretion from a large gland situated in the region of the groin, and present in both sexes. The fur of the musk-rat is the 'musquash' of commerce (this being the Red Indian name for the animal), a fur of sufficient value to have led to the breeding of musk-rats in captivity for their pelts, both in America and Europe. The animals are rapid breeders, and great burrowers and wanderers; in Europe there were soon escapes from fur-farms, and the rats, having few or no natural enemies, quickly increased and became a serious pest. In their home country they normally inhabit large natural marshes where they can do no particular harm. In the British Isles there were a number of escapes, and musk-rats became established in several parts of the country, both in England, Scotland and Ireland.

The musk-rat feeds on aquatic vegetation, especially reeds, and lays up stores of such materials in its burrows for use in winter. Its burrows are so extensive that they undermine banks and dams, and cause riverside trees to collapse into the water. In the autumn the animals build mounds of vegetation in shallow still water; these are primarily stores of food, but are known as 'lodges' because the rats burrow into them, and gradually eat out the centre until only a shell is left. The general effect of a population of musk-rats upon their environment is to turn streams and their neighbourhood into areas of swampy marsh, by diverting the water on to the surrounding land through the collapse of the banks, and by choking the main channels with fallen trees and masses of vegetation that have been cut adrift. Damage of this sort had for some years been a serious problem on the continent, and when musk-rats, escaped from fur-farms, became established in this country, it was quickly evident that similar trouble would arise here unless prompt action was taken. The keeping of musk-rats was prohibited, and a campaign of destruction, mainly by trapping, was undertaken by the Ministry of Agriculture and Fisheries.

Their destruction was by no means easy, for the musk-rat breeds at a very high rate, each female producing six or seven litters of eight during the breeding season, which was longer in Britain than elsewhere because of the mild climate and abundant food, lasting from February to November. The young of the earlier litters migrated away from their native territory to colonise fresh areas in the autumn, those from the later litters in the following spring. So rapid was their increase that in a district in Perthshire, where five females and four males escaped in 1927, no less than 890 musk rats were killed by trapping up to the end of 1933.[7] Similarly in Ireland, an area of 150 square miles was infested between 1927 and 1934 by the progeny of a single pair, and 487 of the animals were trapped in the winter of 1933-34 alone.[82] Whether the numbers would have built up to plague proportions and then have suffered a crash it is impossible to say, but in Canada the musk-rat population has been found to go through a ten-year cycle of abundance and scarcity.[68] The effects of the trapping campaign began to become evident in 1934, the year in which the turning point in numbers was reached; there was a marked decrease during the summer and autumn, and by the end of 1937 the animal had been virtually exterminated throughout the country.[226] Man was not the only sufferer from the musk-rat incident; during two years of trapping in Scotland, in addition to the 945 musk-rats caught in traps set in shallow water, there were also unintentionally killed, 2,305 water-voles, 1,745 brown rats, 2,178 moorhens, 101 ducks, 18 herons, and many other creatures including 36 stoats and 57 weasels.[156] A person releasing a pair of musk-rats does far more damage, and causes far more trouble and expense in clearing up the results of his action, than a person releasing a pair of man-eating tigers.

The long-tailed field-mouse, *Apodemus sylvaticus*, in all its geographical races, is much more completely nocturnal than any of our native voles, and much more omnivorous in its habits. It is a very active animal, a good jumper, and an agile climber. Although it is a devourer of grain and seeds, it also feeds largely upon more succulent things such as berries, roots, and insects. This species is believed to experience periodical fluctuations in its numbers, but it is not known to multiply to the point of producing plagues as do some of the voles, and nothing definite appears to be known about its cycles of increase. Trapping experiments, in which the mice were caught, marked and released, and then caught again, have shown that in general the territorial range of individual mice is quite restricted, and that they do not normally go far from home; 200 yards in a straight line is an exceptionally long distance for a mouse to go in its foraging. The distribution of a population of field-mice in a Berkshire wood was found to be not at random, but to be concentrated in certain areas so that there was a lower density of population in the places between.[71] Further, it was found that when the population as a whole passed from a period of high to one of low density, the survival-rate was greatest in the less densely populated areas. It has therefore been suggested that the normal low density areas that are assumed to be the less favourable

Plate XXIII   *A. R. Thompson*

Harvest-mice

Plate XXIV

John Markham

Harvest-mouse at nest in reeds

environments, are of importance to the species, if not to individuals, in providing a reservoir from which the assumedly more favourable areas can be re-populated after a general fall in numbers.

The field-mouse lives by day within its burrow which may be several feet in length; at the end of the burrow there is a chamber in which a nest of shredded grass is made. The nest, which is about six inches across and contains a cavity about three inches in diameter, is not just a nursery for the young but a home for everyday use. In the nest-chamber, or in a side room of the burrow, a winter store of food is laid up, consisting of seeds, berries, roots and so forth. The mice are very gregarious and several adults are often found living in the same nest.

The breeding season usually begins in March, rises to a peak in July, and subsides to its end in October or November; as in so many small rodents, the males are fertile for a month before the season starts, and the onset of the season must therefore be determined by the state of the females.[9] The average number of young in the litter is five, and litters ranging from two to nine have been recorded; the litters produced at the height of the breeding season are the largest, averaging nearly six young from June to August, slightly over five in June, and less than five after August. The lower numbers in the earlier litters are probably due to some of the eggs released from the ovary not being fertilised, and perhaps sometimes to the re-absorption of some of the developing embryos; but the lower numbers in the later litters appear to be due to fewer eggs being produced. Gestation lasts 25 to 26 days, and the female comes into oestrus directly after the birth of the young, or, if mating is missed or is unsuccessful, five days later. Nursing females can thus be pregnant with a new litter, which is born directly after the young of the first one are weaned. Baker[9] found that 100 per cent of the adult females, in a wild population that he was studying, were pregnant during the months from April to August in one year, and from March to June in another, and that 70 per cent or more were pregnant during most of the remainder of the season. The reproductive rate of the species is thus very high, for the mice can start breeding when only a few months old, and the adult females may produce as many as six litters a year. It is unlikely that the average life-span exceeds, or even equals, twelve months, though individuals may live much longer, and it is improbable that any normally survive a second winter. The mortality is doubtless very high, for field-mice are eaten eagerly by all predators, mammals, birds, reptiles (adders) and even amphibia (large toads). In one census half the population was found to disappear within a month of marking.[71]

The breeding season, however, is not always of the same duration in every year. Baker,[9] who made an intensive study, extending over nearly three years and including three winters, of the field-mice in a wood near Oxford, found a peculiar progressive lengthening of the season during the period. In the first winter no females bred for the space of six months, and all the males were infertile for the first five; in the second winter there were no breeding females during only two months, and all the males were infertile for only one. In the third winter there was only one month in which no pregnant females were found, and at least 18 per cent or more of the males were fertile throughout the winter. The mean temperatures of all these winters were much alike, as were those of the two intervening summers, and the winters with increased breeding activity were not milder than the first; no other naturally varying phenomenon that might have had any influence could be found, and the cause of the progressive increase could not be determined.[10, 11] The figures given do, however, give the impression that the population was on the upward slope of a cyclic increase, as was pointed out by Baker and his colleagues.

Field-mice can hardly be rated as serious pests to agriculture, for they do not as a rule congregate in stacks of grain nor come into granaries or houses, but they can be a considerable nuisance to horticulture. They are particularly destructive to newly-sown beans and peas; gardeners often soak such seeds in paraffin before sowing to make them distasteful to the mice and in the hope that this will prevent them being dug out and eaten. Field-mice are also sometimes very destructive to bulbs in the flower-garden; they have also been recorded as destroying salmon ova in a fish hatchery.[21] A peculiar form of attack by field-mice on cereal crops has been known for some years in the midland counties; it is not clear whether this is a long-standing habit or a new development in the last twenty years.[178] In fields of winter cereals adjoining a wood or spinney, the field-mice come out from the wood every night in the autumn and early winter and graze on the young plants, cutting them down to about half an inch from the ground. Sometimes the damage done is so great that the crop has to be ploughed in and a spring sowing made; where the crops recover, a loss in yield of several quarters an acre may be experienced, and the quality may be diminished by the setback and consequent late harvesting. When the attack is severe, a well-defined grazing front is left every night, marking the limit to which the mice have fed; in one field the line was found to be advanced five yards a night, representing an area of a third of an acre grazed off nightly, so that in five weeks ten acres were completely eaten down. Such attacks can be combated with poison, but, even better, it was found that a ditch containing a few inches of water between the wood and the field completely stopped them.

On the little harvest-mouse, *Micromys minutus soricinus* (Pl. XXIII, p. 184), no modern research has been done. It is a species that appears to have greatly decreased in numbers and wideness of distribution during the last century. The suggestion has been made that the use of reaping machines, which leave a much shorter stubble than does mowing by scythe, has been the cause of this decrease, and it may well be so, but there is no definite information on the point. The harvest-mouse has been recorded at one time or another from practically all the counties of England and Wales, and from some of those of lowland Scotland; it has never been present in Ireland. At the present time it appears to be confined to the southern and eastern counties of England, and even through them it is sporadically distributed, though it is plentiful in some places. It is by far the smallest British rodent, adults measuring from $2\frac{1}{4}$ to $2\frac{1}{2}$ inches in length exclusive of the tail, and weighing 5 to 6 gm.; the house-mouse weighs 35 to 40 gm., and a large brown rat about 400 gm. The colour of the upper parts is a bright yellowish or reddish brown, and of the underside white. The snout is rather short for a mouse, and the tail is partly prehensile, being twisted round a twig or stem for extra support as the animal climbs among bushes or herbage. The harvest-mouse is more diurnal than nocturnal in its habits, and lives in thick vegetation among which it climbs about seeking for seeds, and particularly for insects which appear to form a large part of the summer diet. In autumn it is commonly found in crops of cereals, and at harvest time it is either carried with the sheaves into the ricks, or migrates to them from the open fields. In those districts where it is plentiful, large numbers are frequently found during the winter in ricks, underneath which the winter nests are made. In the fields the winter nest is made underground at the end of a burrow, in which considerable stores of seeds and grain may be laid up.

But it is the summer nest suspended between the stalks of growing corn, or in a thistle-plant, by which the harvest-mouse is generally known (Pl. XXIV, p. 185). This globe, about four inches across, is built of shredded corn-blades and grasses, and may be several inches to a foot or more from the ground, supported by the stalks of tall plants, which are woven into the sides. There is no regular doorway, the mice pushing their way in and out anywhere near the top; some nests are compact, others much more loosely constructed. Each nest is probably not occupied for long, the growth of the vegetation in which it is suspended necessitating the building of a new one or the reconstruction of the old at fairly short intervals. In the summer-nests the young are born; litters ranging in size from five to nine young have been recorded, but the normal number appears to be six or seven. Practically nothing is known of the breeding of this species; several litters are said to be produced during the season, the limits of which are likewise unknown. Judging by analogy with other species of mouse, it is probable that litters follow each other rapidly, and that the nursing females become pregnant shortly after the birth of the young; it is unlikely that individuals normally survive more than their first winter. On the continent the numbers of the harvest-mouse sometimes increase inordinately and the resulting plagues of mice may do serious damage to cereal crops.

The house-mouse of Britain, *Mus musculus domesticus*, is one of the most commensal races of the species, and is associated with man's buildings or cultivation (Pl. 7, p. 169). There is a large urban population commensal in dwelling-houses, factories and warehouses, a rural one attached to farms, and a much smaller feral one living in the fields.[119] The habits of these three divisions differ considerably, but there is nothing to prevent individuals transferring from one habitat to another. In each habitat the animals are very restricted in their individual range, and do not as a rule wander far from home. Of the commensal mice those in dwelling-houses appear to be the ones that have to work hardest for their livings, probably because they are more disturbed by the traffic of man and his household animals, and have to search more diligently for food than those in warehouses and farms. Commensal house-mice breed regularly all through the year, and there is no marked breeding season, but those living in dwelling-houses have a lower overall rate of reproduction than most; they produce an average of 5½ litters a year, a considerably smaller number than is found in other environments. In warehouses the home range may be very small indeed, and it is possible for a mouse to live its whole life inside a sack of grain or flour without ever leaving it. In such places the reproduction rate is higher, and averages just under eight litters a year. The most unexpected environment in which house-mice flourish is that provided by the cold stores in which meat is kept for long periods. Here the mice do well in what would appear to be very adverse conditions. In total darkness, and in a temperature never above 15°F. (about $-10°$ C.), with no food other than meat, the mice breed and live their whole lives. They make their nests of the hessian material in which meat is wrapped, or of the fur and feathers from stored carcasses. Often they eat out burrows in carcasses of frozen meat and make their nests inside. Not only do the mice withstand the severe conditions, but they flourish on them to an unusual extent, so that the average size and weight of cold-store mice is above that of outside mice. Further, their reproductive rate is higher; they produce an average of a little over $6\frac{1}{2}$ litters a year compared with the $5\frac{1}{2}$ of domestic mice; the average number of young in each litter is also greater, being over $6\frac{1}{3}$ against a fraction above $5\frac{1}{2}$.

The rural and feral populations differ considerably from this. In spite of the fact that our subspecies of house-mouse is one of the most highly commensal forms, there is a regular feral population living in the fields and hedgerows throughout the arable districts of the country. This population is so large that during the summer the house-mouse is the third commonest small mammal of the fields in many places, equalling in numbers those of the bank-vole. (The field-mouse is about twice as numerous as either of these.) Some of this population is permanently feral, and shows a peak of breeding in the summer and practically none in the autumn and winter. The part of this population that does not live permanently in the fields spends much of the year in corn-ricks, where it may build up to very large numbers.

Ricks are made during the late summer and autumn, and by the second half of September their temporary population of house-mice is starting to establish itself. Infestation begins with a few mice that are either carried in with the sheaves, or migrate in from the fields on their own, the rest of the feral population remaining permanently in the fields and hedges. Ricks may be threshed at any time up to the following autumn, and at threshing time any mouse population that may have built up is turned out into the fields again. There is a very high mortality, possibly in part due to predators, among the animals thus evicted, and the cycle starts over again in the autumn. The investigations of Southern and Laurie[196] have produced some interesting figures on this subject. A rick provides an ideal environment for the mice; shelter, food, nest-material, an even temperature, and protection from predators, so that numbers rapidly increase. The mice do not leave the rick even for water; corn-grains contain a sufficiently high proportion of moisture to satisfy the greater part of their needs, and the balance is obtained either from dew or from rain on the outside of the rick, all the mice coming to the surface frequently for this purpose.

Starting late in September the population reaches a peak in about eight months time, and does not increase greatly thereafter even if the rick is undisturbed. The population doubles every two months, and thus very heavy infestations can develop from very few original parents. It is common to turn out several hundred mice when threshing a rick, the numbers running at anything from fifty or a hundred, up to over two thousand, representing between 1 and 15 mice per cubic metre of rick (Pl. XXVa, p. 192). Southern relates how impressive it is to see the threshing machine, working a badly infested rick, filling sacks with mouse-droppings instead of dust, or to weigh a sack holding the animals killed and to find that it contains 28 pounds of mice. He calculates that 2,000 mice in a rick will eat up about a stone of corn a day, and the total deficiency on threshing a rick may run into many hundredweights of grain. In addition to the actual loss, the mice nibble great numbers of grains without eating them entirely, producing an unduly high proportion of 'tail' (damaged) corn. They show a decided preference for wheat-ricks, contrary to the general impression that credits them with preferring oats.

In the favourable environment of the rick the reproductive rate is very high. Female wild mice, unlike their tame white relations, generally become pregnant within a day of giving birth to their young, and, for the time that they are in the rick, they produce litters at the rate of over ten a year, nearly double the rate in house-dwelling mice, and closely approaching the theoretical limit of 13 to 14 litters a year. In the crowded conditions of a rick it is common to find communal nests that hold the litters of several females; whether the young are indiscriminately mixed, or are recognised by the mothers when suckling, is unknown. Similar communal nests have been recorded in feral house-mice in America;[160] there they had invaded a building where, though food was abundant, nesting places and nest material were scarce. As many as three females were found using the same nest, and the highest number of young in a single nest at any time was twenty-four. It is calculated that a female mouse will give birth to anything from thirty to about fifty-five young ones in the course of a single year; the average life span is, however, unlikely to exceed a year, or eighteen months at most. One would expect such large populations of mice to attract unusual numbers of predators, an occurrence that does not in fact happen; sometimes a weasel or two, or a nest of young ones, but never a larger number, is found in a rick, and when only a few are present, the number of mice seems to be just as great as usual. There must be a very delicate balance between the rural and feral populations of house-mice and their environment for this yearly cycle to occur without the production of mouse-plagues.

No doubt the feral population of house-mice is yearly added to by the rural mice which, turned out of the ricks at threshing time, take to the fields in the summer and form breeding colonies there. But feral mice appear to be able to live indefinitely without being either outdoor or indoor commensals of man, for Fraser Darling found house-mice living on Lunga, one of the Treshnish Isles, although it had been uninhabited for eighty years; the mice immediately resumed their commensal habits, however, and started to colonise his camp.[49] On the other hand the house-mouse of St. Kilda became extinct very shortly after the island was deserted by its inhabitants in 1930; but in this island the 'wild' habitats away from buildings were already filled by the field-mouse *Apodemus*. In 1931 the total house-mouse population of St. Kilda was estimated to be not more than twenty-five at the utmost (and not less than twelve), and these were only just able to survive in two of the houses that still contained some stores of food.[95] It is probably now extinct.[74a]

Though the house-mouse is the most destructive animal in corn-ricks, the amount of damage that it does in general is not so great as that inflicted by rats, which also injure man by spreading diseases such as food-poisoning in contaminated food-stuffs, and plague, transferred to man by their fleas. When large dumps of food were set up throughout the country during the late war, the threat of rat damage was so serious that widespread action had to be taken. The control of rats on a large scale is, however, no easy matter, and it was soon apparent that the usual methods of dealing with the pests were ineffective. Effective means could not be devised without knowledge of the biology of rats, knowledge which did not exist. An extensive scheme of research was therefore launched, in which teams from the Oxford Bureau of Animal Population, and the Ministries of Food and of Agriculture, collaborated, and from which our modern methods of rodent control were evolved.[12, 13]

The ubiquitous brown rat (*Rattus norvegicus*) is both an indoor and outdoor commensal with man, but the black rat (*R. rattus*) is generally considered to be more restricted to buildings. The latter is certainly confined to towns, mostly ports, in this country; it is also the ship rat, the brown rat seldom going to sea. In the towns where it occurs it is often common, but it has frequently been reported to be absent or uncommon because of confusion with the brown rat, the identity of the brown forms resembling the races *Rattus r. alexandrinus* and *R. r. frugivorus* not having been recognised.[129] All three main colour forms are generally present in any area inhabited by the species, but the numbers of one alone are usually considerably in excess of those of the others. The preponderance of one form is not constant from place to place, nor from time to time, first one and then another dominating any locality successively. Although the numbers of the black rat are assumed to be augmented by new immigrants escaping from ships, the regulations now in force to prevent this occurring, and for 'deratting' ships (usually done by fumigation), must very much reduce the number that successfully get ashore. It thus seems clear that the black rat can maintain itself in some numbers in various types of habitats in British ports without notable additions from ships.

The *alexandrinus* and *frugivorus* forms are usually regarded as inhabitants of roofs and the upper stories of buildings, but there is evidence that the difference in the habitats of the various forms of *R. rattus* and of *R. norvegicus* has been rather over-emphasised, for in America, though not in England[153ab] the 'roof' rats live also in basements and sewers. Across the Atlantic, in fact, all of them will live anywhere in, on, or under buildings, in sewers, or in the ground.[152]

However, *R. norvegicus* lives in the country as well as the town, and there forms a semi-feral population, inhabiting fields and hedges, during the summer months. In the autumn it takes to corn ricks, as does the house-mouse, but does not form infestations of anything like the density found in that species. The rat population of ricks reaches

H. N. Southern

a. Rick of grain damaged and dilapidated by house-mice

H. N. Southern

b. Brown rat cautiously approaching a bait in total darkness: photographed by invisible infra-red rays

Plate XXV

a. Brown rat

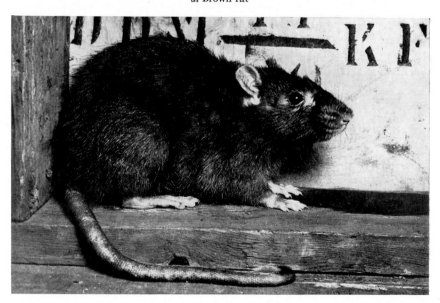

b. Melanistic form of brown rat

Plate XXVI

its peak about April and thereafter declines, most of the animals deserting the ricks, or being turned out during threshing, by June or July.[224] The law now requires that a temporary fence of wire netting be erected round any rick that is being threshed, so that the rats may be killed before they can escape.

The breeding biology of wild *R. norvegicus* differs considerably from that of its domesticated races.[173] Breeding appears to go on at a fairly steady rate all the year round in the population as a whole, but the individual animals do not breed continuously, having periods of breeding separated by comparatively long periods of rest. Among the females there is a high incidence of nursing animals already pregnant with a new litter before the previous one has been weaned, but there is also a large number of animals in a state of complete sexual inactivity, thus proving that individuals experience recurring breeding seasons although the population as a whole may not. There is, however, much variation in this respect between the animals in different environments; as might be expected, populations living where food is abundant and conditions are relatively constant show less seasonal reduction of breeding activity than those in more uncongenial surroundings. Even in favourable circumstances there is a peak in breeding intensity from March to June, and much fluctuation during the winter, but the highest peak-value is not more than three times the lowest value of winter. That the environment can affect the rate of breeding is shown by the fact that in the favourable conditions of a rick, 28 per cent of the females were found to be pregnant from November to February, whereas during the same period only 3 per cent of those living ferally outside, in hedges, rubbish dumps and so forth, were pregnant. There appears to be no seasonal variation in the breeding capacity of the males; at any time the population contains a large proportion of fertile males, so that such seasonal fluctuation as there may be must be determined by the females.

Young brown rats do not start breeding until they are over 100 days old, at an age of between three and four months; gestation lasts about three weeks, and the average number of young in a litter is eight or a trifle less. The mean duration of life in tame rats, subject to none of the hazards of life in the wild[230] has been determined as 669 days for males and 693 days for females; it therefore appears improbable that wild brown rats survive on an average for much more than eighteen months. Prolific as is the brown rat, investigation has shown that there is a considerable mortality of unborn young during gestation. Although the average litter contains seven to eight young, rather more than ten egg-cells are released from the ovaries at oestrus. A high proportion of the fertilised eggs and embryos is thus lost, but on the other hand, the loss is evenly distributed throughout the population and few litters are entirely lost, some at least of the young in nearly all litters surviving to birth. The losses occur at random during all stages of gestation, so that there is no critical stage at which a high rate of loss may occur, as there is in the rabbit. During the intense period of breeding activity, when pregnancies rapidly follow each other, a new set of egg-cells being released from the ovaries within twenty-four hours of the birth of a litter, it is found that gestation is prolonged as a result of the mother suckling her young. This lengthening of gestation is due to a delay in the attachment of embryos in the very early stages of development to the interior of the uterus, and as the breeding season progresses the delay tends to become longer and longer for successive litters, so that eventually as much as ten days may be added to the time required for development.

Apart from the breeding biology, the general habits and behaviour of rats had to be investigated in order to devise sound control methods. Rats live in burrows and travel from them to their feeding places along definite pathways or runs; unlike mice they must have access to water for drinking. The runs of the brown rat skirt the bases of walls and other objects wherever possible, but the black rat is much less disinclined to cross clear spaces and run about on open floors; the black rat too, when living in upper stories, likes attics roofed with pantiles, so that it can peep out from under the curved edges of the tiles and drink rainwater from the gutters. One of the most striking characteristics of rats is their great shyness and sensitivity to any physical change in their usual surroundings, and their avoidance, or apparent fear, of anything new. If any new object is placed in their haunts, or a familiar one is moved to a new position, they generally avoid approaching it for some time, even days, until they have become accustomed to the new arrangement. Curiously enough, they are such creatures of habit that they take no notice of the complete removal of a familiar object, so much so that they will continue to run round the place where an obstruction has stood, instead of crossing the space now opened to them. This shyness leads to the avoiding without discrimination of anything strange, a point that assumes considerable importance when attempts are made to destroy rats by putting down poisoned baits for them. Rats are equally shy of any new food substance, of which they will eat only small quantities until they have become accustomed to it. This shy behaviour has led to the familiar popular stories of the extreme cunning or intelligence of rats, and to the idea that they will not approach anything that has been tainted by being handled. It is not surprising that they will not usually enter a trap as soon as it is put down, but this is not because it has been handled; if it is left in position and baited, but not set, nightly for a week or more, it is easy enough to catch rats when at last it is set, after they have become accustomed to it and to feeding in it.

It is evident, bearing in mind the high reproductive rate of rats, that any control methods, to be effective, must make as complete a clearance of the pests as possible at one swoop, for if the control is only partly effective the numbers will very soon build up again. The control method finally worked out aims at doing this, and also takes into consideration the characteristic shyness of rats, and the fact that they can be accustomed to the presence of new objects and to eating new foods.[12] This method attempts the poisoning of the whole population of an infested area at the same time by the technique of 'pre-baiting', and calls for a high degree of careful organisation if the area is large. The principle is simple; food is put out for the rats so that they may become accustomed to its presence, to its nature, and to the receptacles in which it is placed. This procedure is usually continued for four nights, and what is termed 'token' pre-baiting is adopted. This is merely putting out less food than the rats are capable of eating, and tends to teach the rats to come out for food earlier, and to eat it more quickly, the latter a very important point to ensure that on the fifth night, when the food is poisoned, each shall eat enough to obtain a lethal dose. On the fifth night, when the animals have become well used to feeding at the baits, a full quantity of poisoned food is put out at each point, and if the operation has been carefully carried out there are few survivors. A check on the number of survivors can be made by putting out unpoisoned baits on the sixth night and observing if any are eaten. In very heavily infested areas it is often necessary to repeat the process, but if a repeat is to be made the nature of the baits must be changed and, on the fifth night, the type of poison, for survivors from the first operation become both 'bait-shy' and 'poison-shy' of the substances used on the first occasion.

Some experiments are recorded in which the reactions of rats to a prebaiting and poisoning operation were observed.[219] A small population of between thirty and forty rats, living in some pig-sties in the country, were conditioned to feeding by dim artificial light and then watched from a hide. About a third of them had been trapped alive, clearly marked by removing some of the fur to give individual patterns, and returned to the population, so that the behaviour of individuals could be compared. The experiment took place in February, and watching started each night at 5.30 p.m., as soon as dusk fell. Most of the rats paid very short visits to the bait, but there was much individual variation, both in the time spent on the bait at each visit, and in the total number of visits made. Rats generally run out from cover, seize a mouthful of food, and run back again to eat it under cover. The number of feeding visits to the bait made by individuals varied from none to over a hundred each night, and the time spent at the bait was usually a few seconds only, though some individuals sometimes stayed a matter of minutes. The animals that made no visits to the bait apparently remained under cover and fed by stealing from the others, or by scavenging the fragments dropped by them. After the first night, token-baiting was used, and it was found that as night succeeded night the rats started feeding earlier, paid more visits in the first hour, and ate more quickly.

On the first night feeding started at 7.15 p.m., and practically all the bait, which consisted of wheat, was eaten by 12.30 a.m. On the second night feeding started before 6.0 p.m., and all the bait was gone before 11.45 p.m. On the third and following nights feeding started rather earlier, and all the bait was eaten by 10.45 p.m. on the third, and by 9.0 p.m. on the fourth night. On the fifth night, when the bait was poisoned, feeding started well before 6.0 p.m., and had practically stopped after 35 minutes, completely so after 50, and no more rats were seen, although watch was maintained until dawn at 7.0 a.m. the next day. The whole population was completely wiped out. That this kind of behaviour is typical of rats was later confirmed with a special viewing apparatus, at baits illuminated by infra-red rays,[198] when a flood of "black light", invisible to man or rat, was thrown over the scene (Pl. XXVb, p. 192); further confirmation was obtained from records of feeding made by an automatic device in complete darkness.[42]

The pre-baiting technique has been used in many places on a large scale with success. One of the largest operations took place in the

a. Hibernating dormouse   *Mondiale*

b. Edible dormouse   *John Markham*

Plate XXVII

Plate XXVIII   *John Markham*

Winter drey of the grey squirrel

winter of 1943–44, when the rat population of London's 2,700 miles of sewers was attacked, the campaign lasting ten weeks and employing over 1,100 men. It was carried out in two treatments, using different bait and poison in the second, and achieved a great reduction not only in the density of the infestation but also in the area affected. In the first treatment 60 per cent of the pre-baits of the first night were completely eaten, in the second treatment only 7 per cent, figures that speak for themselves.[12] This method of control is equally applicable to country districts. During a period of just under three years extending from 1942 to 1945 a rural area of over 11,000 acres, containing three villages and over thirty sets of farm buildings, was treated, and a 90 per cent reduction of the rat population was effected at a total yearly cost of about twopence an acre.[224]

The poisons generally employed in rat control are zinc phosphide, arsenic, or red squill; new and more deadly substances ('antu') are also coming into use. A poison of an entirely different sort, that is being studied and may prove useful, is the substance dicoumarol, which causes death by the breakdown of the minute blood-vessels throughout the body. It acts in a very peculiar way because a large single dose is harmless, but a build-up from repeated small doses is fatal. It could therefore easily be fed to vermin by a modified baiting technique, and yet would be harmless to any domestic animal that chanced to eat a bait, or to eat one of the victims. A harmless allied substance, coumarin occurs naturally in clover, and dicoumarol, derived from it, has been found in mouldy hay, evidently being formed during some process of decay; before it was recognised it was responsible for a number of outbreaks of mysterious deaths among animals fed on deteriorated hay. The latest (1950) trials with this substance have, however, been disappointing for although there was some initial success, wild rats soon developed 'shyness' for baits containing this poison, which is evidently distasteful.[7a]

Of the family Gliridae there is only one native British representative, the Dormouse, *Muscardinus avellanarius* (Linnaeus) (Pl. 9, p. 201), restricted to England and Wales. It is regarded as a comparative newcomer to the British fauna, having spread westwards from an origin somewhere in south-central Europe during the Pleistocene. In England it is common in suitable places throughout the southern and western counties, rather scarce and local in Wales, and in the West extends northwards as far as the Scottish borders.

M.   O

Its distribution thins out across the midlands, so that it is absent from most of the eastern counties north of Essex and southern Suffolk; it is absent from Ireland and the Isle of Man. The dormouse is a medium-sized mouse, the head and body measuring 3 to 3½ inches in length, and the tail 2¼ to 2¾ inches; the eyes are large, the ears rather small, and the blunt snout carries long whiskers. The tail is thickly covered with hair but is not bushy; the peculiar ridged character of the molar teeth has already been mentioned (p. 128). The colour of the fur is a rich yellow-brown above, fading gradually into white or creamy-white on the under-parts.

The dormouse is very arboreal in its habits, but it does not live in large trees, keeping to low bushes and shrubs, about which it scrambles with great agility. Its food consists of seeds, berries, nuts, leaves, and insects; it is also said to rob bird's nests of eggs or nestlings. It is nocturnal and solitary, spending the day asleep in a nest built low down in a bush or among tall herbage. The summer sleeping-nest is a small globular construction of grass or leaves and moss, large enough to hold one mouse, each animal in a colony having its own nest. The breeding nest, in which the young are reared, is rather larger and more compact, and is often placed quite close to the ground. The winter nest, which is used for hibernation, is placed on the ground, often beneath piles of dead leaves, in the shelter of the roots of a small tree, or in a stump, or inside a hole in a tree. It is made of grass, dead leaves and moss, and in it stores of seeds and other food are laid up for winter consumption.

There is no recent information available on the life-history or habits of this species; even the length and time of the breeding season are not definitely known. Young have been recorded as being born in May, but litters are commonly found until September or later. It is probable that breeding extends throughout the summer and that several litters are produced, but the frequency with which late litters have been recorded lends some support to the suggestion that the peak of the breeding season falls late in the year. Gestation is said to last four weeks, rather a long time for so small an animal, and litters ranging in number from two to seven have been noted. Nothing is known of the moults of the species, but Miller[161] speaks of a specimen in "full, rich winter pelage," thereby implying that there is an autumn moult.

The dormouse is our only native rodent to hibernate. In the autumn it becomes very fat, and retires into its winter nest. There it rolls up into a ball, the head being bent down so that the chin rests on the belly. The hind feet are curled up forwards about level with the nose, and the hands, clenched into fists, are held either under the chin or alongside the nose. The eyes and mouth are tightly closed, the ears folded back downwards close to the surface of the head, and the tail is tucked forwards between the legs, its tip wrapping over the face and back (Pl. XXVIIa, p. 196). As it sinks into torpidity, the respiration-rate and heart-rate fall, the temperature sinks so low that the animal feels cold to the touch, and the muscles become so rigid that the creature can be rolled along a flat surface without disturbing its pose. When torpid, the mechanism that controls the temperature of the body is altered; the animal in effect becomes cold-blooded and the whole metabolism slows down.

Dormice hibernate from September to April but their sleep is not necessarily uninterrupted, for they may wake up occasionally and eat some of the store laid up in the nest; the longest recorded period of continuous sleep is six months and twenty-three days. The low rate of metabolism during the torpid period is maintained by slowly using up the fat that was accumulated during the autumn; on awakening in the spring the weight of the animal may be little more than half of what it was when hibernation started. The onset of hibernation appears to be brought about by the accumulation of fat, for neither low temperature, length of daylight, nor scarcity of food are believed to affect its beginning; in some tropical mammals, which aestivate during the dry season, the accumulation of fat is known to be one of the causes of torpidity, and the mechanism in the dormouse is probably similar. But the dormouse evidently has a general predisposition to this retarding of the metabolism, for when it sleeps in the summer its temperature drops several degrees, and it thus even then approaches the torpid state. Nothing is known definitely about the natural life span in this animal, but as it spends nearly six months of the year only just on the right side of the borderline between life and death, it probably enjoys a longer total lifetime than most small mammals of comparable size, living for perhaps two or three years.

In addition to our native dormouse another, alien, species is now a member of the British fauna: this is the continental fat dormouse, *Glis glis* (Linnaeus), the species that the Romans fattened for the table (Pl. XXVIIb, p. 196). It has been introduced, and is now fairly common in a limited area; it and several subspecies are distributed throughout central and southern Europe. It is a large dormouse, the head and body reaching a length of 6 to 7 inches, the tail 6 to 6¼ inches. It is very squirrel-like in appearance, the tail being densely haired; but the tail is peculiarly brittle, the end of it being easily broken off, as it is in lizards, especially if the animal is seized by it. The eye is large, the ear small; the colour of the fur is greyish above, white or yellowish below, that on the tail being darkest.

The fat dormouse is nocturnal, and lives in woods and gardens, climbing about in low trees and bushes, where it is very agile and takes astonishing jumps; it rarely descends to the ground, though it sometimes comes into houses in the country, where it can be very noisy, pattering about in attics. The nest, built of vegetable fibres and moss, is placed in a hollow tree, in a crevice behind ivy or some similar place. The food consists of berries, nuts, seeds, fruits and insects; it is said also to include small birds. In the autumn the species becomes excessively fat before hibernating; like the common dormouse it evidently wakes occasionally from hibernation during the winter, for it lays up winter stores in the nest. Breeding is said to occur in June, and the litter to consist of from two to four young, but no detailed or exact recent observations on these points, as of many others in its natural history, have been recorded.

About 1890 some examples of the fat dormouse were liberated by the late Lord Rothschild near Tring in Hertfordshire. From this beginning the species has become established in parts of Hertfordshire and Buckinghamshire, where it appears to be increasing, but it has not made a spectacular invasion of the country as has the grey squirrel. One was found in Shropshire in 1941, but it is difficult to believe that the animal had got so far from headquarters entirely by its own efforts; its journey was probably assisted, either unwittingly or on purpose, by man. It will be interesting to see to what extent this species is able to colonise the land in the future.

The Sciuromorpha differ from the Myomorpha in many anatomical characters, of which the premolars, preceded by milk teeth, have already been mentioned (p. 128), but the most important distinguishing feature is the arrangement of the muscles of mastication, and the modifications in the form of the skull connected with it. In this suborder the infra-orbital canal does not serve as a passage for any part of these muscles (masseter), in the Myomorpha, and still more in the Hystricomorpha, it does; the Sciuromorpha are regarded as the least

Plate 9 DORMOUSE

John Markham

specialised of the rodents, but the simple character of the infra-orbital canal is not necessarily primitive, and there are grounds for believing that its simplicity is secondary, having been derived from a more complicated pattern. The simplicity therefore does not carry the implication that the Sciuromorpha are ancestral to the other sub-orders of rodents whose interrelations are very obscure. On this subject Simpson[190] says, "Their [rodent's] relationships are involved in an in-tricate web of convergence, divergence, parallelism, and other tax-onomic pitfalls. Their great numbers, their marked mutability and variability, their spread over almost every conceivable environment, their remarkable adaptability, the shortness of their generations, their usual great fertility with overpopulation and severe mortality, and other factors give them the possibility of exceptionally rapid evolution and of phyletic connections remarkably difficult to retrace."

If we exclude the extinct beaver, there is only one native species representing this suborder in Britain, the common or red squirrel, (*Sciurus vulgaris*), which is widely distributed throughout the wooded parts of Europe from the northern edge of tree growth to the Mediter-ranean, and from Ireland into Asia. The species is subject to much geographical variation, and there are no less than twelve named sub-species inhabiting western Europe alone; it is therefore not surprising to find that the squirrels of the British Isles have differentiated to form a subspecies peculiar to the islands. This subspecies is called *Sciurus vulgaris leucourus* Kerr, and differs from all the other subspecies in the light, at times almost white, colour of its tail (Pl. 10, p. 208). On the continent the squirrel has two colour phases, one predominantly red, the other very dark brown, usually called black. The northern sub-species belong to the red phase, the southern ones to the dark; in the races inhabiting intermediate territories both phases occur within a single subspecies, some individuals belonging to one phase, some to the other, the proportions of each phase varying with latitude. *S. v. leucourus* contains only the rufous phase, animals of the dark phase being unknown in this subspecies. This dimorphism in the colour of the squirrel on the continent shows that in general the colour of each form, or some physiological peculiarities associated with it, is pre-served through natural selection by the climates or other ecological factors of the various regions inhabited. The pressure of natural selection acts most rigorously against opposite types at the opposite extremes of the range. If the dark phase ever came into this country

when squirrels first inhabited it the environment has completely
eliminated the dark in favour of the light.

The range of the red squirrel covers the whole of England and
Wales, and formerly included Scotland and Ireland, wherever there
are woods, especially woods of conifers. The numbers of the species
have undergone great fluctuation both in historic and recent times,
and are now considerably less than they were half a century ago,
over most of England and Wales. In Scotland the squirrel is believed
to have become practically extinct by the beginning of the nineteenth
century, but since that time it has been introduced again in many
places, so that it has a wide if somewhat sporadic distribution in suitable
localities, and is common in some of them, having spread along the
valleys from the centres of introduction; it is just possible that it was
never completely exterminated and that some of those now living are
descended from the aboriginal stock. In Ireland the squirrel was
exterminated long ago, perhaps sometime in the sixteenth century,
but it was introduced again early in the nineteenth century, since
when it has flourished so that it is now abundant where there are
woods. At the present time the red squirrel is widely spread through
England and Wales, and is not nearly so scarce as has frequently
been stated. It occurs in greater or less abundance over the whole of
the eastern, western and northern counties, except in the most thickly
populated industrial districts; but it is scarce or absent from a tract
of country extending northwards from the sea-coasts of eastern Hampshire and Sussex, through the midlands, and swinging northeast from
Warwickshire to the Wash. The density of the squirrel population
thus varies considerably from place to place, and though the species is
widely but rather thinly distributed, it appears to be increasing in
many places, and is most plentiful in south-west Wales, and the
north.[189]

Apart from the fluctuations of the squirrel population in the distant
past, as in Scotland and Ireland, there was a great decrease in its
size in the decade 1904–14, followed by a considerable recovery in the
1920's. The decrease, contrary to popular belief, is said by the best
authorities[145] to have been quite unconnected with the spread in the
range of the grey squirrel, for there is very little reliable evidence of
any antagonism or competition between the two species. Occasionally
fights between red and grey squirrels have been seen,[111] but then individuals of both species fight amongst themselves, especially in the

spring; encounters between the species therefore, cannot be held to prove a deep-rooted antagonism. The cause of the decrease in the red squirrel is quite unknown; epidemic disease has been suggested, but there is no evidence on the point one way or the other. Where the ranges of the red and grey squirrels overlap the two species exist side by side without apparently interfering with each other; but there is some indication that after an area has been colonised by the grey squirrel for about fifteen years the numbers of the red squirrel begin to decline;[189] time alone can confirm or refute this suggestion. It would appear unlikely that an animal so catholic in its diet, so active and well able to look after itself, would decrease greatly in numbers, in the absence of any indication of epidemic disease, in an environment that had not obviously changed; it is possible, then, that the decrease was part of some long-term cycle comparable with that which occurs with a shorter period in some of the voles, though a cycle longer than ten or eleven years appears to be improbable in an animal no larger than the red squirrel. If a downward phase in the cycle of numbers happened to coincide with the spread of the grey squirrel, the impression might well be given that the increase of the latter was the cause of the decrease of the former.

Perhaps the most characteristic feature of the squirrel is its long and bushy tail, almost equalling in length that of the head and body (8 to 8½ inches). It is thickly furred, the long hairs being directed outwards and backwards so that the bushiness is concentrated at each side, and the tail as a whole appears flattened from the upper to the under surface. There is a growth of long hairs also on the outer surface of the ears, so that they are conspicuously tufted, except in the late summer and autumn when the tufts are lost. There are two moults yearly, a complete one in the autumn, and a partial one in the spring, affecting all the pelage except the tail and the ear-tufts. The winter coat, acquired at the autumn moult, is long and soft, brownish-grey in colour on the back, rufous on the limbs, white or creamy on the under surface; the palms of the hands and the soles of the feet are hairy in winter. At the spring moult this coat is lost and the summer coat, which is much shorter than the winter one, is rich rufous in colour on the back and limbs, the underside being again white or creamy; but the palms and soles are now naked.

At the autumn moult the tail becomes bushy and is a dark buffy-brown in colour. The colour of the tail at once starts to fade, beginning

at the tip, the process of fading extending towards the root, which is
reached about May, when the whole tail is light cream or almost
white. In the spring not only does the tail fade, but the bushy hairs
gradually wear away and fall out, so that by the autumn the tail
appears quite sparse and thin. Before all the white hairs are shed the
new dark winter hairs start to grow, first at the root and then progressively to the tip. Like the hairs of the tail, those of the rest of the
winter coat start to fade almost as soon as it has grown, but this
pelage never becomes bleached to near-white like the tail, for the hair
is replaced at the spring moult before this can occur. The ear-tufts
which grow at the autumn moult are dark brown, and they too, fade
to a cream or a straw colour by the summer, and then fall out, so that
the ears are tuftless during the late summer and autumn. The spring
moult is a gradual process that produces much variation between
individuals during early summer, some showing the full summer
coloration while others are still very grizzled from retaining parts of
the old winter coat.

The bleaching takes place only in those hairs of the coat that
contain the darker brown pigment, and does not affect those containing rufous pigment only. The bleaching is caused by a definite
change in the colour of the hairs, and not by a replacement with new
white hair, as occurs in the mammals that turn white in winter.
The nature of this bleaching process is quite unknown, but the pigment that fades must be very unstable, or the rate at which it bleaches
must be very variable, for Hinton[14] states that young of the first litter
have bushy tails and dark ear-tufts, but that those of the second litter
have not. He quotes an observer who found "young in the nest with
bleached tails and ear-tufts"; if this observation is not erroneous the
bleaching must take place with great rapidity. The bleaching of the
tail practically to whiteness is peculiar to *S. v. leucourus*, and distinguishes it from all the other subspecies.

In habits the squirrel is arboreal, but is not confined to woods of
large trees, though it shows a preference for those of some years'
growth; nevertheless it spends much of its time foraging on the ground.
It shows great agility in leaping from branch to branch, and obtains
some aid from the flattened tail and outstretched limbs as planes
when making a lengthy jump. The red squirrel is cautious up to a
point; if disturbed on the ground it generally runs up into a tree,
keeping on the far side, but having reached a certain height it will

often allow itself to be seen, and even draw attention to itself by its angry chattering cry as it inspects the cause of its alarm. Squirrels are also good swimmers and are known to cross rivers and lakes of considerable width, up to half a mile or more. The food consists of almost anything vegetable from the bark and buds of trees to seeds, fruit, nuts, and fungi; it also includes insects and the eggs and nestlings of birds. Squirrels are destructive pests in plantations of conifers, for not content with pine-cones, the seeds of which are an important part of their diet, they eat the bark off the leading shoots of the trees, thereby deforming them and ruining them for the production of straight timber.

Nothing is recorded of the territorial habits and home range of the squirrel, though doubtless squirrels do have individual territories which centre round the nest, technically known as the 'dray' or 'drey'. This is built high in a tree, of twigs and sticks and is lined with leaves, bark-fibre and moss, wool and feathers; sometimes it is placed inside a hollow tree. When built among tree branches the dray is domed, being somewhat like a magpie's nest in shape and size, but it has no definite entrance, the animals pushing their way in or out through the sides. The female is said to pluck the fur from her belly to make a lining for the dray before the birth of a litter. The dray is not only a nursery for the young but also a home throughout the year, and each animal is said to own more than one, but precise information is lacking on the point.

Our knowledge of the breeding activities of the red squirrel is very incomplete, but some results of a preliminary investigation have appeared.[180] These show that the breeding season, as demonstrated by the times of occurrence of pregnant females, is long, and lasts from December throughout the winter and summer to August or September; nursing mothers were found in all months from February to September inclusive. The figures also hint at the possibility of there being two peaks of breeding in the season, one from late December to April, the other in July to September, separated by a lull in May. The evidence available also points to the probability of a short period of quiescence occurring in October and November. If these indications should be confirmed, it will probably be found that the animals bearing litters during the first peak of the season are the adults over a year old, and that some of the litters produced during the second peak are those of the young of the previous year breeding for the first time, and that others are the second litters of the season of the older adults. The males also have a long breeding season, being fertile at least from November to July inclusive; it is not known whether they have a short infertile season in the early autumn, but it is possible that they do. The average litter-size appears to be about three, but the variation is considerable, and litters ranging from one to six have been recorded. Gestation is said to be from four to five weeks, and the young leave the nest when a few weeks old; but no exact data are available on these matters, or on whether the animals are monogamous, as has been claimed.

The red squirrel does not hibernate, but is out and about in the severest winter weather. In the autumn, from the beginning of October onwards, the animals store up food for winter use, burying such things as acorns and nuts in the ground. When engaged on this task they pick up a nut and run with it for some distance, and then bury it without hesitation as though the place were already decided. They will repeat this many times, using a different place for each nut, pushing it below the surface of soft earth or moss, and smoothing the spot with the hands. Although the action looks very purposeful, and the animals give the appearance of knowing exactly where they are going to bury the food, it is probably quite 'automatic' and directed without intelligence, for they seem to have no memory of the exact places, and appear to rediscover the stores merely by accident when foraging about.[41]

In addition to the red squirrel, we have now to reckon the introduced American grey squirrel, *Sciurus carolinensis* Gmelin, as an established member of our fauna. In form this species is much like a larger red squirrel, without ear-tufts or bushiness of tail, the length of the head and body being from 11 to 11½ inches; it is a speckled grey above and white below (Pl. 11, p. 213). A dark, melanic, variety occurs occasionally, and may be getting commoner in some places. The species is a native of eastern North America, where it has been divided into a number of subspecies in the different parts of its extensive range. It has been liberated in many parts of the British Isles at different times during the last seventy years, and from most of the centres of introduction it has spread, so that its range now covers a large part of the country.[145] One of the largest and most effective introductions was at Woburn in Bedfordshire, towards the end of the last century. By 1914 it was numerous and spreading in that county, in Buckinghamshire and in parts of Hertfordshire. Stock was taken from the Woburn colony and liberated in many other parts, notably in Yorkshire and in several districts in and near London. An early introduction was made into Scotland, in Dumbartonshire, and was followed by others in widely separated places; another was made into central Ireland, in county Longford.

During the nineteen-twenties the grey squirrel made a great increase in numbers and a rapid extension of its range, the spread being always westward and north-west from the main centres of distribution. It reached a high density in many places during 1929 and 1930, but in the winter of 1930–31 there was a great decrease everywhere, which may perhaps have been due to an epidemic, for some evidences of disease were found among the animals. There may also have been some lack of food during that winter, though an animal so omnivorous as the grey squirrel should have had little difficulty in finding enough. By that time, too, the destructiveness of the species had become realised, and it was suffering much persecution at the hands of farmers, foresters, gamekeepers, gardeners and others. Whatever the cause, its numbers reached a low level in 1932, since when there has been a rapid increase everywhere, in spite of the shooting and trapping to which it has been subjected; no further signs of epidemic disease have been noted. A peculiar point about the spread of the species is that, although it goes on steadily westwards, there has been no extension in the opposite direction into East Anglia, where for some unknown reason it does not thrive, separate introductions that have been made in the district having failed to become established.

The present distribution of the grey squirrel extends along the south coast from the east of Kent to the borders of Dorset, and thence as a broad tract trending northwest through the home counties and the midlands, thinning out north of Staffordshire, but increasing in density again in Cheshire and southern Lancashire. The western boundary of this area passes through Dorset and Somerset and rests on the Marches of Wales, while the eastern runs through the western parts of Essex, Cambridgeshire and Lincolnshire. An empty belt separates this area from the population that covers nearly the whole of Yorkshire and extends into parts of Durham. In the south-west there are sporadic colonies throughout Devonshire, the country round Exeter, where an introduction was made, being specially infested. The distribution in Scotland is less well ascertained, but the species is known to be present in several districts in addition to the original area in Dumbartonshire. The grey squirrel appears now to be increasing practically everywhere, even in the face of the widespread control measures being taken against it, through which very large numbers, running into many thousands, are killed annually throughout its range.[145, 164, 189]

In habits the grey squirrel is very similar to the red, but it shows perhaps less preference for coniferous woods, favouring especially woods containing beech trees.[45] In diet it is, if possible, even more omnivorous than its smaller relation, eating anything vegetable from buds and shoots of trees to fruit, nuts, and seeds; it is very destructive to the smaller birds, eating both eggs and young, and the adults too if it can catch them. This species constructs a domed nest much like the dray of the red squirrel, among the branches of trees high above the ground (Pl. XXVIII, p. 197). It does not hibernate, but remains active throughout the winter, as may be seen in many city parks where it has become very tame through being fed by the public.

It is peculiar that the breeding habits of this alien introduced species, like many other particulars of its biology, are much better known than those of our native species; transatlantic importations seem often to attract considerable attention. The breeding season lasts from the end of January to August, there being two peaks in its intensity, the first in April, the second in June to July.[57] The litters born during the first half of the season are those of the adults over a year old; of those born during the second half, some are those of the younger adults which were born in the previous year, and others are the second litters of the season from the older adults. It is unlikely that any of the young, even of the earliest litters, breed in the year of their birth; but some of those from first litters may breed in the first half of the following season, though the majority do not breed for the first time until the second half. Some at least, possibly the majority, of the older adults breed twice in the same year, but as there is no oestrus period immediately following the birth of a litter, the females do not become pregnant for the second time until after the first litter has been weaned. There is in consequence a lull in the intensity of breeding during May, separating the two peaks of the season, and no pregnant females have been found during this period. During the six months from August to January inclusive there is no breeding, and it is therefore surprising to find that the males, or some of them,

Black-and-white photograph by M. S. Wood, coloured

Plate 10 RED SQUIRREL

are fertile at all times during the twelve months. Individuals may pass through periods of sexual inactivity, but there is no season in the year when all the males are out of breeding condition. It is probable that the males do not reach sexual maturity until their second year. The length of gestation is not known, but the average size of the litter is just under 3¾ young, which are born blind and hairless. Because of the sexually quiescent state of the females while nursing their young, there is an interval of about three months between successive litters of the year.

None of the Hystricomorpha is native to this country, but one imported species has gained a foothold, in more than one place, as a result of animals escaping from captivity. This is the coypu, *Myocastor coypus* (Molina), and unless it is deliberately exterminated by man, there appears to be no reason why it should not become permanently established. The coypu is a large rat-like rodent, with a rather large head, a blunt snout bearing long whiskers, small ears, and webbed hind feet (Pl. XXb, p. 165). Full-grown adults are about two feet long from snout-tip to tail-root; the tail, which is nearly naked and scaly like that of the rat, is a little less than 18 inches long; the usual weight of the adult ranges from about five pounds to twenty, and considerably greater weights have been recorded.[120] The enamel of the incisor teeth is dark orange in colour; a similar pigmentation of the teeth occurs in many other rodents. The general colour is brown, the long brown guard-hairs covering the dense and soft greyish brown under-fur, which is the 'nutria' of commerce. The coypu is a native of south America where it is widely distributed over the continent south of the tropic, and where several geographical subspecies have been distinguished. It is a semi-aquatic animal, inhabiting swamps and the reedy banks of rivers and lakes, where it feeds almost exclusively upon aquatic vegetation.

In the nineteen-twenties the new venture of fur-farming attracted much attention in this country, and the coypu was one of the animals that were imported to be bred for their pelts. It is a species that takes easily to captivity, breeds well, and withstands any amount of winter cold without damage, so it is perhaps not surprising that between 1929 and 1939 nearly fifty farms throughout England and Scotland were raising coypu.[225] Inevitably there were escapes, and sporadic occurrences of coypu were reported from many places; in some localities small colonies became established from time to time, but only in two has a permanent settlement been achieved. One of these is on and around a large sewage farm near Slough, and the other in Norfolk, not as might be expected, in the extensive system of broads connected with the river Bure, but in the river Yare and its tributaries, from far above Norwich nearly down to the sea.[120] When the existence of these colonies became known it was feared, particularly in Norfolk, that the animals might prove as destructive as the musk-rat, or more so because of their larger size. In the event, however, this has not turned out to be the case; the damage done has not been very great, and has consisted mostly of raids on crops of sugar-beet and on vegetable gardens. The burrows that the animals make in the banks of rivers, though large in diameter, are not of any great length, a few feet only, and damage to the banks similar to that done by the musk-rat has not occurred. However, control measures were undertaken, and about two hundred were killed in a little over two years; but the animals were not exterminated, and it is probable that they are spreading. As a result of the campaign the Oxford Bureau of Animal Population was able to make investigations on the biology of the coypu in England, and an interesting report on the subject was published by Laurie,[120] from which some of these particulars are taken.

The chief damage done is to reed-beds and aquatic vegetation; the beds of reeds and reed-mace are damaged by being trampled down, as well as by being used as food. Some people have even maintained that the coypu is beneficial in keeping down the luxuriant marsh vegetation, and in helping to keep the ditches clear. The damage is largely to some of the aesthetic amenities of the region, but if the animal becomes at all plentiful it will undoubtedly alter the ecological relationships of much of the flora, and with it of the fauna. In France and Germany, where there have been many escapes of coypu, and a quite extensive acclimatisation, it is not regarded as a pest; indeed, in France one eminent writer has suggested that it is welcome as a new game animal.[23] The coypu is active a good deal by day as well as by night, and comes foraging on land very frequently; because of these habits, and its large size, it is fairly easily seen and shot, a proceeding that is aided by its rather unwary nature.

In addition to burrows, the coypu makes large nests of reeds and other vegetation on comparatively dry land in the reed-swamps, and in these, sometimes at least, the young are born. The latter are very precocious and have been noted as leaving the nest, swimming, and feeding on plants, as early as twenty-four hours after birth. They grow rapidly and reach a weight of four to five pounds at the age of about five months, when they become capable of breeding. But their growth continues for a long time, probably for some years, hence the great weights, of twenty pounds and more, attained by the old ones. Gestation lasts from 120 to 130 days, and the average size of the litter is five young, though as many as nine have been found in Norfolk, and eleven in south America.[5] The females have at least two litters a year, and breeding is not confined to any particular season but goes on all the time. In captivity the coypu has been known to reach the age of twelve years; as the feral animals in Britain have no natural enemies once they are adult, and can very well defend themselves with their teeth, they may be expected to have several years' expectation of life. The teats of the female project from the flanks nearer the back than the belly, and the young are said to suckle while being transported on the back of the mother when swimming, an arrangement that would appear to be hardly necessary in view of the precocious feeding habits of the young noted above. Coypu are sometimes shown in fairs, being exhibited under the title of 'giant sewer-rat' (or, during the war, 'giant rat, caught in the Blitz'), lurid paintings of them resisting capture beneath the foundations of London or Liverpool being used by the 'barker' to lend an air of verisimilitude to his story.

CHAPTER 8

BEASTS OF PREY
(CARNIVORA: FISSIPEDIA)

"You must know that the Great Khan has many leopards, all
excellent for the chase and for catching game. He also has a
large number of lynxes trained to hunt, and very good for the
chase. He has many very big lions too . . . . They are trained
to take wild boars, wild oxen, bears, wild asses, stags, fallow-
deer and other beasts."

MARCO POLO, *Travels*

THE CARNIVORA are typically the flesh-eating mammals, but though
many of them are highly specialised for a diet of animal matter
by no means all of them are; some indeed, notably the giant panda,
make use of a large proportion of vegetable food. The order of carnivores is divided into two parts, the Pinnipedia ('fin-footed') containing the seals and sea-lions, and the Fissipedia ('split-footed')
containing all the others. The Pinnipedia, being very specialised for
an aquatic life and having many features of peculiar interest, form the
subject of the next chapter; the present one is devoted entirely to the
Fissipedia.

The Fissipedia, as their name implies, are land carnivores whose
feet are provided with toes of which there may be five on each foot
though the number is often reduced, especially on the hind feet. The
toes are provided with claws, the structure of which reaches a high
degree of complexity in some species. The teeth of the carnivores are
characteristic in shape and arrangement, in correlation with the diet
of flesh; the full complement of incisors is present (3/3), the canines
are large, but the cheek-teeth are reduced in number and some of them
are highly modified as flesh- and bone-cuters. Most carnivores, and
particularly those whose diet includes little besides animal matter,
do not chew their food; they merely cut it into lumps small enough

Plate 11 GREY SQUIRREL   *John Markham*

to be swallowed. Correlated with this habit is the form of the jaw-joint which allows of an up-and-down hinge movement but not of a transverse one, so that the food can be chopped up, or even crushed in some species, but cannot be ground or triturated. The digestive tract is adapted for dealing with food thus received in lumps, as is well shown in the case of old dogs which have lost all their teeth but get along quite comfortably provided that their food is cut up for them into pieces small enough to be conveniently swallowed. But even a dog with a full set of teeth bolts his food—"wolfs it"—merely cutting up the larger pieces and swallowing all the lumps whole.

Cutting up meat and bone, and seizing living prey and tearing it to pieces require large and strong jaw-muscles that in turn need a large area of bone for their attachment. In consequence the skull of an adult carnivore usually shows a great development of ridges that afford an increased surface for the anchoring of the muscles that work the jaws. These muscles are attached to the side of the skull in the region of the temples, and the surface is increased by the presence of a ridge along the centre line of the hinder part of the skull, and of transverse ones running outwards from the centre above the occiput (fig. 63, p. 214). These ridges can easily be felt on the head of any adult dog.

The brain of a carnivore is large in proportion to the size of the animal, and the surface of the cerebral hemispheres is convoluted so that the area of the outermost layer, where most of the cell-bodies are concentrated, is much increased. Correlated with the large and well-developed brain a high degree of intelligence is found in many carnivores—the fox is proverbially cunning and crafty—and the senses of sight, hearing and smell are acute. And this is scarcely surprising in animals that depend for their livelihood upon catching others that are perpetually on the alert; they live by their wits and need to keep their wits—pretty sharp ones too—about them. There is something about the mental development of the carnivores that makes many of them peculiarly apt for domestication; in addition to dogs and cats, badgers, foxes and many other species throughout the world are easily domesticated if brought up from an early age by man. The friendly responsiveness to human approaches, and the obvious pleasure that domestic carnivores take in the company of man place them on a plane widely separated from that occupied by the other domestic animals. Indeed their behaviour is such that most people are unable

M.   P to resist attributing a higher degree of intelligence and understanding to their pets than is really justified. Nevertheless one may well believe that the simpler mental processes and the emotions of man are in some ways paralleled by those of the carnivores.

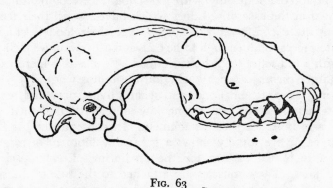

FIG. 63
Skull of badger showing the bony crests extending along the centre ridge the hind end and thence down towards the ear hole

The relation between man and the domestic carnivores differs in a further point from that between man and the other domestic animals, the ungulates, that have been domesticated by conquest, capture and slavery. There is no slavery about the carnivores; they have not been conquered, but have given themselves up, and the partnership is entirely voluntary. The dog, which is at least in part descended from the wolf, undoubtedly became domesticated by degrees, first as camp-follower, then as hanger-on, finally as a dependant of man, the process having been continuous for many thousand years and having started in late palaeolithic times. Something similar probably occurred with the cat, not the wild-cat of northern Europe, but another species native to north Africa.

A feature common to all the fissipede carnivores is the possession of what are euphemistically called scent-glands, but more frequently deserve the name of stink-glands; the polecat, in which they are particularly well-developed, is proverbial for its foul odour, and one of the reasons why the fox is the traditional object of the chase is that it leaves such a plain and unmistakable trail with the scent that emanates from these glands. The scent-glands are modified sebaceous glands, skin-glands are present in nearly all mammals

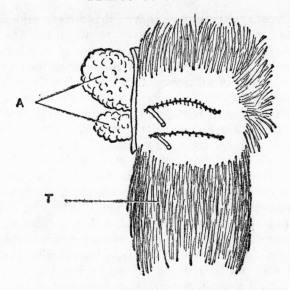

FIG. 64

Dissection to show the anal glands, A, of the badger. A probe is inserted
into the tube leading from the glands of the right side. The upper ones
open at the edge of the anus, the lower ones into a pocket under the root
of the tail, T

and produce a greasy secretion to keep the surface of the skin supple
and the hair waterproof. The stink glands are usually paired, and lie
one on each side of the vent beneath the root of the tail; they may
open separately or they may both open into a pouch in which the
secretion accumulates (fig. 64).

The odour of the secretion is nearly always offensive to human
nostrils and may be completely overpowering as in the skunk, though
occasionally it is pleasing and may even be used in perfumery, as in
the civets. But tastes differ, and odours that may be highly disgust-
ing to man may be delicious to carnivores; one need only remember
how a newly washed dog will delight in rolling in some awful carrion,
or how attractive cats appear to find the unpleasant smell of the drug
valerian. The use of the glands in wild carnivores is normally twofold.
First the scent lays a trail that enables the two sexes to find each
other (it must be remembered that many carnivores live solitary
lives for the greater part of the time), or enables the pack to keep

together in those species, such as wolves, that are gregarious. Secondly it marks out a territory and serves to warn off any trespasser who comes poaching on the hunting grounds of another. In a few instances, as in the skunks where the stink-glands have evolved to a truly awful degree of efficiency, they serve directly to protect the animal from interference by others. Such animals are conspicuously marked with black and white, and have the underside dark so that there is no countershading, a coloration that advertises their whereabouts and warns other creatures not to molest them. This protection gives them such confidence that they show no fear of others, or even man. It is, perhaps, fortunate both for dog and man that the canine scent-glands are not large nor their secretion unduly obvious. The tom cat is, however, notorious for the way in which he can make use of his. The scent-glands are invested with a muscular coat whose pressure squeezes out the secretion. In many carnivores, for example in the badger, the discharge of the secretion is under the control of the animal and can be released or withheld at will, but in others, as in the fox, the scent appears to be released more or less continuously.

These peculiar odours which the carnivores carry about with them are far from blunting the acuteness of their sense of smell, for in very many of them the olfactory is the most important of the senses and is the chief path by which the animal becomes aware of its environment. The badger is a good example; if one remains absolutely still in a suitable place down wind from a badger set at dusk it is possible for a badger to approach within a few feet or even inches without becoming aware of one's presence. If one makes a slight sound the animal immediately stops its activity and stands still, testing the air with its nose in all directions; if the wind remains steady the animal is soon reassured and continues its foraging. But should it get wind of the watcher it immediately panics and rushes back to the set, often not daring to reappear for an hour or more. When suddenly frightened like this the badger will often release the secretion of the scent-glands, the action probably being reflex and quite involuntary; it is possible that this may serve as a warning of danger to any other badgers that happen to be within range. Many carnivores, of course, hunt their prey entirely by scent until the very last stages of the chase when they close in and seize it, and such animals must live in a world of scents quite unimaginable to human beings.

Fox

Plate XXIX

Plate XXX   *Arthur Brook*

Badgers foraging in a Welsh wood

But some carnivores, especially the cats and their close relatives, do not rely so largely upon the sense of smell. One has only to watch a cat hunting field-mice in long grass to see that in them the sense of hearing is the most important and that sight runs it a close second. The ears of the cat are enormous hearing trumpets, their great size in relation to the size of the animal being obscured by the length of the fur; this acuteness of hearing is undoubtedly correlated with the nocturnal habits of the animal. But sight, too, is highly important, the eyes being large and placed so that they both look forward and give a large degree of binocular vision. The size and form of the eye are also related to the habit of nocturnal prowling; in bright light the pupil contracts to a narrow slit, but at night it expands to a large circular aperture to take the utmost advantage of low illumination. There is however no truth whatever in the suggestion that the eyes of nocturnal mammals are sensitive to infra-red radiation, so that they can see mice and other small mammals by means of the radiation produced by the heat of their bodies. Were this possible the small mammals would appear as luminous objects glowing by means of the radiation which they give out. But the lens and other parts of the eye in front of the retina, the layer which is sensitive to light, absorb any infra-red rays falling upon them so that they cannot reach the retina even were it sensitive to them.[139] Further, were the retina able to respond to infra-red radiation the animal would be completely dazzled by the heat of its own body, which produces such radiation actually within the eye itself.

In the otter there is a special adaptation of the sense-organs in correlation with its aquatic habits. The use of the sense of smell is denied to it when it is hunting its prey under water, for it must keep its nostrils tightly shut to keep the water out. When hunting in clear water doubtless much of the work is done with the eyes, but the otter, like the seals, can make a living in waters which are anything but clear, and where sight can be of little help in finding prey. And as in the seals, the facial vibrissae or whiskers of the otter are long and stout, forming a conspicuous moustache. They are, further, set in well-developed pads on the sides of the snout above the lips and their inner ends are rooted in large hair-bulbs, the nerves connected to which are proportionately large. The whole apparatus forms a very sensitive tactile organ which, by responding to small turbulences and differences in pressure, almost certainly enables the animal to be aware of moving

prey at a distance without actually touching it.   The similarity of
these structures in the otter and the seal, both animals which seek
their food in the water, is perhaps an example of convergent
evolution.

The carnivores are the order of mammals that is traditionally
regarded as incompatible with the activities of man, a view that
cannot be contested for the larger species.   Not only may they be
dangerous to man himself but the damage that they do to his flocks
and herds is quite intolerable in any settled parts of the world.   For
these reasons alone the two species of more formidable carnivores
that existed in this country within historical times, the wolf and the
bear, have been exterminated.   The wolf was once numerous throughout the land and was rightly regarded as an unmitigated nuisance.
In the *Brut y Tywysogion*, the Gwentian chronicle of Caradoc of Llan-
carvon, we find it stated that in A.D. 962 King Edgar of the Saxons
"went into Gwynedd, and causing Iago, son of Idwal, to come to him,
he imposed upon him a tribute of three hundred wolves yearly, in
place of that due to him by the old law, with liberty to kill them in
any place they pleased throughout the whole island of Britain; and
so peace was established in Gwynedd.   And that tribute was paid in
Gwynedd for more than five and forty years, until not a wolf could
be found in the whole island of Britain.   After that the king of the
Saxons commuted the tribute for gold, silver and cattle, as formerly."
If this tribute were really paid for the length of time stated some
13,500 wolves would have been slaughtered, but there is some doubt
upon this point, for other versions of the account say that the tribute
was paid for not forty-five but four years, a very different matter.
Furthermore the result of this tributary payment certainly was not
the complete extermination of wolves throughout Great Britain,
though no doubt it greatly reduced their numbers in the more southern
parts of the country.   Yet another version, which gives the year as
A.D. 965, says that the tribute was "three hundred wolves yearly;
which creature was then very pernicious and destructive to England
and Wales.   This tribute being duly performed for two years, the third
year there were none to be found in any part of the Island"; a
sanguine statement that leads one to think that Iago could not have
been really trying to fulfil his obligation.

In the course of time the range of the wolf was gradually restricted
to the wilder and more northerly regions, the animals being driven

farther and farther north until the last ones were killed in Sutherland at the extreme north of Scotland. But this did not happen until nearly half-way through the eighteenth century, sometime about 1740;[96] and in Ireland the species is believed to have survived about thirty years longer.[75]

The bear was probably exterminated before the tenth century, but during the Roman occupation bears were exported alive from Britain to the Roman circuses "where they held them in great admiration."[96] The extermination of other species of large and dangerous carnivores that once inhabited this country cannot be attributed to the action of man. The hyaena, which has left such numerous remains in the cave deposits of many parts of the country, the lion, the lynx, and others became extinct in the last glaciation of the pleistocene period before the end of the great ice age. They flourished when the climate was much warmer than it has been since the final retreat of the glaciers, but had they returned when conditions improved there is no doubt that man would have successfully extirpated them at a very remote period.

The smaller carnivores that offer no direct danger to man have fared a little better and are still with us, though until recently every man's hand was against them, and even now they are subjected to great persecution. Several species that had been brought to the verge of extermination, however, have made some recovery of late years for various reasons, and it is probable that they will remain members of our fauna for the future. In general the larger the animal the worse it has fared, and in consequence our commonest carnivores are the weasel and stoat, the smallest two species. Their larger relations the polecat and marten are now very restricted in their occurrence, but the much larger otter is still fairly plentiful, perhaps partly because of its aquatic habits. Of our other larger species the fox is plentiful because it is preserved for hunting, the badger because it is a quiet animal that keeps out of harm's way and does not make itself particularly troublesome to man; but the wild cat has long been extinct throughout the country except in Scotland, chiefly north of the Great Glen.

The extermination, or near-extermination of most of our carnivores was due originally to two causes. Some of them possess pelts that were valued for their fur in bygone times; such a one was the marten, whose beautiful fur is still an article of commerce in Russia and North

America, though its numbers in this country are too small for it to be of any importance to trade. But the chief reason for the reduction in the population of carnivores has simply been the fact that any flesh-eater has traditionally been regarded as "vermin" so that anybody killing one was thought to be performing a public service. Church-warden's accounts for the seventeenth and eighteenth centuries, are full of payments made for the destruction of various species of carni-vores. One cannot help feeling that a great deal of this persecution was the outcome of the natural destructiveness of man, and the fact that some beasts were classed as vermin provided a splendid oppor-tunity for indulging it and acquiring merit at the same time. The nineteenth century, the great age of game-keeping, was also a bad time for the carnivores, for it is impossible to keep preserves filled with populations of game, far larger than the ground could naturally carry, if predators are not ruthlessly exterminated; the two are incompatible.

In the early years of the present century the marten and polecat were nearly extinct, the wild cat in little better case, the badger was regarded as scarce or even rare, and the otter uncommon except on certain rivers where it was hunted, and in parts of Scotland. There were, however, according to Millais, twenty-one packs of otter-hounds hunting in Great Britain and Ireland in 1904, so that it is evident that the otter was present in some numbers throughout the country. The fox was the only one of the larger carnivores that was abundant, and of the smaller ones the stoat and weasel alone managed to remain common in spite of the attentions of gamekeepers and others.

Since the first world war the position has greatly changed, through two main causes, the decline in game-preserving and the planting of trees over large tracts of country by the Forestry Commissioners. The first has resulted in a diminution of the campaign so long carried on against them, and the second has provided numerous congenial habitats where, far from being persecuted, they are actively encour-aged. For these reasons martens are now on the increase in certain parts of the Highlands and have even turned up spasmodically in parts of the country remote from their normal haunts. These irregular occurrences may often be the result of animals escaping from captivity, but martens are great travellers and it is possible that some of these examples are true wild animals.[140] Polecats, too, are now regarded as almost common in parts of Wales, especially in the area of mid-Wales centred upon the great Tregaron bog. Since a little before 1920 the wild cat has been increasing in the Highlands, and is now quite common in many parts of Argyllshire and Perthshire and the counties farther north.[210] Otters too have increased in numbers and are now common in many rivers throughout the land, but they are seldom seen by casual visitors to the country, for the otter is a very early riser and is an expert at keeping out of sight. Foxes, always common because preserved for hunting, which kept them within reasonable bounds during normal peace-time, increased to such an extent in many parts of the country during the 1939–45 war that farmers were forced to organise shoots to protect their fowls and lambs.

The fox is common throughout Great Britain but is absent from the Scottish isles except Skye; on the continent it occurs all over Europe. Were it not for hunting, the species would have become scarce or even exterminated in the more closely populated parts of the country, though in the mountains of Wales and Scotland, where it has always been regarded as vermin, shooting, trapping and poisoning have failed to reduce its numbers greatly. No estimate can be made of the total numbers in the country, but they are probably very much larger than would be expected. Foxes have increased greatly in Wales during the last ten years, so much that a vigorous campaign against them has been necessary, and in both the years 1947 and 1948 the fox-clubs and pest-officers of eleven counties of Wales killed no less than ten thousand foxes between them; it is scarcely to be expected that this yearly total will be maintained for long.

The badger on the other hand has been unobtrusively going about his business and flourishing for the last quarter-century and has now become a quite common animal in many places even close to large centres of population. It is abundant throughout most of England and Wales, with the exception of East Anglia, built-up areas and mountain tops; it is especially numerous in the south-west. In Scotland it is less plentiful and is scarce in some parts of the highlands, though it occurs right up to the extreme north. The species is present in all parts of Ireland, but is commonest in the south and west. The badger's feeding habits seldom bring it into conflict with man, for it generally avoids hen-stealing and contents itself with things of no interest to its human neighbours. Further, although it is very shy and very clever at avoiding observation, it is not worried by mere proximity of human activities; it is quite content to wait until everyone is safely at home in bed before it starts its nightly foraging. It is surprising how people can be quite unaware of a family of badgers living almost under their very doorstep.

In contrast to the other carnivores, weasels and especially stoats have declined in numbers rather than increased of recent years in many districts. The stoat in particular is very apt to get caught in gins set for rabbits, and in recent years there has been a great increase in the trapping of rabbits both because of their increased market value as food and because of the campaigns organised against them with official backing to reduce their numbers as pests of agriculture. A great many stoats have been incidentally and perhaps unintentionally killed in this way; so much so that in some districts, as for instance in south-west Wales, they have been locally, but probably only temporarily, completely exterminated.

From a purely utilitarian point of view the old-fashioned tradition of killing all carnivores at every opportunity was undoubtedly a mistake, and led to an enormous increase in the numbers of destructive rodents; the present scarcity of stoats and weasels in some districts is to be deplored for this reason. Those in charge of the national forests recognise the value of the carnivores in controlling the numbers of rodents, and wisely discourage destruction of predators in the areas over which they have jurisdiction. Rodents do great damage to young trees by nibbling off the bark when other food is scarce, an injury which usually results in the death of the young tree. The present abundance of the wild cat in many parts of the Highlands is largely owing to this protection, as is the interesting increase in the numbers of the marten and polecat.

All the British carnivores are fur-bearers, that is to say not only are the outer guard-hairs of their coats long and silky but the undercoat of shorter and softer hairs is dense and well developed. Some carnivores of other parts of the world are not fur-bearers for the guard-hairs are stiff and harsh and the undercoat is comparatively poorly developed; a familiar example is the lion. But the majority of carnivores are clothed in fur. This reaches its highest perfection in those species which inhabit the colder regions of the world, an obvious adaptation to the environment. Even in a temperate climate such as that of this country the winter coat of these animals is most beautiful. And the animals know it, or at least behave as though they do, for nearly all our native species are meticulous in the care that they bestow upon their toilet, and if the coat becomes disarranged are obviously uncomfortable until they have smoothed it down into its proper position again. Even the tame cat after being stroked by its closest friend immediately washes itself and arranges the fur to its fastidious requirements. A possible exception to the care of the coat is found in the badger, which perhaps more resembles the dog in this matter of attention to the toilet. A badger's coat always appears to be in good order, but he contents himself with combing it with his claws and does not carefully wash it all over with the tongue as do so many carnivores. One of the first things a badger does on emerging from the set in the evening is to have a good scratch, and a good one it certainly is; the human observer perched in concealment above him could almost imagine that he was tearing his hide to pieces, so vigorous is the use of the claws. But when all is done a good shake settles every hair into its proper place.

The fur of many species of carnivores is made valuable to man by the presence of the rich dense undercoat; this is particularly well seen in the fox, and also in some of the smaller species such as the marten, polecat and stoat. Unlike many other carnivores the fox moults its coat only once a year, the process taking some months for completion and lasting from late spring to autumn; there is considerable individual variation in the time taken, the shedding of the old coat taking from less than two months to nearly three. Shedding starts on the legs and proceeds upwards to the hindquarters, thence to the tail, back and forepart of the body. The hairs become loose, especially those of the undercoat, and fall out or are rubbed off. Almost as soon as the shedding starts the new coat begins to appear, the outer guard-hairs growing more quickly than the underfur so that by the time the old coat has completely gone the new guard-hairs are fully developed, although the new undercoat is by no means complete. As a consequence a fox's coat is not nearly so fluffy in the early autumn as it is later on in the winter because the guard-hairs lie close over the partly grown underfur. A fox in this condition produces a pelt that is known to the trade as a "flat-furred" pelt. The undercoat continues to grow as autumn passes into winter until by the turn of the year it is fully developed and is dense enough to support the guard-hairs so that they no longer lie close but stand up more vertically to the surface, producing a rich dense pelage. At the same time the pigment is withdrawn from the bases of the hairs embedded in the skin so that the flesh side of a raw pelt is changed from dark to light in colour.[89] The final stages of the growth of the underfur, after all the old coat is moulted, are known to fox-fur ranchers as the process of "priming", and when they are complete the pelt is "prime". The degree of priming that occurs appears to depend upon the climate as well as upon the genetic constitution of the animals, for Canadian silver foxes ranched in this country are said to produce pelts of a quality inferior to those raised in colder regions. It is the very practical studies of the fur-rancher that have provided the detailed knowledge of the process of moulting sketched above, the species studied being the silver fox. This is a mutant form of the red fox of North America (*Vulpes fulva*), a very close relative of the European fox, in which the moult is almost certainly very similar if not identical.[15]

The under-fur of the otter also is extremely dense, and serves a further function; in addition to keeping the animal warm, it keeps it dry. When an otter goes into the water the guard-hairs of the outer coat are immediately wetted and lie down closely over the under-fur, producing a surface that offers the least resistance to the water (Pl. XXXIII, p. 244). But the very dense under-fur carries a layer of air trapped among the hairs which are so closely set and soft that the water cannot penetrate between them. The skin of the animal thus never becomes wet at all, nor does the animal become chilled by the water however cold it may be, for there is an insulating layer of air probably at least a quarter of an inch thick all over its body. As soon as an otter climbs out on the bank the water runs off the guard-hairs and causes them to become aggregated together into small bunches so that they no longer form a smooth close coat; each bunch tapers towards its tip, giving the animal a very peculiar spiky appearance (Pl. XXXI, p. 224). If the otter does not intend to return to the water at once a vigorous shaking throws the water out of the bunched hairs so that they are quickly dried and the fluffy character of the fur is again evident. It is interesting to compare the otter with a completely aquatic mammal such as a whale; when submerged both present a perfectly smooth surface to the water so that there is the minimum resistance to movement. But the one has accomplished this by going naked and having no hair at all, the other by having the densest fur possible. Most of the land carnivores seem to object strongly to getting their fur wet, although they can swim perfectly well if they have to.

Plate XXXI

An otter listening, on the alert; it has just left the water and the wet outer fur is bunched into spiky tufts

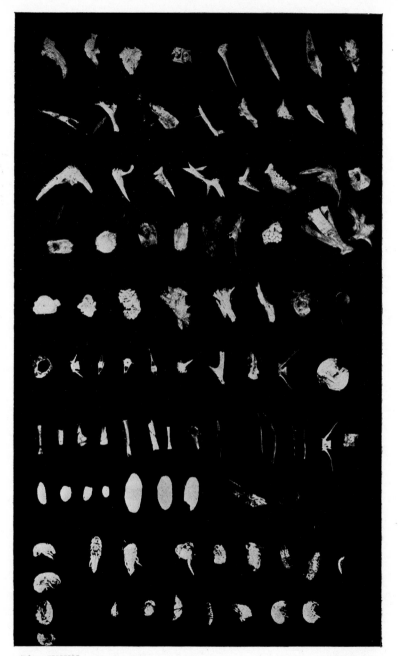

Unlike the fox, many of the carnivores have two moults each year, in spring and autumn, so that the summer and winter coats are quite distinct. This is very well exemplified in the stoat and the weasel, that in the colder parts of their ranges are white during the winter but coloured during the summer. In northern Britain nearly all the stoats become white in winter but in the south very often there is no change, or only a partial one. The change is very rare in the Irish stoat, and it never occurs in British weasels (the weasel is not found in Ireland), though it does in those of the northern and mountainous parts of the Continent. For long it was believed that the change of colour in the autumn was caused by the removal of pigment from hairs that were not lost, the removal being allegedly effected by phago-cytes migrating into the hairs from the tissues of the skin, and destroy-ing the colour. This theory is now known to be incorrect, at least for the change in stoats and weasels, where the alteration is brought about by the growth of a new coat. But it is interesting to note that one form of the Arctic fox, whose distribution is circumpolar in high latitudes, also turns white in the winter. If this species has only one moult each year, as does the common fox, then the colour-change must occur by an actual change in the existing hair. The summer coat is brown to blue-grey, but in the autumn it fades, and in many examples it be-comes pure white in the winter. In the following spring and early summer there is a moult, the white coat being lost and the new one being coloured. Observation of Arctic foxes in captivity in the Zoological Gardens at London has confirmed that the white of winter is acquired without a moult.[175] But the exact means by which this is accomplished are not known. There are two possibilities: either the pigment is removed from the hairs, or else the outer coloured ends of the hairs are worn away as the hairs grow, leaving what were formerly the white inner portions visible when the hairs grow out. This appears to be a point simple enough to elucidate, but there is no exact infor-mation available about it.

A matter that earlier observers found hard to understand in the colour-change of the stoat and weasel is the rapidity with which the change appears to take place. The explanation is that the new white coat grows underneath the old one before the latter is moulted, so that when it is finally shed the nearly full-grown white coat is re-vealed.[179] The shedding may take place very quickly so that the animal turns from coloured to white within the short space of three days. The time taken, however, depends upon the degree of cold to which the animal is subjected, for if the temperature is high the process may take as much as three weeks. The degree of cold, also, at least partly determines whether the winter coat will be white or coloured, experiments having shown that more than half the stoats exposed to cold before and during the moult turn white. Furthermore the temperatures met with during the winter affect the time of the beginning of the spring moult, which starts much earlier in southern England than in the north of Scotland or in Scandinavia. Temperature appears to have no effect on the time of the autumn moult, which always occurs in November and December, whereas the spring moult may start in February in the southern parts of the animal's range but not until much later farther north.

It is very peculiar that temperature can also have a delayed action, for if a stoat is exposed to cold in one autumn so that it turns white it will tend to turn white again in the following autumn even if the temperature is high, though very often in such a case the white hairs are suffused with a yellowish tinge. This may be the explanation of the fact that in southern England white stoats appear to be seen more often in mild winters than severe ones; in the latter they presumably escape observation because of the difficulty of seeing them against a background of snow, but in the former they are conspicuous because they are white through the influence of the change in a previous season. But temperature may not be the only factor involved, and it is quite possible that the length of daylight during the summer in northern regions also has an effect; in the north all stoats turn white in winter, and experiments have shown that temperature affects some, though not all, of the animals subjected to a low degree of cold in the autumn. In the silver fox it has been found[15] that an artificially increased amount of daily illumination during the first part of the summer alters the speed of the moult, so that animals that have experienced the longer days finish the moult sooner than those that have not, and are prime about a month earlier in the winter (fig. 65, p. 227). If day-length can produce this effect in the fox it is not unreasonable to suggest that it may also affect the stoat, though possibly in a rather different way.

There is a little experimental evidence to confirm this suggestion, and though it concerns the American weasel *Mustela cicognanii* it is doubtless not irrelevant to the European species.[22] In these experiments artificially low autumnal temperatures were not used, and there was no response to the normal temperature-range, which did not go below 50°F. But when artificial daylight of abnormal duration was used before the moult the winter coat became partly white, showing that the degree of illumination as well as that of cold can affect the winter colour. The experiment was, however, on a small scale and

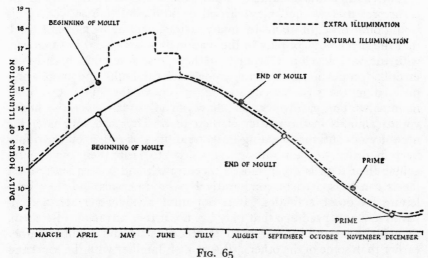

FIG. 65

Diagram to show the effect of illumination on the moult and priming of the coat in the fox. (After Basset, Pearson & Wilke[15])

could well be repeated. It should be noted, too, that in the southern parts of the stoat's range the change to white in winter is often incomplete, parts only of the winter coat being white and the rest brown. Some at least of these partly-coloured animals may be in the process of moult, for when the change is not very rapid as a result of great cold, some parts of the body may be completely white while others as yet show no sign of their approaching moult.

The colour of the summer coat is not affected by the degree of cold experienced before and during the spring moult, for it grows-in brown irrespective of temperature, though the time of the moult may be delayed by exposure to cold. There is much individual variation in the colour-response to temperature and illumination, even between brothers and sisters of the same litter, some changing colour under much less stimulus than others. When the autumn moult takes place very quickly, not only do the hairs of the old coat fall out suddenly, but the new coat grows with great rapidity; on the other hand the spring moult is a much slower process, though it may be actively hastened by the animal, for the American weasel has been noted as pulling out the loosened white hairs with its teeth.[84]

All young animals indulge in play, but it is practically only in the carnivores that we find play carried on into adult life as well. This is no doubt brought about by many factors, yet one cannot but think that the psychology of play in these animals is correlated in some way with the well-developed brain that they possess, a brain both larger in bulk (proportional to the 2/3 power of the bulk) and more complicated in the structure of its higher centres than in many other mammals. The carnivores, too, have an advantage over the herbivorous animals in the matter of their diet. They are not under the necessity of continually eating large quantities of rather un-nutritious food in order to gain sufficient material to keep their metabolism going; their food is much more concentrated, and consequently their meals can be spaced at comparatively wide intervals and they have leisure for other activities. It is not until carnivores reach a comparatively advanced age that play has no further attractions for them, though the cat and its near relatives become staid and dignified rather earlier than some of the others. Everyone is familiar with the eagerness that a dog shows for a game with its friends, human or otherwise, and a similar delight in play is found in many wild carnivores, such as the badger or otter.

Sometimes the play of adults is merely a joining in the play of the young, sometimes it has a sexual meaning when it occurs between the male and female, but at other times it appears to be merely the working-off of superfluous energy. Play in the carnivores usually consists in some form of sham fight, two or more animals wrestling with each other and chasing each other about. The badger even has regular playgrounds, both near to and at a distance from the set, where several animals gather and romp about together. The antics of the stoat are well known, and may be performed by a single individual or a group of as many as fifteen. When several are playing in company they chase each other, box and wrestle together, turn somersaults and leap several feet into the air. In addition to playing together, single stoats make use of antics such as these when hunting,

John Markham

Plate 12 VIXEN

and it is extraordinary that the intended victims do not take fright, for a stoat cutting these capers is able to approach close to feeding rabbits the nearer of which appear to be fascinated by the strange spectacle, while those at a distance take very little notice. Stoats are said to use a similar performance to get close to birds settled on the ground, making a quick dart at one when within easy distance (Pl. XXXVI, p. 249).

Otters too have a very peculiar form of play, that of tobogganing down steep banks, usually those of a river, though they do not necessarily finish up in the water. This game takes place at definite slides where the ground is worn bare, smooth, and slippery with mud by continual use, several otters playing together and taking turns in tobogganing down the slide. In winter the slides are made in the snow, or on the ice of a pond or ditch, and become very fast with use. This habit appears to be more commonly found in the American otter, but slides have been found in this country, especially in winter after a heavy fall of snow.[33]

In the frost of 1940, some observations were made in Norfolk on otter tracks in the snow (Pl. XXXIV, p. 245). Major A. Buxton wrote,[33] "They frequently rolled in the snow and wherever water rising with the tide had overflowed the ice and produced snow slush on the top of it, the otters had every few yards made slides in the slush. There was a sort of twist at the far end of each of these slides, which seemed to show that the otters had galloped and hurled themselves at the slush in a running squirming dive, probably with their legs tucked close to their bodies so as not to check the glory of the resulting slides . . . . On another occasion I followed the tracks of an otter . . . . every mound or bank in his path had been climbed for the sake of a toboggan down the other side; into every pool he had dived, and splashed and then rolled in the snow; on every slippery surface he had broken his canter with a series of dashing slides . . . . A typical slide was 10 feet long from where his nose had hit the snow to where it had left it on the curl at the far end; the slide was 8½ inches wide at the surface of the snow. It was absolutely smooth throughout with the exception of the pad marks of the hind feet landing, about 20 inches from the beginning of the slide, and the two pad marks (again of the hind feet) about 20 inches short of the end of the slide, made by the otter taking off again for the next gallop."

In at least three species of the British carnivora there is some doubt as to whether the animals now existing are pure-bred descendants of

M.   Q the original members of our fauna; these are the polecat, the fox and the wild cat, in all of which there may be some admixture of alien blood. Polecats (Pl. 14, p. 240), are found through northern Europe and Asia, and various local races have been recognised and described, but these appear to be subspecies and it is very doubtful if there is more than one good species. For long, one or more of these races have been domesticated under the name of ferret, and systematists have even gone so far as to give the ferret a separate scientific name, *Putorius furo*, though there now appears to be no valid reason for doing so. The domestic race is largely albino, this character having been fixed by selective breeding, the white colour being preferred for several reasons. Apart from fashion and the more practical point of being more easily seen in dim light, albino, or parti-coloured, strains of many wild animals, are found to be more docile and more easily domesticated than those with the typical wild coloration. But most ferrets cannot be regarded as more than partly domesticated, and throughout the centuries the number of ferrets that have escaped from captivity and returned to the wild must be enormous. Many of the escapers have interbred with wild polecats, and so in effect some of the various subspecies as well as the variations induced by domestication have become mixed in our wild population. Further, man has crossed his ferret back with wild polecats, so that the blood of the latter has been again mixed into the domestic race, producing the coloured ferrets known as "polecat-ferrets".

It has been claimed[216] that the ferret can be distinguished from the polecat by the character of the skull; in the ferret the postorbital region is constricted into a narrow "waist" whereas in the polecat this region is comparatively broad (fig. 66, p. 231). It has been suggested that this difference in the skull is produced as a result of feeding soft food to domesticated ferrets, a suggestion that may have some validity, for the skulls of many species of carnivores brought up in captivity differ considerably from those of their wild relatives. This is because the jaw-muscles are not used so vigorously and consequently do not mould the growing skull to the same extent as in wild animals of the same species. The correctness of this assertion about the ferret could be tested by examining the skulls of polecats bred and born in captivity and fed upon an unnaturally soft diet; their skulls should resemble those of the ferret.

But it has now been found that either as a result of inter-breeding or of accidents of diet, some ferrets and polecat-ferrets can have a skull in which the waist is as little constricted as in the wild polecat. Further, a subspecies of polecat has been described in which the skull has a well-marked postorbital constriction, thus resembling that of the ferret.[212] This subspecies is the polecat of the north of Scotland, which used to inhabit Sutherland, but has been very scarce for many years and may now even be extinct, for no examples are known to have been caught since about 1910.

Thus it is possible that the waist of the skull may be, in part at least, a genetic character, and not merely the result of the quality of the diet during youth, and the variation found in the ferret may be the result of interbreeding by the broad and narrow waist races. On the other hand the carnassial teeth of the ferret are usually smaller than those of the polecat, but here again it is not known if this character is genetic or a result of unnatural food.

The fox of Europe has been classified into several subspecies, one from the Iberian peninsula, one (*Vulpes vulpes crucigera*) inhabiting central Europe, and the third (*V. v. vulpes*) inhabiting Scandi-navia.

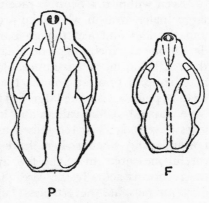

FIG. 66

Skulls of the polecat, P, and ferret, F, seen from above. That of the ferret is very narrow waisted compared with that of the polecat. The skulls of some ferrets are fully equal in size to that of the polecat

The last two are distinguished from each other by the larger size of the teeth and considerably greater dimensions of the skull in the Scandinavian race. It used to be supposed that Great Britain was inhabited only by *V. v. crucigera*; within recent years, however, it has been found that the foxes of this country do not all belong to the same subspecies. The foxes of the greater part of Great Britain and Ireland do belong to the central European race, *V. v. crucigera* (Pl. 12, p. 228). There is nevertheless a considerable amount of individual variation that may in large measure be due to the practice, which has been very widespread in the past, of turning down foxes for the purpose of maintaining stocks for hunting. Importations have been made from the continent into various parts of England, and also from one district to another within the country, especially from those parts of Scotland where foxes are vermin. And it is in those Scottish districts that the second subspecies, *Vulpes v. vulpes*, has now been recognised, the animals found there being on the average much larger than those of the more widespread subspecies and indistinguishable from the race typical of Scandinavia.

Even within this Scottish race two distinct forms are recognised, a larger paler form in which the predominant colour of the fur is red, and the legs and feet though darker are not black, and a smaller darker one in which the predominant colour is grey and dark chestnut, the red being much less noticeable.[214] The weight of the large form may be up to 17 or 19 pounds, that of the small one is generally from 12 to 15 pounds. But the large, red form is not confined, as some writers have claimed, to the valleys and lower lying country. The dark hill-foxes have long been recognised as distinguishable from those of the lowlands and some writers have stated that they are larger; but careful measurement of the few available specimens has shown that the reverse is actually the case. The skulls and teeth of the smaller grey animals are nevertheless larger than those of the subspecies *V. v. crucigera*. It has also been pointed out that all the grey specimens that have been carefully examined have been fully adult, or even old, vixens as shown by the amount of wear undergone by the teeth, and consequently it is quite possible that the greyness is primarily a result of age, and that the small size is correlated with sex, and has nothing to do with geographical distribution. Hill foxes of similar grey colour have been recorded from the higher ground of the English Lake District, but animals from this district and from the more mountainous parts of Wales have not yet been critically examined to determine whether they, too, are indistinguishable from the Scandinavnia *V. v. vulpes*.

In the wild cat there is much variation in size and in the distinctness of the marking of the coat. Some of this variability is no more than would be expected in any wild animal, but some of it is almost certainly the result of crossing with the domestic cat. The origin of the domestic cat is probably to be found not in the wild cat of northern Europe (*Felis silvestris*) but in a species inhabiting north Africa (*Felis maniculata*). However, there appears to have been a good deal of crossing between the two species since the domestication of the latter, the amount of interbreeding increasing in the more northern parts of Europe. The difference in the general appearance of the domestic cat

Plate 13 BADGER   *Ernest Neal*

of the south of Europe and that in the British Isles for instance, is striking. The former is a small, lanky, and close-furred animal, the latter much larger and more robust, having an altogether richer pelage. No exact details of the differences are available, but the general impression formed is that a cline exists with an increasing amount of true wild-cat genes the farther north one looks. But the crossing has of course taken place in two directions and the wildcat has become diluted with domestic cat genes. In spite of this, and contrary to the belief of some writers, there is no indication of any general degeneration in the robustness of the wild-cat of Scotland when compared with the remains left by its prehistoric ancestors, though individual animals may plainly show the effects of recent crossing by their small size and thinly furred tails.

It is rather in the details of its breeding physiology that the wild-cat unmistakably shows the admixture of domestic blood, provided that the information given by those writers who state that there is only one breeding season every year in the true wild-cat, is correct. In the Scottish wild-cat there are two breeding seasons yearly, one about the first half of March and the other at the end of May or in early June, the resulting litters of kittens being born in May and August respectively.[138] Occasionally, too, there is a third breeding season in the autumn, so that litters are sometimes born in the winter, in December or January. The domestic cat also normally has two breeding seasons each year, and the number is often increased to three or even four. The multiple breeding season of the Scottish wild-cat shows the close relationship of this species to the domestic cat, and occurs in specimens that show no other obvious signs of the intermixture. A statistical analysis of the measurements of the body-proportions in over a hundred Scottish wild-cats showed that the population was not homogeneous. Study of the local geographical distribution of the animals examined provided no explanation of their heterogeneous nature, which was probably due to something inherent in the population as a whole, very possibly the admixture of 'domestic' blood.[115]

The suborder Fissipedia is divided into two superfamilies, the Canoidea and the Feloidea, members of both superfamilies occurring in our fauna. The superfamilies are subdivided into families, and the animals are classified in them by the nature of their teeth among other characters. The classification is as follows :—[190]

Superfamily Canoidea
  Family Canidae   (dogs, foxes, wolves)
    „   Ursidae   (bears)
    „   Mustelidae   (stoats, weasels, polecats, martens,
                        badgers, otters)
Superfamily Feloidea
  Family Felidae   (cats)

In the first superfamily there is another family, not represented in our fauna, containing such animals as the raccoon and the panda; similarly in the second there are families containing the mongooses and their allies, and the hyaenas. The flesh-cutting teeth which are diagnostic of the fissipede carnivores consist of one in each jaw, the last (fourth) upper premolar and the first lower molar; these teeth are known as the "carnassial" teeth. In their more extreme form they are modified to form sharp blades that shear past each other, the tooth of the lower jaw lying inside that of the upper jaw when the mouth is shut. In carnivores in which the carnassials are not so highly developed the blade-like form is less pronounced, and a low cusp is present at the front of the inner side of the upper tooth. In bears the carnassials are hardly differentiated from the neighbouring teeth, and are not blade-like but carry broad crushing surfaces. This condition is probably a secondary reversion to a generalised condition, for the bears are believed to have been derived from the early dogs. The presence of carnassial teeth is associated with a deficiency in the number of the other cheek-teeth, the molars at least being always reduced in number, and often in size as well. Figure 67 on page 235 illustrates the various degrees of reduction found in the teeth of the British carnivores, the extreme being shown by the wild-cat, in which the molars are represented by one small tooth in the upper jaw only, all the others being absent. Where the first upper molar is fairly large and functional it is, in many species, wider than long, so that it appears to be set cross-wise in the tooth-row. Where any of the cheek-teeth are particularly small there is a tendency for them to be shed during the animal's lifetime, often even before it is fully adult.

There is a popular fallacy that has been current for many centuries about the jaws of the badger, according to which once a badger has seized anything it cannot be made to let go unless its jaw is dislocated. This yarn has probably arisen from the fact that the jaw-joint of the

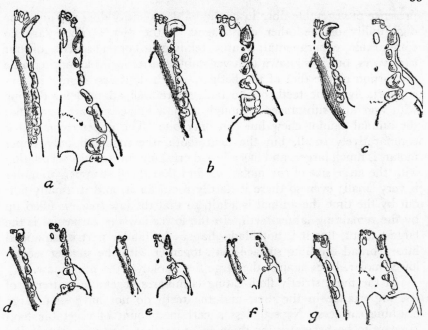

FIG. 67

Teeth of carnivores ; lower jaws to the left, upper to the right. All
on the same scale.

a, fox. *b*, badger. *c*, otter. *d*, marten. *e*, polecat. *f*, stoat. *g*, cat

badger is so constructed that the jaw cannot be dislocated without
breaking part of the socket into which it fits. The front and rear
edges of this socket, the glenoid cavity, are elongated and curved so
that they embrace the hinge, or condyle, of the lower jaw to such an
extent that even in the cleaned and dried skull the lower jaw does
not fall apart from the rest, but remains articulated. But there is no
mechanism for locking the jaws when the badger bites, and if it does
"hold on like a bull-dog", it does so merely by muscular strength and
tenacity.

Although in most carnivores the teeth, and indeed the other parts
of the digestive tract, are especially adapted to dealing with a diet of
animal matter, it by no means follows that vegetable food cannot be
digested by these animals. Experiments have shown that foxes can
digest starch even up to half the dry weight of the food, and that the

presence of vegetable fibre in considerable quantity does not alter the digestibility of the other constituents of the diet.[20] There are no comparable experimental figures relating to other species of our carnivores, but it is known that vegetable matter forms an appreciable proportion of the diet of the badger, which doubtless digests it very comfortably. The teeth of the badger are well adapted for dealing with vegetable substances, although the jaw-hinge is so arranged that the animal cannot chew but can only bite. The upper carnassial is comparatively small, but the next tooth, the first and only upper molar, is much larger, and has a broad crushing surface. In correlation with the large size of the molar we find that the first upper premolar is very small; even so there is hardly room for it, and it usually falls out by the time the animal is adult, so that the jaw space is filled up by the remaining larger teeth. In the lower jaw the carnassial is the largest tooth, but it is not blade-shaped; its hinder part is expanded into a broad crushing surface that, together with the smaller second lower molar, bites against the large first molar of the upper jaw.

In the more strictly flesh-eating carnivores vegetable matter is of less importance in the diet, and the teeth do not have such large crushing surfaces. Nevertheless a certain amount of vegetable food appears to be necessary for them in order that they may obtain the necessary B-vitamins, and it is possible that these come from the food already eaten by the herbivorous animals on which they prey; many carnivores eat the whole of the smaller animals that they kill. It is for this reason that carnivores in captivity generally thrive best when they are at least occasionally given whole animals to eat, and not kept on a perpetual diet of lumps of meat.

The reproductive processes of some carnivores are very peculiar; in many species of the family Mustelidae there occurs the phenomenon known as "delayed implantation". When this happens the egg-cells that are released from the ovary during the breeding season, and are fertilised as a result of mating, do not straight away develop into young animals, but remain dormant for a longer or shorter time after reaching merely the earliest states of differentiation. The egg-cell undergoes development only until the stage known as the "blastocyst" is reached. The blastocyst is barely the size of a pin-head, and consists of a little bag filled with fluid with a small knot of cells, the future embryo, lying just within the envelope at one side (fig. 68, p. 237). This minute object, together with other similar ones if there is to be a litter, passes into the uterus, but instead of becoming attached to the wall of the latter and rapidly growing into a new animal, it remains loose in the central space, sometimes for many months.

In this way the apparent length of the period of gestation is greatly increased, although the actual time during which active development of the embryo is going on is no more than would be expected for an animal of the size concerned. In the badger, for example, pairing occurs from the second half of July to about the end of August, but the blastocysts remain unimplanted until at least the end of the year, and active development of the embryos lasts only about eight weeks, the young being born from the end of February to the end of April.[157] The delay in development may exceptionally last even longer, and appears then to be associated with psychological factors whose mode of action is not understood. Some years ago a female badger was caught alive and brought into the stables at Badminton where she lived alone quite happily; after she had been there for nearly twelve months she produced two young ones.[17] This animal undoubtedly contained dormant blastocysts when it was made prisoner, and it is probable that the upset of being captured delayed the implantation in some way for longer than the normal period, so that gestation did not start until after the animal had quite settled down in its new home. This occurrence is interesting in showing that the blastocysts are able to survive undamaged for such a great length of time.

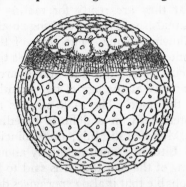

FIG. 68
Diagram to show the structure of a blastocyst.
The upper part of the hollow sphere of cells has been removed to show the knot of cells, that will later become the embryo, attached to one pole. The outer cells will form part of the wrappings of the embryo. The blastocyst is about the size of a pin-head

Delayed implantation also occurs in the stoat and probably in the marten. Both these animals breed but once a year, and practically all female stoats contain unimplanted blastocysts in every month from July to February inclusive.[54, 55] In March the blastocysts of the stoat become implanted and development starts, lasting for about a month,

and shortly after the birth of the young mating occurs. The blastocysts resulting from this mating pass into the uterus and remain
dormant there until the early months of the following year. Young
female stoats reach maturity very quickly, in about two months, so
that they are ready for mating in June and July. In these young
animals, too, the resulting blastocysts remain dormant until the
following spring. The time of the breeding season in this species is
limited not only by the female's time of receptivity for the male, which
occurs soon after the young are born or immediately on reaching
maturity at the age of two months, but also by the period of fertility
in the male. The male stoat is not fertile all the year round, but is
potent only in a definite breeding season that lasts from February
or March until July, thus coinciding with the season of the female.

Little is known definitely about the breeding of the marten, but in
view of the fact that it is said to have only one litter a year it is very
probable that it also experiences delayed implantation. This suggestion
is supported by the record of a pair of martens in captivity that
mated early in January, and whose young were not born until towards
the end of April.[150] If there is no delay this period of gestation is an
exceptionally long one for an animal of the marten's size; it is therefore
probable that delayed implantation does occur in this species, and it is
also probable that in the wild the delay is longer than that recorded for
this captive pair, whose reproductive physiology may well have become irregular from the effects of captivity. In the nearly related
American marten (*Martes americana*) delayed implantation certainly
occurs, mating taking place in July or August, but the young not being
born until the following April.[32]

In the weasel, on the other hand, breeding usually occurs twice in
each season, and there is no delayed implantation associated with it.[56]
Pregnancy can occur in any month from March to August, but it is
most common in April and May. The exact duration of pregnancy
is not known, but it is reliably estimated that pregnancy and lactation
together last about ten weeks. Soon after the first litter of the year is
born mating occurs again, but after the second litter arrives there is no
further breeding activity until the following spring, when the mating
which results in the first litter of the year takes place. The male
weasel is not fertile during the winter, his breeding season finishing in
August or September and not being resumed until the following
January.[100] Curiously enough, in two species of American weasles

(*Mustela frenata* and *M. cicognanii*) delayed implantation does occur, and in these species only one litter is born each year.[232]

In the polecat there is said to be only one litter a year, born in the spring, and the period of gestation is said to be about forty days[150]. The latter figure is probably correct, for in the ferret, which is merely a domesticated polecat, the period is forty-one to forty-three days; there is no delayed implantation in this animal and there is thus likely to be none in the polecat. But it is not at all certain that there is only a single litter a year in the polecat, for in the ferret the mating season lasts from March to August and the young are born from April to September, the later dates in both periods referring to the second litters.[92] By analogy with its domesticated relatives, then, it is to be expected that the polecat has two litters a year, and careful field observations on the subject would be welcome. Should two litters prove to be usual in this animal its breeding cycle would be in agreement with those of the other mustelids in which more than one litter is produced yearly and no delayed implantation occurs.[171]

Very little is known of the breeding of the otter; according to the information available there appears to be no fixed breeding season in this species and young may be born in any month of the year, most frequently in the spring according to some naturalists.[150,43] Two or three young are born after a gestation said to last for sixty-three days; sometimes larger litters are produced and reared, for the female has six teats, though only four of them may be functional. It is not certainly known whether one or two litters are brought forth yearly, and there is likewise no information available about the occurrence or absence of delayed implantation. It is just possible that a delayed implantation period of irregular duration may account for the birth of young at any time of the year; if it is found that the male otter is potent only during a definite mating season this suggestion would be strengthened. On the other hand it is probable that the female does not come into heat for some time after the birth of the young, which are born blind and stay in the holt for some weeks. Even after leaving it they remain in company with the mother until they are almost full-grown, perhaps until she is ready to breed again. With so little definitely known on the subject it is obvious that the whole of the reproductive physiology of the otter still awaits investigation.

As mentioned in an earlier chapter (p. 33), immediately after the eggs are released from the ovary of a mammal the follicles from which they are discharged increase in size and become converted into glandular bodies, the corpora lutea, that release certain hormones into the blood. These hormones act upon the lining of the uterus and cause it to undergo changes in preparation for the arrival of the blastocysts, which normally become implanted in it soon after they reach the uterus. As pregnancy proceeds the corpora lutea undergo changes in size and microscopical structure that are correlated with changes in their activity. In those mustelids in which delayed implantation occurs the cycle of events in the corpora lutea is unlike that found in most mammals. This cycle has been investigated only in the stoat among British mustelids, but the general sequence of occurrences will probably be found to be much the same in the marten and badger.

In the stoat, during the time when the blastocysts remain unimplanted, the corpora lutea are similar in appearance to those found just after ovulation, and it is not until the spring development of the embryos is at hand that any change occurs in them.[55] Shortly before the resumption of development the corpora lutea enlarge and concurrently the uterus increases in size, its microscopical details resembling those of the uterus during the heat period. Thereafter the changes preparatory to the reception of the blastocysts take place and then implantation occurs.

Experiments carried out on the American marten have shown that the length of the delay in implantation can be very greatly reduced by subjecting the animals after mating to the influence of increased illumination.[171] The use of an artificially increased length of day has resulted in a shortening of the apparent length of gestation by three to four months, even though the increased illumination did not start until more than a month after mating. The shortening of the total time of gestation by the stimulus of extra light is brought about by cutting down the period of delayed implantation, and causing the blastocysts to become attached inside the uterus and start their further development. The illumination probably acts, by way of the eye and brain, on the anterior portion of the pituitary gland, which lies underneath the brain. This gland then secretes hormones that in turn act upon the ovary, and the train of events outlined in the last paragraph is started.

From the results of these experiments it is argued that the end of delayed implantation is brought about in spring by the increasing length of the day. This is probably correct, but it is possible that the

Plate 14 POLECAT

John Markham

effect of light is not direct but takes effect through subtle psychological channels, for the increasing length of daylight in January cannot be supposed capable of exerting much direct influence on, for example, the badger, which is a nocturnal animal. In a similar way the resumption of sexual potency in the first few months of the year by the male weasel and stoat is probably the result of the increasing length of daylight. It has already been pointed out that the spring moult is possibly correlated with the lengthening of the day after the turn of the year; the reproductive changes are closely linked with the moult and the connection probably lies in the influence exerted on both by the daily amount of incident illumination.[233]

The Mustelidae thus fall into two divisions, those which breed but once a year and have delayed implantation and those which breed at least twice yearly and experience no delay. To the former belong the badger, marten, and stoat; to the latter the weasel, the polecat almost certainly, and the otter probably. Neither of our other fissipede carnivores, the fox and wild-cat (which are not mustelids), have a delayed implantation, but it is interesting that in the pinnipede division of the carnivores, the seals, there is some indication that delay may occur. Nothing is proven for our two native species, but research now in progress points strongly to the probability of it being a characteristic of some of the antarctic seals.

Precise information is lacking on many points in the breeding of the British fox, though much exact research has been done on that in the silver fox;[182, 169] but all that is known of the British fox suggests that what is true of the latter is equally true of the former, the two forms being really no more than sub-specifically distinct.[170] If this is correct we may say that the fox breeds but once a year, mating occurring most commonly in January. Gestation occupies rather less than two months, the cubs being born late in March or early in April. The male is monogamous and usually mates only once with his vixen; should his mate be killed he usually refuses to take another, forming an example of male faithfulness unknown in other wild animals. Mating is prolonged and, as in the dog, the pair become knotted. The young suckle for about eight to ten weeks, at the end of which they are in process of being weaned, and weigh about $3\frac{1}{2}$ pounds. The average litter-size is rather under $5\frac{1}{2}$; the milk dentition is replaced at about the age of sixteen weeks when the cubs are three-quarters grown; adult size is reached at the age of about twenty-five weeks.[188]

The pure-bred wild-cat is said to breed only once yearly; it has already been pointed out that the wild-cat in Britain breeds twice a year, sometimes three times, and thereby betrays the admixture of the blood of the domestic cat.

The young of all the British carnivores are born in a comparatively helpless state and are cared for by the parent within the shelter of a nest during nursing and for some time afterwards, throughout the rather long period of childhood. But a nest must be protected from the weather, and consequently most carnivores adopt an underground abode, though few of them go to the trouble of excavating it themselves. The badger is the great digger and housekeeper among the carnivores, its burrow or set often being a complicated system of communicating tunnels, for many sets have been inhabited by generations of badgers and in the course of time their excavations become very extensive. The entrance of the set can usually be recognised by the great mass of earth and discarded nest material thrown out. Early in the year the badger spring-cleans the set and throws out the old bedding, often a surprising quantity, that was brought in during the autumn when the ground was carpeted with dead leaves, bracken, and other dried vegetation. When collecting bedding the badger scrapes the material into a heap and then scuffles backwards into the set holding the armful of material in position with its chin. Neal[157] believes that a new nest-chamber for the reception of the cubs is excavated each spring, and that the annual turn-out is connected with this activity. While the cubs are being reared, soiled bedding is brought out at frequent intervals and replaced with new. Badgers prefer wooded country and usually, but not invariably, have their sets in the shelter of a wood or coppice, the entrance frequently being in the side of an earthy bank.

By contrast the fox is a very bad housekeeper and usually makes its den in a ready-made hole such as a big rabbit-burrow which it may take the trouble to enlarge, a field-drain or something similar; quite often the fox shares part of a badger set, or it may lie up in a patch of furze. Unlike the badger the fox makes a habit of bringing food to the earth, and the neighbourhood of a breeding den becomes covered with an untidy litter of mammal and bird remains. The wild-cat makes its den in holes under tree roots, or among rocks and boulders, as also does the pine-marten. The latter, however, being a very nimble tree-climber often makes its nest aloft, utilising an old crow's nest or squirrel's dray. Polecats, stoats and weasels make use of the innumerable holes and crannies that are available to them, from rabbit burrows to crevices in dry-walls. The otter lies up in a burrow, the "holt", among tree-roots or rocks in the bank of a stream, but it has no permanent home apart from the holt in which the cubs are born and reared; frequently one of the entrances is beneath the water-level. But the otter appears to do little excavation of the holt, and merely makes use of an already existing shelter. On the sea coast, caves and crannies in the cliffs are used; away from the sea otters sometimes lie up in reed-beds or furze-brakes.

The baby-coat of all the carnivores differs from that of the adult, being softer, woolier and more fluffy, and usually different in colour. The woolly coat of young fox-cubs is smoky-brown, kittens of the wild cat are light in ground-colour with greyish-brown tabby markings; young martens and polecats are very pale in colour, the former almost white, but young stoats and weasels are duller and greyer than the adults. Only in the badger is the juvenile coat like that of the adult, for the characteristic black, white and grey pattern is present from the first, though the texture of the coat is soft and fluffy. In all our carnivores the eyes of the young do not open until some days, often between a week and a fortnight, after birth. Suckling lasts from two or three weeks in the smaller species to a month or six weeks in the larger. But before suckling has finished the parent starts the process of weaning by bringing in solid food, and then that of education by bringing the young out of the nest and teaching them to catch prey for themselves.

The carnivores are apparently the only British mammals that deliberately educate their young; in all the others the young merely pick up their experience, and are not so definitely taught by the parent. The parental care shown by the mammals and particularly by the carnivores is of a very much more intelligent and adaptable kind than the blind instinctive type found for instance in birds. If a carnivore's breeding place is disturbed the parent will remove the young to a safer place, but if a bird's behaviour pattern is similarly upset it cannot make the adaptation; it usually deserts its brood and at most goes back to the beginning of the story, building a new nest and rearing another brood.

Among the carnivores the education begun when the parent brings disabled but living prey for the young to practise hunting and killing, is never complete; they are notoriously inquisitive, ever ready to examine anything new and adapt themselves to a fresh situation. In most mammals curiosity is mainly an attribute of youth, and by the time that they are adult their reactions to most everyday happenings tend to be stereotyped, and the unexpected leads only to panic flight. Not so the carnivores, which we may perhaps allow, have a higher degree of intelligence; they react by investigating the unusual—every gamekeeper knows, when he sees a stoat or weasel bolt into the crevices of a dry-wall, that he has merely to keep still and wait a few moments, whereupon an enquiring head will be popped out with fatal results to its owner. In larger species the curiosity is combined with a cunning that takes care not to let boldness lead to foolhardy exposure. The inquisitive and even bold disposition of many of the carnivores is undoubtedly correlated with the fact that their whole life is one of aggression; they are the masters and are full of self-assurance.

During the comparatively long period of childhood and adolescence a considerable degree of social structure is developed in the family community, which as a rule does not disperse as soon as the young can fend for themselves. Thus in many species the family keeps together for many months, and occasionally indeed several families combine to make a pack. This sometimes happens in the weasel and in the stoat, where packs of as many as thirty individuals have been seen hunting or playing together. In the larger species, too, as in the otter and the badger, family parties remain together for long periods, and may not be broken up until the onset of a fresh breeding season. Parties of badgers often consist of more than a single family, and such groups are well illustrated by some of Neal's[157] beautiful photographs.

Although many species of carnivores are habitually nomads and have no permanent home, apart from a nursery during the breeding season, each animal has a definite territory, often of considerable extent, which it works regularly and which centres on a den or dens forming the home, temporary or otherwise. Territories are rather in the nature of private property near the centre, but farther afield they become more indefinite, and the bounds of neighbouring territories overlap. Where family parties live together they of course use the same territory, but the individuals do not necessarily keep together when foraging and may then be widely scattered over it. Nearly all mammals are very conservative in many of their ways and prefer to follow a trail rather than break new ground, so that territories become criss-crossed by a network of paths or runs that are used during foraging. The

Plate XXXIII   *Oliver Pike*

Frames from a cinematograph film showing the action of an otter swimming under water

Plate XXXIV   *Anthony Buxton*

An otter's track and three slides in the snow on a frozen ditch carnivores are particularly given to marking out their territories by urinating at definite points on their beats, leaving a sign that apparently warns any stranger that the owner is in possession; the familiar lamp-post habit of dogs is an expression of this instinct. But this method of telling all concerned what animals may be in the neighbourhood is supplemented by another means of communication, by the voice, and this especially at the time of breeding. Foxes are solitary throughout most of the year, the dogs and vixens pairing up only during the breeding season, at which time vixens may be heard at night uttering a loud wailing call to which the dogs reply with a short bark. The wild cat also is particularly noisy at pairing time, much after the manner of the nocturnal concerts of the domestic cat. But the eerie shrieking yell sometimes made by the badger has no such sexual meaning, and neither its significance nor the reason for its utterance are known. Otters give a shrill whistling call, but here again the occasion of its use is not definitely understood. For more intimate use the carnivores have a whole range of growls, snarls, yelps, and purring sounds that are uttered when at close quarters. Stoats, when hunting in a pack, are said to give tongue with a series of chattering cries, but more definite observations on points such as this are desirable.

None of the British carnivores hibernate; it has often been stated, and is widely believed, that the badger does so, but this is incorrect. The badger does not become torpid in winter; at most its activities are somewhat restricted during cold weather, and though individual animals may not come out to forage every night, some of them are out on the prowl even in temperatures as low as 20°F. of frost.[157] Hibernation may perhaps occur on the continent in the more northern parts of its range, but no exact and reliable information appears to be available on the point. Otters certainly do not hibernate, and a good fall of snow gives a splendid opportunity for inferring their movements by means of the tracks that give ample evidence of their winter activities.

There are three ways of finding out what food is eaten by mammals, by directly observing the animals feeding, by examining the contents of the stomach in dead ones, and by identifying any remains of food that may be recognisable in the droppings. The last method has received considerable attention from American students of mammals and has produced much interesting information. They have, indeed, endowed this branch of their studies with the special name of "scatology" from which they have derived the term "scat" for the dropping

M.   R

of an animal, a term useful because there is no corresponding word in
the English vernacular, at least not one suitable for modern ears
polite. Owing to the nature of the food and digestive processes, the
scats of carnivorous mammals are offensive whereas those of herbivores
are not; many people even like the smell of a stable or cow-byre.
Some carnivores such as the cat (and the wild cat is similar to the
domestic tabby in this point) bury the scat, and others have definite
latrines. Badgers always have near their set one or more shallow
excavations or dung-pits in which the scats are deposited; otters often
drop their scats on a boulder in a stream or on regular "seats" on the
bank or near the sea shore, always in some prominent place from which
a good look-out can be kept.[64] Many of these seats are of great age
and have been used by generations of otters, so that they form quite
large mounds, conspicuous because the grass on them is a much
brighter green than that surrounding them. The fox, on the other
hand, has little sanitary sense and not only litters the entrance to its
earth with the remains of its food, but fouls the inside of its den so
much that a periodical change of residence is necessary. Consequently
when making artificial earths in a hunting country it is necessary to
make sure that the roof, especially of the den at the end, is low so that
a fox cannot squat, for otherwise the den will become so fouled that
once the original tenant has left it no other fox will take up its abode
there for many weeks.

The information available about the food of the British carnivores
is not nearly as extensive as it should be, but some exact observations
have been made. The food of the fox is almost entirely animal matter;
an analysis of the contents of the stomachs from a number of animals
showed that during summer rabbits were the commonest food; sheep
came second, followed by small birds, insects, and small mammals.[197]
Some of the mutton may have been carrion, but certainly not all of
it was, for foxes are very destructive to lambs, especially in the hill
districts of Wales. In those districts sheep and small mammals, rats,
field-mice and voles, but not shrews were more frequently eaten than
in the midlands of England; in Scotland the commonest food animals
were rabbits and hares. The wild cat is said to subsist mainly upon
rabbits, but it will doubtless eat anything it can catch. The food of the
badger ranges widely, few reasonably edible objects, animal or vegetable, being rejected. It includes worms, slugs, beetles, wasp-grubs,
rabbits, especially young ones from the nest, hedgehogs (skinned to

avoid spines), beech mast, acorns, apples, grain, bluebell bulbs, roots and many other things (Pl. XXX, p. 217). But badgers rarely raid poultry-houses, though of course occasional rogues occur. Most masters of hounds like (or used up to 1939) to have some badgers in their country if only to lay the blame on them when complaints about poultry losses become too loud; a good badger-dig together with the usual compensation then satisfies everyone.

The otter is above all a fisherman, and sometimes a rather wasteful one, for if fish are plentiful it will often eat only a few bites and leave the greater part of the meal untouched. But the otter is by no means confined to a diet of fish and will take frogs, birds and land mammals such as rats, mice and rabbits. In the sea, otters feed not only on fish such as wrasse, cod and other gadoids and flatfish but also on crabs of various sorts and other crustacea, some of them quite small species such as sand-hoppers[64] (Pl. XXXII, p. 225). The marten, polecat, stoat and weasel all feed upon any of the smaller mammals or birds that they can catch, and also take eggs, lizards and insects.

It is scarcely surprising in view of their great numbers nearly everywhere that rabbits form such a large part of the diet of our carnivores; but the rabbit is not native to the country, although it was introduced many hundreds of years ago, soon after the Norman conquest, and the diet of the carnivores must once have differed considerably from what it is now. But the balance between predator and prey is always in delicate equilibrium, and it is possible that the availability of the rabbit as food has saved both the carnivores, and other species of mammals and birds, from being much scarcer than they are, or even from extinction.

The marten, which is very arboreal in its habits, is expert at catching squirrels, and indeed on the continent the squirrel is said to be its main diet; the polecat, whose chief prey is the rabbit, also feeds upon frogs and other aquatic creatures, and has been known to store large numbers of pithed frogs inside its den. But the rabbit has not only been the means of preserving many of the carnivores as species; incidentally it has also been the means of their destruction in great numbers as individuals. This destruction dates from about the middle of the last century or a little before, and its onset coincides with the introduction of the steel trap or gin. Whatever may be said about trapping animals, it cannot be denied that this is a cruel device that has been responsible for the death of great numbers of the predators as well as of the prey. The species that has suffered most from this invention is perhaps the polecat, formerly a very common animal even close to London up to about a hundred years ago, whose rapid extermination over most of the country began with the first use of gin traps. The example of the local extermination of the stoat in west Wales has already been mentioned (p. 222).

The appearance of our more common carnivores is so familiar that minute descriptions are scarcely necessary here, and a brief mention of the salient points only is made, with remarks upon variation and subspecific forms; a table is appended showing the measurements and weights of the different species (fig. 70, p. 252). Reference has already been made (p. 229) to the variation in three species, the fox, wild cat, and polecat, in which there is reason to believe that the animals found in this country are of mixed racial origin.

The general colour of the fox is reddish to yellowish-brown, frosted with whitish on the hind quarters; white or slaty grey below, the white extending to the chin and upper lip. The tip of the tail is often but not always white, usually with a ring of darker hairs immediately preceding it. The lower parts of the legs, the feet and the backs of the ears are dark brown to black. A dark mark surrounds the eye and often extends down to the mouth (Pl. XXIX, p. 216; Pl. 12, p. 228).

The Scottish wild cat (Pl. XXXVIII, p. 257) has been named *Felis silvestris grampia* Miller, being said to differ from the typical race of central Europe in its darker colour, and more pronounced black markings, especially on the limbs. But the general colour appears to vary seasonally and to be lighter in summer, so this is rather an indefinite character on which to separate a subspecies.[213] The Scottish race is fully as large as, if not larger than, the typical one, and is nearly as big as the large subspecies from Spain. Many more specimens of all the races must be carefully examined before any evaluation of the status of the various named subspecies can be made.

The badger of the British Isles belongs to the typical subspecies (*Meles meles meles* Linnaeus (Pl. 13, p. 233), of most of Europe which bears the trinomial to distinguish it from the lighter-coloured races that inhabit Spain and Crete. The grey colour of the upper parts of the badger is a grizzle of black and whitish, and becomes darker on the back, lighter on the sides. The under parts and legs are black; the chin, face, front edge of the ear, and upper surface of the neck are white, and a broad black stripe extends on each side from just short of the

Plate XXXV

John Markham

Pine-marten

Plate XXXVI   *J. A. Speed*
A stoat springing at a thrush, the tip of whose tail is just visible

muzzle through the eye and ear to the neck, where it fades into the grey of the back.

The otter (*Lutra lutra* Linnaeus), which occurs all over Europe and extends into north Africa, varies considerably both in colour and measurements but not with sufficient consistency for definite geographical races to be recognised, though it has been stated that Irish otters are exceptionally dark in colour, and a subspecific name has been proposed for them. The body is long and slender, tapering off into the tail, which is very wide at its base. The legs are short and the feet webbed to the bases of the terminal toe-joints (fig. 69, p. 250). The ears are small and scarcely project above the dense waterproof fur; both ear and nostril can be shut when the animal submerges. The colour is a rich brown above shading into light brown, buffish, or silvery off-white below; the intensity of the brown on the back is variable but may be seasonal, the darkest colour generally being found in winter. Specimens from Ireland and the northern half of Scotland are said to be darker than those from southern England, but too few examples have been critically compared for a definite statement to be made on the point.[215] There is probably a change of coat in the autumn but there appears to be no observation recorded on any coat-change in the spring; the winter coat may be moulted or may simply wear thin, and further investigation is needed.

The colour of the pine-marten is a rich warm brown, the under parts, legs and tail being rather darker, and the head somewhat lighter (Pl. XXXV, p. 248). On the throat and chest there is a conspicuous patch of creamy or yellowish-buff. The typical race is found all over Europe and bears the trinomial *Martes martes martes* (Linnaeus) to distinguish it from the subspecies found in Sardinia. Another species, the beech-martin *Martes foina* (Erxleben), whose range overlaps much of that of the pine-marten, being distributed over the whole of central and southern Europe, was once thought to occur in this country. It is now known that it is not, and never has been, native to Britain, the confusion having arisen through mistaken identification of faded specimens of the pine-marten. The visible differences between the two species are slight and consist chiefly of some skull and tooth characters, but there is also some difference in the colour of the fur, and particularly in the colour of the throat-patch which is much paler, often almost white, in the beech-marten.

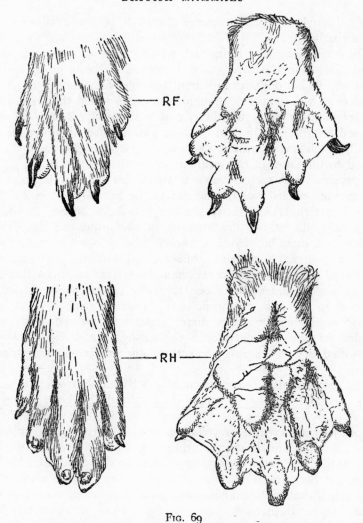

FIG. 69

Right fore, RF, and right hind, RH, feet of the otter, upper and under surfaces to show the webbing of the toes. The claws of the second, third, and fourth toes of the hind foot are worn down to stumps

The general colour of the polecat is a mixture produced by the buffish underfur showing through the long purplish black or dark brown hairs of the outer coat. There is a yellowish patch on each side between the eye and the ear; the lips, sides of the muzzle, and edges of the ears are yellowish-white; and the feet, tail and chest are blackish (Pl. 14, p. 204). The polecat, *Mustela putorius putorius*, inhabits all Europe south of central Scandinavia, there being one little-known subspecies of doubtful validity found in Spain. The polecat of Sutherland has been described as a distinct subspecies, but the specimens known, four only, form too slight a foundation for any conclusion on such a matter.[212] Even the Asiatic polecat, from which the ferret is sometimes claimed to take its descent, is probably no more than a geographical race of the typical species.

Of stoats and weasels, both inhabiting the whole of Europe and extending into Asia, there are many subspecies, distinguished from each other by skull and tooth characters, size, and coat-pattern. Of these, three subspecies of the stoat and one of the weasel are recognised as British. The general coloration of both these species is reddish-brown above and white or yellowish below, the stoat, the larger animal of the two, having the tail tipped with black, a character that is not present in the weasel. Both species turn white during the winter in the colder parts of their range, the areas where the change occurs in the weasel being much more restricted than those where it affects the stoat; weasels do not turn white in these islands. The fur of the stoat in its winter coat, white with black tail-tip, is the ermine of commerce, the black tabs being the ends of the tails.

The British stoat, *Mustela erminea stabilis* Barrett-Hamilton (Pl. XXXVIIa, p. 256), differs from the Scandinavian and Central European subspecies in its slightly greater size and larger carnassial teeth. Its range covers the whole of England and, as far as is known, Scotland. But the stoats from the islands of Jura and Islay have been separated as a subspecies, *M. erminea ricinae* Miller,[151] which is smaller than *M. e. stabilis* and resembles some of the continental subspecies in skull characters. Some stoats of the mainland of Scotland resemble this isolated race, for Miller remarks, "A few small though apparently well-developed skulls from the north of Scotland indicate the possible existence there of a local form somewhat resembling the true *erminea*", the subspecies of Scandinavia. The stoats of Ireland and the Isle of Man belong to another well marked form, *Mustela erminea hibernica* Thomas and Barrett-Hamilton; this has been deemed worthy of full specific rank by some authors, including the original describers, though this is not in accord with modern views. It differs from the

British stoat, which is larger. Its coat-pattern, too, is distinctive, for the line on the sides separating the darker back from the lighter belly is irregular, and there is a marked tendency for the darker colour to encroach upon the light under surface, in some examples to such an extent that it extends right across the belly or throat. Very rarely does the coat turn white or partly white in winter; and a further difference is shown in the number of teats, which are ten to twelve in the Irish stoat but only eight in all the other subspecies.

SPECIES	LENGTH		WEIGHT	
	Head and Body inches	Tail inches	Range	Maximum
Fox	24 – 32	12 – 18	15 – 20 lb.	29 lb.
Wild cat	20 – 25	11 – 14	7 – 13 lb.	15 lb. 10 oz.
Badger	25 – 32	4½– 6¼	22 – 27 lb.	43 lb.
Otter	25 – 32	16 – 18	13 – 23 lb.	37 lb.
Marten	16 – 22	12	2¼– 3¼ lb.	–
Polecat	14½– 17½	5½ – 6¾	1½– 2¾ lb.	–
Stoat	9¾– 11¼	4¼ – 4¾	4 – 11 oz.	–
Weasel	6 – 8¾	1¾ – 2¾	2 – 4 oz.	–

FIG. 70

Measurements and weights of the British carnivores (adults). Data from various sources, some original. Reliable recorded information is scanty

The weasel, in colour and pattern much like a small stoat but without the black tip to the tail, ranges over the whole of Europe and extends into Asia. Most of this area, including Great Britain but not Ireland, is inhabited by the typical race, *Mustela nivalis nivalis* Linnaeus (Pl. XXXVII, p. 256), from which subspecies in Sardinia and in Spain have been separated.

Most of the carnivores show some degree of sexual dimorphism in their size, the males generally being larger than the females, although the difference in many species is not very pronounced. But in the stoats and weasels the difference is very marked, especially in the latter where it is so great that the sexes have often been thought to be different animals, and have been given separate vernacular names, the female being known in some parts of Scotland as the "mouse weasel". Records of weasels trapped have shown that only 27 per cent of the animals taken were females and that males formed 73 per cent of the catch. This was probably because the males are more active, and the females wander less, staying nearer home while they are rearing their two annual broods. In the stoat, which has only one annual litter, the corresponding figures were more evenly balanced, being 55 per cent to 61 per cent of males.[56]

The American mink (*Mustela vison*) has, since 1956, established itself as a member of the British fauna. The feral population is derived from animals escaped from fur-farms and is increasing; mink are at large in many parts of England, Scotland, and Wales, and are most abundant in Hampshire, Wiltshire, Devon, and Lancashire, in Cardigan and Carmarthenshire, and in Aberdeenshire and other counties of Scotland. They are officially outlawed, but it is doubtful whether it will be possible to exterminate them as they are so widespread and well naturalised. Mink are destructive to poultry, to freshwater fisheries, and to the native mammals and birds.

CHAPTER 9

SEALS

(CARNIVORA: PINNIPEDIA)

——Emerging from the wave,
The Phocae swift surround his rocky cave,
Frequent and full; the consecrated train
Of her, whose azure trident awes the main:
There wallowing warm, the enormous herd exhales
An oily steam, and taints the the noontide gales.

> HOMER's *Odyssey*, translation of
> Alexander Pope

THE SEALS are a specialised group of carnivores of ancient origin, and are highly adapted to their aquatic life. They fall naturally into two main divisions, the earless seals and the eared sea-lions (*Phocidae* and *Otariidae*), and a third smaller one containing the walrus (*Odobenidae*). Members of the first division are the only ones that occur regularly in the British fauna, those of the second being confined mostly to the southern hemisphere and only crossing the equator in the Pacific Ocean. The Otariidae are not so completely modified for aquatic life as the Phocidae, and are able to turn the hind legs forwards under the body when on land, thus being then considerably more agile. Their other distinguishing feature is the possession of a small external ear, hence their name. The seals which appear in circuses and in a well known advertisement are Otariid seals, usually Californian sea-lions, which appear to have a natural aptitude for balancing things on their noses.

The Phocidae are much more completely adapted for life in the water. The whole body is more torpedo-shaped and less snaky, with a short neck, and the hind limbs are permanently turned backwards for use in swimming. It is usually stated that the Phocid seals have no external ear pinna—they are often called the earless seals—but this is

254

not strictly correct. It is true that their ears are not so large or so obvious as those of the Otariidae, but there is in fact a very small supporting cartilage that can be felt under the skin surrounding the ear-hole. In some seals, for example the grey seal and the young common seal, this cartilage can be thrust forward so that a perfectly distinct though small ear-pinna is present (fig. 71). The ear-

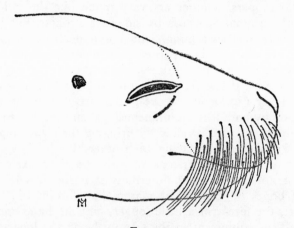

FIG. 71
Head of a new-born common seal with the rudimentary ear flap projecting from its groove

pinna of the earless seals may be small, but their name by no means implies that their ears are in any other way deficient; far from it, for the hearing of seals is acute and, apparently, critical, though in the absence of a pinna it cannot possibly be so directive as in other mammals. Seals are inquisitive creatures, and it is well known that they can be attracted to a boat by the strains of an accordion or a mouth-organ. When they dive below the surface of the water, seals close their external ear-passage by muscular action.

The hind limbs of the Phocidae are permanently turned backwards and are thus of little use for movement on land, but in the water they form a powerful propeller for swimming. The thigh-bone is short but the shank-bones are proportionately longer. The foot contains five long toes: of these the two outer—the big and the little toes—are the longest, the first or big toe being longest of all. The second and fourth toes are smaller and the central third toe is smallest and shortest.

All the toes are connected by a web that reaches nearly to their tips, and each is provided with a small nail on the upper surface a little short of the end (fig. 72, p. 258). The hind-limbs or flippers extend well beyond the tail and in swimming they are turned so that the under-surfaces or soles face inwards. It is generally stated that the toes are then widely separated so that the web is spread out like a fan and the two flippers together act very much like the tail of a fish, propelling the animal forwards by sideways strokes. But this is not the usual method of swimming, which is done by alternate strokes of the hind feet, the web being spread for the active stroke but folded on the recovery stroke. The active stroke is the one during which the sole presses against the water as the limb is brought across the centre line of the body (adduction stroke). Less frequently the swimming stroke is made by both feet simultaneously; then the legs are separated and the swimming stroke is made by bringing them together with the webs spread and the soles facing each other.[183]

The fore flipper of the earless seals is short and fin-like and though externally it appears reduced, internally it is supported by the full number of bones of the typical mammalian fore-limb. The upper arm is short, the fore-arm a little longer, and the hand contains five fingers, the first, equivalent to the thumb, being the longest. All the fingers are closely bound together to form a mitt—they can scarcely be said to be webbed—and each has a nail that projects a little beyond the tip. Little more than the hand projects from the surface of the body, the rest of the limb lying under the skin outside the ribs (fig. 73, p. 259). Nevertheless the hand of the seals is surprisingly mobile. When the animal is swimming the fore-limb is folded back with the palm pressed against the side of the body filling a small depression of the surface, an extension of the armpit, so that no resistance is offered to the forward movement of the animal. On land the palm is applied to the ground and the limb rotated outwards at the wrist to support the body when the seal is moving about. But it is when a seal has pulled out on a rock and is basking in the sun that the full mobility of the arm is seen. As the hair dries and the skin begins to tickle the fore-limb is used for scratching and can reach backwards to the middle of the back, or right forward to scratch the top of the head. The arm can also be brought forward so that the back of the hand can be used for wiping the nose. This great and rather surprising mobility of the fore-limb is no doubt due to the fact

a. Stoat with a dead rat

b. Weasel

Plate XXXVII

Paul Popper Ltd.

Plate XXXVIII

Captive wild cat showing the characteristic bushy tail

that seals have no collar-bone, so that the limb is free to slide to and
fro beneath the skin.

On land the progress of the earless seals is comparatively slow and
difficult, because the hind limbs cannot be brought forwards to support
the rear part of the body. Walking therefore consists of a series of
hitchings forward, and if carefully watched is seen to resemble the
movement of a looper caterpillar (fig. 74, p. 260). The body is first
arched so that the tail end is drawn forward, and then straightened
so that it is pushed ahead from where the pelvic region is in contact
with the ground. At the moment of the forward push the front part
of the body is raised from the ground by the outwardly rotated front
flippers, which also help by hitching the body along. As soon as the
front part of the body is again on the ground the fore flippers are
raised and moved forward to a new position while the body is again
arched ready for a new push off. The rapid succession of these movements can produce quite a surprising turn of speed for a short distance
over level ground, but it is a poor method of progression and a seal
soon tires if it is hurried (fig. 75, p. 261).

Very different are the graceful movements of a seal in the water,
as with little effort it sculls itself swiftly along by easy strokes of the
outstretched toes of the webbed feet. Common seals, and perhaps
other species, appear to be fond of swimming upside-down; this may
enable them to keep an eye on the bottom when they are swimming
near it. When a seal is below the surface the ears and nostrils are
closed, and it must therefore, one would think, find its food entirely
by sight. This is probably to a large extent true, for most kinds of seal
live where the water is clear and the visibility below the surface is
good. But what of the seals that live in estuaries where the water is so
turbid that it is impossible to see a foot ahead, and it is quite dark a
short distance beneath the surface? The common seal is often found
in such places, not as single wanderers from cleaner waters but in
colonies that make the sandbanks of the estuaries their homes.
Fraser Darling,[50] too, has seen and photographed a blind grey seal
whose eyes had probably been destroyed long before in fighting; but
it was nevertheless fat and in good condition and was evidently able
to catch ample quantities of food.

It is difficult to understand how these animals find their prey, the
senses of hearing, smell and sight, being ruled out; one can only
suppose that the sense of touch is employed. The large bristly whiskers

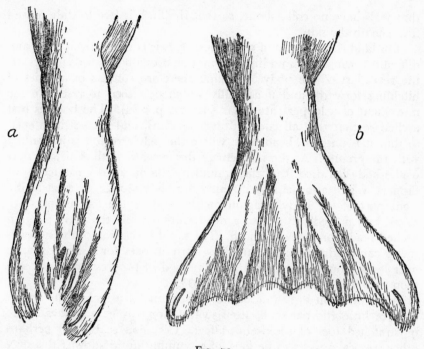

FIG. 72
Right hind limb of the common seal.
a, at rest. *b*, the toes spread to show the webbing

on the snouts and brows of seals are tactile organs, the root of each being connected with a comparatively large nerve, and one may suppose that by means of them the animal is made aware of slight turbulences in the water such as might be produced by the swimming of a fish. But this explanation gives no help in understanding how the seals that eat shellfish, such as whelks and cockles, find them in such circumstances.

The eye of a seal appears to be a liquid dark brown or black in colour, but if one examines it closely one sees that the pupil is comparatively small, and the front layer of the iris is transparent so that a most beautiful and complicated network of blood-vessels can be seen spread out upon its surface. How acute the sight of a seal may be when the animal is on land is not known, but it appears unlikely that the eye can accommodate itself for sharp vision both in water and in air because of the difference in the refractive indices of the two media. There can be no doubt that the seal's eye is capable of seeing clearly in water and therefore it seems likely that it is less efficient in air. Just as objects appear blurred to a human swimmer when below the surface even in the clearest water unless goggles are worn so that the eyes are in contact with air and not with water, it is probable that objects above the surface appear rather blurred to a seal when it

FIG. 73
Upper surface of the right fore limb of the common seal, showing the claws at the ends of the fingers

pokes its head out; but the adaptability to the two media is doubtless greater than in man. The pupil of the eye is capable of great enlargement when the animal is in the dim regions below the surface where the depth of water cuts off much of the light; the pupil then probably expands as greatly as does that of a cat or owl at night, to take as much advantage as possible of every ray.

When seals have been out of the water long enough for their coats to have become dry, their faces are kept wet with the copious tears that flow from their eyes. It has been thought that the tears flow because the eyes are irritated by contact with the air, but this supposition is quite wrong. The tears flow over the face because seals have no naso-lachrymal duct to carry them from the eyes to the nose. This duct is present in all land mammals, and is a channel running from the inner corner of the eye to the inside of the nose. Through it the tears, which are being continually secreted to keep the surface of the

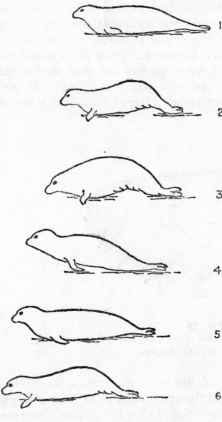

FIG. 74

Diagram of successive stages in the progress of a seal. 1, at rest. 2, 3, hind part of body arched and hind limbs drawn forward. 4, fore part of body raised on flippers and pushed forward by hind end. 5, fore part again on ground. 6, repeat

eye moist, are conducted away; small glands at the bases of the eyelashes secrete a film of grease that coats the edges of the eyelids and prevents the tears spilling over their edges. If the human nasolachrymal duct becomes stopped up, as sometimes happens if one is suffering from a bad cold, the tears overflow on to the face exactly as they do in seals.

Seals spend most of their active life beneath the surface of the sea, but we know little of what occurs in those depths. How is a seal able to perform dives of long duration without being drowned? Although the dives of a seal often do not last longer than a few minutes— five to seven minutes is about the usual time for a seal when fishing—the common seal can stay below for about fifteen minutes, the grey seal for about twenty, and the large elephant-seal of the southern seas is believed to be able to dive for considerably more than thirty minutes. An ordinary man can hold his breath for only about a minute, and even the practised pearl-diver cannot exceed much over two and a half. The seal's metabolism must evidently be very specialised for the animal to be able to hold its breath for such long periods.

The essence of the question is, how can a seal take down sufficient oxygen in its body to last during a dive? As soon as a seal dives it

F. Fraser Darling

a. Herd of grey seals asleep on the shore of North Rona

F. Fraser Darling

b. Grey seals off the west coast of Scotland

Plate XXXIX

F. Fraser Darling

a. New-born grey seal, weight about 30 lb.

Paul Popper Ltd.

b. Grey seal about ten days old, weight about 60 lb.

Plate XL

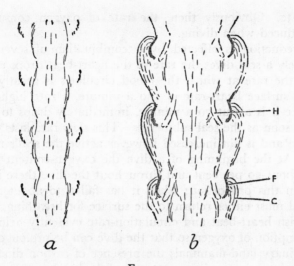

FIG. 75
Tracks left by common seal in firm sand.
a, unhurried; the impressions of the fore claws on each side of
the central skid-way. *b*, hurried; the fore limb has dug in so deeply
that the claw marks are confluent, F. The claws have left parallel
marks in the sand as they were brought forward between paces,
C, and the hind limbs, H, have made impressions by their vigorous
thrusts.
Direction of travel from bottom to top of sketch

usually blows most of the air out of its lungs, probably in part at least
to reduce its buoyancy, so that the amount of oxygen available to it
from the lungs is greatly reduced.[185] On the other hand seals contain
a high proportion of blood, and the amount of oxygen carried in it
is comparatively great. In addition the muscles of seals contain a large
quantity of myoglobin, a substance allied to the haemoglobin of the
blood and able to hold a high percentage of oxygen available for use.
The presence of the myoglobin is responsible for the characteristic
dark colour of the flesh of seals. But all these reservoirs of oxygen—
oxygen depôts as they are termed—are not nearly enough to last the
seal during a long dive if the oxygen is used at the same rate when the
animal is submerged as when it is breathing. The amount of oxygen
carried down in the depôts is not sufficient to last the animal more
than one third of the duration of the average dive if it is used at the

M.   S surface rate. Obviously then, the rate of oxygen consumption is greatly reduced when diving.

This reduction is effected by a combination of several factors. Immediately a seal dives the rate of the heart-beat drops enormously and thus the rate at which the blood circulates is greatly retarded. A normal surface heart-rate of 150 a minute, a rate higher than in man where it is about 70 a minute, immediately drops to only 10 a minute as soon as the seal submerges. This slow rate lasts during the whole dive and is not increased however active the seal's movements may be. At the beginning of a dive the oxygen-content of a seal's blood is about 20 per cent and throughout the dive there is a steady decrease in this proportion; when it has fallen to about 2 per cent the animal must either return to the surface for breathing, or drown. The sluggish heart-beat and circulation-rate evidently help to retard the consumption of oxygen so that the dive can be prolonged.

In ordinary land-mammals the presence of carbon dioxide in the blood stimulates the respiratory centres of the brain so that the breathing rate is increased until the excess carbon dioxide has been removed through the lungs. It is for this reason that carbon dioxide is mixed with the oxygen that is given to patients receiving artificial respiration; and the lack of carbon dioxide in the blood stops the breathing reflex, as can be tried by anyone who takes twenty deep breaths in rapid succession. The deep breathing washes the carbon dioxide out of the blood through the lungs, and there is a long pause before enough of it accumulates in the blood to stimulate the breathing to start again. Seals, however, show a comparatively low sensitivity to increased quantities of carbon dioxide and are therefore able to endure a long dive without feeling the necessity for breathing as would a human diver, for it is not the lack of oxygen but the increase of carbon dioxide in the blood that stimulates our respiratory movements.

The reduced heart-rate greatly cuts down the rate of blood-flow to the muscles during diving, but there is probably a further reduction in the blood-supply caused by a contraction of the walls of the blood-vessels in the muscles themselves. Were this not so there would be a greatly decreased blood-flow through the brain, which would quickly lead to loss of consciousness. The restriction of the blood-flow through the muscles is therefore probably considerable so that the circulation in the brain shall not suffer unduly from the decreased blood-supply due to the lowered heart-rate. As soon as the seal returns to the surface and breathes the heart-rate increases to normal, changing suddenly from 10 to 150 a minute. A few deep breaths wash out the carbon dioxide that has been released from the muscles into the blood, and refill the oxygen depôts.

The reduction of the circulation during diving means that the whole of the animal's metabolism is also reduced. Although the muscles are able to function almost anaerobically, using but little oxygen from the blood together with what is available in the myoglobin of the muscles themselves, the rate of all the other bodily functions must be drastically reduced. This may be one of the reasons for those long periods of lazy basking on rocks and sandbanks or floating at the surface that are so characteristic a feature of the life of seals. It may be then that the internal organs really get to work and digest the food that has been collected during the active hunting hours when the animal has been filling its stomach with prey.

Little is known about the depths to which seals habitually go. A young grey seal on its first deep dive is recorded as reaching 22 metres (72 feet), and young bladder-nosed seals are known to have reached 75 metres (246 feet) on their first attempts at deep diving.[185] It seems unlikely that seals living on the sea-coasts would go to very great depths, say over 100 feet, for they can probably obtain all the food that they need at shallower depths than this. On the other hand the northern seals, which live over deep water, pulling out on to floating ice to rest, may perhaps find it necessary to go to greater depths.

If a human diver goes to a depth of 45 feet or more he is liable to suffer from caisson sickness or "bends" on returning to the surface. This is because the pressure at that depth, about $37\frac{1}{2}$ pounds to the square inch, is sufficient to force the nitrogen in the air that he breathes into solution in the blood and other tissues of the body. On returning quickly to the surface the pressure is released and the excess nitrogen comes out of solution forming minute bubbles in the blood vessels and other parts of the body. This condition at best is very painful and at worst is fatal, the victim dying of gas embolism, the bubbles of nitrogen obstructing the smaller branches of the blood vessels. How is it that seals are able to dive to considerable depths and yet return rapidly to the surface without harm?

Several things combine to give the seal the necessary protection.[185] The first thing that a seal does on deep diving is to blow out a large quantity of air from the lungs, so that the amount taken down in them is very much less than would be the case were the lungs full. This action alone results in there being very much less nitrogen available to be forced into solution in the blood and tissues by the pressure at depth and affords a large measure of protection. When the seal is down deep and is subjected to considerable pressure most of the body, consisting largely of water, retains the volume that it had at the surface, for water is practically incompressible. But the air in the lungs is very compressible and will progressively decrease in volume the deeper the seal goes, the lungs being collapsed by the pressure transmitted to them by the other organs. When this occurs the small subdivisions of the air-spaces in the lungs collapse and their lining membranes become very much thickened. The air is consequently forced out from the finer subdivisions into the windpipe and its ramifications, which are comparatively rigid structures. The nitrogen in the compressed air that then fills the more rigid parts of the respiratory apparatus is very much less easily forced into solution through the comparatively thick walls of these parts. It is similarly prevented from dissolving in the finer air-spaces of the lungs because they are partly or wholly collapsed and their lining membranes are thereby made comparatively very thick.

By the action of these two mechanisms, then, the seal is protected from the liability to caisson sickness on returning quickly to the surface from a deep dive. On the other hand the seal must refrain from going too deep, for even these arrangements will not protect it from the effects of returning rapidly from a very great depth. One instance is known of a bladder-nosed seal that went to a depth of 300 metres and was killed by the formation of a gas embolism on coming to the surface. But perhaps this is a rather inconclusive example, for the seal was taken down experimentally to a depth probably beyond its normal limit and possibly had not emptied the lungs according to the usual habit.

The expelling of air from the lungs at the start of a dive thus serves two purposes; not only does it help to protect the animal from caisson sickness but it also reduces buoyancy so that less effort is required to keep the animal below the surface. In fact a seal with uninflated lungs usually sinks at once, as is well known by people who have shot seals in the water. A swimming seal offers a small target to the shooter, who must aim at the head. If the seal is standing upright, treading water, with his head out, as soon as the fatal bullet strikes him all the air is released from the lungs and the body sinks tail first. But if the seal is lying horizontally on the water and the head drops down as soon as hit, the mouth and nose are brought lower in the water than the lungs which then remain inflated and keep the body afloat long enough for the shooter to retrieve it. Nevertheless seal hunters regard it as almost useless to shoot a seal in the water because the chances of getting a lucky shot with the seal in such a position that it does not sink are remote. But shooting seals for amusement is a poor sort of butchery.

Another adaptation to aquatic life in seals is their possession of a thick layer of blubber underneath the skin. This layer of fat serves to insulate the body and prevent it losing heat to the cold surrounding water. After a good summer of feeding the blubber layer reaches a very great thickness (two or three inches, or more in places), and it is the oil that can be obtained from the blubber that forms one of the main commercial products produced from seals by professional seal-hunters. The coat of blubber, and the gregarious habits of many species at the breeding season, have led to the destruction of countless thousands of seals by man during the last century and a half, a destruction that continues at the present day.

Seals of one sort or another are fairly common round the greater part of the British coasts, least frequent on the south coast. In the past there has been great confusion about the species of British seals, largely because the vernacular name of *Phoca vitulina* is the "common seal" and any seal seen has been uncritically recorded as belonging to this species. On the west coast of England and Wales however the common seal is uncommon, and the seal that is common is the grey seal *Halichoerus grypus*. Broadly speaking the common seal frequents estuaries and coasts where offshore sandbanks or rocks are exposed at low tide, but the grey seal's natural habitat is the rocky coast with cliffs and caves. For the most part each species keeps to its own type of coast, but they follow no hard and fast rule so that, for instance, grey seals are sometimes found in the Wash, and common seals at the rocky Pembrokeshire islands. The two types of habitat are connected, in part at least, with the different breeding habits of the two species. The young of the common seal are born during the summer, mostly in June and July, and are able to take to the water within a few hours of their birth. It is thus possible for the expectant mother seal to come ashore on a sandbank or flat rock as the tide falls, to give

birth to her pup, and for both of them to swim off safely when the tide
rises again. Not so with the grey seal, for in this species the young are
unable to leave the beach until they are several days old. The parent
must therefore find some safe place where the pup may live on land
until it is ready to take to the water. The places selected are quiet
coves beneath high cliffs, with beaches or rocky ledges that are
inaccessible except from the sea, and the pebble beaches and ledges
in the far recesses of sea-caves under cliffs. Here the pups born in the
autumn, mostly in September and October, are able to live safe from
molestation by man, their only enemy. And here they are visited and
suckled by their mothers until they are able to go to sea and fend for
themselves.

The young of all seals are unlike the adults in being clothed in a
coat of soft almost woolly hair, usually different in colour from that
of the adult (Pl. XLa, p. 261). This is shed soon after birth, in anything
from a few days to a few weeks according to the species, when a coat
of the adult character has grown underneath it. The milk teeth of seal
pups are shed or absorbed at a very early age, in many species before
birth, so that the points of the permanent teeth are already through the
gums from the pup's earliest hours. In the common and grey seals,
as in many but not all species, the first puppy coat is white and silky,
and in the grey seal it is retained for about a fortnight. During this
time the pup shuns the sea and indeed may be drowned if it accidentally
falls in the surf, though it can swim, and often does so in sheltered pools.
An autumn gale that brings the swell thundering in on beaches and
through the caves may cause a high mortality among the grey seal
pups by washing them away so that they are battered on the rocks
and drowned.

But the first puppy coat of the common seal is shed at a very early
age, often before birth, so that the pup is without it from the beginning
of its individual life. Even when the pup is born with the white coat,
or parts of it, the silky hairs fall out within a few days, often within a
few hours.[131] This early shedding of the puppy coat of the common
seal has led to contradictory statements appearing on the subject, some
writers claiming that in this species it is shed before birth and others
that it is not; in fact both statements are correct for the coat may be
shed either before or after birth. When the hair is shed before birth it
at first floats in the fluid filling the amnion, the 'bag of waters' in which
the unborn foetus floats inside the uterus. And, like the unborn

foetuses of all mammals including man, the seal foetus drinks its bath-water. In doing so it also swallows the shed-hair, so that young common seals often have their stomachs crammed with their first coat when they are born. Not only does the foetus drink the amniotic fluid, it also excretes into it, and as a consequence the white coat of the grey seal is stained a yellow or cream colour by the faecal matter that has fouled the fluid during the last few days before birth. The pure white colour does not appear until the coat has been well washed by a shower of rain or by a bath in a pool or at the sea's edge. The loss of the puppy coat of the common seal, and the ability to take to the water soon after birth enable the species to occupy a habitat denied to the grey seal. The stage of infantile helplessness has been reduced and, as it were, pushed back in the individual's life so that the most helpless stage is got over before the pup's birth. Nothing definite appears to be known about the length of time that the young of this species are suckled, but it is believed to be not more than four or at most six weeks, and is possibly much less. Opportunities for suckling are limited, for as far as is known, the mother does not feed the young in the water and suckling is therefore confined to such times as the sandbanks are uncovered and the seals can come ashore. Weaning at a comparatively early age would thus be an advantage to the species.

The cows differ greatly in their temperaments when they are with their pups. Some are timid, and escape to sea as soon as an intruder sets foot on the beach; others are reluctant to go, and soon return if the intruder keeps still and does not go too near the pup. But others are fierce and refuse to be driven away from their pups at all; indeed they will make towards the intruder, threatening him with open mouth and menacing cries, and, unless he is stout-hearted, it is he that will be driven away. If, however, he keeps still and quiet he will soon be ignored and can then at very close quarters watch the mother nursing and attending to her baby—a most delightful experience that, with a little patience, can be had by anybody (Pl. 15, p. 281).

Young seals are surprisingly large when they are born; the length of the young common seal is $2\frac{1}{2}$ to 3 feet, and of the grey seal 3 to $3\frac{1}{2}$ feet at birth. Both species grow very quickly, not so much in length as in girth, putting on a great thickness of blubber so that they are soon little barrels of fat (Pl. XLb, p. 261). At the end of the suckling period the grey seal mother deserts her pup and leaves it to fend for itself; the youngster goes hungry for some days during which it gradually takes to the water and learns to find its own food. During this period of starvation it draws upon the fat-reserves that it has built up during suckling. Less is known about this phase in the life of the common seal, but it is probable that the pup is left by the mother to its own resources at an early age.

The habitat of the two indigenous species of British seals is thus determined, in part at least, by the location of suitable breeding grounds; and the suitability of the breeding grounds is determined by the presence or absence of a comparatively long period of infantile helplessness in the life of the pup. But it was not always so; the breeding habits of the grey seal at least have been altered by the influence of man. Apart from the killer-whale, the British seals have no enemy besides man, and from him they are safe when in the water. But in the breeding season when they have to come ashore to nurse their helpless young they are very vulnerable. Hence the choice of remote and inaccessible spots for nurseries by the grey seal, which is at a disadvantage compared with the common seal where the stage of infancy has been largely telescoped into antenatal life. But in past ages when the country was less densely populated by man his interference with the creatures of the wild was smaller, and there must have been many a quiet stretch of coastline and many an off-lying islet where the grey seal could live unmolested. In such places its breeding habits were very different, as we know through the researches of Fraser Darling, who lived for some months on North Rona studying the seals there.[50] This remote island, forty miles north-west of Harris, the northernmost of the outer Hebrides, has been uninhabited by man for about two centuries; here the grey seals are able to live their lives untroubled by him, and have gone back to what were no doubt the habits of their ancestors throughout their range.

All seals are sociable, especially during the breeding season, when many species congregate on their breeding grounds in immense numbers (Pl. XXXIXa, p. 260). At this time, many species leave the water for a considerable time to live on land or floating ice for several weeks. Not all species of seals are known to do this, and the grey seal throughout most of its British range does not: but on North Rona, it does. Here the seals come ashore in autumn and, having the whole place to themselves, they are not restricted to beaches and caves, to be visited furtively with an eye ever on the watch for danger. On the contrary they travel far from the sea, climbing even to the summit of the island nearly 300 feet above sea-level, where they loll at their ease among the cushions of sea-pinks. And here the big bulls have their harems as did their ancestors of old, serving their little groups of females until their procreative instincts are expended, when they are succeeded by their rivals. On this island of North Rona the adult seals may stay ashore for as long as three or four weeks, a striking contrast to the habits of the species elsewhere. There the spells ashore are to be measured in hours only; at least on open beaches, for something similar to the activities at Rona may take place in the far recesses of the sea-caves where no man has intruded on the seal's privacy.

The breeding grounds of the grey seal are few and widely spaced. In Cornwall certain caves and beaches only are used as nurseries; while others, though frequently visited by the seals, are not so used.[204] On the Welsh coast similarly only certain caves and islands are used; others that appear to be entirely suitable are used as hauling grounds but not for breeding. In Scotland too the main breeding grounds are concentrated in a limited number of islands. The seals are loosely gregarious outside the breeding season and the sexes do not keep apart. Towards the end of summer and in early autumn they begin to assemble (Pl. XXXIXb, p. 260), the bulls arriving first and the cows joining them later. On Rona the bulls, or some of them, come ashore and take up territories, where they are joined after a few days by the cows that come ashore to pup, but elsewhere the cows come to land first. The territory annexed by the bull is a small area of beach, or, on Rona, of ground far inland, and here he lies quietly awaiting the arrival of the cows. The latter gradually come ashore as they are ready to pup, and join the bulls. The bulls make no attempt themselves to collect their harem of cows or to prevent cows wandering away to other bulls, but they are quick to defend their own territory and drive off any other bull that may approach or challenge the ownership of it.

Apart from the territories taken up by the bulls the breeding grounds form a sort of neutral territory occupied by seals of both sexes, and act as a reservoir of cows not yet ready to pup and of fresh bulls that take the places of the earlier comers as they become spent and unable to preserve their territories when challenged. The immature seals for the most part keep away from the breeding grounds, which they do not visit until they are about four years old. Only a few late pups and spent bulls remain ashore by the middle of December.

Grey seals are extremely fat when they come ashore at the beginning of the breeding season, having spent all the summer fishing and
feeding, so that the big bulls weigh over a quarter of a ton, some 6 to 7
cwt. (the maximum weight of a bull common seal is about 2 cwt.,
Pl. XLIb, p. 276). This extreme fatness is used up during the breeding
much of that of the cows being transferred to the pups. Pups weigh
about 30 pounds at birth (Pl. XLa, p. 261); they are at first thin
but start fattening within a day or two. Grey seal milk contains more
than 50 per cent of fat (harp-seal's has over 42 per cent[191]), over
ten times the amount in cow's milk, so that the pups are tubby
within a week, and incredibly fat at a fortnight (Pl. XLb, p. 261).
At three weeks the pups weigh three times their birth-weight, have
lost their baby coats, and have been weaned and deserted by their
mothers (Pl. XLIa, p. 276). There is in fact very little difference in
size and weight between young seals a month old and nine months
old, the vulnerable stage of infancy being telescoped and concentrated into the first few weeks after birth so that there follows a comparatively long period of little growth during which the early gains
are consolidated.

The cow seals assiduously attend their own pups, but show much
jealousy and animosity to other cows and their pups. They seem to
prefer to keep a space of a few yards to themselves, but even so there
is much noise, biting and scratching, and woe betide any pup that
wanders too close to a strange cow, for she will bite it savagely. Both
bulls and cows receive considerable damage in encounters with
mothers guarding their pups, and wounds are common. Fraser Darling has found that where breeding grounds are crowded and there is
much quarrelling the cows tend to spend more time close to their
pups, and suggests that though the social habit leads to fighting and
some damage, the species stands to gain by it in the long run because
when predatory land animals such as wolves were a possible danger
to the pups the constant presence of the cows gave them protection.
The cows take great care of the pups when they are endangered by
gales at the time of the high spring-tides in the autumn, lying broad-
side on the beach below the pup to break the force of the surf and
prevent the youngster from being washed away. If the pup does
fall into the surf the cow sometimes shows great persistence in its
efforts to get it back to safety. Nevertheless there is usually a considerable mortality from this and other causes, as much as 10 per cent

of all pups according to the studies of J. Davies on the seals of the Welsh islands.[51]

Grey seals are rather noisy animals on their breeding beaches. The pups, when hungry, call for their mothers with a shrill yapping, and the mothers answer with a high-pitched querulous barking that has a melancholy—almost uncanny—ring as it echoes through the gloom of a sea cave or between the steep walls of some narrow cove. It is the resemblance of these wailing noises to weeping that has given rise to the folk stories of seal-women and water witches that are still current in our Celtic fringe. They have also been seized upon by writers who prefer sentimentality to truth to make up stories of bereaved seal mothers mourning for their lost pups; but the seals make these cries when they are with their pups. When approached or handled the pups show their hostility by hissing and snapping at the intruder.

The food of the British seals consists of fish and other marine animals; but it is doubtful whether seals are always so destructive to commercial fisheries as the fishermen would have us believe. The grey seal haunts rocky coasts where little commercial fishing beyond the setting of lobster-pots is carried on, and where the characteristic fishes are pollack, saithe, wrasses and other species of little commercial interest; Fraser Darling[50] says that the food in Scottish waters comprises saithe, pollack and mackerel. But exact knowledge of the food of this species is lacking; a great opportunity for obtaining information on this point was lost in 1934 when some 177 grey seals were killed on the Cornish coast to appease the feelings of fishermen. "This great and unnecessary slaughter which took place both in and out of the close season (September 1 to December 31), received official condonation although, in part at least, it was a flagrant breach of the law; and none of the victims was submitted to scientific examination."[50] An investigation of the stomach-contents of these animals would have gone a long way to establishing some knowledge of the food of the species on the coast of Cornwall. One may infer that fish and other active creatures are the food of this seal, for each molar tooth usually has only one cusp, which is sharp, curved and well adapted to holding a live fish but of little use for cutting or crushing. It has been ascertained that the common seal eats on an average about 10 pounds of food a day, and G. A. Steven[203, 204] who has studied the seals extensively in Cornwall, suggests that the grey seal, being larger, must therefore eat at least 15 pounds. Putting the Cornish seal population at only 300 to 500 animals the annual consumption of food would thus be about 1,000 tons. Even if half of this consists of unmarketable fishes it represents competition with commercial fishermen to the tune of 500 tons yearly, though this does not imply that the fishermen would necessarily capture them if the seals did not. As a result of his researches Steven favours the control of the numbers of Cornish grey seals by supervised killing of as many as is necessary to keep the numbers within an agreed maximum.

On the food of the common seal we have a little more information, for the contents of some seal-stomachs from the east coast have been examined. The remains of fish, mostly whiting, were found in a few of the stomachs, but the most usual food was found to be shell-fish, chiefly cockles and whelks, as many as two dozen of the latter being found in one seal. In connection with these findings we may note that each molar tooth of the common seal has three or more cusps, one large and two or more small, and appear to be more suited to crushing the hard shells of molluscs and crustacea than the pointed molars of the grey seal. However, stomachs of common seals from the Dutch coast have been found to contain quantities of flat-fish.[98]

It would not be denied that a seal would be likely to take any fish that it encountered, and seals can no doubt be destructive to salmon in estuaries and at the mouths of the rivers up which they run, but until exact information about their food is collected the great destructiveness to commercial fisheries with which they are often charged cannot be blindly accepted. Fishermen are very apt to make seals the scapegoats for a scarcity of fish which may very well be due to quite other causes. It should be remembered that seals have been present on our coasts from time immemorial during seasons both of scarcity and abundance of fish.

Although seals are found practically all round our coasts little is known about their actual numbers. A careful estimate based upon a detailed count gave a population of approximately seven hundred grey seals for the north coast of Cornwall in 1934, an average of about seven seals for each mile of the coast line.[204] A similar density of population was found on the coast and islands of Pembrokeshire. In the breeding season over a thousand grey seals congregated on North Rona and its off-lying skerries. In the Wash the herds of common seal are estimated to total at least a thousand animals, possibly fifteen hundred or more. But of the numbers elsewhere little is known. The

grey seal is found all round the west coasts from the Scillies to the
Shetlands, but apart from the Welsh coast as far north as Anglesey,
it is absent from the Irish sea and the coast of southwest Scotland.
The distribution of this species is concentrated on the coastline exposed
to the Atlantic, with much smaller numbers on the east coast of
Scotland. Some live on the east coast of England as far south as the
Wash, but are not permanently resident in any quantity except for an
isolated colony at the Farne Isles. The headquarters of the common
seal is the west coast of Scotland and the Isles, with Orkney and Shetland. The species occurs on all British coasts but is not at all times so
widely distributed as the grey seal; in summer and autumn it migrates
down the east coast of Scotland in considerable numbers. There is a
large population in the Wash and on the neighbouring coasts, as there
was formerly in the estuary of the Tees where the numbers are said
to be now greatly reduced from the abundance of a century ago.
There are also small colonies in the upper part of the Bristol Channel
and in Liverpool Bay,[63] and elsewhere. Wanderers of both species
may turn up on any part of the coast.

Seals are not always easy to identify in the water when little of the
body is exposed. A side view of the head of a bull grey seal with its
long snout is unmistakable, but a full-face view of the head of a female
or young male often resembles the more rounded head of the common seal (Pl. XLII, p. 277). And the front view of a bull common seal
may easily be mistaken for a cow grey seal. When a bull grey seal
looks straight at the observer he often gives the impression of being
provided with bushy eyebrows. This appearance is caused by the small
ear pinnae, that lie some distance behind the eyes, being protruded as
far as they will go as the seal not only looks intently but listens. The
effect of fore-shortening is to make these little protuberances seem
nearer to the eye than in fact they are, and the resemblance to eyebrows is striking. But the habitat can help with the identification of
a seal: any seal on the coast of Cornwall or Wales or swimming in the
boiling surf of the Atlantic among rocks below the cliffs is likely to
be a grey seal, and any seal on the east coast of England is likely to be
a common seal. Where both species are common in the same places,
as in the Scottish islands, identification of seals in the water is very
difficult. On land the matter is easier. Any seal much over six feet
long will be a grey seal, and any adult seal five feet or less in length
will be a common seal. The head of the grey seal is rather long; that

of the common seal is much rounder. But the colour of the coat is of little help, because it is very variable in both species; it may be light with few dark spots, or very dark through the confluence of many black spots; no two animals are quite alike.

In both species the first coat of the yearlings, which appears when the fluffy baby coat is lost, is steely blue with inconspicuous spots and seems almost white if seen at a distance when dry. At the first moult the yearlings get their adult coats.

In the adult of both species too, a new coat is grown in the late summer or autumn, and before the old one is shed it gets very shabby and faded, becoming a dirty brown in the common seal. The colour of seals appears dark when the coat is wet but becomes very much lighter as it dries. The completely diagnostic character between grey and common seals can, however, rarely be seen except in dead specimens. This is the shape and arrangement of the molar teeth. In the grey seal each molar has usually only a single cusp, but in the common seal there is one large cusp and two or more smaller ones; in addition the axes of the molars are arranged obliquely across the tooth row in the common seal.

The observations of Fraser Darling show that there is a tendency for the grey seals of different breeding stations to differ from each other. Out of the breeding season the seals scatter round the coasts and those from different breeding places no doubt mix together, but when they return to the ancestral headquarters they appear to be segregated into separate clans. The general colour of the bulls on the Treshnish Isles is olive brown, but of those on North Rona steel-grey. There is a difference too in the breeding habits of the Scottish and the Welsh grey seals. On Rona the puppy coat lasts for the first two or three weeks and is then shed, first from the face and limbs and then from the body, the process lasting two to three weeks. But on the Welsh islands the pup is more precocious; many are already partly moulted at birth, and in the remainder the moult of the first coat starts at seven to fourteen days, the process lasting only two to seven days, partly because here the young are far more active and their movements assist in getting rid of the fluff.[51]

The time spent on the beach by the Welsh pups is only two to three weeks, about half the corresponding time of the Scottish ones, and weaning takes place at fourteen to eighteen days instead of three to four weeks. The births do not occur at random all through the pupping season, but the cows come ashore at intervals of about seven days and all drop their pups during the same day or two, practically always when the tide is rising. The birth process is short, lasting only a few seconds, and the pup is very active from the first. The afterbirth is expelled about an hour later and is ignored by the mother (with many animals the mother eats it) and it either drifts out to sea or is devoured by the gulls and ravens. The breeding habits of the Cornish grey seals are almost certainly similar to those of their Welsh rather than their Scottish relatives. In the Baltic the young of the grey seals are said to be born in February, and the adults are believed to keep air holes open in the ice during the winter.[105] The differences between the different clans of seals appear to mark the beginning of different geographical races; the colour differences are undoubtedly genetic, and the differences in breeding habits may be at least partly genetic and not merely individual adaptations to different environmental conditions.

Such being the case it is perhaps surprising that there are not greater differences between the seals of the British coasts and their relatives of the same species elsewhere, for both our species are widely distributed. The grey seal is found on the coasts of both sides of the north Atlantic from Nova Scotia and England northwards to Greenland and the northernmost parts of Norway and in the Baltic. The common seal has an even wider distribution, from New Jersey and Maine to Labrador, Newfoundland and Greenland on the west, and from Spain northwards to the arctic coast of Norway on the east of the Atlantic. In addition it occurs in the Pacific from the coast of California northwards to Behring Strait and along the Asiatic coast to Japan. The Pacific, east, and west Atlantic races have been named as separate subspecies.

Besides our two resident and common species of seal several other kinds have occasionally been found on our shores, all of them northern species that have wandered far to the south of their normal range. Stray examples of them will no doubt turn up again from time to time. They are the harp, hooded, ringed and bearded seals and the walrus, the first two being oceanic seals that do not usually come to land but breed on the floating ice and undertake regular migrations. In some years, known as seal-years in Norway, large numbers of these two species together with ringed seals appear off the Norwegian coast much farther south than is usual; the reason for these unusual migrations is probably that the arctic ice-edge is lying exceptionally far south. All the five species are found on both sides of the Atlantic but the following notes refer mainly to their distribution in the European arctic.[105]

The harp-seal (*Phoca groenlandica*) is a small seal, the normal length of males being from 5 to 5½ feet and of females under 5 feet; it varies greatly in colour. The adult male is yellowish-white, with the nose and face to behind the ears black, and a black band along each side of the body, narrow near the tail but increasing in width towards the front where the bands of each side join over the shoulders. The adult female is bluish-grey above, yellowish below, with the black markings indistinct or in the form of scattered splashes, or wholly absent. The colour of the young after casting the white woolly puppy coat is pale grey, darker above, lighter below, often with small grey spots on the back. At succeeding annual moults the spots become larger and more distinct, and in the fourth year they begin to coalesce so that the full pattern is developed in the fifth year. There is some evidence, however, that the adult pattern may sometimes be attained at an earlier age. The harp-seal is gregarious, gathering in immense herds to breed on the northern ice from the White Sea to Novaya Zemlya, Spitsbergen, Jan Mayen and Greenland. In the White Sea and the eastern arctic the young are born in February and March, and on the western ice to the north of Jan Mayen Island in March and April. They are hunted on their breeding places in the European arctic by the Norwegians and Russians, and farther west by the Newfoundlanders.[44] The newborn young are the chief object of pursuit, though males and yearlings are also present with the breeding herds.

The young are about 2½ feet long at birth, very fat, and covered with a white woolly coat that turns yellowish in a few days and is lost within a month. About three weeks after the young are born the females leave them, after which the moult occurs. The change of coat lasts eight to ten days, during which the young do not feed. After the moult they take to the water but need a few days practice to learn to swim well and to find their food, which at first consists largely of small shrimp-like schizopod crustacea. When the ice breaks up the herds spread with the drift ice and new herds of moulting animals are formed that migrate to the north where they form the 'catch of males' of the second part of the sealing season on the west ice. In the eastern arctic between April and June, large numbers migrate from the White

F. Fraser Darling

a. Grey seal about three weeks old, weight about 90 lb.; the white puppy coat is being shed to reveal the spotted grey hair

F. Fraser Darling

b. An old bull grey seal

Plate XLI

Plate XLII

Sea, where they have wintered and given birth to their young, towards Novaya Zemlya and Spitsbergen, and return in October and November. This species does not keep holes open in the ice during the winter; it feeds on pelagic crustacea and fishes, especially gadoids and herrings.

The hooded seal (*Cystophora cristata*) is a large seal, males being up to eight feet and females up to seven feet in length. The male is dark grey or blackish on the back, lighter on the sides and below. Many light spots are thickly scattered over the skin and frequently become confluent to form rings round large dark markings on the back. The colour of the female is paler with less distinct markings. Under the skin of the top of the muzzle in the adult male there is a sac connected with the nasal cavities. This can be inflated at will, when it becomes a conspicuous hood some nine inches high and twelve inches long extending from the nostrils to behind the eyes. This structure is not present in the female, and is an organ similar to the inflatable trunk of the male elephant-seal of the southern oceans. The hooded seal is numerous in Denmark Strait, and is found along the ice to Spitsbergen and Bear Island. It often occurs on the coast of northern Norway and even strays as far south as Bergen. It breeds only on the drift ice near Newfoundland, Labrador, in Davis Strait and along the edge of the west ice, its breeding grounds being more limited in distribution than those of the harp-seal. The young are born from March to May and stay with the mother two to three weeks; thereafter there is a general northerly migration along the coasts of Greenland and Spitsbergen where the moult occurs in June or July.

The ringed seal (*Phoca hispida*) is a small species, the largest males being only about 5 to 6 feet long and the females smaller. The colour of the adult is brownish-black above, lighter on the sides and yellowish-white below. The back and sides are spotted with a number of oval whitish spots, the centres of which are usually dark grey, giving an effect of dark spots ringed with white, from which the species takes its name. The nose and a ring round the eye are usually black, but there is a wide range of variation in colour between individuals, and the markings on the immature animal are much less distinct. The woolly coat of the newborn young is white or yellowish-white. The seals inhabiting the Caspian Sea and Lake Baikal are very closely related to the ringed seal, if indeed they are not merely subspecies of it. The ringed seal is circumpolar and also occurs in the Baltic and in Lake Ladoga; it is not oceanic but keeps to the neighbourhood of the coasts.

M.   T

In the White Sea it is second only to the harp-seal in commercial importance. It usually occurs singly, and only in the mating and breeding seasons are small herds of several animals found. The young are born in spring until as late as May, but the season is prolonged; in the Baltic breeding occurs in March, sometimes later. The breeding places are usually on the ice and are left by the young when they are about six weeks old, but there are no regular migrations. This species feeds upon fish and crustacea, and during the winter it keeps breathing holes open through the ice.

The bearded seal (*Erignathus barbatus*) is a very large seal, old males having been recorded as reaching twelve feet in length and 1,000 pounds in weight, though ten feet and 500 pounds is more usual, and the females attain up to seven feet. As in most seals there is considerable variation in colour between individuals. The general colour is grey, darker above and lighter below, usually with ill-defined dark spots and splashes on the back. Before the moult the coat fades to a dirty brown. The bristles of the whiskers are strongly curved towards their ends, giving a bushy appearance to the beard.

The bearded seal, the largest northern species, is another circumpolar coastal seal that is neither migratory nor gregarious. It is numerous at Spitsbergen, Novaya Zemlya and farther east in the arctic. It visits the fjords in the autumn and keeps breathing holes open through the ice during the winter. In March when the ice begins to break it hauls out on to a floe for the greater part of the day. Later, when the drifting ice would take it too far from the coast, it takes to sandbanks and similar places, for it usually frequents comparatively shallow water. The young are born in April and May. The food consists of molluscs and crustacea.

The Walrus (*Odobenus rosmarus*) is the only species of a family intermediate between the eared and earless seals, having some of the characters of both those families as well as some peculiar to itself. There are no external ears, but the hind limbs are turned forward under the body when the walrus is out of the water. Male walruses reach a great size and bulk, measuring over twelve feet long and weighing over 2,000 pounds. The most prominent feature in both sexes is the pair of long tusks, the greatly enlarged upper canine teeth, used for digging clams out of the sea-bed, and the stout almost quill-like whiskers that assist in shovelling the excavated clams into the mouth. The skin is covered with short brownish-grey hair which almost completely disappears in the old males, whose skin becomes thrown into a series of deep folds and heavy wrinkles, especially round the neck. The walrus, now greatly reduced in numbers from its former abundance, is mainly confined in the European arctic to the east of Spitsbergen. There is a regular annual migration at the end of June from the west of Novaya Zemlya to the Kara Sea and a return in September. The young are born in May, usually on the ice, and are said to stay with the mother until they are two or three years old, and to be fully grown at four to five. The females and young inhabit comparatively shallow water but the males go much deeper. The food consists almost exclusively of molluscs, especially clams and whelks, the former being dug out of the mud at the bottom of the sea with the tusks.

CHAPTER 10

DEER
(ARTIODACTYLA)

" The mark of a deer's tread is called his *slot*; his haunt is termed his *lair*; where he lies down, his *harbour* or *bed*; where he rolls himself, his *soiling pool*; his breaking place over a hedge, his *rack*; when he goes to water it is called going *to soil*; if headed back, it is called *blanched*; if he stops in a river, or lies down in a pool, during the chase, it is called *sinking himself*."

W. SCROPE, *The Art of Deer Stalking*, 1839

O F THE 'ungulata', or hoofed mammals, there are only two truly wild species left in the British islands, the Red and Roe deer; a few other species exist in a feral state as the result of introduction by man or escape from captivity. None of them is common except in certain habitats where they are comparatively free from molestation, for these grazing and browsing animals are incompatible with human activities in general and with agriculture in particular.

The term ungulata, convenient as it is in a general way, is obsolete zoologically, because the animals included under it are separated into two distinct orders that have only a remote affinity with each other. These orders are the Artiodactyla or even-toed ungulates, containing the oxen, deer, sheep, goats, antelopes, and pigs, and the Perissodactyla or odd-toed ones containing the horses, asses, rhinoceroses and tapirs. Members of both these orders walk upon the tips of the toes, which are protected by hooves equivalent to the claws in other mammals. Their limbs are characteristically long, the length being increased by the tip-toe stance because the elongated toes form part of the vertical portion of the limbs. The possession of long limbs gives the animals a good turn of speed that is used in avoiding predators, for the ungulates are comparatively defenceless against the larger carnivores in spite of the presence of horns in many species, these

Plate 15 Cow Seal suckling calf   *Robert Atkinson*

characteristic weapons being used for defeating or intimidating rivals of the same species as much as for defence against enemies of other kinds. Horns consist of bony outgrowths from the skull, covered with skin. In many forms, such as the antelopes, oxen and sheep, the outer layer of the skin covering the horns is very thick and hard, being in fact "horn"; the horns of these animals (with one exception) are not branched, neither are they periodically shed. In others, the deer, the skin covering the bone is thin and dies after the horns are fully grown, peeling off to leave the bone bare; these horns, or antlers as they are called, are shed annually, a resorption of the bone at the base making a weak place where they break off. New antlers are grown each year with remarkable speed, the new growth starting as soon as the old ones are lost. The only species in which the female carries antlers are the reindeer and caribou; in all other deer the antlers are confined to the males.

Most of the artiodactyls, but not the pigs and some others, are ruminants, having complex stomachs containing several compartments. The first compartment or paunch can be quickly filled during grazing or browsing and in it the food undergoes the beginnings of digestion. When the paunch has been filled the animal settles down in some quiet place and chews the food which is returned to the mouth in small portions. After "chewing the cud" the food passes into the later compartments of the stomach on being swallowed for the second time. The ruminating habit is obviously an advantage to animals that feed upon herbage, which has to be eaten in large quantities because of its unconcentrated nature as a food, and whose defence against predators is fleeing from them. The ruminants preserve their lives by constant vigilance, the senses of smell, sight, and hearing being acute, and relied upon in that order of importance.

The red deer, *Cervus elaphus* Linnaeus, the largest species of deer found in Britain, stands about four feet high at the withers. The general colour is reddish-brown, and the underparts are rather paler; there is a conspicuous light patch, the speculum, on the buttocks. Sometimes a dark line runs along the centre of the back, and dark lines form a border to the speculum. The hair on the neck and throat of the stag is long and forms a well marked mane, especially in the rutting season. The coat of the calf is spotted with white during the first few weeks of life, but the spots fade fast after about a month and have disappeared at the age of about eight weeks. The spots go with the long fluffy baby hair which starts falling at about a month and is replaced by a coat of the adult type, though the depth of colour varies considerably from one to another. The new coat is much softer than that of the adult so that the young animal is more woolly and fluffy until it casts its coat after its first winter.

The spotted coat of the calf is believed to show that the adult coat of the ancestors of the species was also spotted, as is that of the fallow deer, and that evolution has eliminated the spots from the adult. It has been suggested that the spotted pattern helps to make the calf inconspicuous as it lies in the fern, and protects it from possible enemies; the spots have therefore been retained, while in the adults, which are better able to protect themselves or avoid their enemies, they have been lost. A point against this supposition is that most predators hunt by scent rather than sight.

In the deer (and many other artiodactyls) the canine teeth of the lower jaw are shaped like the incisors and placed close to them so that the lower jaw appears to have four incisors on each side. In the red deer the first incisor is larger than the others and about equal in breadth to the combined width of the third incisor and the canine. In the upper jaw of the adult stag the canine is well-developed as the 'tush'; upper canines are also present in the hind, but are smaller.

The antlers, present only in the male, grow from pedicles on the frontal bones, and are at first short and unbranched. In park or hand-fed deer the antlers of successive years quickly increase in size and complexity, but in wild deer the process is less regular. In park deer two years old the first proper horns are simple spikes, often forked at the top; in the next year a branch pointing forward near the base, the brow tine, is added, and frequently another branch near the top, the trez tine, also appears. The following year sees the addition of another tine, the bez, between the brow and trez, and the tip above the trez becomes branched into two, three, or sometimes four points. Thereafter for some years the size and weight of the antlers increase, the number of points arising from the terminal cup becoming greater with increasing age until the animal is past its prime, when it starts to 'go back' and the antlers become progressively lighter and poorer as he loses points. There is not an addition of one point to each antler every year, as it is sometimes supposed, and the number of points does not necessarily correspond with the age of the animal in years.

In wild red deer the development of antlers is not so rapid, nor is it so regular, and it is greatly dependent upon variations of the seasons such as the severity of the weather, and the amount of feed available during the growing period, as well as upon the breed of the individual stag. It is quite impossible to draw a standard pattern of development followed by the antlers of all stags because the variations, produced by breed and local circumstances, are so great; but as a general average the sequence sketched below gives a picture that is probably as accurate a representation of the development of the antlers as can be given. But it cannot be more than a general statement, for no two stags are exactly alike.

Horn growth in stags is usually complete by July, but may sometimes continue for a further month. Calves are generally born in June; a stag will therefore be so many years and about two months old when each year's antlers are full grown. In his first September, when three months old, he is still a suckling and has only just shed his baby coat; a year later he has knobs where his horns will be, and compared with a hind calf his head appears squarer at the top owing to the presence of the knobs. When he is two years old the knobs have been replaced by simple spikes up to four or five inches long; at this age he is known to stalkers as a "wee stirkie" or "knobber". In his fourth year, that is when he is three years and about three months old, his horn growth will have increased considerably and he may, under optimum conditions, have as many as ten points.

Each year, when the horns finish growing, the skin covered with fine hairs, the 'velvet', that clothes them during growth, dies and is shed, as a result of the formation of a coronet or burr where the horns join the pedicles. The coronet or burr is a swelling at the base of the horns; this swelling, when horn growth is complete, constricts the blood-vessels feeding the velvet so that it dies and peels off, exposing the bare bone of the antler. When the antler is to be shed some of the bone between pedicle and burr is resorbed so that the antler drops off taking the burr with it, leaving the pedicle, the top of which is of a spongy consistency.

The sixth year sees the full production of points if conditions have not been too severe; there is, however, no definite order for the appearance of points, though the brow tine is generally the first to be grown. The others may appear successively along the beam, or the terminal cup may throw its points before the intermediate bez and trez are formed. Thereafter the quality and size of the head depend entirely upon breed, feeding and seasons: a stag in his sixth year may throw ten points and the next year be a royal, or he might in the next year go back to eight points and become a royal a year later. On the other hand his head may never improve, or may lose points to become a switch. A royal is a stag with twelve points, brow, bez, trez, and a terminal cup with three points; some stags are royal as young as their fifth year. A switch is an adult stag with no points above the brow tines, a clean switch has not even the brows.

A stag's best years are from seven to thirteen, and he generally carries his finest heads from eight to eleven; wild stags 'go back' rapidly after twelve, their antlers losing points and quality, that is both weight and the beautiful deeply granulated surface that characterises the best heads. But environmental conditions play a great part, and a stag may go back in one year, yet improve again in the next. When a stag is going back his points become thin and needly, and the ones on top are generally the first to be lost. In young stags the suture between the frontal bones is loose and conspicuous in the cleaned skull, but it knits tight with increasing age; the diameter of the pedicle and coronet, too, increases with age so that the pedicle may appear relatively shorter in the older animals. Few wild stags reach an age of over fifteen years, and eighteen is probably the extreme limit.

The range of the red deer covers the whole of Europe south of central Scandinavia, except Italy, but from much of it the species has been exterminated. There is considerable variation between the animals from different parts of the range and numerous subspecies have been described, most of them from quite inadequate numbers of specimens, and the status of many of them is obscure. The red deer of Britain has been named *C. e. scoticus* Lonnberg (Pl. 15, p. 288), and is said to be darker than the nearest related race, which inhabits part of western Norway; but the variation in colour between individual beasts is very great. The species is really a woodland animal, and in the forests of central and eastern Europe it reaches its largest size and greatest development of antler. In Scotland the destruction of the forests has driven the deer to the bare moorlands where, deprived of shelter the size and antler growth are comparatively small. Stags from eastern Germany (Pl. XLIV, p. 293) may reach a body size one third (linear) larger than Scottish ones, and have antlers with as many as twenty-four points whereas anything better than a royal is uncommon in Scotland. The cleaned body-weight of Scottish stags rarely exceeds 115 kg. (18 stone) and in most places the average is about 75 to 90 kg. (14 stone), the animals carrying only about eight points. The weight of continental examples with twenty or more points runs to over 200 kg.

The hard conditions are responsible for some at least of the difference between British and continental animals, for the proprietors of some Scottish forests have improved the size of their deer and the quality of the heads by artificial feeding during the winter. On the other hand, it has been noticed that when afforested areas are available to the Scottish deer they do not forsake the moorlands, and it is possible that a race less suited to forest life, and having a thicker, denser coat, has been naturally selected since the general reduction of wooded forests. The red deer of the herds maintained in parks in many parts of the country are very different from the wild animals. They enjoy an abundance of food and adequate shelter from the weather when they need it, and in many places they have for long years been carefully selected for great size and large antler growth; some herds, too, have been reinforced by the importation of breeding stock from parts of the continent where these desired characters are common. These beautiful semi-domesticated park animals differ so much from wild British ones that they might almost be thought to be a different species. Nevertheless the wild animals are descended from ancestors as large and fine as any of the so-called races now living, as is shown by the remains preserved in pleistocene deposits; the horns from which mesolithic man of these islands made his harpoon heads were as fine as those of any park animals (Pl. XLIV, p. 293).

Red deer inhabited practically the whole of the British islands in prehistoric times, but their wild descendants are now confined to the highlands and islands of Scotland, the lake district, Exmoor and the Quantocks, the New Forest, and part of Kerry. There is, however, some doubt whether they are truly indigenous in the New Forest into which the modern deer may have been introduced after the extermination of the natives. But red deer are at large in many other parts of England where there are big woods and especially in areas planted by the Forestry Commission. These animals are escapes from parks or wanderers from areas where there are wild deer, or descendants from them. A recent survey[209, 211] of afforested areas in England and Wales has shown that those in Durham, Lancashire, Yorkshire, Hampshire,

Wiltshire, Somerset, Devon, and Cornwall contain some red deer; though they are not usually numerous they are plentiful in some places.

The wild red deer, the finest beast of the chase in Britain, has been saved from extermination in south-western England through preservation for hunting, and in Scotland for stalking. Much has been written on all aspects of these sports and on the details and measurements of innumerable heads that make such beautiful trophies when displayed in appropriate settings. But much information about the biology of the wild deer remains to be set down, and those who know most about it, and who have spent their lives watching and stalking deer, are reticent in making definite pronouncements on a subject that their long experience has shown them to be ever full of the unexpected. The present writer gratefully acknowledges his indebtedness to three in particular who have most generously assisted him with their unrivalled knowledge of the deer and their ways.[174]

The red deer is gregarious, and each group of animals belongs to a definite territory from which it does not normally stray. The territories are comparatively restricted and not so extensive as might be expected, but the territories of different groups of animals often overlap considerably. Summer and winter territories are different, the former being higher on the hills and the latter on the lower and more sheltered grounds. Throughout most of the year the sexes keep apart in stag and hind herds, the hind herds being rather more closely bound together as social units than those of the stags, and more closely tied to their territories, the stags showing a greater tendency to wander. The closer structure of the hind groups is due to the presence of the calves and yearlings of both sexes (Pl. XLIVa, p. 309), and of young stags, accompanying their mothers; the young stags do not usually leave the hind groups until their third year. The first hind to be alarmed usually leads the herd to safety and the others follow, her acute scenting powers being always on the alert. A warning bark, like a sharp cough, is often uttered as a first signal of alarm. The stag herds behave in much the same manner.

After the stags shed the velvet from their antlers in late August and early September their herds start to break up for the beginning of the rut. At this time many stags travel long distances and may acquire harems of hinds far from their normal home territories. At the rut not only are the antlers fully grown and clean, but the hair of the stag's neck becomes long and bushy, and the neck itself increases in thickness.

Throughout most of the year the stag has no voice, beyond a grunt when he is worried by flies, but at the rut he acquires a deep and powerful voice which he uses to roar a challenge to all who question his right to hold a harem. If hindless stags approach the harem the owner drives them away if he can, but fights are seldom serious and only take place between well-matched animals; if the stags are not fairly even in strength and weight the weaker invariably gives way before a clash occurs.

The roaring of the red deer usually starts about September 20, and the rut about a week later; but its onset is dependent upon the antecedent weather. If it is wet and muggy the stags hang about roaring in a rather half hearted manner on and off for a few days, and may even stop roaring. The first clear frosty nights set them roaring properly, though rutting may begin and continue despite the absence of roaring.

The rutting stag finds and takes possession of a group of hinds which he keeps together as his harem, and from which he drives all rival stags. The hinds accept him as their proprietor, but it by no means follows that they are all in oestrus and ready for service; the probability is that one or two of the hinds are in oestrus and the remainder not. A hind in oestrus will move to find a stag if there is not one about in her neighbourhood. Once in the harem some hinds appear to be brought into full oestrus by the stimulus of the stag's behaviour, his frequent roaring, and his chivvying and chasing of the hinds as he offers service. It is also possible that his encounters with rival stags help in the process of stimulation to oestrus, for though the hinds appear to take little or no notice of them they form part of the pattern of the rut and a contribution towards the general restlessness and excitement of the time.

The season of rut lasts for about six weeks. Starting about the 27th September, the rut is in full swing about the first week in October, and the big stags, which are generally the first to hold harems, are exhausted and run-out by October 30; stags with harems are in a state of constant activity and feed but little. When the big stags retire the smaller animals have their opportunity, for the hinds do not come into oestrus all at the same time and many of them, particularly the old hinds, lag much behind the others. Many hinds may not be pregnant in October and November, in spite of the occurrence of a normal rut, but most of these do not remain barren; they experience a late oestrus and are covered by small stags who are not yet spent and remain about the hinds. There is a class of small rubbishy stags who may never run harems of their own, but slip in and serve a few hinds, possibly quite late after the big stags are run-out.

The hinds that experience oestrus late in the season may have missed coming into oestrus properly earlier on, or they may have become pregnant, and the development of the embryo may have failed after reaching the earliest stages. An occurrence of this sort is well known in cattle, where sometimes the embryo dies at a very early age and, with its enclosing membranes, is either expelled or absorbed; the cause of this phenomenon is not understood. Whatever the cause, some hinds come into oestrus very late so that they are not served until the end of November, and occasional ones not until December or even January. In November the big stags have gone off to the stag herds and some of the small ones—small in size but not young ones—live with the hinds and serve any that come into oestrus, the product of their service being the calves born late in the following season. A calf still showing the spots has been seen as late as October; service must therefore have taken place in the previous February. Late calves are not uncommon and their occurrence shows that oestrus may sometimes be much delayed.

In some seasons, but rarely, there may be no proper rut, and very few calves are born in the following year. One instance is recorded when the rut appeared to break normally for the stags, but few hinds came into oestrus, and after a short interval the usual excitement died away and the rut was over. A possible explanation of these unsuccessful rutting seasons may be that although the stags come into rut, so few hinds come into oestrus that the stimulus to the stags to herd their harems is diminished, and the rut relapses. The stimulus to mating would thus be reciprocal, for not only would the behaviour of the stags stimulate oestrus in the hinds, but the behaviour of the hinds helps to maintain the stags in a condition of rut. The factors concerned are both complex and obscure, but it is evident that some are those of the environment, such as the weather and the conditions of the feed available during the previous months, and some are internal, arising from psychological processes started by the receipt of stimuli through the senses, and acting upon the glands of internal secretion to increase the amounts of sex hormones which influence the animals both physically and psychologically.

Plate 16 RED DEER SEEN THROUGH STALKER'S TELESCOPE

G. B. Kearey

A further example showing the unexpected result of the inter-action of these complicated factors may be mentioned. An autumn which saw a heavy rut was followed by a very severe winter when large numbers of the deer perished. Most of the calves born to the surviving hinds the next year died, so that in spite of the heavy rut the crop of calves was small. The summer, however, was a good one and the deer made a quick recovery from the poor condition into which they had been brought, many of the hinds being helped by having no calves to suckle. The stags, too, were in splendid condition by the autumn, for the hard preceding winter had eliminated most of the weaker ones. Several early roars were heard, but there was no rut, and very few calves were born the next year. Although the survivors had made a quick recovery from the severe winter its deep-seated effects persisted and were strong enough to upset the entire breeding cycle throughout many forests.

One of the most unusual breeding anomalies of the red deer is the well-attested fact that on more than one occasion a stag has been heard to roar—with a good hearty October roar—in May. The reason for this happening, so unlikely that it is almost incredible to those knowledgeable about deer, is quite unknown, but the suggestion has been made that when both sexes are well fed in the spring, the presence of a hind coming into oestrus much later than the extreme dates mentioned above, might bring on a sort of brief false-rut. But stags also come into rut quite independently of the state of the hinds, as is shown by a small stag-herd that permanently inhabits an isolated corrie; here stags are always to be found, and in the autumn they roar, fight, and chase each other about, although they hold no harems and there are no hinds anywhere in the neighbourhood.

Shortly before and during the rut the stags wallow in pools of muddy peat, often becoming very dark in colour as a result; the reason for their doing this is not known. In the spring both sexes wallow, and rub themselves on trees, posts and such objects to help the shedding of the winter coat, the old hairs of which come away in patches and doubtless make the animals feel as frowzy as they look. At this time of year, too, the larvae of warble flies, living under the skin and producing small sores, emerge and fall to the ground where they complete their development, and wallowing probably helps to soothe the irritation caused by them.

Most of the calves are born in June. The calf gets on its feet shortly after its birth, one calf having been observed to rise to its feet three and a half minutes after birth, but the hind makes it lie down in a patch of cover while she is feeding, in the course of which she may graze up to perhaps half a mile away from it. It is not rare to see two calves running with one hind, but this is no proof that they are twins. Twins are evidently very uncommon, for only two cases are known in which twin foetuses were found inside a hind, and that in the experience of three persons who have had a very long and close knowledge of deer. Hinds have been observed to give birth to calves while in both standing and lying positions.

The heaviest losses among calves are caused by sudden floods and also by very severe winters. Two-, three-, and even four-year old beasts also suffer severely in bad winters. The losses among red deer calves occasioned by foxes and eagles are very small. Lactation lasts about 8 months, and calves probably continue sucking until the hind calves again. The period of gestation is given as 230 to 240 days, or about eight months, this being the interval between service and calving.[114] Darling speaks of delayed development in connection with the red deer,[48] but this phenomenon, which is well known in the roe deer (see p. 298), does not occur in the larger species.

In any herd of hinds there are nearly always some animals that have no calf for one reason or another, some of which have been mentioned above. These calf-less hinds are known as "yeld" and they differ slightly from the milk hinds, so that they can be picked out among the others by the eye of experience. The yeld hinds tend to be more sleek, glossy, rounded, and trim and alert in appearance. These differences are caused by the better condition of the yeld hinds, who can devote all their feed to their own bodies and do not have to turn some of it into milk for a calf.

It is probably rare for a hind to be served in her second year, most of the young hinds coming into use for the first time when they are two years and three or four months old, and producing their first calf at the end of their third year. Stags of similar age come into rut, but they have little chance of holding harems of their own until they are at least five or six years old.

Red deer are very sensitive to variations in the weather and often react to the first signs of an approaching change so subtle that they are imperceptible to man. Deer, being "surer than any barometer", are therefore sometimes credited with a fore-knowledge of the weather through some mysterious means; this is hardly justified, for there is every reason to believe that some of their senses are much more acute than human ones. Apart from the periodic movements caused by the changing seasons, deer are very much more restless under some conditions of weather than others. A bad spell nearly always drives the deer down from the higher hills, and thus concentrates the groups together into larger herds in the corries. It is the sudden changes in the character of the weather, particularly the approach of wind, rain, or storms of snow, that set them on the move, for they always react to sudden changes immediately. When winter has set in, the amount of movement about the territories is not usually so great.

The antlers of stags are concerned with rivalry and combat between the males, that is with inter-male competition within the species, and not primarily with defence against enemies. If antlers were of importance as a protection against enemies the hinds would possess them too, nor would they be discarded annually, leaving the animals defenceless for some months while the new ones are growing. Indeed, while the antlers are in velvet they are a great liability to a stag, for they are extremely sensitive and he takes the greatest care not to hurt them. In addition, it is only at the time of the rut that stags develop aggressive behaviour; after the rut, but while they still have their antlers, they flee from danger and only fight as a last resort when brought to bay. The growth of the antlers must put a great strain on the calcium-metabolism of the animals, for they have to obtain several pounds of calcium salts and phosphorus from the herbage on which they feed in order to build them; it is doubtless for this reason that they chew cast antlers and old bones, often eating the whole of the antlers, in a very short time.

Experiments made at Ardverekie in 1937 and 1938 threw some light on this question. Samples of soil were taken from many areas of the ground concerned, and analysed to discover the deficiencies in calcium and other salts that were thought to be necessary for the animals grazing there. Feeding cubes were prepared containing, in addition to substances of food value, the required proportion of mineral salts that had been found lacking in the soil. The cubes were fed to the stags during the early spring and summer of both years while the stags were growing their horns; no cast antlers were eaten or chewed in any way. For various reasons the feeding of these cubes had to be

discontinued in the following year. Immediately the eating of cast antlers was resumed by the stags, and it has continued in the normal way
ever since. The advantage to the stags with the best heads in securing
and holding harems must, in general, be great for this heavy metabolic
burden to have been imposed by the process of natural selection.

The occurrence of occasional antler-less stags, known as 'hummels'
in Scotland and as 'notts' in Devon and Somerset, presents something
of a puzzle that, at first sight appears to contradict this conclusion.
The hummel does not grow antlers at any time during his life, but he
has rudimentary pedicles in the usual position. The latter have their
tops rounded off as convex domes, which are smooth and have a
surface of the same appearance as the bones of the lower parts of the
pedicles and of the top of the skull itself. There is no sign that there
has ever been any formation of a coronet, however rudimentary, upon
the pedicles. The pedicles are completely covered by the skin, on
which the hair grows exactly as it does on the rest of the head. The
general shape of the skull is the same as that of a normal stag and does
not resemble that of the hind. Hummels are rather rare, their occurrence being perhaps about one to every two or three hundred horned
stags. The cause of their lack of horns is quite unknown.

Contrary to expectation, these antler-less animals are not unsuccessful in maintaining their harems against rivals, but are well able
to hold their own against stags with antlers, which they charge with
their foreheads, like polled bulls. They are often in better condition
than the antlered stags, and so are earlier in coming into rut, no doubt
owing to their being spared the strain of growing antlers; for the same
reason, probably, they are often above the average weight. It is their
heavy weight and earliness in coming into rut that gives them their
advantage over the other stags. But in the long run the advantage is
evidently with the stags possessing antlers; if it were otherwise natural
selection would have caused the hummel to have supplanted the normal type, provided that the hummel character is hereditary. Hummels
are potent, but whether they are also fertile is open to doubt.

The behaviour of the hinds, also, shows that although the antlers
are important in intra-sexual selection, that is in the selection of the
stags which shall have the best chances of fathering the next generation, there is no selection of one sex by the other. The hinds show the
greatest indifference to their proprietor and take little obvious notice
of him where he is herding them; if he gives way to a rival they accept

Oliver Pike

a. Fallow buck with the horns in velvet

Paul Popper Ltd.

b. Sika Deer

Plate XLIII

Plate XLIV   *J. Rödle*
The large German race of the red deer: stag roaring, roebuck in foreground

the newcomer and appear scarcely to notice the change. Further, the success of the hummels in holding harems is incompatible with any idea of selection by the hinds.

Stags may be antler-less for several reasons; the antlers, which are secondary sexual characters, depend, in part at least, upon the presence of an adequate supply in the blood of the male hormone, which is produced in the testes. Stags whose testes have been injured, removed, or are otherwise defective are often one-antlered or antler-less; other causes of the lack of an antler or antlers are injuries to other parts of the body caused by accident, such as old wounds, or direct injury to the pedicles or coronets by fighting or by the animal catching its head in a wire fence or the like. But the growth of antlers cannot be entirely under the influence of the male hormone, because a one-sided injury, and particularly an injury or defect in the testis of one side, usually produces the malformation or absence of the antler on the opposite side of the body only. This points strongly to the influence of some nervous mechanism acting through the brain in addition to the hormonal factor. Were the defect in the antlers solely due to a single testis being unable to produce a large enough quantity of hormone, both antlers should be stunted equally, for the distribution of the hormone in the blood is necessarily impartial. Very rarely indeed the antler of the same side, and not that opposite, may be affected by a defective testis, for one case of this condition has been observed. But more exact information on the occurrences would be welcome. Inconclusive results were obtained from an experiment on two sika stags from each of which one of the testes was removed. In both animals the antlers grown after the operation were smaller than those grown before, and in one of them the 'cross effect' was produced but not in the other.[171a] Zawadowsky[233a] who did some similar experiments on fallow- and red deer in Russia came to the conclusion that any 'cross effect' (which is apparently strongly rooted in hunters' tradition all over Europe) was merely accidental and had no basis in evidence. The number of cases of 'cross effect' reported by reliable observers is, however, so great that further investigation is obviously desirable before dismissing the matter as a fallacy.

Huxley[108, 108a] has claimed that there is an allometric relation between the body weight of adult stags and the weight of their antlers. This relation is the principle of compound interest, and if the one dimension is plotted against the other logarithmically the graph produced shows

M.   U a straight line; the larger the stag, the greater is the fraction of his total weight appropriated to his antlers. This is illustrated in the magnificent heads produced by the heavy park stags, and the huge prehistoric wild deer, when compared with the poor heads grown by undersized animals. The relation between body weight and antler weight is not, however, constant throughout the life of any individual animal; in early life the rate of increase of antler weight is greatest, and when the animal has passed its prime the antler weight decreases. But against this theory it must be emphasized that some of those best qualified to judge from long experience in Scotland state very definitely that there is in general no relation whatever between body weight and antler weight among red deer in Scotland. They add that it is the breeding, the climate and the feeding that produce horn or body or both, and even then there is not by any means a constant relation even from year to year in an individual beast—let alone any relation whatever among stags as a whole. Some areas produce light bodies and big magnificent heads, others heavy bodies and miserable little heads, and there is every gradation between, even in the same areas, all over Scotland.

The small size of the antlers and the light body-weight of the present wild red deer, when compared with those of the prehistoric deer and of park animals, do not necessarily indicate any genetic or subspecific difference. The body-weight is light because the climatic and feeding conditions are less favourable to the wild deer, and the small antlers may be correlated with the light body-weight by the allo-metric principle. Confirmation that this view is correct is provided by what has happened to the red deer introduced from Scotland and elsewhere into New Zealand. Their new home was profusely forest-covered and feed was plentiful; in a generation the stags had become twice the weight of Scottish wild deer, and carried huge heads with more than twenty points. After some time the herds had increased so far that the forests were partly destroyed; "with overcrowding and less favourable food conditions, 'degeneration' set in, and now in many regions the mean and the maximum body-weight and point-number are far below what they were a few decades back."

When stags fight they clash head-on with lowered antlers, and try to push each other back. If one gives way the other attempts to throw him by a twist of the head, and to get in a blow with the antlers on the rival's unprotected flank, such a blow sometimes producing a fatal wound. But stags generally fight only if they are fairly well matched, and after some pushing with lowered heads one of them usually gives up, his main concern being to disengage and get away without exposing his flank to the antlers of the other. Weight for weight the switch often appears to have the advantage in a fight, for his horns do not easily become entangled in those of his adversary. In fighting of this sort, weight of body is as important as size of antler, hence the ability of a heavy hummel to hold his own. Because stags do not fight unless well matched there is a great advantage for any stag to be a heavy animal not only for actual fighting but for the 'bluff' value. Smaller stags will not accept his challenge and consequently do not attempt to oust him from his harem.

In a polygamous animal such as the red deer the successful male's ability to produce descendants is multiplied by the number of females that he possesses. The success conferred by large size and massive antlers on the possibility of leaving offspring may be so great that these characters become greatly emphasised and for all other purposes but breeding they may be a disadvantage. Intra-sexual selection may thus lead to the acquisition of characters that are an embarrassment except at the breeding season. This stage has not been reached by the red deer, but it may have been by *Megaceros*, the extinct giant deer ("Irish elk"), which stood over six feet high at the withers, and carried antlers spanning over nine feet and weighing seventy or eighty pounds. This species became extinct in mid-pleistocene times, and the great strain of annually growing the enormous antlers probably contributed to its decline when conditions became unfavourable.

The only other species of deer native to Britain and living in a truly wild state is the Roe, *Capreolus capreolus* (Linnaeus). This is a small graceful animal, the largest bucks standing little more than two feet high at the shoulders and weighing 40 to 60 pounds. Antlers are normally present in the male only and are short and erect; they do not spread and rarely reach a length of more than nine inches. There are seldom more than three tines, formed by a double bifurcation, which are generally quite short (Pl. XLVIb, p. 309); an error appears to have crept in to the drawing of roe antlers, copied from Millais' photograph, given by Johnston;[112] the two antlers described as from Scottish peat (pleistocene) are almost certainly those of modern Indian hog-deer.

The antlers of the roe, like those of the red deer, show an allometric relation between their weight and that of the body as a whole.

but unlike the relation in the red deer it is negative instead of positive. This means that the weight of the antlers is a smaller fraction of the total body-weight in the larger adult bucks than in the smaller ones. In the life of the individual animal, too, there is a change with age, as in the larger species. The rate of increase in the weight of the antlers at first rises, but it becomes retarded at a much earlier age in the roe, showing that the allometric relation can be modified by biological conditions. One of these conditions may be that the roe lives more in dense cover than the red deer; another may be that the roe goes about in small family parties, and has no harem system with its intense intra-sexual selection.

The coat of the roe is warm red in colour during the summer, the speculum being pale or almost white; in the winter it is greyish and has two white splashes one above the other on the throat; the coat is changed in May and October. The fawns are spotted with white during their first year. The tail of the roe is much reduced and is scarcely apparent externally as a small pimple, though internally there are six tail vertebrae.

The range of the roe extends from Great Britain eastwards into Asia, where it is joined by that of allied species, and from the Mediterranean to southern Scandinavia. Four subspecies have been described from different parts of Europe, differing from each other in size and colour. The race inhabiting Britain is separated as *C. c. thotti* Lonnberg, being rather darker in colour than the allied continental subspecies, and having the face darker than the rest of the body. Wild roe are now to be found only in Scotland, and possibly in some parts of the north of England; in the rest of England and Wales the original stock has long been extinct, and in Ireland it has never been indigenous. Nevertheless roe are at large in many parts of these countries, but they are all descended from animals deliberately introduced by man. One of the oldest of these introductions was made into Dorset, where for many years there has been a considerable population of 'wild' roe. A recent survey of the Forestry Commission's areas in England and Wales has shown that the roe is now very widespread in the wooded districts of the country that are suitable to it; it was noted in the forests in sixteen counties extending from Northumberland to Sussex and Devon, and reported as numerous in some of them.[211]

The roe is a woodland animal, and is mainly nocturnal in its habits, generally lying up in thick cover during most of the day. It is not gregarious like the red deer, but goes in small parties which usually consist of a buck, a doe, and her fawns, but sometimes the group contains five or six animals. Roe are restricted to definite territories like the larger species, but are constantly moving their ground within them; unlike that species, the group is led by the buck, the doe and fawns with perhaps a yearling, following him. The buck is a rather pugnacious animal and will fight others even out of the season of rut, driving other bucks away from his family party; he expels any buck older than a yearling from his group, though the does usually drive off their yearlings when they are about to drop their new fawns.

The social structure of this species is thus entirely different from that of the red deer; there is no system of harems in which the buck devotes his whole attention to the does for a limited time each year, nor any segregation of the sexes into separate herds for the rest of the year. The intra-sexual advantage possible to the buck is here much less because there is only a small number of females to each successful male, and in this point perhaps there lies one of the causes of the negative allometric relation of antler-weight to body-weight.

The fawns, usually twins, are born in May or the beginning of June, each doe retiring by herself at this time and usually driving off the yearlings of the previous season. After about ten days the does return to the bucks with their fawns and remain with them until after the rut. The rut takes place in July and August, when the bucks bark loudly, and the does utter a softer more squeak-like cry that attracts the bucks; indeed a call imitating this cry has been much used, especially on the continent, to lure bucks within range of the gun. After the rut the bucks often wander away for a month or two to higher ground at the upward limit of the forest, where they live alone until they rejoin the family parties. It has been stated that sometimes a second rut then occurs in October, but this is very improbable and more accurate and detailed observations are needed before this matter can be regarded as substantiated. The bucks shed their antlers in November and December, and the new ones are fully grown and clean in April.

The roe is one of the mammals in which delayed implantation of the embryo occurs. The egg-cell is fertilised at the rut, but after the earliest stages of development the growth of the embryos stops and the process of gestation is suspended for several months. The embryos in their small spherical sacs remain loose inside the uterus from August to December, and it is not until the end of the year that development is resumed. The growing embryos only then become attached to the wall of the uterus and establish a close relationship with the maternal circulation. The active part of the process of gestation therefore lasts from December onwards and occupies about five months only, its length being recorded as from 140 to 160 days, although the interval between the rut and the birth of the fawns is more nearly nine months. It is not known what advantage this delay in development may be to the species, nor are the physiological processes that bring it about understood. It is certain, however, that the hormones produced by the pituitary body and the ovary play an important part in the phenomenon of delay, and that the corpora lutea, which replace the follicles in the ovary that produced the egg cells, become larger and apparently more active in secreting hormone at the time when development is resumed.

In many places particular parts of the territory of the roe form centres for the activities of the animals during the rut, though in some localities inhabited by roe they are inconspicuous or perhaps even lacking. These are the racing-rings, more or less circular tracks trodden out by the bucks chasing the does among the trees, round one of which the ring is often centred. If the rings are made in the open they usually centre round a tuft of herbage or rushes taller than the surrounding vegetation. The racing rings are used at the period of the rut, and the origin of the racing habit is probably connected in some way with the so-called courtship activities of reproduction.

Some observers[149] report that the doe allows the buck to chase her round and round the ring, the play sometimes being fast enough, and lasting long enough, for both animals to become temporarily quite exhausted. At the end of a chase pairing takes place, and then racing is resumed and the whole process may be repeated many times. But recently a rather different pattern of behaviour has been described. Roe watched at their rings in Argyllshire in 1948 and 1949 did not race; they walked and only occasionally did the buck break into a slight trot when he fell behind the doe.[34] His activity appeared to be directed towards preventing the doe from leaving the area in which the ring lay. Not only did he follow her but he dodged round in front beneath her nose as if to head her off or stop her. He also shouldered her from one side so that she was guided into a more or less circular course. It is suggested that the rings are probably formed by this action of the buck in herding the doe on a circular track. The doe evidently enjoys this play as much as the buck, for she does not attempt to break away; while a pair were watched walking the ring for half-an-hour the buck served the doe nine times. The fawns, which are about three months old at the time of the rut, are never seen at the rings, and it is believed that the does make them lie down in thick cover from sunset to sunrise while the mothers are on, or grazing near, the rings.

It has been stated that roe return to the rings in October, and that a second rut then takes place. The latest observations, however, do not confirm this entirely. In October the roe do return to the neighbourhood of the rings, but they do not run in them, and merely feed and have their beds in the near neighbourhood. Although the bucks have deserted the does for about a month after the rut the animals that return to the rings are the same individuals that used them earlier in the season, and it is certain that the same buck and doe are paired for the season and not just for the rut. Whether roe pair for life is less certain, and on the whole is improbable.

The rings may be large or small, symmetrical or very irregular in shape, the exact configuration depending upon the nature of the ground. Sometimes an irregular track crosses a large ring, forming a rough figure-of-eight. Some of the rings are of considerable age, being used in successive seasons for many years. Roe are much attached to particular spots for their rings, which are often sited in what appear to be very unsuitable places, for instance near roads where the animals are disturbed by passing traffic. The suggestion has been made that these positions are attractive because of some special feature of their vegetation, and in particular that the presence of a growth of purple moor grass (*Molinia*) infected with the parasitic fungus ergot may be the draw.[35] This theory could be tested only with the aid of a very careful and exhaustive survey of the distribution of ergot, knowledge which we do not possess; but it is not probable that the distribution of this plant is restricted to the neighbourhood of the rings, for it is common enough.

The meaning of the ring-habit in roe is probably similar to that of the 'courtship' activities of so many mammals and birds, and results in more successful mating partly through stimulating the pituitary to the release of gonadotropic hormones into the blood. These act upon the gonads in both sexes so that the reproductive processes are fulfilled. But why the ring-habit should be the form of behaviour adopted to lead eventually to mating we do not know, any more than we know the reason for the exact pattern in any other species of animal in which comparable phenomena occur.

Besides our native deer there are several other species at large in various parts of the country; they have either escaped from enclosures or have been deliberately turned out. The best known of these is the fallow deer, less familiar are the sika or Japanese deer and its sub-species the Manchurian sika, the Siberian roe, and the Chinese munt-jac. There is now a proposal to introduce reindeer into some parts of Scotland where it is believed that they may be able to produce a meat crop from land that is too barren to be otherwise exploited. Two other species, both from India, the axis and the hog-deer are sometimes kept in parks, and it is possible that some individuals have escaped, though doubtful whether the axis can survive winter at large.

Our feral deer live in woods of greater or smaller size, and are often very expert at keeping out of sight so that their presence may be quite unsuspected by the casual observer. They are widely spread through-out England, but are very scarce in Wales, from the greater part of which they are absent. Practically every area that is afforested soon attracts some deer of one or more kinds, but the distribution and abundance of deer in different districts have undergone some changes during the last ten years, largely as a result of the war. In some places they have decreased; causes of decrease mentioned by Taylor[209, 211] are the clear felling of woods for timber, the increased attention given to agriculture and the precautions taken against foot-and-mouth disease, the proximity of military camps, and the shortage of meat. On the other hand there are some areas that have had less disturbance than in normal times, and there the deer have increased. In newly planted forests the roe is one of the first species to appear, and has in this way made considerable gains of territory.

The Fallow deer, *Dama dama* (Linnaeus) is a native of southern Europe, its range extending along the border of the Mediterranean and into Asia Minor, whence it has been introduced into most of the more northern countries. The date of its introduction into Britain is so remote that nothing is now known of it; popular belief credits the importation to the Romans. The species has for long been a favourite ornament for parks, and has also existed in a feral state in such places as the New and Epping forests. Fallow deer at large are now very widely distributed throughout England, few counties being without at least a small population, and in some woodland areas they are numerous.

The fallow deer stands about three feet, or a little more in height at the shoulder; the summer coat, assumed in May, is reddish-fawn ('fallow') dappled with numerous white spots; throughout the winter after the change in October it is uniform greyish-brown without spots. The underside is white, as is the speculum; a dark line along the back extends on to the tail, sending offshoots to outline the speculum. But not all fallow deer are fallow in colour, for there is a dark race in which the summer coat is blackish-brown without spots, in winter similar, but slightly lighter; some park herds consist solely of this race, but it is more usual to see both together. The antlers of the buck have brow and trez tines, but no bez, and the top is palmated, being expanded into a flat plate on the hind edge of which the points appear as notched crenulations (Pl. XLIIIa, p. 292). In many places such as the New Forest, the antlers are poor and the amount of palmation is small; park bucks that are well fed have the most elaborate antlers.[149] The first incisor tooth of this species is much larger than the others; it is expanded laterally so that its lingual surface is almost triangular. There are no upper canines or "tushes".

In parks the fallow deer is gregarious, but in the feral state it is much less so, going about in only small parties. The rut is in October, at which time the bucks gather the does into harems, and drive off their rivals with some show of fighting. After the rut the bucks and does herd together for the rest of the winter, but during the summer the bucks keep apart. The antlers are dropped in May, and the new ones are full grown and clean in August. The fawns, which are spotted like the adults, are mostly born in June. Although the modern fallow deer is not a native of this country, a number of allied species or subspecies, now extinct, formerly existed in pleistocene times, and their remains are common in the deposits of East Anglia.

The Japanese deer or sika is a small relative of the red deer which has been introduced from the far east and, being very hardy, has prospered (Pl. XLIIIb, p. 292). It is present in England, Scotland and Ireland, and is numerous in some parts of the midlands and of the southern counties from Kent to Dorset. This species stands about 2 feet 9 inches high at the shoulder; the summer coat is reddish-brown with yellowish spots, the tail and speculum white, the latter with a black border. The winter coat is dark grey-brown without spots. The antlers have a brow tine, a slightly curved beam with usually no more than two points on top. Two subspecies of this deer have been introduced, the typical species, *Sika nippon nippon*, from Japan, and the larger but otherwise very similar *S. n. mantchuricus* from the mainland of Manchuria. Like the red deer this species is polygamous, the stags fighting and calling during the rut in August and September when they collect the hinds into small harems.

The Siberian roe, *Capreolus pygargus*, is at large in some numbers in parts of the eastern midlands, having spread from Woburn park in Bedfordshire. It is similar to the native roe, but larger in size, with larger antlers, and is less stump-tailed. The Chinese muntjac, *Muntiacus reevesi*, whose distribution and origin in this country are similar to those of the last mentioned species, is a small deer, standing barely eighteen inches in height. Its colour is chestnut red speckled with grey, the legs dark brown, and the throat white. The antlers, merely a few inches long, end in a single spike, and bear a small brow tine only. They are borne on lengthy pedicles along the front of which there is a line of dark hair that extends down as a stripe on each side of the face. In the female the face line ends as a tuft of dark hair in the position of the pedicle in the male. The upper canine teeth of the male are large and project from the mouth as small tusks; they are said to be used in fighting rather than the horns. The muntjacs are sometimes called the "barking-deer" from the characteristic and comparatively loud bark, which is uttered when they are alarmed, and during the rut. There are, in addition, animals of at least three further species at large in Britain, animals that are the feral descendants of recently introduced wild stock. These are the Indian muntjac, *Muntiacus muntjak*; the black-tailed deer of western North America, *Odocoileus columbianus*; and the Chinese water-deer, *Hydropotes inermis*.

There are no wild ungulates other than deer in the British Isles, but feral escapers from domestication exist in various places. Such are the so called wild goats living in the hills and mountains of Wales, Scotland and Ireland, and the ponies of Dartmoor, Exmoor, the New Forest and elsewhere. The herds of feral cattle living or formerly living in various parks such as those of Chillingham, Chartley, Cadzow, Vaynol, Lyme, Dynevor, Leigh Court, and many other places, are said to be descended from the extinct wild aurochs, *Bos primigenus*, but their origin is really quite unknown. Even if they show some resemblance, they are certainly poor dwarfs compared with those giants of the past. Some of the herds are believed to have been driven into the parks in the thirteenth century and to have continued in unbroken descent to modern times, but they were not uninfluenced by man; the characteristic colour of these cattle is white, but that is because they have been artificially selected, the coloured calves which were commonly produced being always killed in order to encourage the desired points. The small breed of horned sheep from Soay of the St. Kilda group, where it lives in a feral state, closely resembles the domesticated sheep of the Iron age, and may be directly descended from it with little change. But these animals descended from domesticated stock hardly come within the scope of a book dealing with the wild mammals of Britain. They form a fascinating study of their own, as do the past and present breeds of domestic animals, and a study of any one of them would provide the substance for a volume.

An exception may perhaps be made in favour of the goat, which is the species that comes nearest to being a true wild animal if it is emancipated from domestication. The domestic goat (*Capra hircus hircus* L.) is descended, with some cross breeding with other races, from the Persian or Grecian wild goat (*Capra hircus aegagrus* Erxleben).[228] In a feral state it is widely distributed in many parts of Scotland, especially in the Highlands and Islands, in Wales, and Ireland. When goats escape from domestication they revert to a wild type within a few generations, often within ten years. Darling[228] attempts to answer the question, what is the influence on their nitrogen metabolism that makes them run increasingly to hair and horn until the standard of the wild goat is reached? He believes that the influence is natural selection, acting chiefly through the climate. The breeding season falls early, the kids often being born in late January and February, and the climatic conditions thus form a "fine meshed sieve in preserving only those that suit the conditions."

Once goats becomes feral they take to the higher parts of the mountains where the drainage is good, for they appear to dislike wet ground. They move about on the most dangerous rock faces, across which they appear to know all the possible paths. They scramble about deliberately and are never in a hurry, the billy leading the party with the nannies and kids following; in the worst places the nannies send the kids ahead and keep them to the path with a prod from their horns if they tend to stray. Parties consist of about half-a-dozen nannies and their kids, led by a mature billy, with a number of yearling billies following loosely on the outskirts. Feral goats are extremely wary; if approached they wait as long as the intruder is in sight, but as soon as he is hidden by the country they disappear and are unlikely to be found again.[228]

CHAPTER II

WHALES IN GENERAL
(CETACEA)

" They row up gently to the *Whale*, and so he will scarcely shun them; and when the *Harpineer*, standing ready fitted sees his Opportunity, he strikes his *Harping Iron* into the *Whale* about or before the Fins, rather than towards the *Tail*. Now the *Harping Irons* are like those which are usual in *England* in striking *Porpus's*; but of singular good Metal, that will not break, but wind, as they say, about a Man's Hand. To the *Harping Iron* is made fast a strong Lythe Rope, and into the Socket of that *Iron* is put a Staff, which when the *Whale* is struck comes out of the *Socket*, and so when the *Whale* is something quiet, they hale him up by the Rope, and it may be, strike into him another *Harping Iron*, or lance him with Lances in Staves till they have kill'd him."

Philosophical Transactions, to the end of the year 1700, Abridg'd

THE WHALES are the most thoroughly aquatic of the mammals, no others having gone so far along the road of adaptation to life in the water. Because they are entirely water-borne and relieved from the necessity of supporting their own weight they have been able to attain enormous size, far greater than would be possible for any land animal. Among the whales are found not only the largest mammals, but the largest animals of any sort that exist or ever have existed. Their vast size and inaccessibility to observation among the waters of the ocean have always excited the interest of naturalists, seafarers and others, so that a fair amount of information has accumulated about some of the interesting details of their lives and structure. But all whales are not giants; the comparatively small porpoises and dolphins of our own coastal waters are no less whales than the leviathans of the antarctic.

The chief distinguishing characters of the whales among mammals are the fish-like form of the body, the absence of hind limbs, the fore

305

limbs in the shape of flippers, the nearly complete absence of hair from the surface of the body, the transverse tail-flukes, and the position of the nostrils or 'blow-holes' on the upper part of the head. All these features obviously fit the whales for their particular manner of life, as do many others to be mentioned in due course (fig. 76).

FIG. 76

The common porpoise, showing the general features of a cetacean, viz. fore limb modified as paddle or flipper, no hind limbs, horizontal tail flukes, torpedo shape

Structurally the whales fall into two natural groups, the toothed whales (Odontoceti) and the whalebone-whales (Mysticeti), distinguish-ed, as the names imply, by the presence of teeth in the one, and of that peculiar arrangement of baleen plates miscalled whale bone in the other. The two groups have many characters in common. Beneath the thin skin lies a thick layer of fat held in the meshes of a network of fibrous tissue, forming the blubber that insulates the animal and prevents loss of heat from the warm body to the cold water. The surface of the body is quite naked and smooth so that skin friction with the water is reduced to a minimum, but that typically mammalian character, the possession of hair, is not completely absent, for on the snout and edge of the lower jaw in most species there is a number of scattered hairs, at least in the young. These sparse beards and moustaches are the last remnants of the hairy covering of their ancestral forms and probably represent the tactile vibrissae commonly present in so many mammals. On the upper surface of the head lie the open-ings of the nasal passages, usually called the 'blow-hole' in whales (fig. 90, p. 344). This migration of the nostrils from the usual position at the end of the snout is an obvious adaptation to aquatic life, for it brings them clear of the water with least effort when the animal comes to the surface to breathe.

The unusual position of the nostrils is accompanied by considerable changes in the form of the facial part of the skull, the nasal bones being greatly reduced in size and the parts forming the jaws much elongated. In the toothed whales, where the nostrils are reduced to a single blow-hole, there is also in many species a great asymmetry of the bones of the facial region in correlation with the reduction of one of the nasal passages to leave the other as a single tube. The torpedo shape of the whale's body excludes the necessity for a mobile neck, and in con-formity with the absence of any externally visible neck region the bones of the corresponding part of the backbone are much reduced. The seven neck vertebrae characteristic of nearly all mammals are reduced in length and may be partly or wholly fused together so that in some species they form a single solid mass of comparatively small size.

Nearer the tail there is another region where the backbone differs

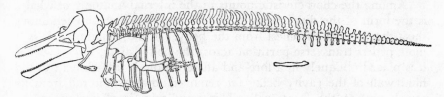

FIG. 77

Skeleton of the common porpoise ; the ribs and limbs of the near side only shown. The breast bone is very short, the bones of the arm and hand flattened and shortened, but those of the fingers increased in number. The hind limbs and pelvic girdle are represented by a slip of of bone embedded in the muscles towards the hind end of the body. There is no bone supporting the back fin, nor the flukes of the tail

from that in most other mammals. This is the region to which in most mammals the pelvic girdle, the foundation that supports the hind limbs, is attached. In whales the body is driven through the water by the action of the tail, and the hind limbs have become unneces-sary for the purpose. The limbs and the girdle supporting them are extremely reduced and represented only by some small bones embedded in the muscles of the hinder part of the belly-wall. The connection between the limb-girdle and the backbone is entirely lost, and the sacral vertebrae, no longer modified to make this connection, have returned to a simpler form, taking their place in an unbroken series extending from the back to the end of the tail (fig. 77). But although the hind limbs are functionless and are represented by trifling rudiments, the reduced pelvic girdle cannot be entirely discarded by the whales. Not only does the pelvic girdle of mammals anchor the hind-limbs, but to it are attached the muscles of the external reproductive organs. And although in the whales the former are rudimentary the latter most certainly are not, and the small representatives of the pelvic girdle are anything but functionless rudiments, for to them are attached the muscles whose action is to support the genitalia during pairing. The fore-limbs are not anchored to the rest of the skeleton by any bony connection but are attached solely by muscles. The bones of their upper parts are reduced in length and those of each finger are increased in number so that the length of the flipper beyond the wrist is augmented. In all whales the fingers and hand are ensheathed in an undivided covering to form the flipper or paddle on which there are neither nails nor claws.

Among the characteristic points in the internal anatomy of whales is the form of the diaphragm or midriff, the muscular and tendinous sheet that divides the chest from the belly. In most mammals it is a more or less transverse partition across the body cavity, but in whales it is placed obliquely in a fore-and-aft direction, its attachment to the hind wall of the cavity being far removed towards the tail from its attachment to the front wall. This peculiarity is of importance in connection with the adaptions to deep diving discussed below (p. 314).

Another character connected with diving is the presence of peculiar networks of arteries massed round the backbone, round the spinal cord, round parts of the brain and elsewhere. Such networks whose anatomical name is *retia mirabilia*, are not confined to the whales, but their luxuriant development in these animals is very much greater than that found in some other mammals. Connected with the aquatic habits, but not particularly with deep diving, is the peculiar form of the kidneys in whales. In the kidneys of mammals the minute bodies known as *glomeruli* which filter water and substances dissolved in it from the blood are massed near the surface. In all but the larger land mammals a kidney of the usual bean-shape is large enough to contain near its surface sufficient glomeruli to cope with the needs of the body.

But in mammals which live in water, and in very large land mammals, the form of the kidney is different. These animals need larger kidneys than most, the first apparently because they imbibe

Plate XLV   *Water-colour sketch by J. Ritchie*

Red deer; the extinct pleistocene form on the left and its small modern descendant on the right

Paul Popper Ltd.

a. Red deer hind and her calf

Mondiale

b. Roebuck (photographed in Germany)

Plate XLVI

greater quantities of water than land mammals of corresponding size, and the second merely because their large size means that there is a great volume of blood to be filtered. The larger whales fall into both categories, and have an added necessity for large kidneys because they have no sweat-glands through which water may be lost. In such animals it is therefore necessary to increase greatly the surface area of the kidney and thus the number of glomeruli, and this is done by dividing the organ up into a number of lobes; a familiar example is the lobulated beef kidney, so conspicuously different from the conventionally kidney-shaped kidneys of sheep and pigs. In the whales the lobulation is carried to an extreme so that the kidney is in effect divided up into a very large number of small kidneys, often many hundreds, packed together closely like an enormous bunch of grapes and compressed so that each grape is faceted by contact with its neighbours. In this way the effective surface area and with it the number of glomeruli is greatly increased without greatly increasing the total bulk of the organ.

The problems confronting the physiology of whales in deep and prolonged diving are similar to those so successfully solved by the seals, but the adaptations achieved by the whales are not the same. The whales, being much more completely adapted to aquatic life than are the seals, are able to dive for much longer periods and to much greater depths. The main problems to be solved are two, how to hold the breath for anything up to two hours, and how to resist the effects of pressure at great depths. It may be said at once that although much has been discovered on these points, our knowledge of the details is by no means complete.

The first point resolves itself into the question, how can life and activity be maintained during prolonged diving without replenishing the reserves of oxygen in the body, and how can sufficient oxygen be taken down to last so long? When a whale dives it takes some oxygen with it in the air held by the lungs, some combined with the haemoglobin of the blood, some with the myoglobin (see p. 261) of the muscles, and a lesser amount dissolved in the tissue fluids. It has been estimated that of the total oxygen store carried down by a fin-whale 9 per cent is contained in the lungs, 42 per cent in the blood, 42 per cent in the muscles and 7 per cent in the tissue fluids.[185] The corresponding figures in a similar estimate for the bottle-nosed whale are lungs 5 per cent, blood 41 per cent, muscles 50 per cent, and tissue fluids 4 per cent. It is thus apparent that the myoglobin of the muscles makes a very important contribution to building up the reserves of oxygen, being of equal or even greater importance than the haemoglobin of the blood. It is the presence of myoglobin in comparatively great quantity that produces the now familiar dark colour of the flesh of whales. In those species that have the longest diving endurance, such as the sperm-whale, the colour of the meat is nearly black because of the great amount of myoglobin contained in it.

It has been calculated that the total of these oxygen stores in a fin-whale 70 feet long amounts to about 3,350 litres. If the oxygen-consumption of the tissues were at the rate that is believed to hold when the animal is at the surface between dives, this would be enough for a dive of sixteen minutes' duration at a swimming speed of five knots. But it is known that fin-whales can dive for at least double this time and can travel under water at much greater speeds; it is practically certain therefore that the rate of oxygen utilisation is much reduced during the dive. If this is so the muscles must function anaerobically during the dive and accumulate an oxygen debt to be discharged when the animal reaches the surface. But although the muscles can safely incur an oxygen-debt, the brain cannot, and must be fully oxygenated all the time if the functions of the body are to continue. And it is in this connection that the retia mirabilia are believed to have their use. It was formerly believed that the retia served as reservoirs of oxygenated blood for use during diving, but this is now known not to be so; for one thing, their volume is much too small for them to be of any importance for this purpose. It appears much more probable that the retia serve as pressure-equalisers for the blood during diving, so that the full normal blood-supply goes through the brain but the supply to the muscles is very greatly reduced. Thus the blood that would go through the muscles were the animal at the surface is diverted during diving and passes through the retia mirabilia, which act as shunts or dummy loads taking the place of the circulation in the muscles. The load on the heart is therefore not greatly changed, but the depletion of the oxygen-content of the blood is greatly reduced, the blood returning to the heart from the veins having passed through the retia without giving up any important amount of its oxygen.

As far as it has been possible to make any observations on the point there is no evidence that the rate of the heart beat decreases when a whale dives. It is very difficult to make accurate observations on this matter, but in the few experiments that have been made the heart-rate was found to be unchanged during dives.[185] But the experiments were made with no whales larger than a porpoise, and under poor conditions, so that the results cannot be accepted as finally settling the matter. If there should in fact be no slowing of the heart-beat, here is a point in which the whales differ greatly from the seals. On the other hand the whales resemble the seals in their apparently great indifference to an accumulation of carbon dioxide in the blood and tissues. They can thus refrain from breathing for long periods because the respiratory centre of the brain is not stimulated by small concentrations of the gas, as in ourselves and most other mammals. There is therefore no urge to respire until the concentration of carbon dioxide is much greater than would produce a feeling of suffocation in a land mammal. The sensation of suffocation in ourselves is produced not by a lack of oxygen but by the accumulation of carbon dioxide compelling the respiratory movements to take place. If, for example, a person breathes an atmosphere of hydrogen so that the carbon dioxide is expelled from the body normally, unconsciousness and death from lack of oxygen follow without any sensation of suffocation.

The power of enduring prolonged dives with reduced consumption of oxygen by the body is correlated with the ability of the tissues, and especially the muscles, to incur a large oxygen-debt; that is to say, the muscles function anaerobically during the dive, but the oxygen which would have been used, had it been available, must be obtained afterwards. Hence when a whale returns to the surface after a long dive it spouts for some time, during which it is repaying the oxygen debt. All mammals can incur an oxygen-debt of this sort, the panting of a runner after, but not during, a burst of sprinting being a familiar example of the repayment of the debt. But the whales can enjoy a greater oxygen overdraft than the others.

When a whale comes to the surface after a dive it usually starts to breathe out just as the head breaks the surface so that a certain amount of spray is thrown up and this, together with the moisture condensed from the breath, forms the visible spout or blow. The spout is not a jet of water expelled by the whale as those delightful figures decorating old maps would suggest, but merely the breath made visible by condensed moisture just as is our own on a frosty day. When spouting a whale exhales with great force and then immediately inhales, the latter action being accomplished with remarkable speed; it is in fact astonishing that the lungs can be refilled so quickly. Between each spouting, that is between each breath, the whale goes beneath the surface, but it does not dive deeply until it has repaid its oxygen-debt and replenished its oxygen reserves; hence it returns to the surface at frequent intervals for further breaths. Then when this is accomplished, or, as the whalers say, it has "had its spoutings out", it "sounds", going deeper for a comparatively long time. When sounding the whale lowers its head, arches its back, and goes down steeply, some species, such as the sperm- and right-whales, bringing the tail-flukes out of the water at the last moment.

Whales fall into two categories as far as their diving powers are concerned; those which do not go very deep for very long, and those which penetrate to great depths and have a long endurance. These two categories do not coincide with the systematic classification of the whales; in the first fall the large whalebone whales and the smaller porpoises and dolphins, and in the second such species as the sperm- and bottle-nosed whales. The normal duration of the soundings in the larger whalebone whales is from five to fifteen minutes, but if the animals are frightened the duration may reach twice the latter figure or more. In the sperm-whale the sounding may last from thirty minutes up to an hour, and for the bottle-nosed whale a case is reliably reported in which the sounding lasted two hours. The length of time spent at the surface, and the number of spoutings, corresponds roughly with the duration of the preceding sounding. Normally the whalebone whales spout four or five times between each sounding, the process lasting about five minutes, sometimes longer; but in the sperm-whale the spoutings are much more numerous, some twenty to forty during seven to ten minutes.

Whales of the first category, that do comparatively shallow diving and have frequent spoutings, possess circulatory and respiratory resources sufficient to support their activities without running heavily into debt for oxygen. But those of the second category, that have prolonged and deep dives during which respiration is suspended and circulation is reduced for lengthy periods, although they take with them greater oxygen reserves than the first, accumulate a much higher oxygen-debt, and thus need a greater time for spouting to make good the deficiency that they have incurred. Experiments on porpoises have shown that the efficiency of the ventilation of the lungs during spouting is very high, that is to say the proportion of oxygen removed from the air inhaled at each breath is greater than is usual in most mammals. There is reason to believe, too, that the lungs are emptied and filled to the greatest degree possible at each respiration, so that there is no shallow breathing as occurs in most mammals when resting or not undertaking violent exercise. Doubtless the respiratory efficiency is similar in all other whales.

The second great problem of diving that has been solved by the whales is that of withstanding the consequences of pressure at great depths. In the human diver one of the most serious consequences of breathing air at high pressures is the condition known as caisson sickness. As explained above (Ch. 7, p. 263), while the diver is under high pressure the nitrogen in the air dissolves in the fluid of the blood, but does not combine with the haemoglobin of the corpuscles as does the oxygen. When the pressure is reduced by the return of the diver to the surface the dissolved nitrogen comes out of solution and forms bubbles in the blood and tissue-fluids; the analogy with soda-water is obvious. The bubbles are liable to block the finer blood-vessels, thus preventing the circulation of the blood, a condition known to medicine as air embolism and to engineering as air-lock. Caisson sickness even if slight may lead to permanent damage of the tissues, and if acute may rapidly result in death.

How does a whale avoid caisson sickness when it dives to great depths? The answer is simple: by not breathing air under pressure. Consider first the human diver who is breathing compressed air. All the time that he is down he is filling and emptying his lungs so that the only limit to the amount of nitrogen dissolved in his body is the capacity of his blood and tissues for dissolving the gas. They will therefore soon become saturated with the gas to their full capacity at the incident pressure. And their full capacity under that pressure is very much greater than under the lesser pressure obtaining at the surface; hence the bubbling out of the excess when the pressure is released. But when a whale dives it is not breathing air under pressure. It takes down with it merely one lungs-full of air, so that the limit to the amount of nitrogen that may be dissolved in its blood and tissues when it is subjected to pressure is set by the capacity of the lungs. The total amount of nitrogen that could possibly be dissolved in the body of the whale is therefore slightly less than four-fifths of the capacity of the lungs and no more, and this only if the entire nitrogen-content of the air in the lungs were to be dissolved. The risk of suffering from caisson sickness is thus very much reduced for whales from the very start of the dive. It has been found that the proportion of lung capacity to body-weight is least in those species of whale that habitually dive deepest. In the fin-whale, which is a shallow diver, this proportion is about two and a half to three per cent, but in the bottle-nosed whale, which goes to great depths, the proportion is only just over one per cent. These figures may be compared with those for man where the proportion is over seven per cent. The proportion of nitrogen in the lungs is thus smallest in those whales habitually subjected to the greatest pressures, so that the proportion of the gas that could be dissolved in the tissues in the most extreme case of pressure is less than in those species that do not normally experience the highest pressure.

In addition to this primary reason for whales avoiding caisson sickness, they possess other protective arrangements. When a whale dives and is subjected to pressure the tissues of the body are not compressed because they are all permeated with watery fluids, and water is not compressible. The only contents of the whale's body that can be compressed are any free gases that may be present, and the only important quantity of these is in the lungs. The effect of pressure therefore will be to compress the air in the lungs, thereby diminishing their volume, the space formerly filled by air being occupied by the viscera which transmit the pressure from outside. This collapse of the lungs under the influence of pressure transmitted from the surrounding water by the abdominal viscera is facilitated by the very oblique position of the diaphragm in whales. By reason of this obliquity a very large part of the lungs is compressed against the back of the chest cavity. The extent to which that part of the chest cavity surrounded by the ribs may be compressed is unknown, but it is probable that a considerable reduction in volume can be produced because the anchoring of the ribs to the breast-bone in front of the chest is much less rigid and extensive than in land mammals. However that may be, the front part of the obliquely set diaphragm is almost certainly pushed forward into the chest cavity by the pressure of the abdominal viscera, thereby causing the collapse of further parts of the lungs. The final result of this collapse of the spongy lung tissue is that the contained air is driven out into the more rigid parts of the respiratory organs. When this happens the minute terminal parts of the air-passages in the lungs, the alveoli, where the exchange of gases between the air and the blood takes place, are emptied of air and the thin elastic membrane lining them is considerably thickened. The air that was in them passes into the rigid air tubes that are branches of the main windpipe, into the windpipe itself, and into the nasal passages leading to the blow hole. All of these structures have comparatively thick walls and are not lined by an exceedingly thin membrane as are the alveoli of the lungs.

There is consequently little absorption of nitrogen from the air in these parts, the blood does not become saturated with the gas, and the whale avoids the risk of suffering from caisson sickness. Experiment has shown that the capacity of the rigid air-passages is about one-eleventh of the total capacity of the passages and lungs together; a simple calculation thus shows that at a pressure of eleven atmospheres, corresponding to a depth of 100 metres, the whole of the air in the alveolar part of the lungs would be compressed and transferred to the rigid passages. At this pressure the invasion-rate of nitrogen would be reduced to nothing in the alveoli and the animal could in perfect safety go to any greater depth. As the animal dives the invasion-rate at first increases but as soon as the pressure begins to restrict the size of the alveoli appreciably and to cause an effective thickening of their elastic lining membrane the invasion rate starts to decrease. Thereafter it continues to decrease no matter how deep the whale goes (fig. 78, p. 316). It is therefore unnecessary to explain the deep diving of whales by assuming, as has been suggested, that the dives are too shallow to cause danger of caisson sickness, or that the amount of air taken down at each dive is too small to cause caisson sickness even if all the nitrogen in the lungs were dissolved during the dive.

A final point needs consideration; will not repeated diving cause an accumulation of nitrogen dissolved in the blood so that caisson sickness will eventually occur? It has been found that whale's blood dissolves nitrogen just as readily as the blood of other mammals, and that if solution takes place under pressure the nitrogen is released in the form of bubbles when the pressure is removed. One investigator thought that he had found in the blood of whales great numbers of minute organisms that were able to remove nitrogen from the blood, thus protecting the whale. But further work has revealed that this was a mistake and that the mysterious organisms were probably bacteria that had contaminated the blood from dirty apparatus

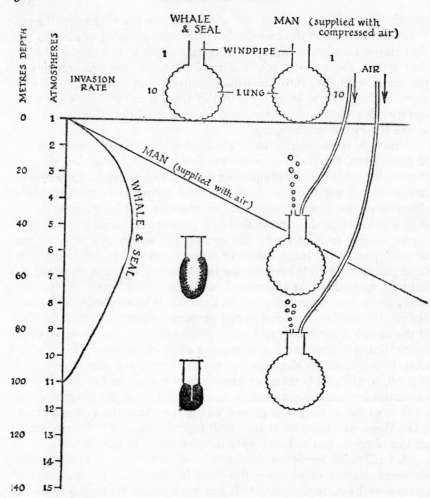

FIG. 78

Diagram to show the relation between the invasion rate of nitrogen
into the blood with increasing pressure. For whale and seal the rate
at first increases, but then decreases to nil when the lungs are completely collapsed at 11 atmospheres. For man, supplied with compressed air, the lungs do not collapse, and the invasion rate increases
indefinitely until saturation for any given pressure is reached. (Adapted
from Scholander[185])

after it had been taken from the whale. Nitrogen accumulation during repeated dives is avoided partly by the very poor invasion conditions during diving, as described above; and partly by the very efficient ventilation of the lungs while the whale is "having its spoutings out".

The speeds attained by whales in swimming are high, a 90-foot blue whale being able to sustain a speed of 20 knots for ten minutes and one of 14 to 15 knots for over two hours.[83] A whale of this size weighs at least 120 tons and would probably need something over 500 horse-power to drive it at the higher speed. The resistance to the movement of a body through the water is largely due to the presence of eddies near its surface and it is to minimise this turbulent flow that the stream-lined form has been developed by engineers. But the shape of a whale's body is not a perfect theoretical stream-line and it is possible that the production of retarding eddies is prevented by the flexure and oscillation of the tail region. A theoretical consideration of the efficiency of swimming in whales shows that the horse-power quoted above is not impossibly high. The efficiency is high because in the first place a whale moves its tail flukes up and down comparatively slowly; the flukes are large, and consequently a large volume of water is displaced astern at a comparatively slow speed. There is thus less loss of power in kinetic energy in the water displaced than if a smaller volume were displaced at greater speed. An output of about 500 horse-power at 20 knots would mean that a whale was producing about 4 horse-power per ton at that speed, and about half the power at 15 knots. The power output of the muscles of an athlete is from 0.01 to 0.02 horse-power per pound,[86] and if we take the lower figure and apply it to the muscles of a 120-ton whale, in which the muscle forms about 40 per cent of the weight, we find that 9 horse-power per ton would be produced, a figure more than twice that given above, so it is evident that the muscles of whales are not inherently more powerful than those of other mammals.

It is when we consider the swimming of porpoises and dolphins, however, that we find it difficult to explain the speeds said to be observed. Dolphins can attain very high speeds for such small animals, and it has been stated that they can touch 25 knots. A six-foot dolphin weighing about 3 cwt. would need some 14 horse-power to drive it at 25 knots, which represents an output of 87 horse-power per ton, and even at 20 knots over half that power would be needed.[83] This is something like six times the power that the muscles of a trained athlete can produce, so that unless the shape of the body, or its movements, greatly reduce water-resistance, the muscular efficiency of these animals must be very high. This is further exemplified by the fact that if the muscular efficiency per pound is the same in large whales and dolphins, a six-foot dolphin should be able to reach only about 9 knots, whereas speeds of at least 20 knots are said to have been observed. The dolphin, on the assumption of equal muscular efficiency per pound, would be unable to reach the higher speed of whales because the volume of the muscles increases as the cube of the length while the water resistance increases only as the square of the length. It is possible that the muscular efficiency is greater in the smaller animals through a higher rate of oxygen utilisation by the muscles or, more probably, through the muscles being able to function anaerobically more efficiently and to incur a greater oxygen debt.

On the other hand it must be remembered that there is some doubt about even the most careful observations that have been recorded on the swimming of dolphins. Sometimes the speeds have been noted with considerable accuracy by pacing against a ship moving at a known speed, but such observations have been made on animals that were not subsequently measured. From the deck of a large ship quite a large dolphin appears as a comparatively small object, and it is easy to guess its length at six feet when in reality it may be twelve. Calculations made on such guesses may lead to results that are wildly inaccurate.

The anatomical basis of swimming in whales is simple; internally the muscles are bunched into two main groups, the epiaxial and hypoaxial muscles, above and below the spinal column, which raise and lower the tail. These muscles cause the tail to oscillate upwards and downwards about a centre of rotation slightly aft of the dorsal fin. The flukes are movable on the tail, also in an up-and-down direction, their centre of rotation being at the level of their insertion into the tail. When the tail is raised, therefore, the pressure of the water causes the flukes to bend downwards, so that throughout the upward stroke they present an inclined plate to the water. At the top of the stroke the tail starts to travel downwards and the flukes rotate upwards so that they are bent upwards on the tail during the downwards stroke, and similarly present an inclined plate to the water. The motion of the inclined plates of the flukes through the water generates a force at right angles to their surface which is resolved into components, one tending to lift or depress the body and the other to drive it forwards; it is the last component that produces the forward motion in swimming.[87, 85]

Some writers have attempted to show that whales, sometimes at least, swim by what they term a sculling movement, implying that the tail strokes are not solely up-and-down, but are at the same time from side to side, as when a boat is sculled by a single oar over the stern. There is no anatomical or observational evidence to support this theory, still less to support the suggestion that a corkscrew-like motion is imparted to the body and tail during swimming.[200, 201] One writer has gone to considerable trouble to convince himself that the angle of the flukes to the tail is adjusted by muscular action during swimming.[161, 162] But there appears to be no need to invoke any such muscular action to explain the observed facts for, provided the flukes were hinged at their centre of rotation and free to move through an angle of not more than ninety degrees, they would propel the animal forward when the tail oscillated up and down, even if they had no connection to the muscles. It is improbable, then, that the muscles play any important part in adjusting the angle of the flukes to the tail. A whale swimming by fluke movements, a boat sculled by an oar over the stern, and a ship driven by a screw propeller, all make use of the same basic principle, that of presenting a moving plate to the water, inclined to the direction of the resultant desired movement of the body as a whole.

It has been calculated that the temperature of a 90-foot blue whale would rise about 3°F during a burst of speed at 20 knots lasting ten minutes. But it is pointed out that getting rid of excess heat is not likely to be an important problem to whales.[163] The layer of blubber corresponds to the deeper layers of the skin in other mammals and, as in them, it is traversed by great numbers of fine blood-vessels that break up into a capillary network a few millimetres beneath the outer surface of the skin. If the capillaries are filled, any excess heat will quickly be lost from the blood to the cold water outside (fig. 79, p. 320). The problem for the whale is obviously the reverse one—how to keep warm—hence the presence of the insulating blubber layer.[220] It has been calculated that the rorquals would need a layer of blubber nearly six inches thick all over the body to insulate them sufficiently for their basal metabolism to run at no higher rate than that of land mammals; the blubber of these whales averages considerably less than this all over the body. It has been suggested that the rorquals may thus have to keep swimming in order to produce enough heat to keep warm, but the figures and assumptions on which this suggestion is based are so arbitrary and unconfirmed that no reliance can be placed upon them. On first principles it appears very unlikely that such highly adapted creatures as whales would have evolved a blubber coating that is an inefficient heat insulator, when by adding to its thickness it could be made fully efficient. On the contrary, it may be taken as certain that the blubber thickness is sufficient to produce all the insulation necessary and, if the figures are correct, it may well be that the basal metabolism of the rorquals does run at a higher level than that of land mammals. It may be significant that in the much more sluggish right whales the blubber layer is very much thicker and probably averages rather more than the calculated minimum of six inches; in these animals the basal metabolic rate may be lower.

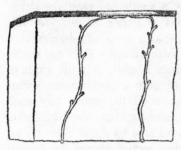

FIG. 79

A block of blubber with the dark layer of thin skin on the outside.

Two blood vessels are shown running towards the surface (diagrammatic); the dark colour has been omitted from part of the skin to show the minute branches from the vessels penetrating into it

The food of the two main groups of whales is very different: the toothed whales are carnivorous animals preying upon active creatures that are caught one at a time, and the whalebone whales may be likened to grazing herbivores, though of course their food is animal and not vegetable, taking in vast numbers of small creatures at each mouthful as they feed on shoals of plankton. And in correlation with these differences in food we find great differences in the mouths of the two kinds of whales.

The toothed whales, unlike other mammals, may have a very large number of teeth, up to fifty or more in each side of each jaw in some species. Unlike those of most other mammals, too, the teeth are not divided up into different sorts, incisors, canines and molars, but are all much alike. They are of simple conical shape and none are provided with multiple cusps as are the molar teeth of most mammals. Such teeth are highly adapted for seizing and holding a slippery living prey, but not for chewing it, so that it must in consequence be swallowed whole or in large lumps after it is broken up. The food of the toothed whales, as far as is known, consists of fish and particularly of cephalopods, in the form of squids and cuttlefish. The latter are a very important prey and, indeed, some species of toothed whales are believed to feed on little else.

Squids of various sorts must be some of the most abundant animals in the oceans, judging from the vast numbers of whales, seals and birds that feed upon them, as shown by their remains that those animals often have in their stomachs. But they are seldom seen and rarely captured by naturalists because they are very active and alert, so that they can avoid the nets and traps used in sampling the inhabitants of the seas. The sperm-whale is known to feed extensively on those giant squids, up to 60 feet long overall, that are so seldom seen but whose gigantic remains are sometimes washed ashore. Some species of these huge molluscs are known only from the fragments of their bodies spewed up by sperm whales in their dying struggles after being harpooned. The skin of these whales is always scarred by the suckers and claws of the squids, which evidently do not fall victims without a determined struggle.

Apart from the undigested soft parts of these animals, that are often of spectacular size, the stomachs of sperm-whales usually contain large numbers of their horny beaks, the parts that are most resistant to the digestive processes. Similarly the stomachs of the smaller toothed whales often hold great quantities of the beaks of smaller squids. In the stomachs of toothed whales, too, there is usually present a great number of fish otoliths, those hard little bones from fishes' ears that are so dense that they long defy the action of the digestive juices. The form of the otolith is distinctive for most species of fish, so that an examination of these bones from the stomach of a whale can tell us the kinds of fish on which the animal has been feeding. One species of toothed whale only is known to feed on animals other than fish and cephalopods, the fierce killer-whale, which will attack nearly anything in the sea. This whale is a great destroyer of seals in the seas where the latter are plentiful, but it is not always successful in catching its intended prey as is shown by the scarred hides of the antarctic seals. In some species of those seals nearly every adult carries the marks made by the teeth of killer-whales that have unsuccessfully snapped at them. Killer-whales often cruise in company, forming small packs, and will then combine to attack even the largest of the whalebone whales which, having no teeth, are comparatively defenceless; they also combine to bump seals, or even men, off ice floes.

It is a curious fact that among many of the medium-sized toothed whales there is a tendency to a reduced number of teeth. Even in the great sperm-whale the teeth are reduced by being restricted to the lower jaw only. The twenty to thirty pairs of pointed teeth in the lower jaw of this species fit into sockets in the gum of the upper jaw when the mouth is closed (fig. 80). Frequently, however, a number of small rudimentary teeth are present in the upper jaw, but they are embedded in the gum and barely appear on the surface. Similarly in many species of dolphins that have numerous teeth in both jaws there are often one or more pairs of reduced teeth concealed beneath the gums at the front of the jaws. But it is in the toothed whales larger than the dolphins that the greatest degree of toothlessness is found. In the bottle-nosed whale there is only a single pair of teeth near the tip of the lower jaw but even these are hidden below the gum so that the animal appears to be quite toothless. In several other species the teeth are likewise only a single pair, but they do cut through the gum, and in the males are often of considerable size. In Sowerby's whale this pair of tusks lies about halfway along the lower jaw; in Cuvier's and True's whales they are at the tip (fig. 81, p. 323). In the old males of Layard's whale, a species of the southern oceans, these teeth grow up round the edge of the upper jaw and curve over it so that the mouth can be opened only to a very limited extent. The food of these whales is believed to be largely cephalopods, but it is unknown how the old males of Layard's whale that can barely open their

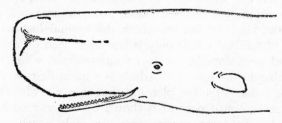

FIG. 80

Head of a sperm whale to show the narrow lower jaw armed with large teeth mouths are able to obtain them. In the narwhal, too, the teeth are few and rudimentary except for the tusk, which is normally present only in the males. In the smallest toothed whales, the porpoises and dolphins, the teeth are usually numerous in both jaws, but it is commonly found that in old specimens of several species the teeth are diseased and many of them may have in consequence fallen out. Though the evolution of the teeth of whales into multiple sharp points appears to be an adaptation, their subsequent reduction in number

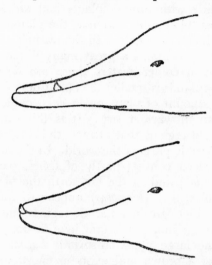

FIG. 81

Heads of Sowerby's whale (above) and Cuvier's whale (below), showing the single tusks present in the males, at the middle of the jaw in the former, at the tip in the latter

seems quite inexplicable. If the multiple teeth are really necessary for capturing active prey how is it that the species with reduced numbers of teeth or none at all can feed successfully on the same food?

The food and feeding of the whalebone whales are very different from those of the toothed whales. All the whalebone whales are of comparatively large size and there are no small ones that might correspond with the porpoises and dolphins among the toothed whales. This is no doubt because there is a size below which the feeding mechanism of these whales, the baleen apparatus, is not an efficient or practicable catcher of food. The smallest whalebone whale, the pygmy right whale of Australian seas, is about twenty feet long, a little smaller than the basking shark, whose feeding mechanism is analogous; all the other species are much larger.

Whalebone whales feed upon animals that are minute compared with a whale's bulk, the largest food known to be regularly eaten by them being fish of the size of herrings. But on their main feeding grounds the food appears usually to be invertebrate animals much smaller than that. The upper layers of the waters of the oceans are everywhere teeming with minute plants and animals that are collectively known as 'plankton', and it is the plankton that forms the sole food of the whalebone whales. In the warmer waters of the world the plankton usually contains a great many different sorts of plants and animals, but in colder waters there are fewer. Though the number of different kinds is smaller the quantities of each are immense, so that the total amount of plankton in each cubic mile of water is much greater than in warmer seas. It is this great abundance of plankton in the cold regions that attracts the whales to the waters of the arctic and antarctic parts of the world. In the arctic the plankton on which whales feed consists partly of fishes, partly of plankton-shrimps (*Boreophausia*); and in the far north the planktonic molluscs known as 'sea butterflies' (*Pteropods*) appear to form an important part of the whale's diet. In the antarctic regions one species of animal alone forms by far the most important item in the plankton eaten by whales; this is the large plankton-shrimp *Euphausia superba*, which reaches the size of a prawn and exists in enormous shoals (fig. 82, p. 326). These shoals are concentrated in the surface waters during the summer and it is then that the large whales migrate far south to fatten on this abundant grazing.

The baleen apparatus by means of which the plankton is collected consists of a number of plates of whalebone or baleen arranged along the margin of the upper jaw. The baleen plates, despite their common name, are not made of bone but of fibrous horny material. The fibres run lengthwise through the substance of the baleen, and at the inner edge of the plate the horny material that binds them together is lacking so that the fibres alone remain and are frayed out to form a hairy edge to the plate. The plates are narrower than they are long and are set closely spaced in the upper jaw one behind the other, each being transverse to the long axis of the mouth (fig. 83, p. 327). The inner edges of the plates are all level with each other so that their

a. Stranded porpoise

b. Bull killer whale, showing the high back fin

Plate XLVII

Kenneth Williamson

a. Ca'ing whales being driven ashore at Grindadráp, Faeroe Islands

Seton Gordon

b. Dead fin-whale at a whaling station: the whale lies on its right side, its head towards the left; its left flipper sticks up among the gulls and the end of the tongue hangs out of the mouth; note the asymmetrical colour-pattern on the area covered by the ventral grooves

Plate XLVIII

hairy fringes are tangled together and form a mat of criss-crossed fibres where the upper tooth-row comes in other animals. The mat is supported by the inner edges of the baleen plates, which are wide at their roots, but taper to a point at their free ends. The outer sides are not frayed out into fibres and are seen as a close-spaced series of plates at the side of the mouth if the jaws are opened. When a whale opens its mouth the lower jaws rotate slightly outwards on their long axes so that the area enclosed between them increases; this is evidently a mechanism that ensures that the ends of the baleen plates are enclosed within the lower jaw and do not slip over the outside edge of it when the mouth is closed again. When feeding a whale opens the mouth and takes in a mass of water with its contained plankton. It then shuts the mouth, leaving a space at the lips, and raises the tongue so that the water is pressed out through the hairy mat and between the baleen plates, the contained plankton being left stranded on the mat. The plankton is then swallowed and another mouthful filtered and so on. The tongue in the whalebone whales is a very large and fleshy structure adapted for use as a sort of piston for forcing the water through the sieve (fig. 84, p. 328).

In many of the whalebone whales (the rorquals) the under-side of the throat is covered by a number of longitudinal grooves or pleats. These are an inch or two deep and have been likened not inaptly to tram-lines. A consequence of the presence of the grooves is that the throat is capable of great expansion when the tongue is depressed and the mouth opened to engulf a shoal of plankton. In those whalebone whales that have no throat-grooves (the right whales) the mouth is proportionately very much larger than in the others and the baleen plates many times longer. The capacity of the mouth is thus increased in two entirely different ways in the two groups of whalebone whales. Doubt has been expressed whether the throat-grooves really are used to increase the capacity of the mouth, but anyone who has seen a whale carcase distended by gases of decomposition will agree that it is at least a possible function. The suggestion[93] that the grooves "decrease the resistance of the water in swimming" may be disregarded as a complete fallacy, for an increase in surface area cannot be expected to decrease resistance.

The feeding of infant whales on their mother's milk is accomplished with less difficulty than might be imagined. The mammary glands are situated rather far back on the under-side of the body

M.   Y beneath the blubber, and the teats lie concealed below the surface in grooves, one on each side of the reproductive aperture near the vent. When the whale suckles its calf the teats are protruded from their grooves and the calf takes one into the corner of its mouth. The milk-gland is then compressed by a muscle that covers it, and the

FIG. 82

Euphausia superba, enormous shoals of which are the "krill " on which the southern whales feed. Length about 2½ inches

milk is forced into the mouth of the calf. It cannot "go down the wrong way" because the larynx of whales is elongated and inserted into the hind end of the nostrils above the roof of the mouth, so that in effect there is a continuous passage from the blow-holes to the lungs with no communication with the mouth. This arrangement is important to a whale when it is feeding under water, not only when it is a suckling, but throughout its life (fig. 85, p. 329). The calves of the larger whalebone whales are suckled for as much as six months after their birth until the baleen has grown long enough for them to be weaned. The birth of a whale must be one of the most critical moments of its life until it has safely put its blow-holes above the surface and taken its first breath. The mother is said to support it carefully during this time but the ability characteristic of whales to refrain from breathing for some time is no doubt present in the calf at birth, so that a little delay in drawing the first breath is probably not important.

Whales are found in all the seas of the world, and some species occur practically everywhere; but although there is no physical barrier to prevent any of them from wandering anywhere they are by no means all of them cosmopolitan. Many are comparatively restricted in their distribution and are found only in their own specific areas. A considerable amount is known about the distribution of the species of whales that are hunted commercially, and also about that of the smaller dolphins and porpoises that inhabit coastal waters. But of many of the others practically nothing is known; they are oceanic species that seldom stray into coastal waters, and not being large

enough to be important commercially it has never been
worth anybody's while to look
farther. They must, presumably, be fairly abundant somewhere sometimes for otherwise
the sexes would stand a very
poor chance of meeting and the
species would become extinct
through lack of opportunity for
breeding. An oceanographic expedition in search of rare whales
and dolphins is a thing much
desired by zoologists interested
in these animals, but is unfortunately scarcely likely to be
realised.

Much information about
rare whales and their distribution has, however, been accumulated through the scheme by
which all whales and dolphins
stranded on the British coasts
are reported to the British Museum (Natural History) by the
coastguards and receivers of

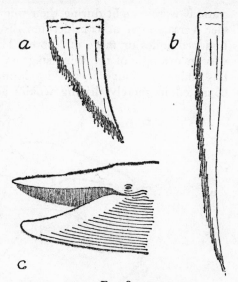

FIG. 83

Plates of baleen, *a*, from a blue whale,
b, from a right whale; the attachment
to the roof of the mouth is at the top,
the smooth outer edges to the right, the
frayed inner edges to the left. *c*, the
mouth of a rorqual showing the baleen
plates in position; seen from the left
side

wreck. This arrangement was started in 1913 by the late Sir Sidney
Harmer, then Director of the Museum, and has continued with great
success ever since. The information collected has been published in a
series of reports issued by the museum from time to time, and a great
many interesting new facts have been established.[93, 76] Another source
of information about the distribution of whales in British seas are the
statistics of the catches made at the whaling stations that formerly
worked at several places on the British coasts in Scotland and Ireland.[218]

People are often surprised to hear that whaling has until quite
recently been carried on in this country; some of the six whaling
stations, four in Shetland, one on Lewis in the Hebrides and one at
Blacksod Bay, Co. Mayo, Eire, worked from the early nineteen-
hundreds to the middle nineteen-twenties. The whales taken at these

stations were caught during their migrations from north to south and vice versa, often at considerable distances from the land, up to a hundred miles or more off shore. This kind of shore-based whaling was an example of the third stage of whaling technique, an art that has undergone four stages of development during its history. The first consisted in merely driving whales ashore, the second in capturing

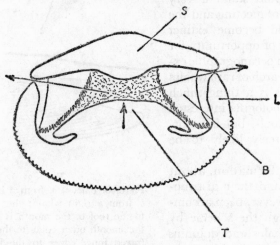

FIG. 84
Diagram of the cross section of the head of a rorqual.
B, baleen plate. L, lower lip. S, snout, cut across. T, tongue. The mouth is filled with water and krill; the tongue is raised in the direction of the vertical arrow, and the water expelled through the baleen plates and lips in the direction of the side arrows. The krill is left on the hairy mat formed by the frayed edges of the baleen

them with hand harpoons. Modern whaling stations were the third stage, in which large harpoons are shot from cannons mounted in small steamers, and the dead whales are towed to a shore factory; and the fourth is the present-day pelagic whaling in which the shore factory is replaced by a large steamer, the floating factory, to which the catchers bring their whales.

Even primitive man appreciated the value of whales, as is shown by the bones sometimes found in ancient kitchen-middens and hut-sites; in fact, a stranded whale must have been a godsend to dwellers near the coast, a position curiously reversed nowadays when the

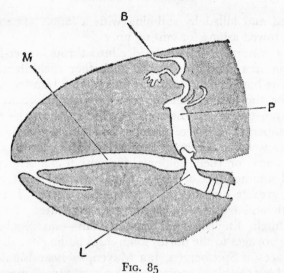

FIG. 85

Diagram of the head of a porpoise split open lengthwise.
From the blowhole, B, a passage, P, descends past several valves. Into
its bottom end fits the tip of the larynx, L, so that the air passage is
cut off from the mouth, M.

responsibility for removing such a malodorous object devolves upon
the owners of foreshore rights. At first, doubtless, the supply of meat
provided by a whale was its chief attraction, but for many centuries
the main value of whales has been the oil that can be extracted from
them. When man had achieved the building of seaworthy boats,
sooner or later he was sure to discover that fortuitous strandings could
be improved upon by deliberately driving whales ashore. This
primitive way of hunting still survives in Faeroe and Shetland, where
to this day schools of ca'ing or pilot-whales—a rather small species not
exceeding 30 feet in length—are annually driven ashore in hundreds and
are there slaughtered, cut up, and boiled down for their oil (Pl. XLVIII,
p. 325). During the middle ages the Basques carried on a profitable
fishery by putting to sea in small boats to hunt and capture the rather
slow-moving and coast-frequenting Atlantic right whales, with such
success that they practically exterminated them on their coasts. They
did not drive the whales ashore, but evolved the technique of har-
pooning them with barbed spears attached to the boat by a line, and
playing them until they were so exhausted that they could be

approached and killed by stabbing with a lance. The dead whales were then towed ashore for cutting up.

When the numbers of whales declined through over-fishing, these enterprising men fitted out ships to go farther afield in search of their quarry. The base of operation was thus merely transferred from shore to ship, for the actual hunting was done as before in small boats lowered from the vessel. Before long, the right whales were so rare off the temperate coasts of Europe that lengthy voyages into high latitudes grew to be the regular practice. Here the whalers found a further reward for their boldness, for within the Arctic circle they discovered another sort of whale, the Greenland right whale, which yielded a greater quantity of oil than any other. Throughout the seventeenth and eighteenth centuries a large fleet of whale-ships—French, Dutch, English, and Scandinavian—was regularly engaged in whaling voyages to the north, some ships boiling out their oil ashore at such places as Spitsbergen, Jan Mayen, or Bear Island, but others merely casking the blubber after cutting it into small pieces and bringing it back to be boiled out at home. The chief British ports concerned were Whitby, Hull, Peterhead and Dundee. The 'Greenland' fishery was for long almost entirely at Spitsbergen, later it extended as well to Davis Strait and Labrador. After the early part of the nineteenth century, northern whaling steadily declined, for Greenland whales were becoming scarce, and towards the end it was only the high value of the whalebone that kept it going. The extinction of the crinoline, together with the substitution of steel busks for whalebone in corsets, and of steel for whalebone ribs in umbrellas, dealt the final blow at the industry; so that since the opening years of the twentieth century sailing ships have no more gone hunting the right whales of the Arctic.

On the New England and Connecticut coasts of America a similar evolution of whaling took place during the eighteenth century, but it was directed not only towards the right whales of the Arctic but also to the sperm-whales of temperate and tropical seas. During the first half of the nineteenth century a very large fleet of Yankee whalers sailed the seven seas; but the civil war and the development of the petroleum industry started the ruin of American whaling, and the first decade of the present century saw the end of it. During the second half of the nineteenth century whaling voyages got longer and longer, up to five years away from home, and there would be visits in pursuit of right whales to the Arctic and Antarctic regions of both the Atlantic and Pacific Oceans, as well as months of cruising after sperm-whales in the tropics. It was on these long voyages that the Americans developed the practice, adopted by whalers of other nations, of boiling out the oil on board ship in tryworks built on deck. The tryworks were a series of cauldrons set in brickwork, and the fuel used was the oil-soaked fibrous scrap remaining after the oil had been boiled out of the blubber. In spite of the danger of boiling such inflammable material on the deck of a wooden ship while at sea, there was not an unduly high loss of ships from fire.

The whaling carried on by means of harpoons hurled from small boats lowered by sailing ships was confined to a few species of whales, mainly right and sperm-whales, because these are the only sorts that float when dead. Other and larger species were inaccessible to this kind of whaling, because they are so large and active that the danger of attacking them, and the difficulty of even approaching such swift-swimming animals, are too great. Further, when dead they sink and would drag down with them any boat rash enough to have 'got fast' to them. But the existence of great numbers of the larger kinds of whales, known collectively as rorquals and individually as blue, fin, humpback, and sei-whales, all immune from attack by the whalers, attracted the attention of Svend Foyn, an inventive Norwegian, about 1860.

Foyn, realising that entirely new methods were required, produced a very large harpoon fired from a cannon mounted in the bow of a small steamer and attached by a stout rope. By using a steamer he got the speed required to approach the rorquals, and the heavy harpoon with its thick whale line gave sufficient strength to hold them when struck. In addition he devised an explosive head for the harpoon, fused to explode a few seconds after it entered the whale, which was usually quickly crippled if not killed at once. When dead the whale sank, but was hauled to the surface by heaving in the line on a steam winch. On arrival there it was made buoyant by inflating it with air pumped in by means of a hose fastened to a pointed pipe plunged into the body-cavity. The carcass could then be towed home to be cut up and boiled down at leisure. This method of whale-hunting is the basis of the modern whaling industry and is essentially that in use on a large scale at the present day. Foyn's methods of hunting were used in conjunction with shore stations—factories at the water's edge of a sheltered harbour—where the whales were hauled on land and the products extracted with the aid of machinery.

The exploitation of the hitherto untapped resources provided by the rorquals led to the establishment of whaling stations, of which the management and practically all the skilled labour were Norwegian, in many parts of the world; while in the tropics the same methods were used for the pursuit of sperm-whales. A prosperous industry became firmly established, though after some years a falling-away in the numbers of whales became obvious at some places.

At the end of the nineteenth century much attention was being turned towards the exploration of the Antarctic, the last remaining great unknown region of the world. In 1902–3 the Swedish South Polar Expedition's ship, the *Antarctic*, was under the command of the veteran whaler captain C. A. Larsen, who noted the abundance of whales in the Antarctic and the suitability of many of the islands of that region for the establishment of whaling stations. After his rescue and return (for the ship was lost) he found financial backing in South America to organise a whaling expedition on modern lines. In 1904 he started the first Antarctic whaling station in a sheltered cove on the island of South Georgia. Whales were abundant and the enterprise was a great success, paying a dividend of 70 per cent in its first year; for the invention of the hydrogenation process for converting oils to fat had created a great demand for animal oils in the margarine and soap trades. Then started a rush for the new El Dorado, and within a few years a number of whaling companies were working on this island, and on the South Orkney and South Shetland islands farther south. The nearest inhabited country to these regions is a British Crown Colony, the Falkland Islands; and though the Antarctic mainland and islands had always been more or less a no-man's-land to the sealers, who were the only people to have used them since their discovery, Captain Cook had formally taken possession of South Georgia in the name of the British Crown when he discovered the island in 1775. The new activities in the south soon came to the notice of the governments, and in 1908 Letters Patent under the Great Seal extended the boundaries of the colony of the Falkland Islands to include a large sector of the Antarctic continent, and its surrounding islands, which now form the Dependencies of the Falkland Islands.

As a result of territorial jurisdiction the British Government was able to introduce regulations to govern the whaling industry, in order to prevent an over-exploitation of the whale population and the consequent ruin of an important world-supply of raw materials. The regulations provided, amongst other things, for the issue of licences to engage in whaling, and the leasing of land on which whaling stations were to be built. They limited the number of hunting steamers or catchers, required whale carcasses to be completely utilised without waste, prohibited the killing of whale calves or their dams, and defined a close season. The application of the regulations was not difficult, because whaling could be carried on only from shore stations or floating factories—large ships provided with the necessary machinery for rendering down the whale carcasses cut up in the water alongside—both of which needed the shelter of harbours within territorial waters. The revenue derived from the licences, leases, and a royalty imposed on the oil produced, provided a fund which was to be used for promoting the interests of the industry. In the course of time this amounted to a very large sum, which has been expended according to intention.

Soon after the start of southern whaling, the Government and its advisers saw the danger of repeating the mistakes made in the past in other parts of the world—as for instance in the Arctic, where over-fishing had ruined a once prosperous whaling industry. An Inter-Departmental Committee on Research and Development in the Dependencies of the Falkland Islands reported in 1920 that a rational regulation of the whaling industry demanded a full knowledge of the life-histories and habits of whales, and all that this implies, and recommended that scientific investigations should be started without delay. A scientific expedition in Captain Scott's old ship, the *Discovery*, was accordingly dispatched in 1925, and from that date until the present day scientific research in all parts of the Antarctic has been carried on by the Discovery Investigations Committee, using first this ship and then her successor, the splendidly equipped research ship *Discovery II*, and her smaller consort the *William Scoresby*. The results achieved have been of the greatest value, both to science and to whaling.

Before the *Discovery* researches began it had been assumed that whales grew slowly and attained a considerable age in reaching their full size. Among the first facts to emerge was the surprising one that they reach maturity very quickly, and their full size at a remarkably early age. Of the many thousands of whales examined by the expedition, only one was found whose age was estimated at about thirty years, and the vast majority were not older than five or six. The

largest species of whale is the blue whale, which when fully grown may
reach a length of nearly a hundred feet; it is about twenty-five feet in
length at birth and grows up quickly, reaching a length of over
seventy feet, and being ready to breed, in two years. The period of
gestation is roughly twelve months, that of suckling about six, and a
further period of about six months elapses before breeding occurs
again. The female blue whale thus produces a calf once every two
years. The growth of the whale foetus from an ovum so small as to be
only just visible and weighing a fraction of a milligram, to an infant
twenty-five feet long and weighing twelve or fifteen tons, within the
space of twelve months, is by far the most rapid growth known anywhere in the animal or plant kingdoms. The majority of the calves
are born about the southern midwinter, but not in the cold Antarctic
seas, for the whales have regular migrations and move north to temperate waters during the winter, and the young are usually several
months old before they accompany their mothers to the south. The
blue whale and a rather smaller species, the fin-whale, which reaches sexual maturity at a length of about sixty feet and whose life-history is very
similar, together make up the major part of the Antarctic catch; a third
and smaller species, the humpback, is of minor economic importance.

The southerly migration during the Antarctic spring and summer
is entirely a feeding migration. The plankton of the south is very rich
and is characterised by the presence of vast quantities of the crustacean, much like a large shrimp—'krill' or *Euphausia superba*—which
there forms practically the whole diet not only of the whales but of
many of the seals, penguins, and other members of the fauna. Whales
quickly fatten on this rich and abundant food, and their blubber is
conspicuously thicker and richer in oil soon after they reach the
southern feeding grounds. The life-history of the helplessly drifting
krill is a complicated one.[77] The eggs are laid near the bottom in
deep water, 500–1,000 metres down, and the young when hatched
drift in the current of comparatively warm water that flows south
deep below the surface and wells up near the ice-edge of the Antarctic
continent. Here the adolescent krill become concentrated and then
drift north again in the cold Antarctic surface current, probably
taking several years to become adult.

By about 1935, so much information had been accumulated on
whales, their food, migrations, and the hydrological and meteor-
ological factors governing their distribution, that it was evident that

the whaling industry could with profit base its activities on this foundation of comparatively exact knowledge. But a new factor had now entered the problem of whaling, making impossible the application of regulations by a system of licensing shore-stations, to the industry as a whole: this was the development of pelagic whaling. In 1925-30, when new whaling ventures could no longer obtain licences, the revolutionary move was made of fitting out a floating factory to operate entirely on the high seas, and to be completely independent of harbours. The many technical difficulties of such an undertaking were successfully overcome, and the advantages of being free from regulations, licences, and royalties, and of being able to cruise where whales were most abundant, were demonstrated. Once again the pioneering success was followed by many imitators, and there ensued an over-production of oil so great that the industry was forced to refrain from sending any expeditions south for a whole season, until the surplus was absorbed by the market.

The only remedy for this state of things was international agreement, and accordingly a conference of the interested nations met in London and drew up regulations for the industry. Each year now the amount of oil to be produced is decided upon before the expeditions sail south, and the season during which, and the places where, whales are to be hunted are laid down. Hunting is thus confined to those regions where the whales are in best condition, and is prohibited in those where their exploitation is wasteful. It was hoped in this way to conserve the stock of whales so that an annual crop could be gathered safely, though a disquietingly high proportion of immature whales continues to be shown in the returns of the catches. All nations interested in whaling accepted the regulations except Japan; but Germany, though signing the agreement, did not observe it.

The modern pelagic whaler is a large ship of 20,000 tons or more, fitted with a ramp up which the dead whales may be hauled out of the water on to the flensing deck, where they are dismembered and the products extracted by the aid of elaborate machinery. She carries a crew of several hundred men, and is completely self-reliant, having on board sufficient fuel for the factory and her attendant catchers as well as for steaming, and for distilling the large amount of fresh water required. Her chief homeward cargo is, of course, oil, which is used in the manufacture of margarine and soap, but, in addition, the whale meat and bones are used, after extraction of the oil, for producing

feeding stuffs, guano, and bone-flour. During the ten years before the
late war the annual world catch has varied from 24,000 to 44,000
whales, producing from about 400,000 to over 540,000 tons of oil.

Nearly all species of whales about whose habits anything is known
are sociable and gregarious animals, being often found in schools of
very large size. No doubt whales congregate where their food is plentiful, but their gregarious habit
must also be of use to the species
in allowing the sexes to find each
other at the breeding season. But
their sociability, and perhaps
their curiosity, goes farther than
that, as is shown by the well-
known habit in porpoises and
dolphins of accompanying ships
for a while when they meet them,
swimming close alongside or under the forefoot and appearing to
find pleasure in matching the
vessel's speed. It may have been
this combination of curiosity and
gregariousness that started the
famous Pelorus Jack, a Risso's
dolphin, in his habit of escorting
ships through Cook Strait between the north and south islands

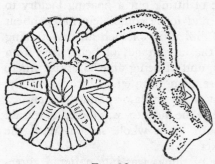

FIG. 86

A large acorn-barnacle (*Coronula*)
growing on the skin of a whale: on
the acorn-barnacle is growing a stalked barnacle (*Conchoderma*). Humpback whales often carry many of
these barnacles, the stalked ones
nearly always growing on the others
and not directly on the skin of the
whale

of New Zealand for so many years. So well known did he become
that a special Order in Council was made to protect him. He was
on his beat regularly for thirty-two years, and was last seen in 1912.
A rather similar habit has been developed by a dolphin in Baltimore
Harbour, Eire, where it has lived for some years, and doubtless
there are other examples. The habit in the smaller whales of jump-
ing clear of the water, so characteristic that 'porpoising' has become
a descriptive word, appears to be a form of play. It is of no advantage to the animals as far as is known, and seems to occur merely
because they are excited and in high spirits. Even the large whales
indulge in something similar, though their breaching is a much less
graceful performance. Sperm-, sei- and humpback-whales frequently
jump quite clear of the water, but they do not curve forward and enter

it again head first, merely falling back with a tremendous splash. It has been suggested that they do this in an effort to rid themselves of parasites or lampreys sticking to the skin, but it is much more probable that breaching is a form of play, and may be specially manifested as sexual play during the breeding season. The writer has also seen a southern right whale poking its head out of the water, for about a third of its body-length, apparently in order to look at a small sealing vessel at anchor nearby.[136]

Whales do have skin parasites, and are alleged to rub themselves against rocks in order to get rid of them, an occurrence about which there is no really reliable observation (they certainly have been seen to scratch themselves on rocks). There are several sorts of barnacles, both of the acorn and the stalked kinds, that are found on whales, some of them nowhere else (fig. 86. p. 336). They are for the most part confined to the slower-moving species of whales, especially the humpback, probably because the larval stages are unable to settle on a surface over which the water-flow exceeds a certain moderate speed. Barnacles can do little harm to the whales on which they grow, but other parasites are not so benign. There

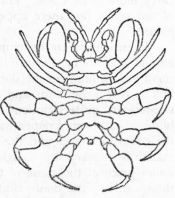

FIG. 87
The whale-louse (*Paracyamus*). These may be found on any whale, but are particularly numerous on humpback and right whales, occurring in hundreds in the 'bonnet' of the latter. Size, up to half-an-inch long

is another crustacean, the copepod *Penella*, which settles as a free-swimming larva on the skin of whales and then sends long branching rootlike processes ramifying into the blubber, from which the parasite extracts its nourishment. Finally, when its growth is complete, all that appears on the surface are the long egg-sacs protruding like tags from the wound of entry. When the parasites' life-cycle is complete with the production of a new generation it dies and the wound heals over leaving a small light-coloured scar.

Another crustacean, an isopod known to the whalers as the whale-louse, infests whales, more particularly right whales. Whale-lice grow up to an inch in length, and have very strong recurved claws on each leg by which they retain their hold (fig. 87, p. 337). In the right whales there is a patch of roughened skin forming an excrescence on the snout, and similar smaller ones along the lower jaw; there is always a large number of whale-lice clinging to the irregularities of these growths. Humpback whales, too, are often infested with whale-lice, but the larger rorquals are usually free, and rarely carry more than a few. The lice are believed to feed upon the skin of the whale but there appears to be no exact information on this point.

When whales are in temperate or subtropical waters during their annual migrations they are liable to attack by something that makes small oval wounds in the skin, about three inches long by one-and-a-half to two inches wide and an inch deep. When first inflicted these wounds are quite clean-cut and look as though a piece of skin and blubber had been scooped out with a sharp-edged spoon. Gradually the edges heal over and the hollow is filled in, the place being permanently marked by a light-coloured and slightly depressed scar. Exact proof of the cause of these wounds has never been given, but there can be little doubt that they are produced by lampreys, which are commonly found sticking to whales, large sharks, and so on. Though the lamprey has no jaws its sucker-like mouth is provided with rows of horny teeth and the similarly armed tongue or radula appears to be a suitable instrument for cutting out a chunk of blubber. Whales, like most mammals, carry internal parasites as well as external ones. They are mostly worms of different kinds such as nematodes in the gut and kidneys, and cestodes in the intestines, some of the latter being enormous tape-worms on a truly cetacean scale.

Whales are not known to have any voice. When they blow they of course produce a loud puffing noise, which in the larger kinds has a peculiar hollow sound that gives a tinny character to the noise of the blow in some species; but these sounds are not produced by vocal cords. Several observers[79, 118] have reported that whales and dolphins sometimes make a very high-pitched whistling sound when they are completely under water. This noise is believed to be made by the animals allowing a fine stream of bubbles to escape from the blow-hole. Indeed the beluga or white whale when under water makes a low liquid trill 'reminiscent of the cry of curlews in the spring time', a sound from which these whales have been named 'sea canaries' by the

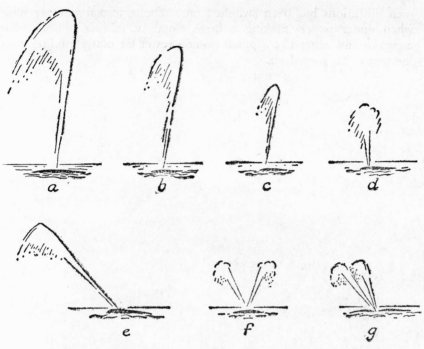

Fig. 88
Whale blows.
a, blue whale, about 25 feet. *b*, fin whale, about 15 feet. *c*, sei whale,
about 10 feet. *d*, humpback, low and bushy. *e*, sperm whale, directed
obliquely forwards. *f*, *g*, right whale, double and directed obliquely
forwards; *f*, from directly behind; *g*, the whale swimming from right
to left and slightly away from the observer

whalers of times past.[217, 184] Whales are far from deaf although they
have no external ears; the ear-passages become very narrow and
practically obliterated, completely so in some species, as they approach
the surface of the body. Whalers well know that everything must be
kept quiet when they are near a whale, any loud sound, a shout or
a bucket dropped on deck, will at once frighten it away; the whale
is 'gallied', as the old whaling term puts it. Several observers have
noticed that whales are apparently sensitive to ultrasonic vibrations,
for nearby whales have been seen to depart at once from the neighbourhood of a ship as soon as an echo-sounding apparatus producing

such vibrations has been switched on. Whales also frequently blow when under water, making a large cloud of minute bubbles that hangs in mid-water like a patch of soda water for many minutes after the whale has passed on.

CHAPTER 12

WHALES OF BRITISH SEAS

"There spouting whales the billows lash to foam,
Then plumb the gloomy caverns of their home;
Relentless there the finny tribe pursue
Till, bellies fill'd, their gambols they renew—
The chief among 'em leads his fav'rite spouse
To coral grottoes, there to hold carouse
Most strangely in their wat'ry nuptial bed:
For lo! the spermaceti's in his head."

SAMUEL MARTINS, 1687–1763, *Verses upon several occasions*

THIS CHAPTER presents some particulars of the specific characters
and of the life-histories of the whales and dolphins known from
British seas. For more detailed information the reader is referred to
the reports by Dr. F. C. Fraser of the British Museum (Natural
History) on the cetacea stranded on the British coasts.[76]

The British cetacea are classified into families as follows:

ORDER   Cetacea.
SUBORDER   Odontoceti.
    Superfamily   Delphinoidea.
          Family   Phocaenidae.   (Porpoises)
               ,,   Delphinidae.   (Dolphins)
               ,,   Monodontidae.   (Narwhal & White whale)
    Superfamily   Physeteroidea
          Family   Physeteridae.   (Sperm & Pygmy Sperm)
               ,,   Ziphiidae.   (Beaked whales)
SUBORDER   Mysticeti.
          Family   Balaenidae.   (Right whales)
               ,,   Balaenopteridae.   (Rorquals, Finner whales)
               ,,   Rhachianectidae.   (Grey whales: extinct in
                                    Europe)

The Odontoceti (toothed whales) are distinguished by the absence of baleen and the presence of teeth, though the latter may not cut the gum during life. The mouth is not very large, and there is a single blow-hole. Whales belonging to four families of the Odontoceti, the Phocaenidae, Delphinidae, Physeteridae and the Ziphiidae are known from British seas.

PHOCAENIDAE AND DELPHINIDAE

These families contain the porpoises and dolphins, of which there are many species. They are mostly of moderate size, from about six to twelve feet long, though a few reach twenty or thirty feet. In most of them the teeth are numerous and present in both the upper and the lower jaws, and in most of them there is a dorsal fin, though there are exceptions to both these points. The nostrils are united to form a single median blow-hole (fig. 90, p. 344).

The common porpoise (*Phocaena phocaena*) is by far the commonest cetacean in British seas, and the smallest (Pl. XLVII, p. 324). It does not exceed six feet in length, and few specimens have been seen as long as that. The snout is not prolonged into a beak as it is in many of the dolphins, but ends bluntly; the dorsal fin is low and triangular. The coloration is a general dark blackish above and white below, but there is great individual variation in the extent of the areas occupied by the two colours. The flipper is dark on both surfaces; the line dividing the dark upper surface from the white lower side of the body frequently passes through the insertion of the flipper. Sometimes it passes above this point, and when this occurs there is usually a dark streak extending down from the black upper parts to the roots of the flipper. The underside of the tail flukes and the root of the tail are also dark coloured. Occasionally the light colour extends right up on to the back, and the line separating light and dark may be rather indefinite, the dark shading through grey into white. In many porpoises the front edge of the dorsal fin is studded with a series of small hard tubercles, which may be from ten to twenty in number. These tubercles, that may be present in as much as fifty per cent of porpoises, were once thought to characterise a second species. This was named *Phocaena tuberculata*, but it is now known that there is no specific difference between porpoises with and without tubercles. The shape of the teeth is characteristic, the flattened crowns being wider than the roots so that they have a spade-like shape, which may, however, be obscured when the crowns are much worn down in old animals (fig. 89). They vary in number from about 22 to 26 on each side of each jaw. In the lower jaw, at the front end of the tooth row, there are usually two small teeth that do not cut through the gum and are therefore invisible during life. In the young animal some of the teeth are commonly set obliquely in the jaw because, owing to their spade shape, there is not room for them to stand longitudinally until the jaw has lengthened with increasing overall size. In all whales

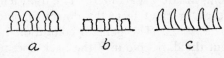

FIG. 89

The spade-shaped teeth of the common porpoise, *a*, and the same when worn down in an old individual, *b*. *c*, the pointed teeth of the common dolphin

the reproductive aperture and the vent are contained within a single groove on the under surface of the body in the female, but are separated in the male. In the male porpoise the distance separating these apertures is unusually great, so that the latter lies far forward on the under surface of the body at the level of the dorsal fin.

The common porpoise is widely distributed in the waters of both sides of the north Atlantic, and an annual migration is believed to bring it in large numbers to the waters of Britain during the summer, though it is not clear whence the migrating animals come nor whither they go. Porpoises are commonest in our coastal waters in late summer and early autumn, scarcest in January. They are said to spend the three months from November to January inclusive in the Baltic sea and to be absent from it for the rest of the year. But it is scarcely credible that the majority of the porpoises of European seas go there during the winter. On British coasts the greatest number of strandings reported to the British Museum (Natural History) occurs in the southern part of the North sea and in the English Channel, but the animals are undoubtedly present in all coastal waters, though perhaps less abundant elsewhere than in those parts. The common porpoise often travels up large rivers to great distances from the sea.

Porpoises pair in the late summer, the birth of the young occurring in the following summer; the exact length of gestation is not known but it is unlikely to be more than eight or nine months. The young porpoise is nearly half as long as the mother at birth. The food of this species, as far as is known, consists chiefly of fish; stomachs which have been examined have contained the remains of large numbers of whiting or herring. These two fishes appear to form an important part of the diet of the species.

In the common dolphin (*Delphinus delphis*) the snout ends in a sharply demarcated narrow slender beak, five to six inches or more long in adult specimens. The total length of the animal may be up to seven or eight feet; the dorsal fin is comparatively high and curved backwards. The general coloration is black above and white below, but the dark colour of the back does not extend far on to the sides nor usually reach the insertion of the flipper. The latter is dark on both

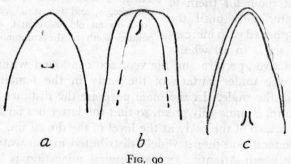

FIG. 90
Upper surface of the head of porpoise *a*, sperm whale *b*, and rorqual *c*.
Not all to same scale.
In the porpoise the blowhole is symmetrical and crescentic, in the sperm whale it is S-shaped and lies on the left, in the rorqual it is double and symmetrical

surfaces and is inserted in the white part of the body, but a streak of dark colour runs from its base to join the darker upper parts. The under side of the tail flukes and the caudal peduncle are dark. The line separating the dark and light areas is not sharp, the two grading into each other through shades of grey, brown and yellow with darker patches and smears, so that a very streaky appearance is given to the sides of the body. The area surrounding the eye is often darker, forming a patch that may be prolonged forwards as a dark streak. Individual variation in the disposition and colour of the markings is great. The teeth are forty to fifty in each side of each jaw, and are conical and slender (fig. 89, p. 343). There are from three to five further small teeth concealed beneath the gum at the front of the row during life.

The common dolphin is an inhabitant of the warmer parts of the Atlantic, and the Mediterranean, coming as far north as the British Isles. It is particularly common in the English Channel, and is also common in the southern part of St. George's Channel and off the Irish coasts. It is less frequently noticed off the west of Scotland and is usually rare in the North Sea in which it has seldom been found. In 1933 an exceptional influx of Atlantic water took place round the north of Scotland into the North Sea, bringing with it many species of animals not usually found there, including large shoals of common dolphins. A similar irruption occurred in 1937 when it was found that they were feeding upon the shoals of squid that had invaded the North Sea. Dolphins sometimes enter fresh water, though less commonly than porpoises; in 1937 one was captured in the Thames at Putney. These occurrences are, however, exceptional. It appears probable that the shoals of common dolphins approach the British coasts from a south-westerly direction in late summer and autumn, and leave again during the spring, probably withdrawing to the more offshore parts of the Atlantic. These inshore migrations are possibly correlated with the yearly migrations of the shoals of mackerel and, off Cornwall, of pilchards. The young are born in June and July while the adults are away from coastal waters. The food consists of various fishes, especially mackerel, herring and pilchards, and of cephalopods, and to a lesser extent of crustacea.

The euphrosyne dolphin (*Prodelphinus euphrosyne*) is a rare and beautiful species that has only twice been recorded on the British coasts, the first time in 1937 from South Devon. In size and general form it closely resembles the common dolphin but may at once be distinguished by its colour pattern. The upper parts are black and the under parts white, the line of separation passing from the base of the beak through the eye to the under side of the tail root. The flipper is dark and is inserted in the white part. A dark ring encircles the eye, and from it a dark line runs along the flank to the vent. This gives off a branch which extends obliquely towards the belly from a little behind the insertion of the flipper, fading out about half-way along the body. The eye ring gives off two further dark lines which run obliquely to the base of the flipper. The teeth which are conical and slender number about fifty on each side of the upper jaw, and less than forty-five on each side of the lower. The diagnostic character that distinguishes dolphins of this genus from those of *Delphinus* is, however, the form of the palate bones which bear two longitudinal grooves in *Delphinus* but are without them in *Prodelphinus*; this character is only to be seen in the cleaned skull. Nothing is known of the life and habits of this species, which is generally regarded as being oceanic. Nevertheless it evidently occurs, or did once occur, plentifully in the Mediterranean sea (where the common dolphin is also found), for the characteristic pattern is plainly to be recognised in the dolphins depicted on the frescos and vases of the ancients.

Three species of much larger dolphins with short beaks are found in British seas; the white-sided dolphin (*Lagenorhynchus acutus*), the white-beaked dolphin (*L. albirostris*), and the bottle-nosed dolphin (*Tursiops truncatus*). The first two of these reach an adult length of eight to nine feet or a little more, never exceeding ten feet, but the last is distinctly larger, attaining a length of twelve feet. These animals may be distinguished by their form and colour, and by the number and character of the teeth. In both the white-sided and the white-beaked dolphins the beak is short, only about two inches long, and the tail root is strongly compressed laterally so that it is comparatively deep from above to below.

The white-sided dolphin is black above, the colour extending down to include the beak and eye, and sweeping back obliquely over the side to the mid line of the belly in the neighbourhood of the vent, so that the caudal peduncle and both sides of the tail flukes are dark. The remainder of the under-surface is white, shading off into light grey at the front under the lower jaw. The flippers, inserted in the white part, are black, and a dark streak runs forward from their bases towards the lower jaw. But the distinctive feature of the pattern is the large splash or streak of light colour on each side in the black area, extending from below the dorsal fin nearly as far back as the tail flukes. These "white sides" are not pure white but yellowish, shading into brown behind and at their junction with the darker colour. There are about thirty teeth on each side in each jaw; they are comparatively small, being not more than 1/6 inch in diameter. The white-sided dolphin is a northern species and is particularly common in the northern parts of the North Sea and round Orkney and Shetland. Very occasionally it has been found as far south as the Wash and the Atlantic coast of Ireland. It is a gregarious species, occurring in large shoals that have been described, by guesswork, as numbering many thousands. Little is reported of the food or life-history of this species, but the scanty information available indicates that the young are born during the summer in June or July. There is too, no information about any migratory movements, but the presence of the animal in northern Scottish waters has been noted in most months of the year.

The coloration of the white-beaked dolphin is characteristic. In general it is black above and white below, the line separating the colours running from the base of the beak which is left white, to the angle of the jaw, thence to the base of the flipper and sweeping along the side to reach the mid-line of the under-surface at the base of the caudal peduncle. Both surfaces of the flippers and the tail flukes are black, and there is generally a greyish area on the sides extending obliquely from below the dorsal fin to the root of the tail. There are also sometimes some greyish patches on the chin and sides of the throat. The teeth are larger than in the last species and may reach rather more than $\frac{1}{4}$ inch in diameter; they are from twenty-two to twenty-six in number. In British waters the white-beaked dolphin is chiefly an inhabitant of the North Sea, where it is abundant. It has very rarely been found in the English Channel, from which it is usually absent, but it occurs in small numbers in the Bristol and St. George's Channels and on the Atlantic coasts of Ireland and Scotland. In the North Sea there appears to be a migration northwards during the summer and a return south during the autumn and winter. This species is less gregarious than the last, being usually seen in small schools of from twenty to thirty. There is no general information on the food of the species, but the remains of herring and cod are reported to have been found in the few stomachs that have been examined. The young appear to be born about mid-summer. Large, and therefore old, animals of this species are frequently found to be suffering from a disease of the teeth, many of which are often missing.

The bottle-nosed dolphin, considerably larger than the last two species, has a beak that is distinctly longer in porportion to the rest of the body, reaching a length of about $4\frac{1}{2}$ inches. The dark colour of the upper surface, black or grey, extends down to include the beak and the eye, and is continuous with the dark colour of the upper surface of the flipper, which is also dark beneath. The under surface is white, and behind the flipper the white area extends up the side above the level of the mouth and eye. Farther back the dark area reaches the under surface of the body at about the level of the vent, the tail and both sides of the flukes being dark. The white of the underside usually extends along the edge of the beak to form a white line along the upper lip. The teeth are rather large, being from 1/3 to nearly ½ inch in diameter. and are usually from twenty to twenty-two in number on each side in each jaw. Though the bottle-nosed dolphin has been recorded from British seas in all months of the year, there is a great increase in its abundance during the summer. This is the result of an annual migration that approaches our coasts from the south-west in early summer, and spreads up the English, Bristol, and St. George's Channels and the west coast of Ireland. Some of these dolphins pass through the Straits of Dover but they seldom go farther north in the North Sea than the coasts of Suffolk or Holland. On the Atlantic coasts it is rare off the coast of Scotland. This species does not appear in any numbers in British waters until May; it reaches its peak in August, after which it becomes scarcer. The autumn migration away from the coasts is believed to be in the reverse direction to the spring approach from the south-west, but what its destination may be is unknown. Bottle-nosed dolphins are gregarious and sometimes occur in shoals of considerable size. As with most dolphins, the young are born about midsummer. Old individuals, like those of the white-beaked dolphin, are very liable to disease of the jaws leading to ulceration and the loss of teeth. This species is common on the east coast of North America, where there was at one time a commercial fishery for it on the North Carolina coast.

The killer (*Orcinus orca*) is the largest of the dolphins and is easily identified by its striking colour pattern. There is a very great difference in the size attained by adult females and by males, the former reaching a length of about fifteen feet but the old males growing to twice that length. In females and half-grown males the dorsal fin is high and curved backwards (falcate), but in the adult male it is triangular with straight edges and reaches a height of about six feet (Pl. XLVII, p. 324). The killer has no beak, and flippers bluntly oval in shape. The colour pattern is black and white, the black of the back including the upper jaw and eye. At the level of the flipper it extends far down towards the under side, includes the insertion of the flippers, and runs back to the tail flukes. The white of the underside of the head passes as a narrow band between the flippers and along the belly to the level of the dorsal fin where it gives off a large oblique splash which extends up the side between the dorsal fin and the tail. The underside of the tail flukes is white. Just above and behind the eye there is an oval white patch on the side of the head, and another triangular one on the side of the back just behind the dorsal fin; the latter mark is often rather indistinct and is sometimes absent, especially in females. The white coloration is often strongly tinged with a yellowish hue. In the old males not only is the dorsal fin very large but the flippers also reach a great size, measuring over six feet in length. The teeth are large and conical, and may be up to two inches in diameter in old bulls; in the females they are smaller and in young animals they are slightly curved. They number from ten to twelve on each side in both jaws.

Killer-whales are usually found in small schools which consist of an adult bull and several cows, but lone bulls are also frequently seen. Killers fully justify their name, being very fierce and voracious animals feeding on seals, porpoises and fish. They are known to attack the larger whales, and it is said that a pack of them worrying a large whalebone whale seizes upon its tongue and tears it to pieces. It is surprising, considering that the killer is so fearless and has no known enemies, that it is not more numerous. It occurs in all the seas of the world and though not uncommon it is never seen in the vast schools usual with some of the other whales. There must be some unknown factor that controls and prevents an inordinate increase in its numbers, for at first sight it appears to have everything in its favour. Killers seem to be consistently rovers and are always on the move, but they are not known to have any regular migrations. They are to be found at any time of the year in British waters and though never abundant cannot be regarded as uncommon. The young are born in November and December, to judge from the records of occurrences of young specimens and of full sized but as yet unborn animals.

The false killer (*Pseudorca crassidens*) is a dolphin of great interest because it is an oceanic species that occasionally comes into coastal waters in large schools and there comes to grief by getting stranded. It has been liable to this accident for thousands of years, for up to 1927 the only British examples known were three sub-fossil skeletons from the fens. Since then the living animal has turned up, and a piece of another sub-fossil skeleton has been found forty to fifty feet below the surface in the Thames gravel beneath London. In 1927 a large school numbering about 150 animals ran ashore in the Dornoch Firth, and in 1934 a smaller school was stranded on the coast of South Wales. In 1935 there were further strandings of considerable numbers on the North Sea coast of Lincolnshire and Yorkshire and in the estuary of the Tay.[78] The cause of these periodical visitations, so disastrous for the animals, is unknown; they may occur at any time of year.

The false killer is a large dolphin, the males reaching a length of nearly twenty feet, the females probably not more than sixteen. There is no beak, the snout being rounded and projecting slightly beyond the lower jaw. The dorsal fin is recurved, resembling that of the females and young males of the killer, but it never attains the great height nor assumes the triangular shape of the dorsal fin of the old bull killer. The flipper is pointed, and proportionately smaller than in the killer. The colour of the false killer is black all over without any white patch on the belly or elsewhere. The teeth are conical, from $\frac{1}{2}$ to $\frac{3}{4}$ inch in diameter, and number eight to eleven on each side in each jaw. Little is known of the life of this animal, but the food is known to include cephalopods. The breeding season appears to be spread over a fairly extensive period of time, and not to be confined to any particular month. The false killer inhabits all the seas of the world with the possible exception of the arctic and antarctic, and schools have been stranded on the coasts of all the continents.

The blackfish, pilot-whale, or ca'ing whale (*Globicephala melaena*) is a dolphin which may reach a length of twenty-eight feet, though the specimens reported from British waters have seldom been over twenty feet in length. The head is rounded or swollen so that it is almost globular in front, and there is a very short beak forming a slight projection at the tip of the upper jaw. The flippers are long, narrow and pointed; the dorsal fin is recurved and the length of its base is greater than its height. The colour is black all over except for a white or greyish patch beneath the chin, and a white streak in the centre of the belly. The throat patch is not always present, and may be divided partly or completely by a central streak of dark colour; the streak on the belly may likewise not be present. The teeth are fairly large and number about ten on each side of each jaw; they are confined to the front part of the jaws, the hinder halves being toothless. The blackfish is gregarious, and is often found in schools numbering many hundreds. It is on the whole a northern species, being specially abundant round Orkney and Shetland, but it may be found off any part of the British coasts. In northern waters large schools often enter a bay or sea loch where their retreat may be cut off by a line of boats; they can then be frightened and driven ashore by splashing the water with oars. Fisheries for blackfish oil, carried on in this way, have existed for centuries in Orkney, Shetland and the Faeroes (Pl. XLVIII, p. 325). The young are probably born during the summer; July and August may be the usual time. The food of this species is fish and cephalopods.

The general form of Risso's dolphin (*Grampus griseus*) is similar to that of the blackfish, but it is a smaller animal, not exceeding twelve feet in length. The head is rounded and blunt, but less globular than in that species; the beak is very small, forming only a slight projection at the tip of the upper jaw. The flippers are rather long and narrow but less so than in the blackfish. The colour of this species changes considerably with age. In fully adult animals the dorsal fin and the back behind it are black; in front of the fin the colour shades into grey which in turn shades into near-white on the front of the head. The under surface is light grey, and a patch of white extends up the sides behind the dorsal fin; the flippers and tail flukes are dark. The light colour is dappled with darker and lighter markings and the surface of the body is covered with irregular light streaks and spots. In the young animal the back is black and the underside white, the division between the colours being much sharper than in the adult, and the irregular light streaks and spots are few or absent. There are three to seven rather large teeth on each side of the front part of the lower jaw only. There are usually no teeth at all in the upper jaw, but specimens are sometimes found with one or two rudimentary teeth there. The headquarters of this species is evidently somewhere to the south-west of the British Isles, for it has usually been found on the south-west coast of England and the south and west coasts of Ireland. Occasionally it strays farther north to Scotland and has even, but very rarely, been found in the North Sea. It is a species not very frequently met with in British waters, but is liable to turn up in any month of the year, so that its visits give no indication of any regular migration. Practically nothing is known of its life-history, but it is considered probable that the young are born in the summer.

Two further species of dolphin have very rarely been found in British waters, the beluga or white whale (*Delphinapterus leucas*) and the narwhal (*Monodon monoceros*). These are arctic species that have seldom strayed to our coasts. Both differ from our other dolphins in having no dorsal fin, and both are of rather large size.

The beluga sometimes reaches a length of eighteen feet, but is more commonly twelve to fourteen feet long. The head is bluntly rounded, and the flipper is oval and rather wide. The adult is pure creamy white all over, but the young are dark brown-grey on which white mottlings appear with advancing age until finally all the darker colour has disappeared. The teeth are from eight to ten on each side of each jaw, but the numbers above and below, or on opposite sides, may not be equal. In the young animal the teeth bear lobes in front of, and behind, the main cusp, but in the adult the lobes disappear through being worn away.

The narwhal, or unicorn, is similar in general shape to the beluga but reaches a rather greater size, from fifteen to twenty feet in length. The young animal is grey all over, but with advancing age the upper parts become darker, and the under lighter, and when full grown the upper side is covered with dark spots. The teeth are reduced to two only, in the upper jaw. In the females these remain embedded in the bone and do not cut the gum, but in the males the tooth on the left side grows out as a long spirally marked tusk projecting horizontally from the upper lip; this tusk may reach a length of nine feet or more. Very rarely a tusk is developed in a female, or both tusks are developed in a male; occasionally, too, it is the right and not the left tusk that grows in the latter sex. The spiral, on both left and right tusks, is always a left-handed thread. Only five narwhals have ever been recorded from British waters, one in each of the years 1588, 1648, 1800, 1808; and one stranded on the Essex coast of the Thames estuary in February 1949.[80]

PHYSETERIDAE

The only member of this family found in British waters is the sperm-whale. A character that distinguishes this family from all other whales is the presence of a single blow-hole on the left side only, that of the right being suppressed.

The sperm-whale (*Physeter catodon*) reaches a large size, and may at once be identified by the bulk and form of the head. The head measures in length about a third of the entire body-length, and is bluntly truncated in front. There is no well-marked dorsal fin, but a low hump occupies the usual position for a fin, followed by four or five smaller ones between it and the tail flukes. The flippers are rather rounded, and along the sides of the body the surface is raised into a number of low longitudinal ridges. The lower jaw is very long but narrow, and the palate against which it bites is correspondingly narrow and seems disproportionately small below the immense head; the jaw, however, does not reach to the end of the snout. The eye lies a little above and behind the angle of the mouth, and the single blow-hole shaped like an elongated 'S' lies a little to the left of the mid line at the front of the top of the head (fig. 90, p. 344). The colour is black, often black all over, but there is frequently some white on the under surface, usually round the jaw and farther back on the belly. The amount of white colour is very variable, and in old bulls the front end of the head, too, may become very light. There are from eighteen to about thirty conical teeth in each side of the lower jaw; they are of very large size and fit into sockets along the upper jaw when the mouth is closed. The upper jaw is without functional teeth, but a number of small rudimentary ones is often present in the gum and sometimes they just cut through it to appear on the surface. They are not rooted in sockets of the bone as are those of the lower jaw. There is a great difference in size between the adult males and females, old bulls reaching a length of about sixty-five feet but females seldom exceeding thirty.[135]

The sperm-whale is essentially a species of the tropics where it is gregarious, roaming the oceans in schools that often contain many individuals. It also occurs regularly outside the tropics, but these wanderers are nearly always bulls; in high latitudes they are large bulls travelling alone. It is said that the latter are old ones that have been driven out of the herds by younger and more vigorous rivals, for the sperm-whale is a polygamous species. But most of the bulls that visit British seas are not of the largest size, and may well be schools of comparatively young ones that have been driven away from the schools of cows by the larger and older bulls. In the warmer seas the sperm-whale appears to undertake regular migrations; the old whalers used to seek it at different times of the year on recognised 'grounds', though these grounds might be far from land or from shallow water. The sperm-whaling grounds lie in all the oceans, for this species enjoys a world-wide distribution. Sperm-whales feed upon fish, and especially upon oceanic squids, some species of which reach a great size.

Sperm-whales are not common in British coastal waters, where occasional stragglers only are found. Nevertheless they regularly occur in the Atlantic to the west of our coasts in the neighbourhood of Rockall and St. Kilda, but they do not usually come much closer to our coasts than the eastern edge of the warm ocean current lying roughly over the hundred fathom line. The schools that visit these regions are composed almost entirely of bulls, cows being very rare. They arrive in early summer and are most abundant in August.

Apart from the oil that may be obtained from the blubber of the sperm-whale there are two other substances of commercial importance that are produced by this species, spermaceti (from which the species takes its name) and ambergris. Sperm-oil and spermaceti are liquid waxes and differ from the oil obtained from whalebone whales. They are both esters produced by the combination of fatty acids with mono-hydric alcohols, whereas ordinary whale oil is an ester of a fatty acid with the trihydric alcohol, glycerine. At the temperature of the whale's body they are both liquid, but whereas on cooling the sperm oil remains fluid the spermaceti solidifies. They are mixed together in the tissues of the whale, but the proportion of spermaceti greatly preponderates in the head. In the part of the head above the jaw and in front of the brain case, that forms the main bulk of the head, there is a space, or rather series of spaces, filled with spermaceti and surrounded by a meshwork of fibres and tendinous tissue. This hollow part is known as the 'case', and from it the spermaceti can be bailed out or poured off; as soon as the spermaceti cools down it sets to a firm white wax. What use the case with the spermaceti may be to the whale is unknown. The special part, the spermaceti organ, in which the wax is produced is derived from the suppressed right nostril.

Ambergris is found in the intestine of some sperm-whales, but its exact origin is unknown. It is said to be found only in whales that are sickly, but how, why or where it is formed is not explained. When found in the whale it is a black greasy substance with a horrible smell, but if it is exposed to the air it becomes harder, lighter in colour, and loses its bad odour, gaining a characteristic faintly aromatic earthy smell. The best sort is not obtained directly from the whale's intestine but is found floating in the sea or washed ashore; it has then had ample time to undergo its natural refining process, probably an oxyda-tion. Embedded in the ambergris there is often a number of horny beaks from the squids that have been eaten by the whale. Ambergris is used in cosmetics to fix and intensify perfumes; it fetches a very high price, and at least one whaling company that had come on hard times has been saved from bankruptcy by the timely discovery of a large quantity of ambergris in a sperm-whale.

ZIPHIIDAE

This family consists of medium-sized toothed-whales. All have a dorsal fin, a well-developed beak not marked off from the body by a groove, teeth reduced in number, no notch at the junction of the tail flukes, and a pair of longitudinal grooves under the throat.

Old males of the bottle-nosed whale (*Hyperoodon rostratus*) reach a length of a little over thirty feet, females not more than twenty-five at the utmost. The beak is very distinctly demarcated from the rest of the head, but not by a groove, and behind it the forehead rises in a rounded protuberance which becomes very large and almost globular in the old males. The colour is black all over in young animals but with increasing age it fades, finally becoming yellowish or almost white, the beak and forehead being white and the belly greyish-white. No teeth are visible in the mouth as a rule, but one or two pairs are present at the tip of the lower jaw concealed below the gum; in old males one or both of these may cut the gum and appear on the surface. The food of this species appears to consist mainly of oceanic squids, and it is surprising that such active prey can be successfully caught by a toothless animal. The bottle-nosed whale is an Atlantic species which migrates to the arctic during the summer and returns south during the autumn and winter. Its northerly migration takes it well to the west of the British Isles, but during the southerly journey many pass through our coastal waters. At that time the species may be found anywhere in the surrounding seas, on the Atlantic coasts and in the North and Irish seas. These whales, however, probably represent only the eastern fringe of the southwardly migrating schools, for those that have been examined have usually been females or young males; and the full grown males, which are very rare British animals, are believed to keep farther to the west. Bottle-nosed whales are hunted by the Norwegians and produce an oil of the same type as sperm-oil, known to commerce as "arctic sperm-oil".

Cuvier's whale (*Ziphius cavirostris*) is a rather smaller whale than the bottle-nosed, reaching a length of about twenty-six feet. The beak is shorter than in the former species and is not so sharply marked off from the forehead, which slopes gradually to the beak. The colour is variable, some specimens being black above and light below, others dark over the greater part of the body but with the back in front of the dorsal fin, the upper part of the head, and the beak, white; there may also be a number of light streaks in the dark area. There are two teeth at the tip of the lower jaw; they are fairly large and exposed in the old male, but in the female and young male they are smaller and concealed in the gum. Cuvier's whale is an Atlantic species which occasionally comes into British waters, and has been found on the Atlantic coasts of Scotland, Ireland and south-west England. It was once thought to be extremely rare, but is now known to be not very scarce. Nothing is known of its life-history.

True's whale (*Mesoplodon mirum*) reaches a length of sixteen to seventeen feet, and has a rather long narrow beak that passes gradually into the rest of the head, from which it is not sharply demarcated. The colour varies, and may be dark above and light below with some greyish colour on the belly; or the upper parts may be light with some darker mottlings. Only one or occasionally two pairs of teeth are present at the extreme end of the lower jaw, concealed beneath the gum in the female, but the larger front ones, strongly compressed from side to side, appearing on the surface in the male. True's whale is a rare and little known Atlantic species that has been recorded in British waters only four times, all on the west coasts of Scotland or Ireland.

Sowerby's whale (*Mesoplodon bidens*) reaches a length of about sixteen feet or a little more. The long narrow beak merges gradually with the head, which is rather slender. The colour is black, sometimes partly white below and sometimes with irregular white splashes and streaks on the upper parts. The teeth are a single pair in the lower jaw about half way along its length. They are small and remain below the surface in females and young males, but they cut the gum and are comparatively large in old males. There may be a few additional rudimentary teeth beneath the gum in both jaws. Sowerby's whale is another Atlantic species that sometimes comes into British coastal waters, where it has been found on both the eastern and western coasts, more particularly off the north-east of Scotland. Practically nothing is known of its life-history.

*   *   *   *   *   *   *

Six species of the Mysticeti (Whalebone-whales) are known as British, but most of them are seldom seen in coastal waters, for they usually keep well out in the Atlantic to the west, the hundred fathom line roughly marking the limit of their approach. The six species are distributed between two families, one in the Balaenidae and five in the Balaenopteridae. All are provided with baleen in the mouth and none have teeth, though the tooth-rudiments are present in both jaws of the unborn young. The nostrils form paired blow-holes (fig. 90, p. 344).

To the Balaenidae belongs the Atlantic right whale (*Balaena glacialis*), a species fifty to sixty feet long when adult. There is no dorsal fin, the flippers are wide and rounded, and the upper jaw is long, narrow, and highly arched. The lips of the lower jaw are greatly enlarged at the sides to meet the arched upper jaw and close the mouth (fig. 91). The baleen plates are about 230 in number; the largest are six to nine feet long and nine to twelve inches wide. The baleen plates and their hairy fringes are entirely black in colour; there is no series of parallel grooves on the throat as in the other family. On the

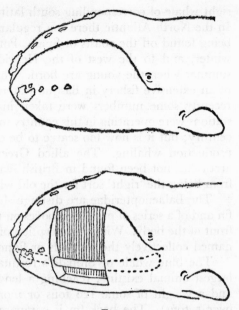

FIG. 91

Side views of the head of the right whale.

Above, showing the shape of the mouth, and the position of the bonnet and minor excrescences. Below, part of the lower lip is shown, diagramatically, as cut away, exposing the baleen hanging from the upper jaw, and part of the lower jaw bone. The rest of the lower jaw bone is indicated by a dotted line. The lower lip rises to a great height above the lower jaw bone

snout there is an area of thickened and roughened skin known as the 'bonnet', and along the lower jaw there are several similar but smaller patches. These areas are usually infested with whale-lice (*Cyamus ceti*); their function, if indeed they have any, is unknown. In colour the Atlantic right whale is black all over, but there are often some irregular patches of white of greater or lesser extent on the under surface. The distribution of this whale covers the north Atlantic but may be wider, for it is not certain whether the closely allied southern right whale of corresponding south latitudes is really a distinct species. In the North Atlantic there is a regular yearly migration, the animals being found off the coasts of Spain, Portugal, and north Africa in the winter, and to the west of the Hebrides and thence north in midsummer when the young are born. This species was once the subject of an extensive fishery in Basque waters and farther north, and more recently some numbers were taken in British waters when whaling stations were operating in this country in the earlier years of the present century; but it is now too scarce to be of importance to modern massproduction whaling. The allied Greenland right whale of the far arctic has not been found in British seas. The species get their name from being the 'right' sort for the old whalers.

The Balaenopteridae are distinguished by the presence of a dorsal fin and of a series of parallel grooves on the throat and underside of the front of the body. With the exception of the humpback whale they are named collectively the rorquals or finner whales.

The blue whale or Sibbald's rorqual (*Balaenoptera musculus*) is the largest animal existing, reaching a length of about one hundred feet and a weight of some 120 tons or more (a very big elephant is not over 5 tons). The back fin is comparatively very small, and placed far back towards the tail. The throat grooves are from 70 to 120 in number and average about 90. A variable number of short hairs is present on the chin, the edge of the upper jaw, on the centre line of the snout, and near the blow-holes; the number on the chin averages about thirty. The breadth of the baleen plates is about three-quarters of their length; they vary in number from a little under 300 to nearly 400 on each side of the upper jaw. The baleen plates and their hairy fringes are a uniform blue-black in colour. The colour of the body is an all over bluish-grey on which are splashed numerous white specklings. A slightly darker streak extends upwards and backwards from the region of the eye and fades out on the side of the head.[126] The blue whale, or sulphur-bottom as it is called by the Americans, is found in all the seas of the world, and in both hemispheres there is a migration to high latitudes in summer and a return to lower ones in the winter. The migration to cold waters is a feeding migration which takes advantage of the plentiful plankton there, the most important food being shrimp-like Euphausian crustacea: *Euphausia superba* in the southern hemisphere, and *Boreophausia inermis* in the northern. These planktonic crustacea are termed 'krill' by the whalers. It is during the winter when the whales are in the warmer waters of lower latitudes that the young are born; but the whales feed little and become quite lean during this part of their wanderings. In the Atlantic to the west of the British Isles this species is most abundant from July to September.

The fin-whale or common rorqual (*Balaenoptera physalus*) (Pl. XLVIIIb, p. 325) is next in size to the gigantic blue whale, attaining a length of sixty to seventy, sometimes of over eighty feet, the females commonly reaching the greater lengths. The general form of the species is similar to that of the blue whale, but the dorsal fin, set far back towards the tail, is proportionately considerably larger. In colour it differs greatly from that species, being slaty grey to nearly black above and the purest white below. The under surfaces of the flippers and tail flukes are also white, the white of the underside of the flipper creeping round on to the upper side along the hind edge to form a white line. The whole pigmentation is asymmetrical, being shifted slightly towards the left so that the dark colour extends farther towards the belly on that side, and on the left the lower jaw is pigmented, but on the right it is white. A black band several inches wide runs upwards and backwards from the eye and fades out on the side of the head, and there is a white streak running backwards from the minute ear-hole. The throat grooves average about 85 to 90 in number, and may total anything from 70 to 115 in different individuals. The baleen plates which are in width rather less than three-quarters of their length, number from about 260 to 470, 350 to 400 being the usual range. Most of the baleen plates are of a dark slaty colour with yellowish longitudinal streaks; all of them on the left side are thus coloured, as are the hinder two thirds of those on the right side. But the front third of the series on the right is white or yellowish-white, the change in coloration being quite abrupt. The hairy fringes of the inner edges of all the baleen plates, both of the dark and of the light ones, are white. It is believed that the asymmetry of the coloration is correlated with a tendency of fin-whales to swim not on an even keel but slightly on the right side when they are feeding below the surface.[126] Fin-whales, like blue whales, are found in all the waters of the world and have similar feeding and breeding migrations to high and low latitudes. Off the British coasts they travel north in late winter and spring and return south during the autumn. The food also of this species is similar to that of the blue whale, but it is known sometimes to include herrings as well when there is a scarcity of krill. Like the blue whale, too, the fin-whale seldom approaches our Atlantic shores to within the hundred fathom line, though occasional stragglers to inshore waters are not so rare and have been recorded from all parts including the North Sea coast down to the Straits of Dover.

The sei-whale or Rudolphi's rorqual (*Balaenoptera borealis*) is a smaller and more slender rorqual, adults being from 40 to 45 feet long, sometimes exceeding 50 but very rarely reaching 60 feet. The flipper is relatively smaller than in the fin-whale, and the dorsal fin is proportionately much larger and more curved, being deeply notched behind. The throat grooves are much fewer than in the blue and fin-whales, numbering from forty to about sixty, the average being less than fifty. They do not extend so far back as in those species and end level with each other some distance in front of the navel. The coloration is rather variable; on the back it is grey, usually lighter than in the fin-whale but sometimes darker, and it becomes lighter on the under surface. There is an area of pure white on the throat grooves but the extent of it is very variable and may cover most of the groove area or be reduced to a small streak in the middle line. The edges of the white colour are irregular in outline, and there may be uneven splashes and spots of lighter colour on the darker parts. The under-surface of the tail flukes is pigmented and may be as dark as the upper surface. In some sei-whales there is a tendency for the pigmentation to be asymmetrically shifted slightly to the right as in the fin-whale, but it has been denied that this species turns on to its side when feeding as does that species. On the chin, lower jaw, and upper surface of the head there is a number of scattered hairs, usually rather less than thirty on the chin. The baleen in this species is of fine texture and the hairy fringe is soft, silky and curled. The number of plates on each side of the mouth averages about 340, not many less than in the blue and fin-whales.[137] The texture of the baleen is thus necessarily finer than in those species, for if a similar number of plates is to be packed into a much smaller mouth obviously they must be thinner. The width of individual plates is also less, being not more than half the length. Most of the baleen plates are dark in colour, nearly black, but a number of white plates is often present at the front end of the series on one or both sides. The hairy fringe inside the plates is always white or greyish-white, and occasionally plates are found partly white and partly black.

The sei-whale is a cosmopolitan species, being found in all the seas of the world. Like the blue and fin-whales it has a summer feeding migration to high latitudes and a winter breeding migration to lower ones. This whale also feeds on krill, but because of its finer baleen it is able in addition to make use of much smaller planktonic animals than are the larger species. In the northern hemisphere it is known to feed upon planktonic copepods (water-fleas) as well as the larger crustacea. The migrations of the sei-whale in general follow a similar course to those of the blue and fin-whales, roughly following the hundred fathom line to the west of the British Isles where the greatest abundance of the species is reached during June. But this species comes inshore much more frequently than the others, and during the summer is not uncommonly to be found among the western isles of Scotland. Elsewhere it is rarely seen and has never been recorded from our North Sea or English Channel coasts.

The piked whale or lesser rorqual (*Balaenoptera acutorostrata*) is the smallest rorqual, seldom exceeding thirty feet in length. The dorsal fin is hooked and notched behind as in the sei-whale, and the throat grooves number about fifty. The colour is greyish-brown above and white below, including the underside of the tail flukes. The upper surface of the flipper is greyish with a white patch occupying about the middle third, a unique colour pattern among whalebone whales. The baleen plates are narrow and all of them, including their hairy fringes, are white or yellowish-white, this also being a distinctive character. They are fine in texture and number from 270 to about 320 on each side. The piked whale also is a cosmopolitan species, but little is known of its migrations because it is too small to be worth hunting commercially and consequently there are no records of its capture available from the whaling stations; as far as is known its migrations are similar to those of the other rorquals. In British waters it is commonest in late summer when it enters the North Sea round the north of Scotland, but it does not usually travel farther south than the Wash, nor has it been found in the English Channel. Elsewhere it has been found from time to time round all parts of the Atlantic coast and the Irish sea. This species is said to feed on fishes as well as the smaller planktonic animals. Since 1939 it has been hunted extensively by the Norwegians for the Whale-meat market.

The humpback-whale (*Megaptera boops*) is a short tubby whale, usually not much exceeding fifty feet in length, but having proportionately a great girth so that the body is not nearly so streamlined as in rorquals. The flipper is very long and narrow, measuring about a quarter of the body length. The dorsal fin is small and is set on the summit of a low hump, behind which lie several smaller elevations of the surface. The front edge of the flipper is beset with a number of irregular lumps that give it a wavy outline, and the hind edge of the tail flukes is irregularly notched. On the upper surface of the head and along the side of the lower jaws there is also a number of large wart-like lumps or knobs, each of which bears one or more short coarse hairs. The throat grooves are spaced much more widely than in the rorquals and are consequently fewer in number, being from 20 to 36 and averaging from 25 to 30. The colour of this whale is very variable but is always black above and may be white below. But the black of the back may extend so far down the sides that the white area on the belly is greatly reduced or is even sometimes completely absent. The proportions of black and white also vary on the flipper which may be nearly entirely black, black above and white below with a white fore edge, or nearly wholly white. The baleen plates and their hairy fringes are coarse, the plates dark grey to black in colour and the fringes white to greyish-white; sometimes some of the plates at the front end of the series are white or partly white. The width of the plates is a quarter to a third of their length, and they range in number from about 320 to something short of 400 on each side of the jaw.[134] The humpback whale is cosmopolitan in its distribution, and migrates to high latitudes to feed in the summer, returning to lower ones for breeding in the winter. Animals of all the types of coloration are found everywhere, but there are indications that particular types tend to be commonest in particular localities, showing that there is likely to be some segregation of the schools. This species is not common in British waters, but some individuals come in as far as the hundred fathom line to the west during their migrations, and are most plentiful during July and August. In some parts of the world, particularly in lower latitudes, the humpback is very definitely a coastal species coming into shallow water close under the land especially at calving time. The food, as that of the rorquals, consists of plankton and especially euphausian crustacea, but the humpback is also a great eater of fish such as herring and others that congregate in shoals.

There is a species of whalebone whale that is found in the Pacific, the Pacific grey whale (*Rhachianectes glaucus*), and migrates

along the coasts of America and Asia to the Arctic in summer returning as far south as California in winter. It is a small species, only
about forty to forty-five feet long, has no dorsal fin, and no more than
two throat grooves. Until 1936 it was unknown outside the Pacific
but in that year parts of the skull and of the skeleton of one were dug
up in Holland in a reclaimed part of the Zuider Zee.[222] The bones
were of pleistocene age, but other specimens have since come to light
which show that the species must have occurred along the European
coasts at least until 500 A.D., and that at least one specimen was
stranded on the coast of Cornwall. In the light of these facts a new
interpretation has been given to old records, and it is now believed
that the species must also have been present along the American coast
of the Atlantic until at least the end of the first quarter of the eighteenth
century, where it was at that time hunted commercially. The species
was evidently an inhabitant of British seas in early historical times,
but it is not likely ever to be one again.

CHAPTER 13

THE ORIGIN OF THE BRITISH
MAMMAL FAUNA

Why doth Africa breed so many venomous beasts, Ireland none?
Athens owls, Crete none? Why hath Daulis and Thebes no
swallows (so Pausanias informeth us) as well as the rest of
Greece, Ithaca no hares, Pontus asses, Scythia wine? whence
comes this variety of complexions, colours, plants, birds, beasts,
metals, peculiar almost to every place? Why so many strange
birds and beasts proper to America alone, as Acosta demands,
lib. 4. *cap.* 36. were they created in the six days, or ever in Noah's
ark? if there, why are they not dispersed and found in other
countries?

ROBERT BURTON, *Anatomy of Melancholy.* 1628

THE EXISTING mammal fauna of the British Isles is, geologically
speaking, of very recent origin, and did not become established
until the later phases of the pleistocene period or ice-age. The pleistocene began less than a million years ago, perhaps about 600,000 before
the present, and forms a very small fraction of geological time. The
beginning of the palaeozoic era, whose rocks contain the remains of
the earliest known forms of life, is placed at rather less than 500 million
years B.P. (before the present). But life must have existed on the earth
long before that, although it has left no traces in the pre-cambrian
rocks that are believed to have an age of at least three times the
length of all that has been deposited since, the age of the oldest rocks
thus being perhaps 2,000 million years. Mammals of the class now
existing in most parts of the world (Eutheria, placental mammals)
first appear in the palaeocene period at the beginning of the tertiary
era, 60 to 55 million B.P.; mammals of a more primitive type were
already present in the late Jurassic over 100 million B.P., and all are
believed to have evolved from synapsid reptilian ancestors that
flourished in the triassic period of the mesozoic era some 90 million

years earlier than the palaeocene. Just as the reptiles were the dominant group of vertebrates during the mesozoic era, the mammals became dominant early in the tertiary. They reached their peak in numbers and diversity of form in the late miocene and early pliocene periods, 15 to 10 million B.P., since when they have been declining, so that the present mammal fauna of the world is only an impoverished remnant of that which once adorned its surface. At first an increasing dryness of climate, which produced ever greater areas of arid and desert land, and later the succession of glaciations simultaneously with the rise of man appear to have been the main causes of the decline, a decline which, during the last few centuries, has been hastened with mounting speed by the activities of man; all the larger species will inevitably soon be extinct, except perhaps a few that may be preserved in artificial sanctuaries.

The character of the present fauna was determined by the conditions of climate, vegetation, and geography that prevailed during the pleistocene period. But although the period was of comparatively short duration, the conditions were far from constant; it is loosely spoken of as the ice-age, but it contained at least four ice-ages or glaciations, separated by long inter-glacial periods, in some of which the climate was warmer than that of the present day. There was, of course, no sharp division between these succeeding phases, nor between the preceding pliocene period and the pleistocene, the transitions taking thousands of years. During the glaciations part, sometimes nearly the whole, of the country was covered with ice-caps and glaciers that were completely uninhabitable to mammals; and the parts not actually covered with ice must have had a cool or sometimes very cold climate. In addition to these changes others were produced in the level of the sea, by the locking-up of enormous quantities of water as ice so that the sea level was lowered, and places that are now islands were joined to neighbouring land masses by the dry sea-bed. Conversely, changes in the level of the land produced alterations both upwards and downwards in the shore-line.

A great quantity of research has been carried out on the geology and palaeontology of the pleistocene period. This has been critically reviewed and set out as a history of the period by Zeuner,[234] whose book must form the basis of any account of the fauna that evolved during this time—immensely long by human, but extremely short by geological standards. The deposits of the pleistocene period are divided by geologists into the lower, middle, and upper series, which are subdivided as here tabulated, the approximate dates being those assigned by Zeuner :

Lower pleistocene. 600,000 B.P.   First (Early) glaciation.
First (Antepenultimate) inter-
glacial.
Second (Antepenultimate)
glaciation.
Middle pleistocene. 425,000 B.P.   Second (Penultimate) interglacial.
Third (Penultimate) glaciation.
Upper pleistocene. 180,000 B.P.   Third (Last) interglacial.
Fourth (Last) glaciation; followed
by the Holocene or Post-glacial
(extending to the present).

But this table conveys an impression of precision greater than is justified, for although the glaciations and interglacial phases lasted for very long periods of time the conditions characteristic of each did not rise gradually to a central peak and then decline; glaciation advanced and retreated within each phase, some of the fluctuations having been great enough to leave their mark on the deposits, so that they are now recognised as interstadial phases.

The sequence of the glaciations throughout the pleistocene period has been fitted to a time-scale by combining the information obtainable from astronomy and geology. Zeuner taking the date, of c.600,000 B.P. for the beginning of the period, gives a scale approximately as follows (fig. 92, p. 367). The first glaciation lasted c.60,000 years (600,000–540,000 B.P.), and had two maxima of cold at c.590,000 and 550,000 B.P., with a milder interstadial phase between them. The succeeding first interglacial period also lasted c.60,000 years (540,000–480,000 B.P.) during which the climate was temperate and much like that of the present day.

The second glaciation was slightly shorter, lasting 55,000 years from 480,000 to 425,000 B.P.; it also had two maxima of cold, at c.476,000 and c.435,000 B.P. with a warmer interstadial intervening. The last of these maxima brought the heaviest glaciation of the pleistocene, and during it little if any mammalian fauna can have remained anywhere in the British Isles. Then followed the enormously long second, or great, interglacial lasting about 185,000 years from c.425,000 to c.240,000 B.P., during parts of which the climate was considerably warmer than that of the present.

The third glaciation, which was less severe than the preceding one, lasted about 60,000 years from c.240,000 to c.180,000 B.P.; it had two

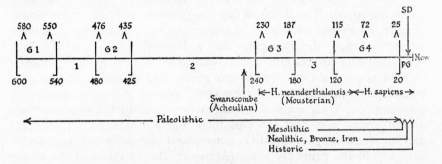

FIG. 92
A time scale for the Pleistocene period.
The dates in thousands of years before the present, the peaks of the glaciations shown as points above the line. G1, G2 etc., first, second etc. glaciations. 1, 2, 3, first, second and third interglacials. PG, post glacial. SD, final opening of the Straits of Dover

maxima of cold, in c.230,000 and 187,000 B.P., separated by an interstadial during which the climate was milder. The third interglacial which followed was of about the same length, lasting from c.180,000 to c.120,000 B.P., and during part of this time the climate was warmer than now.

The fourth and last glaciation covered about 100,000 years, from c.120,000 to c.20,000 B.P. Three maxima of cold occurred in this period at c.115,000, c.72,000 and c.25,000 B.P., and two milder interstadials separated them. The post-glacial period, which has lasted at least 15,000 and probably 20,000 years, had a climate during its middle stages that was warmer than at present; it has been getting cooler for the last 10,000 years but another glaciation need not be expected before the lapse of at least an equal period of time, and possibly one many times longer—or, indeed, ever.

Throughout most of the pleistocene period the British Isles were connected to the continent so that animals could pass freely over to them from the south and east. At times the connection was broken by changes in sea-level, but the final severance did not occur until quite recently, the straits of Dover being finally opened only some seven thousand years ago, about 5,000 B.C. When heavy glaciation covered the country, therefore, the fauna was driven out to the south, and probably also to the south-west, into lands now destroyed by denudation and erosion, from which it returned when conditions again improved. The fauna of the late pliocene, living in a temperate climate, continued without change into the early pleistocene. Zeuner points out that the European fauna immediately before the first glaciation had an eastern, Asiatic character, shown by the presence of wild pigs of a typically eastern group and of tapirs, and that it contained many essentially new-world genera such as mastodons, primitive elephants some of which carried tusks in the lower as well as the upper jaw, and sabre-toothed 'tigers' (*Machairodus*). Several species of monkeys, zebra-like horses, and antelopes are character-istic, as are the primitive voles (*Mimomys*) the ancestors of the living *Arvicola*, whose molar teeth were provided with roots, and the gigantic elephant *Elephas meridionalis*, some examples of which are calculated to have been fifteen feet in height. Bears, wolves, lions, hyaenas and many smaller carnivores preyed upon the horses, antelopes, deer of many species, pigs, hares, beavers, voles and squirrels, and probably sometimes also on the larger herbivorous mammals such as the mastodon, elephant, rhinoceros, hippopotamus, and tapir. All the mammals making up this fauna belonged to species that had become extinct by the middle pleistocene.

The first glaciation, which in the west of the old world consisted of an ice-sheet spreading across the North Sea from Scandinavia, began about 600,000 B.P., and some 30,000 years later a milder phase was accompanied by a temporary retreat of the glaciation, during which the Norwich crag deposits were laid down. After this the glaciation advanced again and did not withdraw until the first interglacial period, during which the Cromer Forest bed was formed about 485,000 B.P. During the first glaciation the fauna was in general similar to that of the pre-glacial period, but some new species, such as an otter, appear, and after its end mastodons are no longer present. The succeeding first interglacial supported a rich fauna characterised by late forms of *Elephas meridionalis*, sabre-tooths, the Etruscan rhinoceros, and including as new arrivals the red deer, elk, roe, and several extinct fallow deer. During this time, too, elephants resembling the mammoth and others approaching the straight-tusked elephant first appear. Wild pigs, hippopotamus, a number of deer related to the red deer, several species of giant deer, bison, horses and rhinoceroses filled out the total of herbivores, and provided food for the numerous carnivores. These included several species of huge bears, lions, sabre-tooths, the wolf, fox, otter, marten, and several hyaenas, none of them belonging to existing species, though a weasel occurred that is indistinguishable from that now living. Of the smaller mammals there were several insectivores, a mole little different from that of the present, shrews, a hedgehog, and a desman; among the numerous rodents there were hares, susliks (ground-squirrels), several voles, including one much like the living bank-vole, squirrels, beavers, and field-mice. At least one species of monkey was present, as was a human maker of very primitive stone implements, but what manner of man he was is unknown.

The increasing cold accompanying the approach of the second glaciation added to the fauna forms such as the musk-ox and glutton, typical of more northern climates. During the first cold phase of this glaciation, which reached its peak about 476,000 B.P., the earlier form of elephant, *E. meridionalis*, became extinct, leaving the straight-tusked *E. antiquus*, an inhabitant of forests, and *E. trogontherii*, which lived in more open country; the sabre-tooths are not found after the next interstadial. During the first cold phase, too, the voles of the genus *Mimomys* evolved molar teeth without roots, being transformed thereby into *Arvicola*,[104] though not into species now living. With the approach of the second cold phase of this glaciation the reindeer joined the fauna, and the zebra-like horses became extinct, as did the Etruscan rhinoceros.

It was during this second cold phase that the greatest degree of glaciation experienced by Britain in any part of the pleistocene occurred. The whole of the northern part of the country was covered with an ice-cap, and the ice-sheet extended over all of Ireland and of England as far south as the Thames. The entire fauna must have been driven from the greater part of the land, and it is probable that for a long time the parts not actually under ice were so cold and inhospitable that few animals could have lived there. The foundation of the present fauna of the country must therefore have been laid when the animals migrated in after the second phase of the second glaciation had passed its maximum, for the two glaciations which were to occur in the far distant future were much less severe; thus the fauna was not again completely driven out, but could remain at least in the southern regions.

About ten thousand years after the peak of the severest glaciation the second, or great, interglacial period started c.425,000 B.P., and lasted for about 185,000 years to c.240,000 B.P. The climate went through a number of fluctuations, and was sometimes warmer than it is at present, but throughout the whole of this great length of time it never became glacial. The fauna that returned when the land again became habitable resembled in a general way that which had been expelled by the glaciation, but many of the animals were sufficiently different from the previous ones to be separable as distinct species, and most of the older forms that were more characteristic of the pliocene had disappeared. Some of the species were already the same as those now living, and others so near that they have been separated only as subspecies. The fox was the same as the species of the present day, and the wild cat and the spotted hyaena differed only slightly from their living descendants. Others of the carnivores have since become extinct everywhere, such as some of the bears and the cave-lion, or locally, as the wolf. Horses were abundant, but were now true (caballine) horses, and not zebra-like species. Two species of two-horned rhinoceros now replaced the ancestral Etruscan rhinoceros, *Dicerorhinus merkii*, an inhabitant of forests, and *D. hemitoechus*, an inhabitant of more open grassy lands. Pigs resembling the present wild boar but very much larger, a hippopotamus, red and roe deer, an extinct fallow deer and more than one species of giant deer occur, together with at least two species of ox, one of which was the huge aurochs (*Bos primigenius*), a bison, and a goat. The elephants derived from *E. meridionalis* show two lines of specialisation, one represented by the forest-living *E. antiquus*, and the other by *E. trogontherii*, which developed a more complicated pattern on the crowns of the molar teeth by means of which it was able to feed upon the coarser herbage and grasses of the open plains. The former became extinct later in the pleistocene when conditions became unfavourable for it, but the latter, taking advantage of the great quantities of less succulent food available to it, continued to flourish and develop yet more complicated teeth until it later gave rise to the mammoth.

Among the smaller mammals there were several species of vole, one not very different from the present bank-vole (*Clethrionomys*), several species of short-tailed vole (*Microtus*) and of water-vole (*Arvicola*), and a beaver indistinguishable from the living species. Shrews and water-shrews of several species occurred, but less is known of these small mammals because their fragile remains are not preserved as often as the bones of larger ones. In the early part of this interglacial a species of monkey (*Macaca*) was living in the south of England but appears to have become extinct long before its close. During the final third of the period a type of man arrived who differed little in cranial characters and development of brain from ourselves; his remains are little known apart from the Swanscombe skull, but his flint implements, of the Acheulian type, are plentiful. Acheulian man replaced the makers of the more primitive Chellean and pre-Chellean implements of earlier times, but towards the end of the great interglacial he was himself replaced by yet another race. The newcomer was a very different person, low in stature and with small brain and beetling brow, so unlike modern man that he is classified as a separate species, *Homo neanderthalensis*; his implements are what is known as Mousterian in type and differ fundamentally in the method of their manufacture from those of Acheulian man, generally being made from flint flakes struck from cores and not being solely heavy hand-axes, from which the flakes were discarded as waste.

The third glaciation marked the end of the great interglacial at c.240,000 B.P. and lasted for about 60,000 years to c.180,000 B.P.; it had two maxima of cold at about 230,000 and 187,000 B.P. In neither of them was the whole country ice-covered, southern Ireland, most of south Wales, and England south of Yorkshire being free, though glaciers extended as far south as the Wash on both east and west coasts. The climate of the ice-free parts was cool, and the land tundra-like without forests. These conditions are reflected in the fauna which, however, is not as well-known as those of some other phases of the pleistocene. Cold-climate animals such as the reindeer, musk-ox, and woolly rhinoceros, the latter being a new arrival from the steppes and tundras of the east, were typical of the times. During this glaciation *Elephas antiquus* is believed to have retired to the south away from temperate Europe, leaving its relative *E. trogontherii* which was becoming more and more mammoth-like. Neanderthal man, or Mousterian man as he is known from his implements, was the only human representative in this fauna.

The third and last interglacial lasted about as long as the **third** glaciation, from c.180,000 to c.120,000 B.P.; its climate was temperate but, during part of it, was warmer than that of to-day. During the cooler parts the forests were not extensive but formed scattered woods among open park-like land over which roamed the bear, wolf, lion, horse, rhinoceros, red and giant deer, aurochs, bison and mammoth. In the warmer phases the forest cover was widespread and harboured in addition the hyaena and hippopotamus, but the horse and rhinoceros were less plentiful. During these times, too, the mammoth migrated away to the open steppes of the north and east, being replaced by the straight-tusked elephant (*E. antiquus*), which returned to the north from the more southern regions whither it had retreated during the preceding glacial period. The fauna of this interglacial contained many species identical with those now living, either in this country, or elsewhere if they have been locally exterminated. Such are the fox, badger, otter, marten, wild cat, watervole, red and roe-deer, all of which have probably remained in uninterrupted occupation since those times; and the wolf, lynx, and beaver, which live on the continent although lost to us. Throughout most of this interglacial the only species of man inhabiting the country was *H. neanderthalensis*; Piltdown man (*Eoanthropus*) is believed to have lived in the earlier part of it.

The fourth or last glacial period, although not nearly the most severe, was much longer than any of those that preceded it, enduring for 100,000 years from c.120,000 to c.20,000 B.P. Unlike previous glaciations it had three, instead of two, maxima of cold, at c.115,000, c.72,000, and c.25,000 B.P. and therefore two interstadials. During the maxima the mountain valleys of the north were filled with glaciers, but extensive ice-caps were not developed, and the steeper mountain-tops were probably not buried. Even during the peaks of glaciation much of the country was inhabited by man and animals, which also occupied the territory released by the retreating glaciers during the interstadial phases. Zeuner, speaking of the faunas of the three cold phases of this glaciation, says, "By this time, immigration and adaptive evolution had supplied a large number of species well fitted for the periglacial biotopes. Many, present in small numbers in earlier cold phases, now become abundant; arctic fox, varying hare, lemmings and susliks (*Citellus*), caballine horses, woolly rhinoceros, reindeer, musk-ox, mammoth (*E. primigenius* s. str.)". Even in the early phase of this glaciation very many present-day species are found, totalling more than in the last interglacial, for there were in addition shrews, several species of bats, the brown bear as well as the extinct cave-bear, the stoat, polecat, bank-vole, water-vole, long-tailed field-mouse, squirrel, and wild boar. Some others are now totally extinct or extinct in Europe, such as the lion, woolly rhinoceros, mammoth, aurochs, hyaena, giant deer, and Neanderthal man.

Neanderthal man, like the giant deer, seems to have disappeared sometime about the second peak of glaciation, c.72,000 B.P. He was replaced, perhaps exterminated, by *H. sapiens* of an entirely modern type, men like ourselves who probably migrated into Europe from Asia. Professor Le Gros Clark[122] points out that although Neanderthal man had a "brutish appearance" he does not represent a direct stage in the evolution of modern man from ape-like ancestors, but is a specialised offshoot from the main human family tree. Proof of this is given by the discovery of pre-Mousterian, Acheulian man in the Swanscombe skull, which shows that a type scarcely different from the modern existed before Neanderthal man. It is possible that at least in some regions there may have been some intercrossing of the two species, so that modern man may be hybrid in his origin and may contain some Neanderthal genes. Modern man's behaviour certainly does nothing to refute the suggestion of this possibility. Since the extinction of *H. neandertalensis* successive waves of immigration by different races of *H. sapiens* have succeeded each other down to historic times.

The last glacial age came to an end about 20,000 years ago. Geologists have agreed that this should be used to mark the end of the pleistocene period, the post-glacial or holocene period being taken as extending from then until the present. The climate at first was dry and cold, almost sub-arctic, and the country a tundra inhabited by great herds of reindeer. Later the summers became warmer and the land steppe-like; in these conditions the horse became one of the most characteristic animals of the fauna. There were, however, considerable oscillations of climate, so that cold conditions returned after warmer periods. When the climate improved so that it was suitable for the growth of trees, forests spread over the country, first of birch, then of pine and finally hazel. About 15,000 years ago, or perhaps rather less, the palaeolithic cultures of man gave way to the mesolithic, the transitional stage leading to the neolithic. During the times in which this culture flourished there were considerable changes in sea-level caused by the rising or sinking of the land, as shown by the present-day raised beaches and submerged forests. When the final cutting of the Straits of Dover occurred about 7,000 B.P. this caused, according to Stamp,[199] an abrupt change in the British climate, which became wetter and milder, so that forests of deciduous trees covered the country during the neolithic, bronze, and iron ages, though during the bronze age the climate was probably again drier than at present. By this time the fauna contained only a few species that are not members of it now, species that have been exterminated within historic times by man, such as the wolf, bear, beaver and wild boar.

Throughout the pleistocene period the character of the fauna was approaching more and more to that of the present, but the gradual change was not a continuous process going on in the same territory without interruption. There were, no doubt, progressive changes during the interglacial periods, but each glaciation brought much more drastic alterations, most of them driving the fauna to the southern parts of the country and at least one of them completely expelling it. This latter was the second, or great, glaciation during which the entire fauna must have taken refuge in lands to the south, and when the ice retreated the fauna that returned was of a definitely pleistocene character, nearly all of the older forms that had survived from the pliocene into the first interglacial period having disappeared. Thus, though some species were able to survive in the south during the later glaciations, there can be little doubt that continuity of occupation goes back no more than about 425,000 years to the beginning of the second interglacial period. But few species can have a history of unbroken occupation in the British Isles as long as that, for conditions at the end of the last glaciation, only about 20,000 years ago, were almost subarctic, and can have been favourable to no more than a few of our present species, such as the stoat and mountain hare.

The presence of subspecies of mammals peculiar to the British Isles, and of subspecies having a restricted distribution within them, may give some clue to the probable course of events in the formation of the present fauna. Because Britain was not finally separated from continental Europe until about 7,000 years ago, our present species must have been isolated for at least that space of time, and many of them for much longer, for when the connection became narrow there would have been less chance of species finding the isthmus. On the other hand, in the absence of geographical isolation, 7,000 years is generally considered not nearly long enough for the evolution of new species; Zeuner points out, on the evidence of the fossil elephants that were by no means a slowly evolving group, that it needs something of the order of half a million years for a new species to become completely differentiated. But the conditions that produced the present British fauna were different from those influencing the evolution of elephants.

Subspecies, which may be considered as species in the making, would be expected to need less time than this to become established, but some writers have questioned whether the time since the separation from the continent has been long enough to produce some of the more well-marked subspecies such as the British squirrel. To overcome this supposed difficulty the possibility has been suggested that many of the subspecies peculiar to Britain were differentiated, or in the course of differentiation, before the last glaciation, and that they retreated to the south during that period, returning again when conditions improved. If this occurred it is supposed that the allied subspecies now inhabiting the continent also retreated to the south so that there was an alteration of territories, the entire European population of a species moving to the south as a whole and then returning to the north again without the various local races becoming mixed together. It is, however, very improbable that these hypotheses are correct.

The species that probably came into the British Isles earliest after the last glaciation are those that have the widest distribution throughout England, Scotland, Ireland and the smaller islands. But the problem of the origin of the subspecies peculiar to the various smaller islands cannot be settled definitely, because the geologists have not yet been able to determine the probable times when the islands were finally separated, nor even when the isthmus joining the north of Ireland to the Isle of Man and southern Scotland was severed. It is probable, however, that none of them was finally cut off until post-glacial times, within the last 20,000 years. It is probable, too, that many of them were separated and rejoined more than once during this period by alterations in sea-level.

Post-glacial connection with the mainland appears to afford the most satisfactory explanation for the presence of peculiar subspecies of mammals in many of the smaller islands, especially those of Scotland. Their presence might, in fact, be considered as evidence that such connections must have existed in those times, for it appears highly improbable that small mammals could have existed in the northern islands during any of the glaciations. Even in the less severe glaciations, when a varied fauna remained in southern England, Scotland and the isles must have been unsuitable territory for them.

The suggestion made by Beirne[18] that subspecies differentiated in the north took refuge in lands, now lost, lying to the west during glacial stages of the last glaciation is not entirely acceptable. It is true that during some of the more severe glacial stages the level of the sea was very much lower than at present, as much as 400 feet, according to Zeuner. A lowering to this extent would make the whole of the British Isles part of the continent and would add a great extent of dry land to them on the west. Beirne suggests that the coastal parts of this territory on the Atlantic shore would not have been ice-covered, and would have formed an area of refuge for mammals driven out by the glaciation of the more easterly parts. It is possible that this may have happened, but would it not be more probable that the ice-sheet would extend beyond the western shore as a floating barrier, in a glaciation severe enough to cause so great a eustatic lowering of the sea level? These hypothetical western lands should not be confused with the connection with south-west Europe that existed for a time, by which the so-called 'Lusitanian' flora and fauna of the south of Ireland and the south-west of England may have arrived from the Iberian region—though some authorities suggest that the 'Lusitanian' species were inadvertently introduced by megalithic man invading the British Isles from south-west Europe and the Mediterranean. The hypothesis that the inhabitants of the northern and western islands are all post-glacial immigrants appears to be the best explanation of their presence on the evidence yet available. Further researches may bring nearer a more satisfactory answer to the question of their origin.

Among the British shrews the pygmy shrew is, judging by its distribution, our oldest species, for it is very widely spread over the whole country, including Ireland and the islands. The common and water-shrews must have arrived much later, and cannot have spread into southern Scotland until after the connection with Ireland had been severed, for they are absent from the latter country and from the Isle of Man, as well as from Orkney and Shetland, all the outer and many of the inner Hebrides. And yet both these species are subspecifically different from their relatives on the continent, whereas the pygmy shrew is not, although it has had a very much longer time for differentiation. There is no satisfactory explanation of these differences; saying that the common and water-shrews are more plastic species than the pygmy shrew, as is often done, is merely a cloak for ignorance and does no more than state in obscure terms what we well know already, that of the former there are several subspecies but of the latter none. The Scilly shrew, which has no relatives of even the same genus elsewhere in Britain, must be a relict from a time when the Scillies were connected with the continent, but it is difficult to understand why it should not have spread on to our mainland, from which no congeneric fossils are known. Its presence in the Scillies might be considered as good evidence that the islands were cut off at a very remote time and remained comparatively temperate in climate during the glaciations that covered most of the rest of the country. On the other hand it is possible that it has been introduced by man, for it is very closely allied to the subspecies of the nearest coast of the continent.

The mole, whose burrowing habits unfit it for life in frozen soil, cannot have spread northwards until the last glacial phase had passed, and its present distribution, confined to the mainland of England, Wales, and Scotland, shows that its spread throughout the land was delayed until after the severance of Ireland and the islands. The hedgehog, on the other hand, whose habit of hibernation would allow it to follow closer in the wake of the retreating glaciers, has a much wider distribution, being present in Ireland, Orkney and some of the Inner Hebrides.

Most of our carnivores are relatively ancient members of our fauna. Some such, as the badger and otter, have been present in the country from early in the pleistocene period, and it is possible that they have never been absent since the second interglacial period, though they would have been confined to the southern parts of the country during the subsequent glaciations. They would have been able to spread northwards again as soon as the glaciers retreated, and have thus spread into Ireland and some of the islands. They did not, apparently, arrive at the extreme north until after the outer Hebrides, Orkney, and Shetland were cut off, for all carnivores except one are absent from those islands. The exception is the otter, which required no land-bridge to penetrate to them, its powers of swimming being ample to take it to all the off-lying islands. The stoat must have been one of the earliest migrants to the north, for it is found not only throughout the inner Hebrides and Ireland but also in the Isle of Man, from which all the others, except the otter, are absent. The absence from the Isle of Man of many species, not only of carnivores but of other mammals that occur in Ireland and Britain, probably indicates that the island was cut off before the isthmus connecting Ireland with southern Scotland was severed. On the other hand the stoats of Ireland and Man are thought to be the same subspecies, differing from those inhabiting the rest of Britain and the Isles of Jura and Islay; if this is correct it implies a later connection between Ireland and Man. The restricted distribution of our rare species such as the wild cat, marten and polecat has no connection with the early history of these animals, for they were once wide-spread, and have been reduced to their present scarcity by man within historic times. The latest arrival among our carnivores is evidently the weasel, for it is confined to England, Wales, Scotland and some of the inner Hebrides; nevertheless it is a late arrival only as a member of our present fauna, because weasels indistinguishable from the living species were present as early as the first interglacial period, after which they must have been completely driven out by the second glaciation.

It is difficult to apply the same theory, of colonisation following the retreat of the glaciers, to the distribution of the smaller rodents, because there are numerous subspecies among the voles and mice inhabiting the Hebrides, Orkney and Shetland. If the carnivores were unable to reach these places before they were cut off from the mainland it is difficult to understand how these small mammals could have succeeded; of course it might be said that the predators could not have lived there until there was first a population of smaller mammals upon which they could prey, but presumably they could have kept level with their food in the movement towards the north. As has already been mentioned, a theory has been put forward that these small mammals are descended from ancestors that took refuge during glacial periods in land formerly existing to the west; but had such a refuge been available surely the carnivores would have been there too? It is not at all easy to imagine how the mice and voles reached these islands if the carnivores could not; transport on drifting timber is not very convincing, though the possibility of accidental introduction by early man is not entirely ruled out. By whatever means they may have reached their destinations, it is undoubted from what is known of genetic processes that comparatively small populations of mammals may become differentiated as subspecies in a relatively short time; there is evidence to show that the house-mice of Faeroe have become a distinct subspecies even within recent historic times.

The suggestion, set out in chapter 5, that the different subspecies of the bank- and short-tailed voles owe their origin to successive waves of immigration from the south of genetically distinct races, necessarily assumes that the island subspecies reached their present homes before they were severed from the mainland. But the sea-depths between Orkney, Shetland, the outer Hebrides and the mainland are such as to suggest that these islands may have been separated before the end of the pleistocene period; if the severance was before the end of the last glacial phase the populations of small mammals must have survived it, an occurrence that appears improbable in islands so far to the north. One is forced to the conclusion that these populations probably entered the islands at the earliest possible moment after the last glaciation and that the islands were not cut off before the early part of the post-glacial period. This view avoids the necessity for assuming the existence of habitable lands to the west during glacial phases, an assumption impossible of proof or disproof, and one which postulates theoretical inhabitants about which we have no shred of information.

Similar early entry after the last glaciation must have occurred with the Scottish and Irish hares, and the water-voles. The squirrel, however, must be a post-glacial arrival, and not a particularly early one, for it would have been unable to colonise the country during the sub-arctic times after the last glaciation and would have had to await the growth of woods before it could join the fauna. It had, of course, formerly been a member of the fauna during earlier interstadials. The brown hare was evidently a late-comer, for it is absent from Ireland except for deliberate introduction by man. Its presence also in the outer Hebrides, and in Orkney and Shetland is due to introduction by man, because the species is certainly a later arrival than the Scottish hare, which is not present in the last two. It is not at all surprising that such a favourite game animal, and one so excellent on the table, should have been introduced into these islands. The restricted ranges occupied by the dormouse and by the harvest mouse show that both species were quite late additions to the fauna at some time well on in the post-glacial period. The rabbit, though now universally distributed, was not introduced until late historic times and does not form part of the truly indigenous fauna.

Both our native ungulates, the red deer and the roe, are probably survivals from the pleistocene, conditions in the extreme south of England having been suitable for their continuance during the glacial phases of at least the last glaciation. Our subspecies of red deer, *C. elaphus scoticus*, if it be a good one, is now an open-country, almost a barren-grounds, race, adapted to the poor conditions on the margin of the main area of distribution of the species, and is descended with little genetic difference from the forest-living subspecies that reached such splendid proportions of body and antler in the earlier interglacial periods (Pl. XLV, p. 358).

The distribution of bats might not be expected to throw much light on their history, because their powers of flight suggest that at least short sea-crossings would be no bar to their dispersal. But although some species are known to have regular migrations in other parts of the world, our own species appear to be much restricted and it is probable that individuals seldom go far from their home roosts. A further illustration of the restricted home ranges of bats is given by the extreme rarity of the occurrence in Britain of any of the continental species that are quite common on the European coasts opposite our shores, though it must be admitted that the chances of any casual strangers being recognised are not great. The British Isles are evidently at the extreme edge of the area where environmental conditions make possible the distribution of many of our species, all of which are insectivorous and able to survive the winter, when there is no food for them, only by hibernation.

Our two hardiest species, the pipistrelle and the long-eared bat, are found throughout the British Isles, the second alone being absent from Orkney and Shetland; this universal distribution points to the probability that they were both early arrivals in the post glacial period. Daubenton's bat, too, was probably an early comer, for although it is restricted to the neighbourhood of fresh-water, either standing or flowing, it is widely distributed except in the highlands and islands of Scotland. Several species occur in Ireland and in the south and west of England, but not elsewhere, a range which suggests that they came into the British Isles from the south-west, and lends some support to the idea that they may have survived the last glacial phase, as part of the 'Lusitanian' fauna on land now submerged in that direction. These species are Leisler's, Natterer's, and the lesser and greater horseshoe-bats. The whiskered bat has a distribution much like that of many terrestial mammals, extending through England to the South of Scotland and covering Ireland, though thinly. It was probably a fairly early post-glacial arrival and may have entered Ireland by the land-bridge from southern Scotland. The remaining species are all late arrivals; the noctule being widely spread through England but not elsewhere, the barbastelle less widely in the south and east only, and the serotine and Bechstein's bats both being restricted to comparatively narrow ranges in the extreme south and east. None of the British species of bats has become differentiated into subspecies distinct from those found on the continent, though sub-specific names have been given, on apparently inadequate grounds, to both our species of horseshoe-bats.

The shortness of time that has elapsed since the last glaciation has been thought by some to make a difficulty in finding an explanation to fit the facts of the occurrence of subspecies among our mammals, and their present distribution. But if the islands were populated early in the post-glacial phase while they were still attached to the mainland, and the inhabitants were thereafter trapped upon them by changes in sea-level it is admitted that the differentiation of small populations into new subspecies might be attained comparatively quickly.

It will not be until geology can offer zoology more precise information on the approximate dates at which the various islands were separated from each other and the mainland that the problems of the origin of our peculiar subspecies can be entirely solved. At present the distribution of the fauna is sometimes used to uphold theories of the probable course of geological phenomena; what zoology awaits is a chronology derived entirely from the facts of geology so that the zoological details can be fitted to it without making geological assumptions of doubtful validity.

Two main points emerge from a study of the origin of the British mammal fauna during the pleistocene period; first, the great changes that have occurred during that very small fragment of geological time, and secondly, the much shorter time during which the mammal fauna has had a general character similar to that of the present. Yet even in this short time many subspecies have been differentiated in different parts of the country; although no mammal has evolved to a

distinct species confined to our islands it is interesting to note that one
bird has done so—the red grouse.

The outstanding fact with nearly all our subspecies of mammals is
that they are geographically isolated from their nearest relatives, being
usually confined to off-lying islands. Regarding each species as a
whole, and its European or even wider range, all our species are, of
course, confined to islands, and it might be expected that they would
all be subspecifically different from their relatives found on the continent. But although some, such as the British squirrel, are; others,
such as the badger, are not, showing that some animals more readily
form subspecies than do others—they are more 'plastic'.

On the other hand it must be remembered that although different
species may inhabit the same country, they do not inhabit the same
habitats, and that the ecological habitats of one species here and
elsewhere may differ, although only slightly, and those of another may
not. So many factors of this sort are involved, that a very small genetic
difference arising by mutation may give an advantage that can be
acted upon by natural selection in one species, while one of a similar
magnitude in another species may not. If the difference gives a real
advantage in competition with other species, or with other members
of the same species, it is likely, however slight, to be perpetuated.
However, differences giving an advantage in one direction may be
linked genetically with differences giving a handicap in another, a
handicap that may be so great that the differences are not preserved. The essential requirement for the formation of a subspecies
is the isolation of a population by physical means in an environment
different, however slightly, from that of the parent population, so that
natural selection can act upon small genetic mutations in a population
where they will not be swamped by back-crossing with the original
parent stock.

Summarising the history of the British mammal fauna, we may say
that none of our species (except those introduced by man, and possibly
some bats) has entered the country during the last 7,000 years, and
that many of them have probably been in continuous occupation for
20,000 years, some of them probably for very much longer, perhaps
as much as 400,000 years. But it is only during the last 20,000 years
that the fauna has again distributed itself over the whole of the country
after the end of the last glaciation; and in the earlier part of that period
populations, large or small, of many species became cut off on various

islands where they have evolved to recognisable subspecies. On the processes of nature man has imposed his influence to an increasing extent in the last two thousand years, often only in the direction of destruction; now that his inquisitiveness is at last giving him some inkling of the processes with which he is interfering we may hope, probably in vain, that he may be sufficiently disinterested to avoid wanton meddling in the future.

APPENDIX
A LIST OF LIVING BRITISH MAMMALS

Excluding feral animals descended from domestic stock
Feral animals descended from introduced wild stock marked*

(As explained in the text, the value of many of the subspecific names is doubtful; nor is it known whether many of the alleged subspecies are real biological entities. Many that have been described have been omitted entirely and deliberately.)

SCIENTIFIC NAME	COMMON NAME
Order INSECTIVORA	
Superfamily ERINACOIDEA	
Family ERINACIDAE	
Erinaceus Linnaeus	
Erinaceus europaeus Linnaeus	Hedgehog
Superfamily SORICOIDEA	
Family SORICIDAE	
Sorex Linnaeus	
Sorex araneus Linnaeus	Common Shrew
Sorex araneus castaneus Jenyns	(British) Common Shrew
Sorex araneus granti Barrett-Hamilton & Hinton	Islay Shrew
Sorex minutus Linnaeus	Pygmy Shrew
Neomys Kaup	
Neomys fodiens Schreber	Water Shrew
Neomys fodiens bicolor Shaw	(British) Water-Shrew
Crocidura Wagler	
Crocidura cassiteridum Hinton	Scilly Shrew
Family TALPIDAE	
Talpa Linnaeus	
Talpa europaea Linnaeus	Common Mole
Order CHIROPTERA	
Family VESPERTILIONIDAE	
Nyctalus Bowditch	
Nyctalus noctula (Schreber)	Noctule
Nyctalus leisleri (Kuhl)	Leisler's Bat
Pipistrellus Kaup	
Pipistrellus pipistrellus (Schreber)	Pipistrelle
Eptesicus Rafinesque	
Eptesicus serotinus (Schreber)	Serotine
Myotis Kaup	
Myotis daubentoni (Kuhl)	Daubenton's Bat

SCIENTIFIC NAME	COMMON NAME

Order CHIROPTERA (Contd.)
- *Myotis mystacinus* (Kuhl) — Whiskered Bat
- *Myotis nattereri* (Kuhl) — Natterer's Bat
- *Myotis bechsteini* (Kuhl) — Bechstein's Bat
- *Myotis myotis* (Borkhausen) — Mouse-eared Bat
- *Plecotus* Geoffroy
- *Plecotus auritus* (Linnaeus) — Long-eared Bat
- *Plecotus austriacus* (Fischer) — Grey Long-eared Bat
- *Barbastella* Gray
  - *Barbastella barbastellus* (Schreber) — Barbastelle
  - (In this family also *Vespertilio murinus* Linnaeus, the Parti-coloured Bat has been recorded, perhaps incorrectly, as a vagrant)
- Family RHINOLOPHIDAE
  - *Rhinolophus* Lacepède
    - *Rhinolophus ferrum-equinum* (Schreber) — Greater Horseshoe-Bat
    - *Rhinolophus hipposideros* (Bechstein) — Lesser Horseshoe-Bat

Order LAGOMORPHA
- Family LEPORIDAE
  - *Oryctolagus* Lilljeborg
    - *Oryctolagus cuniculus* (Linnaeus) — Rabbit
  - *Lepus* Linnaeus
    - *Lepus europaeus* Pallas — Brown Hare
      - *Lepus europaeus occidentalis* de Winton — (British) Brown Hare
    - *Lepus timidus* Linnaeus — Blue Hare, Mountain Hare
      - *Lepus timidus scoticus* Hilzheimer — (Scottish) Blue, or Mountain Hare
      - *Lepus timidus hibernicus* Bell — Irish Hare

Order RODENTIA
- Suborder *MYOMORPHA*
  - Family CRICETIDAE
    - Subfamily MICROTINAE
      - *Clethrionomys* Tilesius
        - *Clethrionomys glareolus* Schreber — Bank-Vole
          - *Clethrionomys glareolus britannicus* (Miller) — (British) Bank-Vole
          - *Clethrionomys glareolus alstoni* (Barrett-Hamilton & Hinton) — Mull Vole
          - *Clethrionomys glareolus erica* (Barrett-Hamilton & Hinton) — Raasay Bank-Vole
          - *Clethrionomys glareolus skomerensis* (Barrett-Hamilton) — Skomer Vole
      - *Microtus* Schrenk
        - *Microtus orcadensis* Millais — Orkney Vole
          - *Microtus orcadensis orcadensis* Millais — Orkney (Mainland) Vole
          - *Microtus orcadensis ronaldshaiensis* Hinton — South Ronaldshay Vole
          - *Microtus orcadensis rousaiensis* Hinton — Rousay (Orkney) Vole
          - *Microtus orcadensis westrae* Miller — Westray Vole

SCIENTIFIC NAME	COMMON NAME

Order RODENTIA (Contd.)

Microtus orcadensis sandayensis Millais — Sanday Vole

Microtus agrestis (Linnaeus) — Short-tailed Vole

Microtus agrestis neglectus (Thompson) — (Scottish) Short-tailed Vole

Microtus agrestis exsul Miller — Hebridean Vole

Microtus agrestis macgillivraii
    Barrett-Hamilton & Hinton — Islay Vole

Microtus agrestis mial
    Barrett-Hamilton & Hinton — Eigg Vole

Microtus agrestis fiona Montagu — Gigha Vole

Microtus agrestis luch
    Barrett-Hamilton & Hinton — Muck Vole

Microtus agrestis hirtus (Bellamy) — (English)Short-tailedVole

Arvicola Lacepède

Arvicola amphibius (Linnaeus) — Water-Vole

Arvicola amphibius amphibius (Linnaeus) — (British) Water-Vole

Arvicola amphibius reta Miller — (Highland) Water-Vole

Ondatra Link

Ondatra zibethica (Linnaeus) — Musk-Rat

Family MURIDAE

Apodemus Kaup

Apodemus sylvaticus (Linnaeus) — Long-tailed Field-Mouse

Apodemus sylvaticus sylvaticus (Linnaeus) — (Mainland) Long-tailed Field-Mouse

Apodemus sylvaticus hebridensis (de Winton) — Hebridean Field-Mouse

Apodemus sylvaticus hirtensis (*?)
    (Barrett-Hamilton) — St. Kilda Field-Mouse

Apodemus sylvaticus fridariensis (Kinnear) — Shetland Field-Mouse

Apodemus flavicollis (Melchior) — Yellow-necked Field-Mouse

Apodemus flavicollis wintoni (Barrett-Hamilton) — (British) Yellow-necked Field-Mouse

Micromys Dehne

Micromys minutus (Pallas) — Harvest-Mouse

Micromys minutus soricinus (Hermann) — (Western) Harvest-Mouse

Mus Linnaeus

*Mus musculus** Linnaeus — House-Mouse

*Mus musculus domesticus** Rutty — (Western) House-Mouse

*Mus musculus muralis** Barrett-Hamilton — †St. Kilda House-Mouse

Rattus Fitzinger

Rattus rattus (Linnaeus) — 'Black' Rat

Rattus norvegicus (Erxleben) — 'Brown' Rat

Family GLIRIDAE

Muscardinus Kaup

Muscardinus avellanarius (Linnaeus) — Dormouse

† Recently extinct.

SCIENTIFIC NAME	COMMON NAME

rder RODENTIA (Contd.)

    Glis Brisson

      Glis glis* (Linnaeus) — Fat Dormouse

Suborder *SCIUROMORPHA*

    Family SCIURIDAE

      Sciurus Linnaeus

        Sciurus vulgaris Linnaeus — Red Squirrel

          Sciurus vulgaris leucourus Kerr — (British) Red Squirrel

        Sciurus carolinensis* Gmelin — Grey Squirrel

Suborder *HYSTRICOMORPHA*

    Family MYOCASTORIDAE

      Myocastor Kerr

        Myocastor coypus* (Molina) — Coypu

der CARNIVORA

Suborder *FISSIPEDIA*

    Superfamily CANOIDEA

      Family CANIDAE

        Vulpes Oken

          Vulpes vulpes (Linnaeus) — Fox

            Vulpes vulpes vulpes(*?) (Linnaeus) — (Northern) Fox

            Vulpes vulpes crucigera (Bechstein) — (Central European) Fox

      Family MUSTELIDAE

        Meles Brisson

          Meles meles (Linnaeus) — Badger

            Meles meles meles (Linnaeus) — (European) Badger

        Lutra Brisson

          Lutra lutra (Linnaeus) — Otter

        Martes Pinel

          Martes martes (Linnaeus) — Pine-Marten

            Martes martes martes (Linnaeus) — (European) Pine-Marten

        Mustela Linnaeus

          Mustela erminea Linnaeus — Stoat

          Mustela erminea stabilis Barrett-Hamilton — (British) Stoat

          Mustela erminea ricinae Miller — Islay Stoat

          Mustela erminea hibernica

              Thomas & Barrett-Hamilton — Irish Stoat

          Mustela nivalis Linnaeus — Weasel

            Mustela nivalis nivalis Linnaeus — (European) Weasel

          Mustela putorius Linnaeus — Polecat

            Mustela vison Schreber — American Mink

    Superfamily FELOIDEA

      Family FELIDAE

        Felis Linnaeus

          Felis silvestris Schreber — Wild Cat

            Felis silvestris grampia Miller — (Scottish) Wild Cat

Suborder *PINNIPEDIA*

    Family PHOCIDAE

      Halichoerus Nilsson

SCIENTIFIC NAME	COMMON NAME

Order CARNIVORA (Contd.)

   Halichoerus grypus (Fabricius) — Grey, or Atlantic, Seal

   Phoca Linnaeus

     Phoca vitulina Linnaeus — Common Seal

     Phoca hispida Schreber — Ringed Seal

     Phoca groenlandica Fabricius — Harp-Seal

   Cystophora Nilsson

     Cystophora cristata (Erxleben) — Hooded Seal

   Erignathus Gill

     Erignathus barbatus (Fabricius) — Bearded Seal

  Family ODOBENIDAE

   Odobenus Brisson

     Odobenus rosmarus (Linnaeus) — Walrus

Order UNGULATA

  Family CERVIDAE

   Muntiacus Rafinesque

     *Muntiacus muntjak** (Zimmermann) — Indian Muntjac

     *Muntiacus reevesi** (Ogilby) — Chinese Muntjac

   Dama Hamilton Smith

     Dama dama(*?) (Linnaeus) — Fallow Deer

   Hyelaphus Sundevall

     *Hyelaphus porcinus** (Zimmermann) — Hog-Deer

   Sika P. L. Sclater

     *Sika nippon** (Temminck) — Sika

     *Sika nippon nippon** (Temminck) — Japanese Sika

     *Sika nippon mantchuricus**(Swinhoe) — Manchurian Sika

   Cervus Linnaeus

     Cervus elaphus Linnaeus — Red Deer

     Cervus elaphus elaphus(*?) Linnaeus — (European) Red Deer

     Cervus elaphus scoticus Lönnberg — (British) Red Deer

   Odocoileus Rafinesque

     *Odocoileus columbianus** (Richardson) — Black-tailed Deer

   Capreolus Gray

     Capreolus capreolus (Linnaeus) — Roe

     Capreolus capreolus thotti Lönnberg — (British) Roe

     *Capreolus pygargus**(Pallas) — Siberian Roe

   Hydropotes Swinhoe

     *Hydropotes inermis** Swinhoe — Chinese Water-Deer

Order CETACEA

  Suborder *ODONTOCETI*

   Superfamily DELPHINOIDEA

    Family PHOCAENIDAE

     Phocaena Cuvier

      Phocaena phocaena (Linnaeus) — Common Porpoise

    Family DELPHINIDAE

     Delphinus Linnaeus

      Delphinus delphis Linnaeus — Common Dolphin

SCIENTIFIC NAME	COMMON NAME
Order CETACEA (Contd.)	
Prodelphinus Gervais	
Prodelphinus euphrosyne (Gray)	Euphrosyne Dolphin
Lagenorhynchus Gray	
Lagenorhynchus acutus (Gray)	White-sided Dolphin
Lagenorhynchus albirostris (Gray)	White-beaked Dolphin
Tursiops Gervais	
Tursiops truncatus (Montagu)	Bottle-nosed Dolphin
Orcinus Fitzinger	
Orcinus orca (Linnaeus)	Killer
Pseudorca Owen	
Pseudorca crassidens Owen	False Killer
Globicephala Lesson	
Globicephala melaena Traill	Ca'ing Whale, Blackfish
Grampus Gray	
Grampus griseus (Cuvier)	Risso's Dolphin
Family MONODONTIDAE	
Delphinapterus Lacepède	
Delphinapterus leucas (Pallas)	White Whale, Beluga
Monodon Linnaeus	
Monodon monoceros Linnaeus	Narwhal
Superfamily PHYSETEROIDEA	
Family PHYSETERIDAE	
Physeter Linnaeus	
Physeter catodon Linnaeus	Sperm-Whale
Family ZIPHIIDAE	
Hyperoödon Lacepède	
Hyperoödon rostratus (Muller)	Bottle-nosed Whale
Ziphius Cuvier	
Ziphius cavirostris Cuvier	Cuvier's Whale
Mesoplodon Gervais	
Mesoplodon mirum True	True's Whale
Mesoplodon bidens (Sowerby)	Sowerby's Whale
Suborder *MYSTICETI*	
Family BALAENIDAE	
Balaena Linnaeus	
Balaena glacialis Bonnaterre	Atlantic Right Whale
Family BALAENOPTERIDAE	
Balaenoptera Lacepède	
Balaenoptera musculus Linnaeus	Blue Whale
Balaenoptera physalus (Linnaeus)	Fin Whale
Balaenoptera borealis Lesson	Sei Whale
Balaenoptera acutorostrata Lacepède	Lesser Rorqual, Piked Whale
Megaptera Gray	
Megaptera boöps Fabricius	Humpback

M.

BIBLIOGRAPHY

1. ADAMS, L. E. (1903.) A contribution to our knowledge of the mole (*Talpa europaea*) *Mem. Manchr. lit. phil. Soc. 47:* no. 4.

2. — (1906). Observations on a captive mole. *Mem. Manchr. lit. phil. Soc. 50:* no. 9.

3. — (1911). Reported in footnote in *Barrett-Hamilton & Hinton, (1910–21), 2:* 121. q.v.

4. ALLANSON, M. (1934). Seasonal variation in the reproductive organs of the male hedgehog. *Philos. Trans. Lond., 223B:* 277–303.

5. ALLEN, G. M. (1942). *Extinct and vanishing animals of the western hemisphere*, New York, Amer. Cttee. Internat. Wildlife Protection.

6. ANON. (1933). *The musk rat.* London, Min. Agr. Fish. Form No. A 767/LP.

7. — (1934). Musk rats in Scotland. *Scot. J. Agric. 17:* 94–98.

7a. ARMOUR, C. J. & BARNETT, S.A. (1950). The action of dicoumarol on laboratory and wild rats, and its effect on feeding behaviour. *J. Hygiene. 48:* 158–70.

8. BAINES, J. M. (1940). Analysis of lepidoptera eaten by bats. *Entomologist, 73:* 139–40.

9. BAKER, J. R. (1930). The breeding season in British wild mice. *Proc. zool. Soc. Lond. 1930:* 113–26.

10. BAKER, J. R., & RANSON, R. M. (1932). Factors affecting the breeding of the field-mouse (*Microtus agrestis*). Part I—Light. *Proc. Roy. Soc. Lond. 110B:* 313–32.

11. — (1932). Factors affecting the breeding of the field-mouse (*Microtus agrestis*). Part II—Temperature and food. *Proc. Roy. Soc. Lond. 112B:* 39–46.

12. BARNETT, S. A. (1948). *Principles of rodent control*, in: *Pests of stored grains.* Washington, F.A.O. Agric. Publns. No. 2.

13. BARNETT, S. A., LAWRENCE, M. D. A. & JENSON, A. G. (1946). *Infestation control: rats and mice.* London, H.M.S.O. pp. 70–492.

14. BARRETT-HAMILTON, G. E. H. & HINTON, M. A. C. (1910–21). *A history of British mammals.* London, Gurney and Jackson.

15. BASSETT, C. F., PEARSON, O. P. & WILKE, F. (1944). The effect of artificially-increased length of day on molt, growth, and priming of silver fox pelts. *J. exp. Zool. 96:* 77–84.

16. BEALE, G. H. (1945). Recent biological work in Finland. *Nature, Lond. 156:* 357–59.

17. BEAUFORT, H. G., THE DUKE OF. (1949). Unpublished information.

18. BEIRNE, B. P. (1947). The history of the British land mammals. *Ann. Mag. nat. Hist. ser. 11, 14:* 501–14.

19. BELL, T. (1837). *A history of British quadrupeds.* London, Van Voorst.

20. BERNARD, R., SMITH, S. E. & MAYNARD, L. A. (1942). The digestion of cereals by minks and foxes with special reference to starch and crude fiber. *Cornell Veterinarian 32:* 29–36.

21. BERRY, J. (1937). The long-tailed field mouse (*Apodemus sylvaticus*) as a destroyer of salmon ova. *Rep. Avon. biol. Res. Southampton, 1936–37:* 67–69.

22. BISSONETTE, T. H. (1942). Anomalous seasonal coat-colour-changes in a small male Bonaparte's weasel. (*Mustela cicognanii cicognanii* Bonaparte). *Amer. Midland Nat. 28:* 327–33.

23. BOURDELLE, E. (1939). American mammals introduced into France in the contemporary period, especially *Myocastor* and *Ondatra. J. Mammal. 20:* 287–91.

24. BOURLIÈRE, F. (1947). La longévité des petits mammifères sauvages. *Mammalia, 11:* 111–15.

25. BRAMBELL, F. W. R. (1935). Reproduction in the common shrew (*Sorex araneus* Linnaeus). *Philos. Trans. Lond. 225B:* 1–62.

26. — (1944). The reproduction of the wild rabbit. *Proc. zool. Soc. Lond. 114:* 1–45.

27. BRAMBELL, F. W. R. & HALL, K. (1937). Reproduction of the lesser shrew (*Sorex minutus* Linnaeus). *Proc. zool. Soc. Lond. 1936:* 957–69.

28. — (1939). Reproduction of the field vole, *Microtus agrestis hirtus* Bellamy. *Proc. zool. Soc. Lond. 109A:* 133–38.

29. BRAMBELL, F. W. R. & MILLS, I. H. (1946). Presence of fibrinogen in the yolk sac contents of rabbits. *Nature, Lond. 158:* 24.

30. — (1947). The occurrence of fibrin in the yolk-sac contents of embryos during and immediately after implantation. *J. exp. Biol. 23:* 332–45.

31. BRAMBELL, F. W. R. & ROWLANDS, I. W. (1936). Reproduction of the bank vole (*Evotomys glareolus* Schreber). I. The oestrus cycle of the female. *Philos. Trans. Lond. 226B:* 71–97.

32. BRASSARD, J. A. & BERNARD, R. (1939). Observations on breeding and development of marten, *Martes a. americana* (Kerr). *Canad. Field. Nat. 53:* 15–21.

33. BUXTON, A. (1940). The frost of January–February 1940. *Trans. Norfolk Norw. Nat. Soc. 15:* 102–05.

34. — (1948). Roe deer and their fairy rings. *Country Life, Lond. 104:* 1,266–67.

35. — (1949). Roe deer and their fairy rings: a sequel. *Country Life, Lond. 106:* 1,367–68.

36. CABRERA, A. (1922). *Manual de mastozoologiá.* Madrid, Calpe.

37. CALMAN, W. T. (1949). *The classification of animals.* London, Methuen.

38. CARLIER, E. W. (1893). Contribution to the histology of the hedgehog. *J. Anat. Physiol. 27:* 85–111, 169–78, 354–60, 508–18.

39. — (1896). On the pancreas of the hedgehog during hibernation. *J. Anat. Physiol. 30:* 334–46.

40. CARLIER, E. W. & EVANS, C. A. L. (1903). A chemical study of the hibernating gland of the hedgehog. *J. Anat. Physiol. 38:* 15–31.

41. CHAPPELLIER, A. (1939). Notes sur l'écureuil. Les cachettes. *Trav. Sta. zool. Wimereux, 13:* 69–75.

42. CHITTY, D. & SHORTEN, M. (1946). Techniques for the study of the Norway rat (*Rattus norvegicus*). *J. Mammal. 27:* 63–78.

42a. CHRISTIAN, J. J. (1950). The adreno-pituitary system and population cycles in mammals. *J. Mammal. 31:* 247–59.

43. CLAPHAM, R. (1922). *The book of the otter.* London, Cranton.

44. COLMAN, J. S. (1937). The present state of the Newfoundland seal fishery. *J. anim. Ecol. 6:* 145–59.

45. COLQUHOUN, M. K. (1942). The habitat distribution of the grey squirrel (*Sciurus carolinensis*) in Savernake forest. *J. anim. Ecol. 11:* 127–30.

46. COWARD, T. A. (1907). On the winter habits of the Greater Horseshoe Bat, *Rhinolophus ferrum-equinum* (Schreber), and other cave-haunting bats. *Proc. zool. Soc. Lond. 1907:* 312–24.

47. — (1908). Notes on the Greater Horseshoe Bat, *Rhinolophus ferrum-equinum* (Schreber), in captivity. *Mem. Manchr. lit. phil. Soc. 52:* no. 11.

48. DARLING, F. FRASER. (1937). *A herd of red deer.* Oxford, University Press.

49. — (1938). Atlantic seals and their west highland home. *Geogr. Mag. Lond. 7:* 145–60.

50. — (1939). *A naturalist on Rona.* Oxford, Clarendon Press.

51. DAVIES, J. L. (1949). Observations on the grey seal (*Halichoerus grypus*) at Ramsey island, Pembrokeshire. *Proc. zool. Soc. Lond. 119:* 673–92.

52. DEAN, F. (1946). A note on the food of the water vole. *Naturalist, Lond. 1946:* 153.

53. DEANESLY, R. (1934). The reproductive cycle of the female hedge-hog. *Philos. Trans. Lond. 223B:* 239–76.

54. — (1935). Growth and reproduction in the stoat. *Philos. Trans. Lond. 225B:* 459–92.

55. — (1943). Delayed implantation in the stoat (*Mustela mustela*). *Nature, Lond. 151:* 365–66.

56. — (1944). The reproductive cycle of the female weasel (*Mustela nivalis*). *Proc. zool. Soc. Lond. 114:* 339–49.

57. DEANESLY, R. & PARKES, A. S. (1933). The oestrus cycle of the grey squirrel (*Sciurus carolinensis*) *Philos. Trans. Lond. 222B:* 47–78.

58. DEANESLY, R. & WARWICK, T. (1939). Observations on pregnancy in the common bat (*Pipistrellus pipistrellus*). *Proc. zool. Soc. Lond. 109A:* 57–60.

59. DEGERBØL, M. (1940). *Mammalia*, in: *The zoology of the Faeroes.* Copenhagen.

60. DEPARTMENT OF ANIMAL HEALTH, ABERYSTWYTH. (1948). Unpublished information.

61. DRANE, R. (1895). The hare in captivity. *Proc. Cardiff Nat. Soc. 27:* 101–04.

62. EADIE, W. R. (1938). The dermal glands of shrews. *J. Mammal. 19:* 171–74.

63. ELLISON, N. F. (1945). Increase of seals in the Dee. *Northw. Nat. 20:* 268.

64. ELMHIRST, R. (1938). Food of the otter in the marine littoral zone. *Scot. Nat. 1938:* 99–102.

65. ELTON, C. (1942). *Voles, mice and lemmings.* Oxford, Clarendon Press.

66. ELTON, C., DAVIS, D. H. S. & FINDLAY, G. M. (1935). An epidemic among voles (*Microtus agrestis*) on the Scottish border in the spring of 1934. *J. anim. Ecol. 4:* 277–88.

67. ELTON, C., FORD, E. B. & BAKER, J. R. (1931). The health and parasites of a wild mouse population. *Proc. zool. Soc. Lond. 1931:* 657–721.

68. ELTON, C. & NICHOLSON, M. (1942). Fluctuations in numbers of the muskrat (*Ondatra zibethica*) in Canada. *J. anim. Ecol. 11:* 96–126.

69. EVANS, A. C. (1948). The identity of earthworms stored by moles. *Proc. zool. Soc. Lond. 118:* 356–59.

70. EVANS, C. A. (1938). Observations on hibernating bats with especial reference to reproduction and splenic adaptation. *Amer. Nat. 72:* 480–84.

71. EVANS, F. C. (1942). Studies of a small mammal population in Bagley wood, Berkshire. *J. anim. Ecol. 11:* 182–97.

72. EVANS, F. C. & VEVERS, H. G. (1938). Notes on the biology of the Faeroe mouse (*Mus musculus faeroensis*) *J. anim. Ecol. 7:* 290–97.

73. FENTON, E. W. (1940). The influence of rabbits on the vegetation of certain hill-grazing districts of Scotland. *J. Ecol. 28:* 438–49.

74. FINDLAY, G. M. & MIDDLETON, A. D. (1934). Epidemic disease among voles (*Microtus*) with special reference to *Toxoplasma*. *J. anim. Ecol. 3:* 150–60.

74a. FISHER, J. (1948). St. Kilda a natural experiment. *New Nat. J. 1:* 91–108.

75. FISHER, N. (1934). The last Irish wolf. *Irish Nat. J. 5:* 41.

76. FRASER, F. C. (1934–46). *Reports on cetacea stranded on the British coasts.* nos. 12–13. London, British Museum (Natural History).

77. — (1936). On the development and distribution of the young stages of krill (*Euphausia superba*). *Discovery Rep. 14:* 1–192.

78. — (1936). Recent strandings of the false killer whale, *Pseudorca crassidens*, with special reference to those found at Donna Nook, Lincolnshire. *Scot. Nat. 1936:* 105–14.

79. — (1947). Sound emitted by dolphins. *Nature, Lond. 160:* 759.

80. — (1949). A narwhal in the Thames estuary. *Nature, Lond. 163:* 575.

81. GALAMBOS, R. & GRIFFIN, D. R. (1942). Obstacle avoidance by flying bats: the cries of bats. *J. exp. Zool. 89:* 475–90.

82. GARVEY, T. (1935). The muskrat in Saorstat Eireann. *J. Dept. Agr. Dublin, 35:* 189–95.

83. GAWN, R. W. L. (1948). Aspects of the locomotion of whales. *Nature, Lond. 161:* 44–46.

84. GLOVER, F. A. (1942). Spring colour change in a New York weasel. *Pennsylvania Game News, 13:* 18, 32.

85. GRAY, J. (1933). Studies in animal locomotion. I. The movements of fish, with special reference to the eel. *J. exp. Biol. 10:* 88–104.

86. — (1936). Studies in animal locomotion. VI. The propulsive powers of dolphins. *J. exp. Biol. 13:* 192–99.

87. — (1948). Aspects of locomotion of whales. *Nature, Lond. 161:* 199–200.

88. GRIFFIN, D. R. & GALAMBOS, R. (1941). The sensory basis of obstacle avoidance by flying bats. *J. exp. Biol. 86:* 481–506.

89. GUNN, C. K. (1932). Phenomena of primeness. *Canad. J. Res. 6:* 387–97.

90. GUTHRIE, M. J. (1933). The reproductive cycles of some cave bats. *J. Mammal. 14:* 199–216.

91. HACKER, H. S. & HACKER, A. P. (1949). Local variation, wandering powers and chances of interbreeding in *Apodemus sylvaticus*, the long-tailed wood mouse. *Proc. Linn. Soc. Lond. 161:* 9–10.

92. HAMMOND, J. & MARSHALL, F. H. A. (1930). Oestrus and pseudo-pregnancy in the ferret. *Proc. Roy. Soc. Lond. 105B:* 607–30.

93. HARMER, S. F. (1914–27). *Reports on cetacea stranded on the British coasts.* nos. 1–10. London, British Museum (Natural History).

94. HARRISON, D. L. & DAVIES, D. V. (1949). A note on some epithelial structures in microchiroptera. *Proc. zool. Soc. Lond. 119:* 351–57.

95. HARRISON, T. H. & MOY-THOMAS, J. A. (1933). The mice of St. Kilda, with especial reference to their prospects of extinction and present status. *J. anim. Ecol. 2:* 109–15.

96. HARTING, J. E. (1880). *British animals extinct within historic times.* London, Trubner.

97. HARTRIDGE, H. (1920). The avoidance of objects by bats in their flight. *J. Physiol. 54:* 54–57.

98. HAVINGA, B. (1933). Der Seehund (*Phoca vitulina* L) in den Holländischen Gewässern. *Tijdschr. ned. dierk. Ver. ser. 3, 3:* 79–111.

99. HERTER, K. (1938). Die Biologie der europäischen Igel. *Kleintier u. Peltztier.* Leipzig, *14:* 1–222.

100. HILL, M. (1939). The reproductive cycle of the male weasel. *Proc. zool. Soc. Lond. 109B:* 481–512.

101. HILL, W. C. OSMAN. (1948). An undescribed structure in the rodent rhinarium. *Nature, Lond. 161:* 276–77.

102. — (1948). Rhinoglyphics: epithelial sculpture of the mammalian rhinarium. *Proc. zool. Soc. Lond. 118:* 1–35.

103. HINTON, M. A. C. (1924). On a new species of *Crocidura* from Scilly. *Ann. Mag. nat. Hist. ser. 9, 14:* 509–10.

104. — (1926). *Monograph of the voles and lemmings* (Microtinae). London, British Museum (Natural History).

105. HJORT, J. & KNIPOWITSCH, N. (1907). Bericht ueber die Lebensverhaltnisse und den Fang der nordischen Seehund. *Rapp. Cons. Explor. Mer. 8:* 1–125.

106. HODGSON, S. B. (1943). Bats feeding on moths at sallow. *Entomologist, 76:* 147–48.

107. — (1944). Lepidoptera eaten by bats. *Entomologist, 77:* 62–63.

108. HUXLEY, J. S. (1931). The relative size of antlers of deer. *Proc. zool. Soc. Lond. 1931:* 819–64.

108a. — (1932). *Problems of relative growth.* London. Methuen.

109. — (1942). *Evolution: the modern synthesis.* London, Geo. Allen & Unwin.

110. JOHNSEN, S. (1914). Über die Seitendrüsen der Soriciden. *Anat. Anz. 46:* 139–49.

111. JOHNSTON, F. J. (1938). The grey squirrel in Epping forest. *London Nat. 1937:* 94–99.

112. JOHNSTON, H. H. (1903). *British mammals.* London, Hutchinson.

113. KELWAY, P. (1945). The water shrew. *J. Soc. Pres. Fauna Emp. pt. 51:* 20–22.

114. KENNETH, J. H. (1947). Gestation periods. *Technical communication No. 5.* (2nd ed.). Edinburgh, Imperial Bureau of Animal Breeding and Genetics.

115. KIRK, J. C. & WAGSTAFFE, R. (1944). A contribution to the study of the Scottish wild cat. *Northw. Nat. 19:* 14–23.

116. KOLOSOV, A. M. (1941). The biology of reproduction in the hare (*Lepus europaeus* Pall.). *Zool. Zh. 20:* 154–72.

117. KON, S. K. (1945). Synthesis of vitamins by micro-organisms of the alimentary tract. *Proc. nutrit. Soc. 3:* 217–29.

118. KULLENBERG, B. (1947). Sound emitted by dolphins. *Nature, Lond. 160:* 648.

119. LAURIE, E. M. O. (1946). The reproduction of the house-mouse (*Mus musculus*) living in different environments. *Proc. Roy. Soc. Lond. 133B:* 248–81.

120. — (1946). The coypu (*Myocastor coypus*) in Great Britain. *J. anim. Ecol. 15:* 22–34.

121. LAWRENCE, B. (1945). Brief comparison of short-tailed shrew and reptile poisons. *J. Mammal. 26:* 393–96.

122. LE GROS CLARK, W. E. (1949). *History of the primates.* London, British Museum (Natural History).

123. LESLIE, P. H. & RANSON, R. M. (1940). The mortality, fertility, and rate of natural increase of the vole (*Microtus agrestis*) as observed in the laboratory. *J. anim. Ecol. 9:* 27–52.

124. LOCKLEY, R. M. (1940). Some experiments in rabbit control. *Nature, Lond. 145:* 767–69.

125. LYMAN, C. P. (1943). Control of coat color in the varying hare *Lepus americanus* Erxleben. *Bull. Mus. comp. zool. Harvard, 93:* 393–461.

126. MACKINTOSH, N. A. & WHEELER, J. F. G. (1929). Southern blue and fin whales. *Discovery Rep. 1:* 257–540.

127. McLAUCHLAN, J. D. & HENDERSON, W. M. (1947). The occurrence of foot-and-mouth disease in the hedgehog under natural conditions. *J. Hygiene, Camb. 45:* 474–79.

128. MADSEN, H. (1939). Does the rabbit chew the cud? *Nature, Lond. 143:* 981–82.

129. MATHESON, C. (1939). A survey of the status of *Rattus rattus* and its subspecies in the seaports of Great Britain and Ireland. *J. anim. Ecol. 8:* 76–93.

130. MATTHEWS, L. HARRISON. (1935). The oestrous cycle and intersexuality in the female mole (*Talpa europea* Linn). *Proc. zool. Soc. Lond. 1935:* 347–82.

131. — (1936). The pelage and ear pinna of a newly-born common seal (*Phoca vitulina* L.). *Proc. zool. Soc. Lond. 1936:* 315–16.

132. MATTHEWS, L. HARRISON. (1937). The form of the penis in the British Rhinolophid bats compared with that in some Vespertilionid bats. *Trans. zool. Soc. Lond. 23:* 213–23.

133. — (1937). The female sexual cycle in the British horseshoe bats. . . . . *Trans. zool. Soc. Lond. 23:* 224–66.

134. — (1938). The humpback whale, *Megaptera nodosa*. *Discovery Rep. 17:* 7–92.

135. — (1938). The sperm whale, *Physeter catodon*. *Discovery Rep. 17:* 93–168.

136. — (1938). Notes on the southern right whale, *Eubalaena australis*. *Discovery Rep. 17:* 169–82.

137. — (1938). The sei whale, *Balaenoptera borealis*. *Discovery Rep. 17:* 183–290.

138. — (1941). Reproduction in the Scottish wild cat. . . . . *Proc. zool. Soc. Lond. 111B:* 59–77.

139. — & MATTHEWS, B. H. C. (1939). Owls and infra-red radiation. *Nature, Lond. 143:* 983.

140. — & MAYES, W. E. (1946). Occurrence of the pine marten near Bristol. *Proc. Bristol Nat. Soc. 27:* 121–22.

141. — (1949). The occurrence of Leisler's bat (*Nyctalus leisleri* (Kuhl)) at Bristol. *Proc. Bristol Nat. Soc. 27:* 486.

142. MARSHALL, A. J. (1949). The breeding seasons of animals. *New. Nat. Lond. 2:* no. 5; 15–18.

143. MAYNARD, C. J. (1889). Singular effects produced by the bite of a short-tailed shrew, *Blarina brevicauda*. *Contr. Science, 1:* 57–58.

144. MEITENS, H. (1909). Zur Kenntnis des Thymusreticulum und seiner Beziehungen zu dem der Lymphdrüsen, nebst einigen Bermerkungen über die Winterschlafdrüse. *Jena. Z. Naturw. 44:* 149–92.

145. MIDDLETON, A. D. (1930). The ecology of the American grey squirrel (*Sciurus carolinensis* Gmelin) in the British Isles. *Proc. zool. Soc. Lond. 1930:* 809–43.

146. — (1931). A contribution to the biology of the common shrew *Sorex araneus* Linnaeus. *Proc. zool. Soc. Lond. 1931:* 133–43.

147. — (1932). Syphilis as a disease of wild rabbits and hares. *J. anim. Ecol. 1:* 84–85.

148. — (1935). The distribution of the grey squirrel (*Sciurus carolinensis*) in Great Britain in 1935. *J. anim. Ecol. 4:* 274–76.

149. MILLAIS, J. G. (1897). *British deer and their horns*. London, Sotheran.

150. — (1904–06). *The mammals of Great Britain and Ireland*. London, Longmans, Green, 3 vols.

151. MILLER, G. S. (1912). *Catalogue of the mammals of western Europe*. London, British Museum (Natural History).

M. 2D

152. MILLMORE, D. K. (1943). Harborage of *Rattus r. alexandrinus. Publ. Health Repts. 58:* 1507–09.

153. MONTAGU, I. G. S. (1923). On a further collection of mammals from the inner Hebrides. *Proc. zool. Soc. Lond. 1922:* 929–41.

153a. MORGAN, M. T., FISHER, J. & WATSON, J. S. (1942). Rodent control in the Port of London. *Medical Officer, 68:* 189–91, 197–98, 205–07.

153b. — (1943). Rodent control in the Area of the Port of London Health Authority. *Medical Officer, 70:* 37–38, 45–46.

154. MOROT, C. (1882). Mémoire relatif aux pelotes stomacales des léporidés. *Rec. Méd. vét. Paris, 59:* 635–46.

155. MORRISON-SCOTT, T. C. S. (1939). A key to the British bats. *Naturalist, Lond. 1939:* 33–36.

156. MUNRO, T. (1935). Note on musk-rats and other animals killed since the inception of the campaign against musk-rats in October 1932. *Scot. Nat. 1935:* 11–16.

157. NEAL, E. G. (1949). *The Badger.* London, Collins *New Naturalist.*

158. NICHOLSON, C. (1937). Moths eaten by bats. *Entomologist, 70:* 188.

159. OLDHAM, C. (1905). On some habits of bats, with special reference to the lesser horseshoe bat (*Rhinolophus hipposiderus*). *Mem. Manchr. lit. phil. Soc. 49:* No. 9.

160. ORR, R. T. (1944). Communal nests of the house-mouse (*Mus musculus* Linnaeus). *Wasmann Collector, 6:* 35–37.

161. PARRY, D. A. (1949). The swimming of whales and a discussion of Gray's paradox. *J. exp. Biol. 26:* 24–34.

162. — (1949). The anatomical basis of swimming in whales. *Proc. zool. Soc. Lond. 119:* 49–60.

163. — (1949). The structure of whale blubber, and a discussion of its thermal properties. *Quart. J. micro. Sci. 90:* 13–25.

164. PARSONS, B. T. & MIDDLETON, A. D. (1937). The distribution of the grey squirrel (*Sciurus carolinensis*) in Great Britain in 1937. *J. anim. Ecol. 6:* 286–90.

165. PEARSON, O. P. (1942). On the cause and nature of a poisonous action produced by the bite of a shrew *Blarina brevicauda. J. Mammal. 23:* 159–66.

166. — (1944). Reproduction in the shrew (*Blarina brevicauda* Say). *Amer. J. Anat. 75:* 39–93.

167. — (1946). Scent glands of the short-tailed shrew. *Anat. Rec. 94:* 615–29.

168. — (1947). The rate of metabolism of some small mammals. *Ecology, 28:* 127–45.

169. PEARSON, O. P. & BASSETT, C. F. (1946). Certain aspects of reproduction in a herd of silver foxes. *Amer. Nat. 80:* 45–67.

170. PEARSON, O. P. & ENDERS, R. K. (1943). Ovulation, maturation, and fertilization in the fox. *Anat. Rec. 85:* 69–83.

171. — (1944). Duration of pregnancy in certain mustelids. *J. exp. Zool. 95:* 21–35.

171a. PENROSE, C. B. (1924). Removal of the testicle in a sika deer followed by deformity of the antler on the opposite side. *J. Mammal. 5:* 116–18.

172. PERRY, J. S. (1943). Reproduction in the water-vole, *Arvicola amphibius* Linn. *Proc. zool. Soc. Lond. 112A:* 118–30.

173. — (1945). The reproduction of the wild brown rat (*Rattus norvegicus* Erxleben). *Proc. zool. Soc. Lond. 115:* 19–46.

174. PILKINGTON, S. M., MACKINTOSH, F., & MATHESON, D. C. (1951). Unpublished information.

175. POCOCK, R. I. (1905). Observations upon a female specimen of a Hainan gibbon (*Hylobates hainanus*) now living in the Society's gardens. *Proc. zool. Soc. Lond. 1905:* 169–80 (footnote p. 169).

176. POULTON, E. B. (1929). British insectivorous bats and their prey. *Proc. zool. Soc. Lond. 1929:* 277–303.

177. RANSON, R. M. (1941). New laboratory animals from wild species. Breeding a laboratory stock of hedgehogs (*Erinaceus europaeus* L). *J. Hygeine, Camb. 41:* 131–38.

178. ROEBUCK, A., BAKER, F. T., & WHITE, J. H. (1944). The grazing of winter cereals by the wood mouse (*Apodemus sylvaticus*). *J. anim. Ecol. 13:* 105–09.

179. ROTHSCHILD, M. (1942). Change of pelage in the stoat, *Mustela erminea* L. *Nature, Lond. 149:* 78.

180. ROWLANDS, I. W. (1938). Preliminary note on the reproductive cycle of the red squirrel (*Sciurus vulgaris*). *Proc. zool. Soc. Lond. 108A:* 441–43.

181. — (1939). Reproduction of the bank vole (*Evotomys glareolus* (Schreber)). II. Seasonal changes in the reproductive organs of the male. *Philos. Trans. Lond. 226B:* 99–120.

182. ROWLANDS, I. W. & PARKES. A. S. (1936). Reproduction in foxes (*Vulpes* spp.). *Proc. zool. Soc. Lond. 1935:* 823–41.

183. SCHEFFER, V. B. & SLIPP, J. W. (1944). The harbor seal in Washington State. *Amer. Midland Nat. 32:* 373–416.

184. SCHEVILL, W. E. & LAWRENCE, B. (1949). Underwater listening to the white porpoise. (*Delphinapterus leucas*). *Science, 109:* 143–44.

185. SCHOLANDER, P. F. (1940). Experimental investigations on the respiratory function in diving mammals and birds. *Hvalråd. Skr. 22:* 1–131.

186. SCHWARZ, E. & SCHWARZ, H. K. (1943). The wild and commensal stocks of the house-mouse, *Mus musculus* Linnaeus. *J. Mammal. 24:* 59–72.

187. SELYE, H. & TIMIRAS, P. S. (1949). Participation of 'brown fat' tissue in the alarm reaction. *Nature, Lond. 164:* 745–46.

188. SHELDON, W. G. (1949). Reproductive behaviour of foxes in New York State. *J. Mammal. 30:* 236–46.

189. SHORTEN, M. (1946). A survey of the distribution of the American grey squirrel (*Sciurus carolinensis*) and the British red squirrel (*S. vulgaris leucourus*) in England and Wales in 1944–5. *J. anim. Ecol. 15:* 82–92.

190. SIMPSON, G. G. (1945). The principles of classification and a classification of mammals. *Bull. Amer. Mus. Nat. Hist. 85:* 1–114.

191. SIVERSTEN, E. (1941). On the biology of the harp seal *Phoca groenlandica* Erxl. *Hvalråd. Skr. 26:* 1–166.

192. SMYTHE, R. H. (1943). The hedgehog suckling theory. *Vet. Rec. 55:* 174.

193. SOUTHERN, H. N. (1940). The ecology and population dynamics of the wild rabbit (*Oryctolagus cuniculus*). *Ann. appl. Biol. 27:* 509–26.

194. — (1942). Periodicity of refection in the wild rabbit. *Nature, Lond. 149:* 553–54.

195. — (1948). The persistence of hydrogen cyanide in rabbit burrows. *Ann. appl. Biol. 35:* 331–46.

196. SOUTHERN, H. N. & LAURIE, E. M. O. (1946). The house-mouse (*Mus musculus*) in corn ricks. *J. anim. Ecol. 15:* 134–49.

197. SOUTHERN, H. N. & WATSON, J. S. (1941). Summer food of the red fox (*Vulpes vulpes*) in Great Britain: a preliminary report. *J. anim. Ecol. 10:* 1–11.

198. SOUTHERN, H. N., WATSON, J. S. & CHITTY, D. (1945). Watching nocturnal animals by infra-red radiation. *J. anim. Ecol. 15:* 198–201.

199. STAMP, L. DUDLEY. (1946). *Britain's structure and scenery.* London, Collins *New Naturalist.*

200. STAS, I. I. (1939). Recording of the dolphin's body movement in the sea. *C. R. Acad. Sci. URSS. 24:* 536–39.

201. — (1939). Once more on the recording of the movements of the dolphin in the sea. *C.R. Acad. Sci. URSS. 25:* 668.

202. STEVEN, D. (1949). (Edinburgh). Unpublished information.

203. STEVEN, G. A. (1934). A short investigation into the habits, abundance, and species of seals on the north Cornwall coast. *J. Mar. biol. Ass. U.K. 19:* 489–501.

204. — (1936). Seals (*Halichoerus grypus*) of Cornwall coasts. *J. Mar. biol. Ass. U.K. 20:* 493–506.

205. SUOMALAINEN, P. (1939). Artificial hibernation. *Nature, Lond.* *144:* 443–44.
206. SVIRIDENKO, P. A. (1940). The nutrition of mouse-like rodents. *Zool. Zh. 19:* 680–84.
207. TANSLEY, A. G. & ADAMSON, R. S. (1925). Studies of the vegetation of the English chalk. III. The chalk grasslands of the Hampshire-Sussex border. *J. Ecol. 13:* 177–223.
208. TAYLOR, E. L. (1939). Does the rabbit chew the cud? *Nature, Lond. 143:* 982–83.
209. TAYLOR, W. L. (1939). The distribution of wild deer in England and Wales. *J. anim. Ecol. 8:* 6–9.
210. — (1946). The wild cat (*Felis sylvestris*) in Great Britain. *J. anim. Ecol. 15:* 130–33.
211. — (1948). The distribution of wild deer in England and Wales. *J. anim. Ecol. 17:* 151–57.
212. TETLEY, H. (1939). On the British polecats. *Proc. zool. Soc. Lond. 109B:* 37–39.
213. — (1941). On the Scottish wild cat. *Proc. zool. Soc. Lond. 111B:* 13–23.
214. — (1941). On the Scottish fox. *Proc. zool. Soc. Lond. 111B:* 25–35.
215. — (1945). Notes on some specimens of the British otter. *Proc. zool. Soc. Lond. 115:* 189–93.
216. — (1945). Notes on British polecats and ferrets. *Proc. zool. Soc. Lond. 115:* 212–17.
217. THOMAS, D. H. (1939). *Tracks in the snow.* London, Hodder & Stoughton.
218. THOMPSON, D'ARCY W. (1918–19). On whales landed at the Scottish whaling stations, especially during the years 1908–14. *Scot. Nat. 1918:* 197–208, 221–37; *1919:* 1–16, 37–46.
219. THOMPSON, H. V. (1948). Studies of the behaviour of the common brown rat (*Rattus norvegicus*, Berkenhout). *Bull. anim. Behav.* No. 6, 26–40.
220. TOMILIN, A. G. (1946). Thermoregulation and the geographical races of cetaceans. *C.R. Acad. Sci. URSS. 54:* 465–68.
221. TOPSELL, E. (1607). *The historie of foure-footed beastes.* London, Jaggard.
222. VAN DEINSE, A. B. & JUNGE, G. C. A. (1937). Recent and older finds of the California grey whale in the Atlantic. *Temminckia, 2:* 161–88.
223. VENABLES, L. S. V. (1943). Observations at a pipistrelle bat roost. *J. anim. Ecol. 12:* 19–26.
224. VENABLES, L. S. V. & LESLIE, P. H. (1942). The rat and mouse populations of corn ricks. *J. anim. Ecol. 11:* 44–68.

225. WARWICK, T. (1935). Some escapes of coypus (*Myopotamus coypu*) from nutria farms in Great Britain. *J. anim. Ecol. 4:* 146-47.

226. — (1937). The occurrence of disease among musk-rats (*Ondatra zibethica*) in Great Britain during 1934. *J. anim. Ecol. 6:* 112-14.

227. — (1939). Some habits of pipistrelle colonies. *Scot. Nat. 1939:* 68-70.

228. WATT, H. B. (1937). On the wild goat in Scotland. With supplement; Darling, F. Fraser. Habits of wild goats in Scotland. *J. anim. Ecol. 6:* 15-22.

229. WELLS, A. Q. (1946). *The murine type of tubercle bacillus (the vole acid-fast bacillus).* Med. Res. Council. special Rept. ser. No. 259. London, H.M.S.O.

230. WIESNER, B. P. & SHEARD, N. M. (1935). The duration of life in an albino rat population. *Proc. Roy. Soc. Edinb. 55:* 1-22.

231. WOLLASTON, A. F. R. (1921). *Life of Alfred Newton.* London, Murray.

232. WRIGHT, P. L. (1942). Delayed implantation in the long-tailed weasel (*Mustela frenata*) and the short-tailed weasel (*Mustela cicognani*) and the marten (*Martes americana*). *Anat. Rec. 83:* 341-53.

233. — (1942). A correlation between the spring molt and spring changes in the sexual cycle of the weasel. *J. exp. Zoo. 91:* 103-10.

233a. ZAWADOWSKY, M. M. (1926). Bilateral and unilateral castration in *Cervus dama* and *Cervus elaphus*. *Trans. Lab. exp. Biol. Zoopark, Moscow, 1:* 18-43 (In Russian; English résumé: 44-48).

234. ZEUNER, F. E. (1945). *The pleistocene period.* London, Ray Society.

INDEX

Abbé Spallanzani 103
Alexandrine rat 170
American grey
  squirrel 206–209
American marten, delayed
  implantation 240
Antler weight, deer 294
Antlers, deer 281; Fallow
  deer 301; Red deer 282–
  284; 292–294; Roe deer
  295, 296
Apodemus 159–165
Apodemus flavicollis 161, 164
Apodemus flavicollis wintoni
  164
Apodemus fridariensis 163
Apodemus hebridensis 162
Apodemus hirtensis 162, 163
Apodemus sylvaticus 160, 161,
  164, 165, 184, 185
Apodemus sylvaticus butei 162
*Apodemus sylvaticus fridari-
  ensis* 164
*Apodemus sylvaticus hebri-
  densis* 164
Apodemus sylvaticus hirtensis
  164
Apodemus sylvaticus sylvaticus
  161–163
Appendicular skeleton,
  mammals 22–24
Arctic fox, fur 225
Arms, bat 76, 78
Arvicola amphibius 158, 159;
  breeding season 181, 182
Arvicola amphibius amphibius
  158
Arvicola amphibius reta 158
Atlantic right whale 357,
  358
Axial skeleton, mammals
  16–22

Badger 221; appearance
  248; breeding 237; de-
  layed implantation 237;

Badger, (*Cont.*)
  diet 246; fur 223; jaw
  234, 235; play 228; set
  242; teeth 236
Balaena glacialis 357, 358
Balaenoptera acutorostrata 361
Balaenoptera borealis 360.
  361
Balaenoptera musculus 358,
  359
Balaenoptera physalus 359, 360
Bank-vole 148–153; breed-
  ing season 180, 181;
  length of life 180
Bank-vole, Raasay 149,
  151, 153
Barbastella barbastellus 121
Barbastelle 121
Barrett-Hamilton and
  Hinton 7
Bat, Bechstein's 119, 120;
  Daubenton's 117, 118;
  Greater Horseshoe 122;
  Leaf-nosed 121–123;
  Leisler's 114; 115; Lesser
  Horseshoe 122, 123;
  Long-eared 120, 121;
  Natterer's 119; Noctule
  83, 84, 85, 95, 113, 114;
  Pipistrelle 115, 116; Serotine 116, 117; Whisk-
  ered 118
Bats 75–123; arms 76, 78;
  breeding season 99;
  colonies 94; colour 81;
  diet 75, 87, 90, 91; distribution 95; ears 82, 86,
  105; echo-location 102–
  109; eyes 83; fleas 92;
  flies 92, 93; flight 85–88,
  103, 106; feet 77; fur 81,
  84; gestation period 98;
  glands 84; glandular
  buccal pads 84, 86, 87;
  grooming 92; hands 76;
  hibernation 95–97; key

Bats, (*Cont.*)
  for identification of British species 110–112; legs
  77, 78, 79; length of life
  101; mammary glands
  98, 99; method of feed-
  ing 90; migration 95;
  milk teeth 80, 81, 82, 83;
  mites 92; nose-leaf 108;
  number of young 100.
  101; *Nycteribiidae* 92, 93;
  origin 380, 381; parasites
  92, 93; reproductive
  tract 100; skeleton 77,
  78, 79; skull 79, 80;
  sleeping position 88, 89;
  summer colony 94; swim-
  ming 90; tail 77; teeth
  80, 81; territory 92, 93;
  ultrasonic squeak 105,
  106; ultrasonic waves
  102–108; vocal organs
  106, 107; wings 76, 77;
  winter colony 94; young
  97, 98
Bats, Horseshoe, breeding
  season 99; captivity 94;
  eyes 83; flight 86, 88;
  fore-limb 78; length of
  life 101; method of feeding 90; nose-leaf 85, 87;
  reproductive tract 100;
  sleeping position 88, 89;
  subspecific name 95; tail
  82, 86; teeth 80, 81
Bats, Vespertilionid, ears 82,
  86; flight 86, 88; glands
  84; length of life 101;
  reproductive tract 100;
  sleeping position 88, 89
Bearded seal 278
Bears 219
Bechstein's bat 119, 120
Behaviour, coypu 210; grey
  squirrel 208; rabbit 137,
  138; red squirrel 204,